The Historical C
the Jesus of Faith

The Incarnational Narrative as History

C. STEPHEN EVANS

CLARENDON PRESS · OXFORD

OXFORD

UNIVERSITY PRESS

Great Clarendon Street, Oxford OX2 6DP

Oxford University Press is a department of the University of Oxford.
It furthers the University's objective of excellence in research, scholarship,
and education by publishing worldwide in

Oxford New York

Athens Auckland Bangkok Bogotá Buenos Aires Calcutta
Cape Town Chennai Dar es Salaam Delhi Florence Hong Kong Istanbul
Karachi Kuala Lumpur Madrid Melbourne Mexico City Mumbai
Nairobi Paris São Paulo Singapore Taipei Tokyo Toronto Warsaw
with associated companies in Berlin Ibadan

Oxford is a registered trade mark of Oxford University Press
in the UK and in certain other countries

Published in the United States
by Oxford University Press Inc., New York

British Library Cataloguing in Publication Data

Data available

Library of Congress Cataloging in Publication Data
The historical Christ and the Jesus of faith: the incarnational narrative as history / C.
Stephen Evans.
Includes bibliographical references and index.
1. Jesus Christ—Person and offices—Biblical teaching. 2. Jesus Christ—Historicity.
3. Bible. N.T. Gospels—Criticism, interpretation, etc.—History—20th century—
Controversial literature. 4. Bible. N.T. Gospels—Evidences, authority, etc.
5. Incarnation—Biblical teaching. 6. Atonement—Biblical teaching.
I. Title.
BT205.E83   1996   232.9'08—dc20   95–41328
ISBN 0-19-826382-1
ISBN 0-19-826397-X (Pbk)

3 5 7 9 10 8 6 4

Printed in Great Britain on acid-free paper by
Biddles Ltd., Guildford and King's Lynn

The Historical Christ and
the Jesus of Faith

Preface

Iᴛ is difficult to imagine a story that has had more impact on human history than the story of Jesus of Nazareth. A huge part of the power of the story has always rested on an understanding that the narrative is not merely an imaginative story; it is a story of what really happened. The historicity of the story has, however, been subjected to intense critical scrutiny for the last two hundred years. The outcome of that scrutiny has not always penetrated popular consciousness, at least if theologian Van Harvey is to be believed: 'Anyone teaching the origins of Christianity to college undergraduates or divinity students cannot help but be struck by the enormous gap between what the average layperson believes to be historically true about Jesus of Nazareth and what the great majority of New Testament scholars have concluded.'[1]

Fortunately or unfortunately, the situation Harvey describes is surely changing. The wide publicity given to and sought by the work of the 'Jesus Seminar', for example, has gone far to make the layperson aware of what many New Testament scholars think about these questions, though to what extent people are changing their beliefs is anybody's guess.[2] The Jesus Seminar, a group of mostly American scholars, has become famous or infamous for producing a version of the Gospels, *The Five Gospels*, in which supposedly authentic words of Jesus are printed in red, with other colours used to print other words, graded in order of descending authenticity.[3] Decisions

---

[1] Van Harvey, 'New Testament Scholarship and Christian Belief', in R. Joseph Hoffmann and Gerald A. Larue (eds.), *Jesus in History and Myth* (Buffalo: Prometheus Books, 1986), 193.

[2] See *Time* magazine's article, 'Jesus Christ, Pure and Simple', 10 Jan. 1994, 38–9.

[3] Robert W. Funk, Roy W. Hoover, and the Jesus Seminar (eds.), *The Five Gospels* (New York: Macmillan, 1994).

were made at meetings twice a year in which members voted by dropping colour-coded beads in a box.

The theatrics behind the Jesus Seminar may obscure the real problem that Harvey points to: Can a person of intellectual integrity continue to take the story of Jesus that the Christian Church has traditionally recounted to be historical in its main outlines? That problem must be considered in relation to others: Does the historicity of the story even matter? Why does it matter? These are the questions I have tried to address in *The Historical Christ and the Jesus of Faith*.

The title is of course a twist on the distinction some theologians have attempted to draw between 'the historical Jesus' and the 'Christ of faith'.[4] The distinction is appealing because it represents an attempt to isolate what is religiously significant about Jesus from the difficulties that arise from entanglement with history. However, much of what is religiously significant about Jesus lies precisely in the historicity of his story, and much is lost when the story is emptied of that historicity, as many critics of Bultmannian theology have pointed out. My own title reflects my thesis that the story of Jesus as told by the Church—the story of Jesus as the Christ, the Son of God—can be reasonably accepted as historically true. Throughout the book I shall describe the Church's version of this story as 'the incarnational narrative', a phrase that is described in more detail in the first chapter.

It is often said that such a view of Jesus cannot be justified by history, but is only arrived at by faith. This claim is a half-truth. It is certainly correct that a conviction that the Church's story is true must be rooted in faith. However, the claim that the Church's story must be accepted by faith, as usually understood, is misleading for two reasons. For it is often thought that it means that believers hold their convictions by faith and not reason, while serious historical scholars base their views solely on reason. However, to say that the Church's story must be accepted by faith does not mean that such faith cannot be reasonable, or that it can or should be isolated from critical scrutiny. And the suggestion that it is only the Church's

---

[4] For a good example of this tendency, see Martin Kähler, *The So-Called Historical Jesus and the Historic Biblical Christ*, ed. Ernst Wolf, trans. Carl Braaten (Philadelphia: Fortress Press, 1964).

version of the story that it requires faith to accept is mistaken. The truth is that there is no story of the historical Jesus that can be isolated from faith convictions, and this is as true for the stories told by 'scientific, critical historians' as it is for the story told by the Church. The story of Jesus is always a story of a Jesus of faith.

It would probably be helpful to say something about the point of view from which this book has been written. First of all, it is not really a work of apologetics. That is, though I discuss the prospects for arguments designed to convince unbelievers of the historicity of the story, this is not itself such an argument. Rather, the book aims to give a convincing account as to why knowledge of the story is important, and also argues that ordinary people who claim to have knowledge of the truth of the story of Jesus of Nazareth may be quite reasonable in making such a claim. Specifically, I claim that the reasonableness of such a claim is not undermined by modern critical biblical scholarship. It should be obvious that an argument such as mine is quite different from the kind of argument that would need to be offered to try to change the minds of those who do not accept the biblical story.

To whom is the book addressed? I do, of course, hope the story I tell will be convincing to Christians. However, the book is by no means addressed solely to a Christian audience. My hope is that a non-Christian who understands my account will gain a new respect for the integrity and intellectual vitality of Christian faith in the contemporary world. My aim is not to convert such a person, but to help that person understand and appreciate the logic of the standpoint of faith. Perhaps such a person will consider the story afresh and even take seriously the apologetic arguments that could be offered on behalf of the story.

My professional training is as a philosopher, and it is of course with fear and trembling that I offer the world a book such as this, one that freely crosses the disciplinary boundaries of biblical studies, theology, history, philosophy, and literary criticism, to name just a few. The name of the game in modern academe is 'specialize, specialize', and a book such as this may appear to be an act of *hubris* if not madness. However, a careful look at the history of philosophy reveals that a concern for clarification and even defence of theological claims has been important to many philosophers.

In any case, this is a book that I had to write, and my sense of call was confirmed when I was named a Pew Evangelical Senior Scholar by The Pew Charitable Trusts to work on these issues. This generous grant gave me two years with a reduced teaching load, and one year off entirely, to attempt to fill some of the big gaps in my education in the fields of theology and biblical studies, and to provide time to write. I owe therefore an enormous debt to The Pew Trusts and to the selection committee for the Pew Evangelical Scholarship Initiative. Of course The Pew Charitable Trusts does not endorse and is in no way responsible for the content of the work. I am also grateful to St Olaf College for structuring the grant in such a way as to allow me the maximum benefit from the award. Finally, I must thank Calvin College for appointing me William Spoelhof Teacher-Scholar in Residence in 1994, a position that has allowed me the time to make necessary final revisions.

Despite the reading I have done over the last three years, in a variety of fields but especially in biblical studies, my work has simply deepened my sense of how ignorant I am and how vast the problems are. So it is important for me to affirm that my book not only wishes to consider the situation of the layperson; it is itself written from that standpoint, with respect to many of the issues addressed. I am also emboldened by my recent discovery of a work by a New Testament scholar, N. T. Wright, *The New Testament and the People of God*.[5] Wright spends a good deal of space at the beginning of his book dealing with the crucial philosophical issues that he sees at the root of New Testament scholarship. If biblical scholar and theologian Wright is bold enough to write as a philosopher, because of a sense that the problems will not stay within neat disciplinary boundaries, then perhaps I am right to trespass a little as well.

It is my sincere hope that no one will read this book as an attack on the value of historical biblical scholarship. As I have read the works of people such as E. P. Sanders, John Dominic

---

[5] N. T. Wright, *The New Testament and the People of God* (Minneapolis: Fortress Press, 1992).

Crossan, N. T. Wright, and others, I am full of admiration for the learning and diligence their labours manifest. Any critical remarks on such historical scholarship in this work must be understood solely as directed to claims made on its behalf to undermine the possibility of knowledge on the part of ordinary people of the founding Christian narrative. These criticisms reflect no denigration of the intrinsic value of biblical, historical scholarship. Nor do I wish to question the fact that such scholarship can have positive value for the life of the Church.

Books can be long and life is short, and I recognize that not all readers will have the time to peruse the whole of this work. I have tried to be relatively comprehensive in treating a broad range of significant questions concerning the historicity of the incarnational narrative, and the book as a whole is one sustained and—I hope—coherent argument. Nevertheless, certain sections could be omitted by readers who are less interested in some of the issues. Readers who are already convinced that the historicity of the events of Jesus' life matters and that the category of non-historical myth is religiously inadequate for understanding the narrative could skip Chapter 3. Readers who have either no doubts or no interest in the significance of Jesus' life and death as an atonement could skip Chapter 4. Someone who is already convinced that it is crucial to know about the story if it is true could dispense with Chapter 5. Those with no worries or interests in the question of the logical coherence of the story could omit Chapter 6. Other readers may have few worries about the possibility that miracles could occur and be known, or that critical historians could embrace miracles. If so, Chapters 6 and 7 could be skipped. The epistemological heart of the book is a sustained argument that is found in Chapters 9 to 12; this section could be read as a more or less self-contained unit. Finally, readers who are most interested in the question of whether contemporary New Testament scholarship undermines faith in the incarnational narrative should look chiefly at the last two chapters.

Some portions of this book had an earlier life. An ancestor of some of the material in Chapters 10 to 12 appeared in the *International Journal for Philosophy of Religion*, 35 (1994), 153–82, under the title 'Evidentialist and Non-Evidentialist

Accounts of Historical Religious Knowledge'. A careful reader will notice some significant changes between that article and the current book, particularly with respect to the relation between evidentialism and internalist epistemology. An earlier version of Chapter 3 appeared as 'The Incarnational Narrative as Myth and History', in *Christian Scholar's Review*, 23/4 (1994), 387–407. An earlier version of part of Chapter 8 appeared as 'Critical Historical Judgment and Biblical Faith', in *Faith and Philosophy*, 11/2 (1994), and an earlier version of another section of that same chapter appeared as 'Empiricism, Rationalism, and the Possibility of Historical Religious Knowledge', in *Christian Perspectives on Religious Knowledge*.[6] My thanks to the respective editors and presses for permission to include revised versions of these essays.

There are many other people I wish to thank. One of the most important is Professor Richard Swinburne, who secured me an invitation to be a member of the Senior Common Room at Oriel College, Oxford University, during 1993–4, and also provided me with detailed critical remarks. Oxford provided a wonderful environment to complete this project and Professor Swinburne's help was invaluable. Others who read the book or parts of it and offered me the benefit of their criticism include several anonymous readers for Oxford University Press, Charles Taliaferro and Ed Langerak of St Olaf, the members of the philosophy department of Calvin College, several other Calvin College colleagues, including David Hoekema and Dan Harlow, David Holwerda and Ronald Feenstra of Calvin Theological Seminary, Eleonore Stump of St Louis University, Bruce Langtry of the University of Melbourne, and Nicholas Wolterstorff of Yale University.[7] My student research assistant at Calvin, Ray Van Arragon, also read through the manuscript, checked notes and references, and prepared the index. I owe all of them a deep debt.

It is customary to end such a preface by thanking one's spouse and family for their help, patience, and understanding. I hope the customary character will not obscure the genuine debt I owe to my children for their patience and understanding,

---

[6] C. Stephen Evans and Merold Westphal (eds.) (Grand Rapids, Mich.: Wm. B. Eerdmans, 1993).

[7] I should also offer apologies to anyone whom I have overlooked.

and most of all to my wife Jan, for her love, faith in me, and hopes for this project. This book is dedicated to her.

C.S.E.

Calvin College
March, 1995

Contents

I

The Incarnational Narrative and the Problem of Its Historicity

IN a trivial sense every human religion is a historical phenomenon and has historical roots. Every human religion has some
kind of historical foundation, in the sense that its origins lie in
some set of historical events. Nevertheless, there are large
differences both between different religions and even within a
single religion in the significance attached to these historical
origins. The historical origins of Hinduism seem lost in the
mists of time, and Hinduism seems none the worse for that.
Buddhists certainly revere Gautama, but Theravada Buddhists
do not think that enlightenment is in any way contingent upon
historical knowledge of Gautama's life. It is rather the timeless
truths that Gautama discovered that are important.

History seems more important for Islam and Judaism.
Devout Muslims believe that God revealed himself to Muhammad, and that the right path to submission to Allah is found
in the revelation thus given. Nevertheless, the focus of the
revelation is not on Muhammad, but on Allah. One should
accept Muhammad as a faithful revealer of Allah, but the locus
of faith is Allah, not Muhammad. History seems still more
important for Jews, for Orthodox Judaism has always seen
itself as grounded in the claims that God chose a historical
people for a particular destiny, delivered that people from
oppression, and continued to deal with that people in history,
to fulfil God's own purposes for the human race. It is an open
question, one still debated by Jewish theologians, to what

degree Judaism is dependent on the historical truth of the narrative of this interaction.

I. THE INCARNATIONAL NARRATIVE

Though there are many historical narratives in the Bible that are significant for Christians, orthodox Christian faith has traditionally understood itself as rooted supremely in the life, death, and resurrection of a historical person, Jesus of Nazareth. Whether Judaism could survive the discovery that Moses never existed and the Exodus never occurred is not for me to say, but it has seemed to many Christians that Christian faith could not survive if Jesus did not live, die, and rise from the dead. This story of Jesus I shall call 'the incarnational narrative'. I shall use this phrase to designate the story of Jesus of Nazareth, taken from the New Testament as a whole, as that story has traditionally been told by the Christian Church.[1] Thus understood it is not a story about a mere human being, but an account of Jesus as the Son of God, a unique, divine person. 'The incarnational narrative' is therefore my way of designating a particular account which is theologically rich. I do not, however, wish to endow the narrative with more theological baggage than is necessary. In so far as possible, I shall assume a version of the narrative that does not take sides on questions that are disputed in-house among different streams of historic Christian orthodoxy.

Of course many will say that to understand the story of Jesus as an incarnational narrative is already to endow it with too much theological baggage. Clearly, I have already tipped the scales in the direction of the orthodox understanding of Jesus, simply by taking the New Testament story *as that document has been interpreted by the Church*. The narrative in

[1] Obviously one could object at this point that there is not one Christian Church but many. In speaking of the Church I mean to refer to all branches of Christianity that continue to affirm the early ecumenical creeds, and when I refer to the Church's teachings, witness, or convictions, I mean to refer to the central affirmations of those Churches that are consistent with those creeds and with each other. Clearly these affirmations are a limited subset of the actual affirmations of any particular Church. This is roughly equivalent to what C. S. Lewis called 'mere Christianity'.

which I am interested is a 'thick' one, not one that is theologically bare or neutral. Still, it is the narrative itself upon which I wish to focus. There have been, of course, many attempts on the part of Christians to capture the significance of the incarnational narrative, many attempts to express in propositional form what the story is about, why it is important, and what it implies. One can question any such attempt without questioning the fundamental importance of the narrative itself. One can even question whether or not one can and should try to articulate the meaning of the story, as has been done by some recent 'narrative theologians', without doubting in any way the crucial significance of the story itself.

Of course many New Testament scholars today argue that one cannot meaningfully speak of one coherent story found in the New Testament; rather they argue that the message of the New Testament is irreducibly plural. In one sense this contention is absolutely correct. The New Testament was written by diverse authors with diverse concerns and aims, and the various books lend themselves to studies of 'the theology of Paul' or 'the theology of Mark'. Nevertheless, despite this diversity, the Church has historically regarded the New Testament as a unified revelation from God, inextricably tied to the Old Testament, and one which contains a unified story in and through its diversity. That is in fact how the Church has traditionally read the Bible.

There is a vast literature dealing with questions concerning how the Church moved from whatever historical events lay behind the New Testament documents to the New Testament, and how the Church developed, from those events and from those documents, orthodox Christian doctrines.[2] In this work I shall not address such questions. I shall not discuss how the New Testament came into existence, or 'the making of Christian doctrine'. By largely ignoring such issues I do not mean to imply that they are not important. I ignore them for three reasons: (1) I lack the competence to treat them adequately; (2) it does not appear necessary to me to deal with

---

[2] See e.g. C. F. D. Moule, *The Birth of the New Testament* (London: A. & C. Black, 1962) and *The Origin of Christology* (Cambridge: Cambridge University Press, 1977); and Maurice F. Wiles, *The Making of Christian Doctrine* (Cambridge: Cambridge University Press, 1967).

them in order to treat the questions in which I am interested; and (3) no single book can deal with every issue, and this one is, if anything, over-ambitious in scope already.

Of the three reasons given, only the second seems likely to be controversial. How can I examine the truth of the incarnational narrative as the Church's story without discussing such questions as how the New Testament was developed, whether the Church's interpretation of the New Testament is sound, or whether the distinctive doctrines of the Church can be generated from the narrative? Interesting and important as those questions are, it does not seem to me that one must have answers to them prior to any consideration of the truth of the Church's narrative. Regardless of how the New Testament was written and developed, it is a fact that the New Testament exists, and is put forward by the Church as a faithful witness to the truth. Thus it seems perfectly legitimate for someone to examine and reflect on the content of that witness, even if one is not sure as to how the witness came into being.

As for questions of interpretation, it is today a vexed question even to say what it might mean for the Church's version of the story to be the 'correct' interpretation, and many would deny that there can be such a thing. While I would certainly not wish to deny that some interpretations are better than others, and some are just plain wrong, it seems unlikely, in this post-modern era, that one will find any particular interpretation to be *the* correct reading of a text. And in fact the history of New Testament interpretation strongly suggests that the New Testament under-determines its own interpretation; it seems foolish even for a Christian believer to claim that an honest, reasonable interpreter of the New Testament would necessarily arrive at readings consistent with Christian orthodoxy, *if the interpretative process proceeded independently of the guidance of the Church and the Holy Spirit.*

However, within the plurality of interpretations of the New Testament that can be and are offered, once more it is undeniable that the Church's reading of this document, and of its central narrative, *exists* as an offering in the marketplace of ideas, whatever one may want to do with it. And what I wish to do with it is examine it and reflect on the truth of the story as thus interpreted, rather than debate the 'correctness' of the interpretation as an interpretation. The Church's story is one that continues to be offered to all comers, and there is no good reason why we should not ask whether the story, with its historical claims, could be true, and whether it is true.

There are well-known difficulties with the harmonization of the four Gospels. The Gospels not only present differences in coverage and emphases, but certainly appear to contain inconsistencies. I take it that most of these difficulties concern the details and not the major outlines of the story, and thus that it is possible to read the New Testament as providing a *basically* coherent narrative about the life, death, and resurrection of Jesus. That it is possible to read the New Testament in this way is proved by the fact that the Church has for centuries given it just such a reading. Furthermore, it continues to be read in that way, even by individuals who are well aware of the results of contemporary biblical scholarship.[3]

The Church's story, the one I am calling the incarnational narrative, is an account of how the divine Word took on human flesh, was born as a baby, lived a life characterized by miraculous healing and authoritative teaching, died a cruel and voluntary death for the sake of redeeming sinful humans, was raised by God to life, and now abides with God, awaiting the time of his glorious return and ultimate triumph. So much at least seems common ground among orthodox Christians, be they Catholic, Orthodox, or Protestant.

As noted above, I shall also omit any discussion as to how the Church moved from telling this story to the development of fully articulated credal Christianity. Nor shall I discuss the question of the general credibility of such fully developed faith. Rather, I wish to discuss just one facet of Christian faith, the credibility of its founding narrative. Within this question I shall pay special attention to the historicity of the narrative. Is the basic narrative historically reliable? Do the four Gospels, along with speeches in Acts and references to Jesus in the Epistles, present a *basically* reliable record of the life, death,

---

[3] See e.g. Arthur Wainwright, *Beyond Biblical Criticism: Encountering Jesus in Scripture* (London: SPCK, 1982), particularly pp. 21–46. Wainwright shows convincingly that the differences in the New Testament accounts are secondary to the underlying similarities.

and resurrection of Jesus? It should be obvious that such a concern for the basic reliability of the narrative is quite distinct from a concern for the 'inerrancy' or 'infallibility' of the Bible. My concern is not with the Bible as a whole, but only with the central elements of the story of Jesus, as the Church has distilled the story. Someone who embraces this story as true is not for that reason committed to any stronger claims about the truthfulness of the Bible.

The incarnational narrative is of course a unity, and it cannot be neatly separated into theological and historical components. An assertion that Jesus as the Son of God died on the cross for the sins of the human race is a complex claim, and its truth can be challenged from many different perspectives. Most obviously, the claim is historically false if Jesus was not in fact crucified. However, the claim as a whole is also false as an historical claim if its theological preconditions are false. If, for example, Jesus was not the Son of God in the intended sense of 'Son of God' then it is false that Jesus was crucified as the Son of God. If it makes no sense to say that a particular person could atone for the human race, then it is false that Jesus atoned for the sins of the human race on the cross. The defence of the narrative as historically true must therefore involve the consideration of theological and philosophical issues, as well as 'pure' historical ones.

At least until the Enlightenment period, the overwhelming main body of Christians was united in holding to the fundamental importance of the historicity of this narrative. Virtually all Christians believed, in addition to such purely theological propositions as that God created the heavens and the earth, that Jesus was born of a virgin, and that he was crucified, buried, and resurrected on the third day. The fundamental importance of this is attested by the historical reference in the Apostles' Creed: Jesus 'suffered under Pontius Pilate'. Though Pilate himself would otherwise surely bask in well-deserved oblivion, he is immortalized by the need early Christians felt to link the passion of Jesus with secular history.

Such beliefs were never, for example, an issue between Catholics and Protestants at the time of the Reformation. Catholics and Protestants alike not only affirmed the historicity of these crucial events, but unhesitatingly viewed the four Gospel accounts as historically reliable, even in the face of well-known discrepancies in the accounts.

I.2. HISTORY AND THE HISTORICAL: CLARIFYING THE TERMINOLOGY

I wish to say something about why the historicity of the incarnational narrative is important, though this subject will be treated in depth in later chapters. However, I need first to clarify how I shall use such key terms as 'history' and 'historical'. The first point to be made is the often-noticed one that the English term 'history' has two importantly different senses. Sometimes when we speak of 'history' we speak of *events*, what has actually happened. At other times we mean to speak of the *accounts*, the narratives, given by historians and others about those events. I want to argue that the historicity of the incarnational narrative is important in both of these senses of 'history', but first I need to say a bit about each of them.

What does it mean to say that an *event* is historical or is part of history? I mean nothing exotic or fancy, but intend to use whatever rough concept we all employ in judging that the assassination of John F. Kennedy was an historical event, but that the death of Superman in a Marvel comic book story was not, though the writing and publication of the story was historical. I will not attempt a full philosophical analysis of 'history' in the sense of events. Rather, I will simply say that an event or series of events qualifies as historical if it can be assigned a date and if it enjoys meaningful relations, including causal relations, with other events in that stream of datable events that includes human doings and sufferings. Anyone who does not know how to identify that stream can only be told that it is that stream that includes the doings and sufferings of his or her own life.

There are some distinctions commonly made by theologians that will play no role in my account. One of these is the distinction between the historic and the historical Jesus. What is historic can be distinguished from what is historical by virtue of its importance and significance. However, the relation between the historic and the historical is not always clear and seems to be understood differently by different authors.[4] Some view what is historic as just a subset of what is historical, so that to say that an event is historic is to affirm that it is both historical *and* has a certain kind of importance. However, others use the term 'historic' to denote an alleged event that has had this kind of importance, whether historical or not. For example, someone using the term 'historic' in this way might say that the story of Adam and Eve is historic even if it is not historical. So on some usages, what is historic is automatically also historical, while on other usages this is not so. Given the potentiality for confusion, I shall avoid any discussion of 'the historic Jesus', since it is obvious that the life of Jesus had the kind of importance in question. The object of inquiry is whether the story can be affirmed as historical.

I shall also put aside as unhelpful the distinction some draw between 'the real Jesus' and the 'historical Jesus'. The idea behind this distinction is the correct insight that the accounts given by historians about Jesus of Nazareth can never be completely certain or complete. John Meier, for example, noting these points, goes on to say that we should distinguish between the 'real Jesus', the Jesus who walked the roads of Palestine in the first century, and the 'historical Jesus', who is 'a modern abstraction and construct'.[5] The historical Jesus is the 'fragmentary, hypothetical reconstruction of him by modern means of research'.[6] Meier goes on to say that it is a confusing anachronism to say that the Gospels at points present 'the historical Jesus'. Presumably Meier means by this that by definition 'the historical Jesus' refers to the accounts of Jesus given by modern historians, and so cannot be found, even in a fragmentary way, in the Gospels.

I find this unhelpful for a number of reasons. First of all, Meier's usage here flies in the face of ordinary language, in which to say that an account given of some event is historical is not merely to say that it occurs in a narrative given by a

---

[4] John P. Meier, in *A Marginal Jew: Rethinking the Historical Jesus*, i. (New York: Doubleday, 1991), points out this confusion and gives several helpful examples. See pp. 26–31.

[5] Ibid. 25.

[6] Ibid. 31.

modern historian, but that the event really occurred. If the incident of George Washington chopping down the cherry tree and then confessing the deed did not occur, then we would surely say it is not historical, and in so doing, we would not just be saying that modern historians fail to include it in their accounts. We would also be saying the incident never happened. What Meier calls 'the historical Jesus' would better be termed 'the historians' Jesus'.

One hardly needs to make a conceptual distinction between the historical and the real in order to recognize that there is a difference between the reality of a series of events and the narratives that later historians recount. Of course a narrative is not itself the reality that it attempts to portray. And of course all such narratives are incomplete, some more so than others, and subject to the usual failings of finite human knowers. But the conceptual distinction Meier wishes to draw actually muddies the water. For if we ask what is the aim of historians in giving their historical reconstructions, surely part of the answer is that they are attempting to describe what really happened. Of course the accounts that historians give are always selective and reflect the interpretative framework and ends of the historian, but they none the less aim at the real. Speaking of these accounts as 'the historical Jesus' (or Jesuses) is confusing because it treats attempts to represent reality as if they were themselves the reality being represented. If the 'historical Jesus' is simply an account given by a historian, then no account given by a historian can fail to be historical. It seems preferable to maintain an 'event' sense of history, in which to say that an event is historical is simply to say that it really happened. Narratives, which we shall consider in a moment, can be said to be historically true to the degree that they accurately represent the events which occurred.

Biblical scholars such as John Meier, who are also Christian believers, have another reason for distinguishing between 'the historical Jesus' and 'the real Jesus'. The reason is that there is often a tension between the picture of Jesus that emerges from the work of the historian and the picture that the faithful believer who is part of the Church must affirm. By insisting that the 'historical Jesus' is not identical with the 'real Jesus', Meier leaves open the possibility that the 'Jesus of faith' or 'the theological Jesus',[7] may also capture part of the 'real Jesus'. For this reason, Meier emphasizes that the historical Jesus must be regarded as 'a scientific construct, a theoretical abstraction of modern scholars'.[8]

Now, if Meier changed his terminology and did not speak of the 'historical Jesus' but rather of the distinction between the 'historians' Jesus' and 'the Jesus of faith' I should not object very much to this. His point is that the picture (or rather pictures) of Jesus presented by modern critical historians must be regarded as a picture that derives from a particular 'game' with a particular set of rules. '[I]n the quest for the historical Jesus, the "rules of the game" allow no appeal to what is known or held by faith.'[9] Doubtless, Meier is rightly describing the actual practice of most historians. Nevertheless, questions can and should be raised about this practice, for the 'game' of the historians is one that attempts to justify itself on the grounds that it is the best way of getting at the truth about the real Jesus. As Meier himself says, 'only a careful examination of the Gospel material in the light of the criteria of historicity can hope to yield *reliable* results'[10] (emphasis mine).

A dilemma arises at this point. What about the conclusions that can be arrived at by faith? Is faith a reliable way of reaching conclusions about Jesus? If so, and faith therefore helps one reach truth, then why should not the historian take the methods of faith into account, if the historian is interested in truth? On the other hand, if relying on faith does not lead to reliable conclusions, why should anyone accept these conclusions? If faith does not provide a reliable way of reaching truth, then faith begins to look like an unjustified standpoint, a 'personal choice' that looks arbitrary.

Meier and others like him may well argue at this point that the picture of Jesus that the historian gives may not be the only reliable picture; it is simply a picture that 'provides an

---

[7] It is unclear whether or not Meier wishes to identify these two, and I do not assume they are identical.

[8] Meier, *A Marginal Jew*, ii (New York: Doubleday, 1994), 4.

[9] Ibid. 112. These rules of the game for Meier also exclude any acceptance of miracles as real events, though he also says they exclude dogmatic claims that miracles cannot occur; see ibid. 11. I discuss at length in Ch. 8 whether critical historians must avoid any acceptance of miracles.

[10] Ibid. 5.

academically respectable common ground and starting point for dialogue among people of various faiths or no faith'.[11] I would agree that it is a worthwhile endeavour to see what kind of picture might emerge from a conversation of people of various faiths. For the sake of participating in such a conversation, the participants might well decide to bracket some of their beliefs, as Meier recommends. So I do not object to this enterprise as one method of studying the real Jesus. However, I see no reason to assume that the rules of such a conversation provide the *only* reliable way of getting at the real Jesus, and no reason therefore to regard such rules as binding on all historians for all purposes. Rather, they ought to be seen as binding on those who choose to participate in a conversation that is governed by such rules. Other conversations, equally pluralistic in character, might operate by different rules. For example, a Christian might wish to know what a Jew who does *not* bracket his faith thinks of Jesus. The rules Meier has in mind define *a* historical method, but they are not part of *the* historical method, if indeed there is such a thing.

In Chapters 8 to 10 I shall argue that contemporary epistemology is open to the idea that faith perspectives may contribute in a positive way to gaining knowledge. The old dichotomy between what we 'know' on the basis of objective evidence and what we 'believe' on the basis of subjective commitment is no longer tenable. Knowledge is not rooted in 'pure objectivity' but is suffused with subjective commitments; hence faith cannot be separated from knowledge. At the same time genuine faith should not settle for the status of arbitrary, subjective commitment; faith ought to reflect on whether what it is committed to is really so, and therefore must be open to critical reflection and questioning.

1.3. WHY HISTORY (IN BOTH SENSES) MATTERS

If we consider the 'event' sense of history, it is clear that Christianity has traditionally affirmed that in the life, death,

---

[11] Ibid. 5.

and resurrection of Jesus, *something happened*, something that has fundamental importance for the entire human race and even for the whole created order. This something has been understood variously: as a victory over Satan, the satisfaction of a penalty, the offering of a sacrifice, the plundering of hell, the effecting of a reconciliation between God and an alienated humanity, making possible the glorification of the human race, and the overcoming of powerful spiritual forces. All such theories agree in understanding these events as playing a crucial role in making it possible for the human race and the created order to be redeemed and restored. The importance of history follows clearly from this: if these events are regarded as decisive in making salvation possible, then if they did not occur, salvation has not in fact been made possible, at least in the manner that Christians affirm.

As was noted at the beginning of this section, the English word 'history' can refer not just to the events themselves, but also to the accounts we give of those events, and Christianity affirms the importance of the historicity of the incarnational narrative in this second sense as well. Christians do not simply say that it is vital that the events occurred; they also affirm the crucial importance of *knowing* about those events. The author of the fourth Gospel, who attempted to give a narrative account of these events, put it this way: 'Now Jesus did many other signs in the presence of his disciples, which are not written in this book. But these are written so that you may come to believe that Jesus is the Messiah, the Son of God, and that through believing you may have life in his name.'[12] It is through coming to know the story that one can acquire faith in Jesus as the Christ, and having such faith is the key to life. So in affirming the importance of the historicity of the incarnational narrative, Christians affirm both that it is important that the events which the narrative depicts actually occurred, and that we have some means of becoming acquainted with the narrative and knowing or believing that the events thereby depicted occurred.

Many questions can of course be raised at this point. Are all the events depicted in the narrative important? Are they of

---

[12] John 20: 30–1. All biblical quotations are from the NRSV.

equal importance? Why are the events important? How detailed must our knowledge of the narrative be? How accurate must our knowledge be? How do we gain such knowledge? These are important questions and many of them will be discussed later on, but for the moment we must bracket them to focus on the fundamental importance of the basic historicity of the narrative. These other questions might be answered in many different ways by a person who consistently continued to affirm that the historical character of the founding narrative is essential.

1.4. WHY BELIEF IN THE NARRATIVE HAS BECOME DIFFICULT

Despite the fundamental importance of the historicity of the incarnational narrative, since the Enlightenment that historicity has become deeply problematic for Christians. To put it bluntly and simply, we have become unsure whether the events happened, and uncertain about whether we can know that they happened, even if they did. The problematic character of the historicity of the narrative is no secret among mainstream academic theologians; one of the few things liberal theologians, neo-orthodox theologians, process theologians, feminist theologians, and post-modernist theologians would probably all agree on is that it is very doubtful that the New Testament Gospel narratives represent reliable history.

Why has something that was taken for granted by almost everyone in the West prior to the Enlightenment become recognized by almost everyone in the West as a problem since then? The quick answer is simply 'modernity'. That is, the assumptions and mind-set of the Enlightenment have made it difficult for us to affirm the historicity of the incarnational narrative. Though this answer cries out for development, so much is neutral and uncontroversial. When we begin to say whether this way of thinking we call 'modernity' represents an advance or a decline, or both, the debate begins. Some would claim that it is hard for us to affirm the historicity of the incarnational narrative because we have advanced beyond the

mythological, pre-scientific patterns of thinking that domi-
nated the ancient world, when the narrative came into being.
We have overcome the credulity that characterized people of
earlier times and developed new standards of critical history.
Others might say the change is not so much a mark of intellectual advance as a sign of a deterioration of our imaginative
powers and spiritual earnestness. Regardless of one's opinions
here, it is possible to trace out some of the aspects of modernity
that have created the difficulties. I shall briefly discuss four
factors here, though each will be given additional consideration
later.

1.4.1. *Post-Enlightenment Scepticism about the Supernatural*

Both the metaphysics and the epistemology of the Enlightenment provide rocky soil for belief in a narrative that embodies accounts of angelic appearances, exorcisms, mysterious
healings, and resurrections. To look first at metaphysics, the
Enlightenment saw the development of deistic and mechanistic
views of the natural world that left no room for miracles and
the supernatural. Even though most of the great seventeenth-
century scientists were devout Christians, the picture of the
natural world they developed, in which events in nature are
the product of impersonal, mechanistic laws, seemed to fit
poorly with a picture of the world as shaped by a loving
providence. In such a world, miraculous and supernatural
events seem like alien intrusions, and there is a strong tendency
to discount supernatural explanations and look for natural
ones.

Equally important is the fact that the epistemological positions characteristic of the Enlightenment, either in rationalist
or empiricist forms, are not hospitable towards belief in the
veracity of stories involving miracles and supernatural agents.
The tendency in rationalist epistemology is to see essential
religious knowledge as knowledge of necessary truths, knowable a priori.[13] From such a perspective, miracle stories have too
much of a contingent, accidental character, and the empirical

---

[13] See the discussion of 'religious rationalism' in Ch. 8 for a detailed discussion of
these issues.

grounds for such beliefs do not look like the sort of foundation that really important knowledge requires. Perhaps such stories can be reinterpreted as expressions of rational truths; that at least is what Immanuel Kant attempted in his *Religion with the Limits of Reason Alone.* In such a case, however, their factual, historical character becomes inessential and insignificant.

An empiricist view of knowledge might appear to provide more promising soil for stories of the miraculous, but here the monumental figure of David Hume looms, along with a host of lesser lights.[14] Hume's attack on belief in miracles in his *Enquiry Concerning Human Understanding* has inspired many rejoinders, but even conservative, orthodox Christians continue to feel the weight of his argument.[15] Essentially, Hume assumes that the question of belief in a miracle boils down to a question of evidence. He assumes the kind of evidentialist epistemology that is so characteristic of the Enlightenment, and argues that the improbability of miracles, when compared with the frequency with which witnesses lie or are mistaken, implies that it will always, or nearly always, be more probable that the testimony in favour of a miracle is mistaken than that the miracle occurred.[16]

Whatever else may be true of the incarnational narrative, it is abundantly clear that it is full of apparently miraculous and supernatural elements. In the Gospels, Jesus is represented as having a miraculous birth, being born of a virgin, with angels appearing to announce and celebrate the occasion. In his public ministry, Jesus shows supernatural knowledge, and performs many miracles and exorcisms. Finally, and most crucially, his execution is followed by his own resurrection from the dead. One might argue that many of the miracle stories belong to the 'details' rather than the basic outline of the story, and thus that the credibility of the narrative does not rest on the accuracy of any individual story. Even if this is so, however,

[14] See R. M. Burns, *The Great Debate on Miracles* (Lewisburg, NJ: Bucknell University Press, 1981).
[15] See I. Howard Marshall, *I Believe in the Historical Jesus* (Grand Rapids, Mich.: Wm. B. Eerdmans, 1977), 59.
[16] See David Hume, 'Of Miracles', in *An Enquiry Concerning Human Understanding* (Indianapolis: Hackett Publishing Co., 1977).

one could hardly argue that the narrative as a whole is reliable if *all* the miracle stories are historically false. And even if some or all of the earlier miracles are regarded as peripheral and dispensable, the Church has always regarded the resurrection of Jesus as its very foundation. For better or worse, the story seem inextricably tied to the miraculous, and a world that has difficulty believing in miracles cannot help but have difficulty accepting such a narrative as historical.

1.4.2. *The Divorce of Fact and Value and the Denuding of the Meaning of History*

The metaphysics of the Enlightenment, with its implicit or explicit embracement of a mechanistic view of nature, views the objective world as devoid of meaning and value; values and meanings must reside in the subject if they are to have any purchase at all in such a world. There is a profound divorce between facts and values. The world is as it is; 'values' are rooted in our attitudes towards it.

In such a world, it becomes difficult to see how *any* historical fact could have the profound significance traditional Christians ascribed to the incarnational narrative. In the words of C. S. Lewis, describing his attitude prior to his becoming a Christian, 'what I couldn't see was how the life and death of Someone Else (whoever he was) 2000 years ago could help us here and now—except in so far as his *example* helped us'.[17] This means that even those who might see the *story* of the incarnation as significant in some way, have difficulty in seeing the importance of its factual, historical character. If contemporary people are to take seriously the historical character of the incarnational narrative, they must be able to see how it is possible for a historical event to have the kind of meaning traditional Christians claim.

---

[17] *They Stand Together: The Letters of C. S. Lewis to Arthur Greeves (1914–1963)* ed. Walter Hooper (New York: Macmillan, 1979), 427.

1.4.3. *Moral Difficulties with the Atonement*

Of course part of the traditional Christian answer to the question as to why the incarnational narrative's historicity is significant to people in every age is the doctrine of the atonement. Though there are many theories of atonement, many answers to the question as to how the life, death, and resurrection of Jesus constituted a victory over sin and death, most theories of atonement, and certainly the dominant ones, agree that the story recounted an objective achievement, an achievement with implications for everyone for whom Christ died.

Theories of atonement, however, especially the popular forms of 'substitutionary' atonement, rather than being the solution, are often seen as part of the problem. The idea that God forgives human sin by virtue of punishing an innocent figure in our place raises a host of moral difficulties. The Enlightenment emphasized a view of individuals as morally autonomous agents; I am responsible only for my own choices. Such a moral perspective poses many questions for theories of atonement: Why must God punish at all? If punishment is indeed necessary, how can guilt be transferred to someone else? How can the suffering of an innocent person take away my guilt? Perhaps these questions can be answered, but in the individualistic post-Enlightenment age, substitutionary theories of atonement seem unintelligible and morally dubious to many.

1.4.4. *The Development of Critical Views of the New Testament*

In the late eighteenth century, critical examination of the New Testament, and especially the four Gospels, began in earnest. Prior to this period, discrepancies between the accounts given in the four Gospels had of course been noticed, but there was a general assumption that such differences could be 'harmonized', though it was acknowledged that this was not always easy to do. Early in the eighteenth century, English deists and free-thinkers such as Anthony Collins, Thomas Woolston, Peter Annet, Thomas Chubb, and Matthew Tindal

had critically attacked orthodox defences of the reliability of
the Gospels, focusing on difficulties with alleged miracles,
supposedly fulfilled prophecies, and general discrepancies and
historical implausibilities in the narratives.[18]

Nevertheless, many follow Albert Schweitzer in viewing so-
called 'higher' critical study of the New Testament as stemming
from the fragments of the work of H. S. Reimarus (1694–1768)
published by G. E. Lessing in 1778. Reimarus was a deistic
free-thinker who developed a reading of the Gospels which
saw them as a deceptive attempt on the part of the disciples to
cover up the death of Jesus. Reimarus believed that hidden
within this unhistorical account one could discern the outlines
of the real Jesus, who was a failed revolutionary. Though the
'fraud hypothesis' of Reimarus is generally dismissed, his theories anticipated many later developments in historical criticism. Reimarus is important for simply treating the Gospels as
ordinary historical documents, with no presumption of divine
inspiration or even reliability. Perhaps even more important is
the attitude of critical suspicion adopted towards the documents, the sense that to learn what really happened one must
look through the texts and not take them at face value.

What began as a trickle with Reimarus became a flood after
the publication of D. F. Strauss's *Life of Jesus* in Germany in
1835.[19] Prior to Strauss there had been no shortage of rationalists who were sceptical of the miraculous and supernatural
elements in the Gospels, but, with some exceptions, the
assumption had been that the accounts had the credibility of
eyewitness sources, and thus the tendency had been to look
for naturalistic or reductionistic explanations of the supposed
miracles. Strauss clear-headedly followed Reimarus in dis-
carding the notion that the Gospels are eyewitness accounts,
by viewing them as containing great amounts of legendary and
mythical accretions of the sort that frequently grow up around
religious leaders after their death. The way was clear to investigate these documents to determine if any genuine historical

---

[18] Robert Morgan with John Barton, *Biblical Interpretation* (Oxford: Oxford University Press, 1988), 56. For more extended treatments of such figures see Hans Frei,
The Eclipse of Biblical Narrative (New Haven: Yale University Press, 1974).

[19] D. F. Strauss, *The Life of Jesus Critically Examined* (Philadelphia: Fortress Press,
1972). Originally published as *Das Leben Jesu* in 1835.

knowledge could be wrested from them, or, as was the case for Strauss himself, to attempt to extract from the mythical material itself a true philosophical meaning.[20]

With Strauss the floodgates to this kind of historical-critical analysis opened, initially in Germany, but eventually extending to England and the United States as well. Such 'higher criticism' (the term distinguishes this kind of historical criticism from the less controversial textual or 'lower' criticism) is today pursued on all sides using a variety of sophisticated methods. The Gospels are analysed from such perspectives as 'source criticism', 'form criticism', and 'redaction criticism'. Source criticism examines the text to discern what earlier sources may be discerned within it. With respect to the four Gospels, for example, it is commonly argued that Mark was written prior to Matthew and Luke. The latter two Gospels draw not only on Mark, but on another hypothetical document, designated 'Q'. Source criticism looks not only for obvious cases of literary dependence, but for tensions, discrepancies, 'fissures' in the text, that point to divergent sources that the final author or editor has combined.

Form criticism examines the Gospel narratives by looking at more or less self-contained passages or 'pericopes', which are assumed to be elements that were circulated and passed down in the Early Church, and which underwent a process of reshaping through such transmission. These pericopes were then arranged in various ways by the authors of the Gospels. The task of the critic is not only to classify the various types of material by their 'forms' but to understand them in light of the sociological situation of the Early Church which preserved and perhaps in some cases created them. From this perspective, much of the material in the Gospels tells us more about the problems and needs of the Early Church than about the historical Jesus.

Redaction criticism views the evangelists, and their predecessors who authored whatever sources the authors of the Gospels employed, not so much as passive compilers of inherited traditions, but as active authors, who edited or

---

[20] See the discussions of Strauss in Morgan with Barton, *Biblical Interpretation*, and in Frei, *Eclipse of Biblical Narrative*.

'redacted' the materials for theological purposes. Redaction criticism is a quite different enterprise from form criticism, though the two ways of looking at the texts are by no means incompatible. There is in fact an underlying similarity; both tend to assume that the documents are not reliable history. Rather, redaction criticism sees the evangelists as authors who felt free to rewrite or even create narratives for theological purposes, much as form criticism sees pericopes as created and shaped by the larger Church communities for their purposes.

In all of this work there is a general assumption that the writers of the Gospels had little genuine historical interest, and almost no critical historical judgement in the contemporary sense. Rather, there is a strong presumption that many of the incidents described in the Gospels are recounted for theological, liturgical, or polemical reasons, rather than because they occurred. If any genuine historical knowledge can be extracted from the Gospels, it can only be wrested from them with great ingenuity, and, in comparison with traditional beliefs, what can be gained looks quite scanty to many critics.

This is far from true of all biblical scholars. It would be a mistake to think that the defender of the incarnational narrative must necessarily be opposed to such critical study of the Bible. Though many of the critics have come to conclusions that seem to undermine the credibility of the narrative, others argue that at least the basic outlines of the narrative can survive such critical scrutiny intact. It would in any case be foolish to deny that such historical, critical studies of the Bible have led to important new discoveries and insights, including ones that have positive significance for the life of the Church. For the defender of the narrative, the problem is not critical study of the Bible *per se*, but the conclusions and assumptions of particular critics. Nevertheless, although such critical methods themselves do not necessarily lead to scepticism about the narrative, it seems clear that they have created a cultural situation in which widespread scepticism is easier and belief in the historical credibility of the narrative is more difficult. The defender of the narrative, therefore, will rightly look with a critical eye at the assumptions embedded in the methods of particular critics, while being careful not to oppose critical studies in general. After all, the truly critical scholar will be open to critical reflection on the methods of criticism itself, and methods that make possible new insights and discoveries may also contain limitations and blind-spots.

It is a very interesting question as to whether sceptical attacks by critical scholars on the veracity of the New Testament are more a product or a cause of the anti-super-naturalistic attitude which the Enlightenment produced. I am inclined to say that originally such work is best viewed as an outgrowth of the kind of Enlightenment assumptions I have briefly discussed. Such critics as Strauss simply assumed that the universe is a closed, naturalistic system, and that miraculous accounts must be legendary or mythical. However, once biblical criticism is in full flower, I believe the relationship becomes more complex. One barrier to anti-supernaturalism is precisely a vigorous belief that miracles have occurred; people who read the Gospel narratives as historically reliable naturally reject a world-view that posits the impossibility of supernatural events. The development of plausible accounts of the New Testament that dismiss such events as unhistorical thus can strengthen the kind of naturalistic view that originally gave rise to such readings.

1.5. THE POST-MODERN SITUATION

In light of these Enlightenment-inspired developments, it is easy to see why many theologians have grave doubts about the wisdom of linking Christian faith to the historical character of the incarnational narrative. To say that the intellectual climate of modernity has not been hospitable to traditional Christian faith would be an understatement.

It is generally recognized, however, that our intellectual situation has changed significantly. We now live in a 'post-modern' world, though there are many radically different accounts of what this new situation is supposed to be like. Theologians and Biblical scholars have certainly recognized this intellectual shift to various degrees and in various ways. I am convinced, however, that a great deal of what is presented as 'post-modern theology' still continues to incorporate some of the Enlightenment assumptions that constitute the essence of modernity. The time is ripe for a thorough rethinking of the problem of the historical foundations of Christian faith, and the modern biblical and historical scholarship that has shaped the terms of the debate.

What do I mean in speaking of the post-modern intellectual situation as contrasted with the mind-set of modernity? Let me first say what I do not mean. I do not wish to claim, as do many post-modernist thinkers, that we must embrace a perspective that mixes together relativism, subjectivism, and scepticism. I have no doubt that there is an objective world, and that it is possible for human beings to have knowledge of it and reasonable, true beliefs about it. Rather, as I am using the term, to accept our situation as post-modern is simply to recognize the collapse of the metaphysical and epistemological assumptions of the Enlightenment.

Specifically, in our post-modern situation, we have no good grounds for assuming that the natural world is a closed mechanistic system. Nor do we have any good reasons for accepting the epistemological assumptions common to both rationalists and empiricists since the Enlightenment: those of classical foundationalism. The classical foundationalist affirms that human knowledge must rest on foundations free from the possibility of error, or as free from error as possible, and that the beliefs built on these foundations must be constructed by equally sturdy means. Such epistemologies are often linked with an ethic of belief that holds that beliefs not held on such grounds are improper. I believe that much theology and historical, biblical scholarship from the Enlightenment to the present is strongly shaped by a blend of this kind of evidentialist epistemology and often unconsciously held naturalistic metaphysical assumptions.

Of course, historical biblical scholarship is the product of many other factors as well; it stems from genuine historical curiosity, tensions and inconsistencies in the Bible itself, and many other things, and it would be a gross exaggeration to say that it merely is the product of Enlightenment philosophy. My claim that a changed philosophical scene means the time is ripe for rethinking such scholarship is by no means to be construed as a wholesale rejection of contemporary biblical scholarship.

Still, my own sense is that if biblical scholars really engaged

with contemporary epistemological theories, the field would
be significantly altered, and altered for the good. The implications of this would be particularly dramatic with respect to
the scholarly quest for the historical Jesus. New Testament
scholars have certainly sensed that the post-modern intellectual situation will change things, and have responded in a
variety of ways. One possibility that has been explored is to
give up the quest for historicity altogether and be content with
literary analyses of the Gospels.[21] I will say more about the
value of these kinds of study as well as the difficulties connected with the loss of concern for historicity later on. At this
point I simply want to say that on my view the post-modern
situation provides new opportunities for looking at the historical issues. On this point, at least, I am pleased to cite
respected New Testament scholar Ben Meyer as concurring:
'It follows that with a *basic breakthrough* in the account of
knowledge the modern Christian dilemma might be radically
resolved, cracked open, and the way cleared for constructive
projects irreducible to theological salvage operations.'[22]

Contemporary Biblical scholarship in its more sceptical
forms and the theology that is based on it needs to be critically
examined from its foundations to its conclusions, given the
post-modern intellectual situation. I do not propose, however,
simply to argue from a sociological situation. That is, we are
not entitled to assume that, because our intellectual situation
has changed, the change represents progress, and it would be
simply unphilosophical to assume that we must uncritically
accept the convictions of 'post-modernism', even if we could
identify them. That kind of intellectual error can be found in
the writings of the theologians and biblical scholars I propose
to criticize; writers such as Rudolf Bultmann and Gordon
Kaufman frequently seem to assume that we must somehow
take for granted the thought-forms of 'modern man'.[23] I make

---

[21] The amount of work developing such a literary approach to the Bible is already
large. For a good example of a critic who bypasses historical questions, see R. A.
Culpepper, *Anatomy of the Fourth Gospel* (Philadelphia: Fortress Press, 1983). See p.
56 where Culpepper discusses how 'his story' can be true even if it is not 'history' if
we learn to look at the text as a mirror instead of seeing it as a window.

[22] Ben F. Meyer, *The Aims of Jesus* (London: SCM Press, 1979), 15–16.

[23] See e.g. Bultmann's famous statement that 'it is impossible to use electrical light
and the wireless and to avail ourselves of modern medical and surgical discoveries,

no such assumptions on behalf of either modernity or post-modernism. That is not to make the silly claim that I, unlike those modernist scholars, am free from the biases of my age. It is simply to affirm that no such bias is beyond challenge.

1.6. THE PLAN OF ATTACK

I propose to begin with a brief review of the responses of modernity to the Enlightenment challenge to historically rooted religious faith, and an analysis of the unsatisfactory character of each of those options. I shall then take a fresh look at why history matters for Christian faith by giving an account of what would be lost if it were determined that the *events* recounted in the incarnational narrative did not occur. In this connection we must take a look at the question as to whether theological doctrines such as the atonement still have existential relevance and make intellectual sense. Following this, I shall argue for the value of historicity in the other sense of 'history', in which reference is made to the narrative itself as an account. Granted the importance of the *events*, it is crucially important to have knowledge of those events as well.

Of course it is one thing to argue that it is important for Christians that the events occurred and that we have knowledge of them. It is quite another to ask whether they *did* occur, and whether we *do* have knowledge of them. The main body of this book will tackle these questions. I shall look first at the possibility of the narrative: could the story be true? Is the story logically coherent, and consistent with contemporary scientific knowledge? We must examine the charge that the narrative

and at the same time to believe in the New Testament world of spirits and miracles', in *Kerygma and Myth* (New York: Harper & Row, 1961), 5. Much of Gordon Kaufman's theological work begins from the assumption that the philosophical conclusions of Kant and Hume have made traditional religious belief untenable. See for example his book, *God the Problem* (Cambridge, Mass.: Harvard University Press, 1972). Bultmann's claim is in fact false as sociology; there are many educated persons who use electricity and visit physicians, and continue to believe in miracles and spiritual beings. If Bultmann has some argument up his sleeve designed to show that they are irrational to behave in this way, then this argument needs to be placed on the table. Kaufman's claim reflects a deplorable tendency on the part of theologians to defer to what is perceived as assured philosophical conclusions, when the truly philosophical attitude puts into question whether there can be such a thing.

embodies logically contradictory ideas, and the basic question as to whether a story that embodies supernatural and miraculous elements can be taken seriously.

It is of course not enough to know that the story could be true. What we want to know is whether it is true, and whether we can know it to be true. Here we must examine the contemporary epistemological terrain, and see if there are viable theories of knowledge and belief that will allow us to construct a plausible account of how anyone could have such knowledge.

I shall examine two different types of theological accounts of how knowledge of the incarnational narrative is possible, and assess their viability in the contemporary epistemological situation. These two accounts are an evidentialist model, that understands knowledge of the story as derived from ordinary historical evidence, and what I shall term the Reformed account, that describes the knowledge as the product of the work of the Holy Spirit within the life of the person. I shall try to show that these two stories are not really rivals but are complementary. Both have difficulties but these difficulties can be overcome if we reject the Enlightenment epistemologies that have often framed the discussion. I shall try to show the value of one particular contemporary epistemological theory, that of externalism. There are many different forms of externalism but I shall take the core insight as a sense that knowledge is something that is achieved when the knower has the right kind of relation to reality. We gain knowledge when our beliefs can be said to 'track' reality, to use Robert Nozick's suggestive phrase.[24] Knowledge is not necessarily a matter of having evidence, though that is one way a belief can acquire a 'truth-conducive ground'. Knowledge may simply be the result of reliable processes, or truth-oriented faculties, operating as they were designed to operate. Such an epistemology is particularly helpful in showing how these two different theological accounts may be combined.

In the end, I argue that though each account has a plausible story to tell, a combined account provides the best picture of how such religious historical knowledge is possible. In the

[24] Robert Nozick, *Philosophical Explanations* (Cambridge, Mass.: Harvard University Press, 1981), 167–288.

light of this account, I shall argue that the claim to know the truth of the incarnational narrative as historical is reasonable and plausible. The defence of this claim will require an analysis of both the value and the limitations of some kinds of contemporary critical New Testament scholarship for those who are not New Testament scholars, among whom I certainly class myself. I shall try to show that despite the large amount of valuable scholarly work done on the questions, in the end individuals must answer for themselves the question, 'What do I know about the historical Jesus?' Having answered that question, one can then go on to ask the really important questions: 'What is the significance of this Jesus?' 'In the light of what I know about him, what should my relation to him be, and what does that mean for the way I live my life?' This book, however, will focus mainly on the preliminary question, for if Jesus is not an actual historical figure whom I can know, then it is all too likely that the Jesus to which I attach significance will be merely a creation of my own imagination.

2

Modernity's Responses to
the Problem

IN the last chapter we looked briefly at the challenge posed to
the historicity of the incarnational narrative by Enlightenment
epistemology and metaphysics. We shall now take a brief look
at the responses to this problem that have been characteristic of
modernity. In one sense, of course, the variety of responses has
been immense, almost uncountable; the corpus of 'historical
Jesus' material and theological and philosophical literature
bearing on the issues related to the incarnational narrative is so
massive as to make it virtually impossible for one individual to
master all of it. Nevertheless, I believe that most of this material
can be usefully classified as falling into one of a small number of
categories. Though differences in details are enormous, there
are only a few responses that clearly differ in logical structure
as answers to the problem. I shall look briefly at four types of
response and correlative attitudes towards traditional Christian
faith: (1) Defence of the narrative as historical—defence of traditional Christian faith. (2) Rejection of the narrative—rejection
of Christianity. (3) Revision of the narrative—revision of Christianity. (4) Divorce of the meaning of the narrative from its historicity—divorce of Christian faith from history.

2.1. DEFENCE OF THE NARRATIVE AS HISTORICAL—
DEFENCE OF ORTHODOX CHRISTIANITY

There have of course been numerous theologians and apologists who have attempted to argue that the historicity of the

incarnational narrative is still defensible, and thus that traditional Christian faith is still a viable option. What is most
important to understand is why such attempts have seemed so
unconvincing to so many.

It is important, I think, to distinguish two kinds of defence
of orthodoxy: appeals to authority as opposed to attempts to
rebut critical historical attacks on their own grounds. Each has
its characteristic strengths and weaknesses.

Appeals to authority are often written off as obscurantist
and irrationalist, and certainly this has often been the case.
However, an appeal to authority is not necessarily a rejection of
reason; most of what human beings know is based on accepted
authority, and one can have good reasons for regarding an
authority as trustworthy. The appeal to authority in this case
can be to the authority of the Church, the creeds, or the Bible
itself. All such appeals necessarily have an *ad hominem* flavour,
in that they can only usefully be addressed to those disposed
to accept the authority in question. That by no means implies
that such appeals have no rational value to anyone, however.
If I believe, and think it reasonable to believe, that the Church
is a reliable, authoritative teacher, then if the Church teaches
that the Gospel narratives are historically reliable, I have a
good reason for believing that they are historical.

Some, though by no means all, of the work of the great
Princeton theologian B. B. Warfield serves as an excellent illustration of this kind of appeal to authority. Warfield is a complex
and subtle thinker. Some of his work could be used to illustrate
the second response to the problem, one that attempts to
defend the Bible by examining the evidence in an impartial
way. 'By all means', he says, 'let the doctrine of the Bible be
tested by the facts.'[1] Here Warfield reveals his roots in the
'common sense' tradition of Scottish realism that had a major
influence on American intellectual life. Yet a careful look at
the way he views the problems and the evidence for the Bible's
reliability shows that the appeal to authority also has an
important role in his thought.

Warfield wants to argue that the teaching of the Scriptures

---

[1] B. B. Warfield, *The Inspiration and Authority of the Bible* (Philadelphia: Presbyterian and Reformed Publishing Co., 1948), 217.

about themselves is that they are inspired by God and fully truthful.[2] Those who wish to accept the authority of Scripture should accept its account of itself. Such an appeal contains an obvious circularity problem, and Warfield attempts to circumvent this by grounding the authority of Scripture in the authority of Jesus and Jesus' view of Scripture. This still seems circular since we know Jesus through the Scriptures, but it is not. Even though we know about Jesus through the pages of Scripture, Warfield thought we could gain some reasonable knowledge about the historical Jesus without assuming the inspired character of the Gospels. If we begin by examining the Scriptures simply as ordinary historical testimony, we can still know something about Jesus' own views of the Old Testament, and also about the authority Jesus entrusted to his disciples. Someone who has met Jesus in the Gospels and has accepted his authority can reasonably go on to accept Jesus' view of the Scriptures, Warfield thought.[3]

Warfield is well aware of problems posed by the Gospels, and the difficulties in producing harmonizations. Nor is he opposed in principle to attempts to resolve such problems; he is in fact confident that solutions are possible in principle, and tries to give solutions to some problems.[4] In this respect Warfield differs from some of the Dutch Calvinist theologians, such as Bavinck, who not only make appeals to authority but also eschew particular appeals to evidence, looking instead to the importance of fundamental presuppositions.[5] Still, for the most part Warfield's attitude is that we must continue to accept

---

[2] See Warfield's article on 'Inspiration' in the *International Standard Bible Encyclopedia* (Chicago: Howard-Severance, 1915), iii. 1473–83. Repr. in Warfield, *Inspiration and Authority*.

[3] See the argument in 'The Real Problem of Inspiration', in Warfield, *Inspiration and Authority*, 213.

[4] See Warfield, 'Inspiration and Criticism', in *Inspiration and Authority*, 435–7.

[5] See Warfield's critical essay on Herman Bavinck reprinted in Mark Noll (ed.), *The Princeton Theology: 1812–1921* (Grand Rapids, Mich.: Baker Book House, 1983), 302–7. In this essay Warfield makes it clear that he is no 'presuppositionalist' in the Dutch Kuyperian tradition. Warfield is by no means unwilling to consider and respond to particular problems. Nevertheless, some of Warfield's own arguments, particularly when he is engaged in ecclesiastical polemics where presumably his opponents are at least nominally considered to be recognizing a common authority, function in a way very similar to the Dutch arguments.

the Scriptures as authoritative and therefore reliable, whether we can resolve particular problems or not.

Warfield claims that given the authoritative backing of the Scriptures, he is entitled to accept them as fully inspired and even infallible. This in turn means that one should not accept an error or contradiction until it has been *proved* to be an error or contradiction.[6] The mere possibility that a historical claim could be true is all that is needed to continue to accept it as true. In other words, the appeal to authority gives the Scriptures such weight that the burden of proof on a critic who wishes to show unreliability becomes practically impossible to meet. In *practice*, then, however committed in theory to common-sense realism and an 'inductive' approach to Scripture, once the argument for the authority of the Scriptures has been accepted, Warfield meets critical objections to the veracity of the Bible by relying heavily on this authority. In theory, his commitment to biblical inspiration is open to empirical test, but in practice no critical objections are allowed to count.

Still, since Warfield is not a pure 'presuppositionalist', who thinks the whole matter is decided by the assumptions one holds by faith, he is willing to begin by considering the Bible as an ordinary historical document, and thus the door to criticism has been left open. This concession to historical argument has turned out to be crucially important in undermining the effectiveness of Warfield's case in the long run. Plainly, to accept Warfield's argument, one must accept the picture of Jesus as provided in the Gospels as reliable, especially with respect to what Jesus thought of the Old Testament, and with respect to the authority he intended to vest in his followers. If someone thinks the New Testament picture of Jesus is radically untrustworthy, then there is little reason to think the picture given of Jesus' view of Scripture to be trustworthy, even if one were inclined to accept that view on the basis of Jesus' authority. Already in Warfield's day, few scholars in Europe who accepted critical historical investigation of the Gospels would have agreed that the picture of Jesus presented in them is necessarily reliable on these scores, and the situation would quickly become very similar in the United States.

---

[6] Warfield, 'Inspiration and Criticism', 438–9.

Of course Warfield appealed to the authority of the Church and of creeds as well. In the midst of the controversies in the Presbyterian Church of the time, he argued that the Westminster Confession, which his denomination accepted as normative, contained a strong affirmation that the Scriptures were inspired and infallible, and he argued that such views were held by the Fathers, such as Augustine, and the Reformers Luther and Calvin as well.[7] Such arguments had some force to those who accepted such creeds and wished to regard themselves as following the traditional teachings of the Church, and they perhaps therefore 'bought some time' for those who wished to uphold orthodoxy within the Church. They could hardly, however, have much impact towards making orthodox Christian views viable in the broader culture, and more specifically, in the growing universities.

Even within the Church, such arguments could always cut in two directions. If the positions defended by authority begin to seem quite implausible, then the effect of the appeal to authority can be to undermine the credibility of the authority. To the extent that Warfield was content to appeal, in a 'deductive' manner, to authoritative teaching, and not to descend to the level of argument about particular problematic passages and critical historical passages, he may unwittingly have undermined faith in the authority of the Church, creeds, and Scripture itself.

The second type of orthodox defence was to argue the case for the reliability of the narrative on ordinary historical grounds. Though the advocates of such a view may have personally believed that the Scriptures were inspired and even inerrant, they believed that the critical attacks could and should be met using the methodology of the critics themselves. Often the difference between this type of defence of the narrative and the appeal to authority is put in terms of the question as to whether or not the Scriptures should be treated as an 'ordinary historical document' or rather be put in a special category where ordinary historical critical principles do not apply. The

---

[7] See Warfield (with A. A. Hodge), 'Inspiration', in Noll (ed.), *Princeton Theology* 220–32.

second type of defence of orthodoxy claims to avoid any special pleading.

The work of many British scholars could be used to illustrate this approach. In the late nineteenth century, the triumvirate of B. F. Westcott, F. J. A. Hort, and J. B. Lightfoot provided convincing historical evidence that the critical conclusions of F. C. Baur in Germany had a flimsy historical basis. Baur had argued that the New Testament must be understood as arising out of a conflict between Judaizing and Hellenizing parties, and he believed that many of the Pauline Epistles were spurious and stemmed from very late in the second or even from the third century. Westcott, Hort, and Lightfoot provided powerful evidence that these dates were much too late, and that some of the Pauline Epistles must date from around AD 55. The story is told very nicely by Stephen Neill in his *The Interpretation of the New Testament*, and Neill draws from the tale the moral that the Church must welcome historical investigation, securely confident that good work will be an aid to faith.[8]

This triumvirate worked mainly on the Epistles and did not deal with the problems posed by the Synoptic Gospels, but much British scholarship on the Synoptics has continued in this tradition of taking on critical historical scholarship on its own ground, even though this type of work can no longer be regarded as dominant. The twentieth-century work of people such as F. F. Bruce, N. T. Wright, and I. Howard Marshall provide excellent examples.[9] Nevertheless, this approach, like the appeal to authority, is not without its problems. Two opposite difficulties, which may appear in fact to cancel each other out, are evident.

Both problems relate to the underlying Enlightenment ideal of objectivity that this type of defence of the narrative embodies. The essence of this strategy is to claim that an objective, neutral historical study of the Gospels confirms the basic reliability of the narrative. The proponents agree with the

---

[8] Stephen Neill and Tom Wright, *The Interpretation of the New Testament: 1861–1986* (Oxford: Oxford University Press, 1988), 1–64. See esp. 33–4, where Neill forthrightly declares that critical historical investigation must be unimpeded and will ultimately strengthen belief in inspiration.

[9] See e.g. I. Howard Marshall, *Luke: Historian and Theologian* (Grand Rapids, Mich.: Zondervan Press, 1971), and N. T. Wright, *The New Testament and the People of God* (Minneapolis: Fortress Press, 1992).

sceptical critics that the Gospels must be studied as 'ordinary historical documents' by 'ordinary historical means' and with no 'special pleading'. The first difficulty is whether adopting these methodological presuppositions necessarily undermines Christian orthodoxy, regardless of the intent of the defenders.

Everything hinges around the question as to what 'ordinary historical documents' and 'ordinary historical methods' involve. Ordinarily, human beings do not observe miraculous and supernatural events, and do not speak or write as divinely inspired, divinely authorized messengers. Yet the Gospel narratives clearly describe Jesus as having such miraculous powers and as making claims to speak with that kind of authority. If we regard the Gospels as ordinary documents, does this commit us in advance to discounting such claims? For example, if Jesus is represented as prophesying the destruction of Jerusalem and the temple, must we conclude that this narrative was written after the destruction of the city in AD 70? Is it special pleading to take seriously the possibility that Jesus had a knowledge of the future derived from his relationship to God?[10]

A look at the practices of historical critics, as well as theoretical accounts of what historical method involves, makes it evident that many scholars would claim that ordinary historical methods do require such a bias against the supernatural.[11] If that is the case, then defending the historicity of the narrative using 'ordinary' historical methods will necessarily be a losing battle. This raises the question as to whether the defenders of the narrative have essentially given away the contest by accepting the terms of the engagement of their opponents. Though lip service may be given to the recognition that total objectivity is impossible, the defenders of the narrative have accepted the Enlightenment assumption that knowledge is acquired through supposedly objective, neutral means. Theories must be tested by appeal to objective facts, facts that anyone can recognize. In practice, such a criterion of what counts as a fact is heavily weighted against those supernatural

[10] This assumes that such foreknowledge would have been supernatural in origin. Actually, as some critics have noted, it is quite conceivable that an astute observer of 1st-c. Palestine politics could have anticipated such an event without supernatural aid.

[11] See Van Harvey, *The Historian and the Believer* (New York: Macmillan, 1966). This issue is given a fuller airing in Chs. 7 and 8.

events not 'everyone' will recognize. I do not myself wish to challenge the validity of the ideal of impartiality this view attempts to embody, but one still must question whether this type of defender has given sufficient attention to the question as to how objective 'ordinary historical methods' are and can be.

The other type of objection raised against these defences of the narrative comes from the opposite quarter. Critics often question whether these defenders of the narrative measure up to the ideal of objectivity they profess. The suspicion is that the actual conclusions to be reached are predetermined by theological commitments, and then historical evidence is marshalled to support those conclusions, while claiming a willingness to follow the evidence wherever it leads. D. E. Nineham provides an illustration of this type of criticism when he speaks of 'mediating theologians' who try to be historical scholars, but for whom 'in the end religious considerations get in the way of a scientific judgment', using the words of Albert Schweitzer.[12] The claim is not necessarily that such theologians lack integrity (though there is a hint of this suggestion in Nineham). Rather, they simply exhibit unconscious bias.

The defender of the narrative at this point can and often does respond that the accuser is equally biased, and the counter-charge is usually plausible. Both sides in fact usually admit the impossibility of total objectivity, and affirm only that they are striving to put aside bias. Nevertheless, the accusation reinforces the need for a rethinking of the entire epistemological situation. It does not appear accidental that orthodox Christians usually appear to read the historical record differently from many others. It does not follow from this that their readings are mistaken or unjustified, but it does suggest that presuppositions play a larger role than those committed to an 'inductive' method would allow. What has become clear is how crucial it is to rethink the epistemological foundations of the debate.

---

[12] D. E. Nineham, 'Schweitzer Revisited', in *Explorations in Theology* (London: SCM Press, 1977), 118. Also see Nineham's comments that some who profess to follow the historical method do so with 'serious mental reservations'.

2.2. REJECTION OF THE NARRATIVE AS HISTORICAL— REJECTION OF CHRISTIANITY

The distinction between an individual who rejects the incarnational narrative and thereby rejects Christianity and one who merely wishes to revise the narrative and thereby reform Christianity can be difficult to draw. In fact, people with basically the same religious outlook might well be placed on both sides of this divide, since the individuals in question might have different conceptions of what is essential to Christianity. As is shown by the controversy embodied in the *Fundamentals* book series in the early twentieth century, one individual might see the virgin birth of Jesus as an essential Christian doctrine, so that abandoning it amounts to rejecting Christian faith altogether, while other thinkers might see such an element of the narrative as peripheral and inessential.

While keeping this imprecision in mind, it is still important to recognize the difference in mental outlook between the categories of the 'rejecters' and the 'revisers'. Quite a few individuals, when confronted by the difficulties of the narrative, concluded that traditional Christian faith simply had to be rejected. Regardless of whether one agrees with this position, many of its advocates exemplify virtues it is difficult not to admire: intellectual clarity and honesty, and often, in the case of seventeenth- and eighteenth-century representatives, personal courage.

Though this option can be seen in some of the eighteenth-century English deists and free-thinkers, it can be seen most clearly in the nineteenth century in positivists and humanists such as Comte. By the time we reach the twentieth century university, it perhaps becomes harder to find intellectuals who do not embody this option than those who do.

It is important to recognize that eighteenth-century English deists such as T. Woolston, M. Tindal, W. Wollaston, and P. Annet were neither atheists nor sceptics. They were sincere religious believers, and some of them certainly could be classed with the 'reformers of Christianity', in so far as they believed that the 'natural religion' they defended was in fact identical with 'true Christianity'. However, they were generally clear-headed enough to understand that the religious stance they were defending was essentially different from the Christianity of their opponents. The deists clearly argued that true religion was rooted in natural reason rather than in authoritative revelation, and thus a great deal of their polemical activity was directed against the historical reliability of the Gospel narratives.[13] As the deists saw it, orthodoxy stood or fell with the reliability of the historical narrative and the apologetic force of the miracles it contained. The deists did not all reject miracles, or even the miracles of the New Testament, as genuine, but they rejected the idea that such miracles could be historically established so as to provide rational evidence for orthodox Christian faith.[14]

By the time we reach Auguste Comte, the ambivalent attitudes the deists had towards Christianity have vanished. Comte sees religious faith in general and Christianity in particular as rooted in pre-scientific modes of thinking that are incompatible with a modern outlook.[15] For him the narrative has simply become incredible, so much so as to make serious historical argument unnecessary. For Comte the religious needs of the human race must henceforth be met by the worship of 'man'. Though the religious trappings of Comte are probably an embarrassment to contemporary secular humanists, a careful look at the 'Humanist Manifestos' of the American Humanist Association shows that the transference of faith from a religious historical narrative to a narrative about human progress is still deeply entrenched in secular humanist thought.[16]

[13] For a very clear account of the controversy between deists and orthodox theologians in the 18th c. see R. M. Burns's excellent study, *The Great Debate on Miracles: From Joseph Glanvill to David Hume* (Lewisburg, NJ: Bucknell University Press, 1981). Burns focuses particularly on the deists' attack on the miraculous elements in the narrative. For a good discussion of Anthony Collins's attack on the claims in the Gospels to demonstrate the fulfilment of Old Testament prophecies, see Hans Frei, *The Eclipse of Biblical Narrative* (New Haven: Yale University Press, 1974), 66–85.

[14] See Burns, *Great Debate on Miracles*, 73. Burns demonstrates clearly that Hume's famous argument against miracles was unoriginal in most respects, since the deists had made most of the points.

[15] Comte's view of myth is briefly discussed in the next chapter. For an account of Comte's views, see G. H. Lewes, *Comte's Philosophy of the Sciences* (London: G. Bell & Sons, 1904). To see how influential Comte's view of science has been, see the first part of B. F. Skinner's *Beyond Freedom and Dignity* (New York: Bantam Books, 1972), which repeats Comte's views quite precisely.

[16] See Paul Kurtz (ed.) *The Humanist Manifestos I and II* (Buffalo: Prometheus Books, 1973).

Among those who still regard it as worthwhile to give serious arguments against Christian faith, the problematic character of the historical narrative still figures prominently as a reason to reject Christianity. For example, Michael Martin's recent work, *The Case Against Christianity*, spends roughly the first half of the book arguing that we have little reason even to believe Jesus existed, but if he did, there are massive difficulties in accepting the resurrection and the virgin birth, not to mention other miracles that figure less prominently in the narratives.[17]

Rejection of the narrative clearly is regarded by many as a viable option, and by some as the only viable option. Nevertheless, I think it is fair to say that many of those who embrace this option do not find it fully satisfying. As Basil Mitchell has argued, those who reject Christian faith and accept instead some materialist outlook on human life have difficulty making sense of the human freedom that we unhesitatingly believe we have in ordinary life.[18] Nor does the materialist have a ready-made, convincing answer to questions about the meaning and purpose of human life. It is doubtless for just these kinds of reasons that alternative spiritual outlooks seem to be flourishing at present in the West. There is not only strong interest in Hinduism, Buddhism, and other eastern religions, but also renewed attention being paid to Native American religions, to gnostic and pagan religions, particularly those which emphasize the role of a goddess, and to a host of other religious perspectives that are loosely grouped under the 'New Age' label.

These alternative spiritualities certainly show that secularism is not the only standpoint from which the incarnational narrative can be rejected. However, the plurality of views embraced is testimony to a continuing spiritual hunger that belies the modernist myth of inevitable secularization, and provides some reason to think that no one alternative has emerged that really speaks to the needs of contemporary humans. In such a situation it is certainly not foolish to look

[17] Michael Martin, *The Case Against Christianity* (Philadelphia: Temple University Press, 1991).

[18] See his essay in *How to Play Theological Ping-Pong* (Grand Rapids, Mich.: Wm. B. Eerdmans, 1991), 29.

once more at the narrative that has been so foundational to Western culture. While recognizing the importance of this narrative to the West, it is important, however, not to regard it as an exclusively Western possession. The narrative was created and first flourished in the Middle East, and at this time perhaps has more vitality in Africa than in Europe or North America. The time is certainly ripe to rethink the reasons for its decline in the West.

2.3. REVISION OF THE NARRATIVE—REVISION OF CHRISTIANITY

The third option is perhaps the most common response to the crisis that has engulfed the narrative—but also the most commonly criticized. The strategy here is simple: if the incarnational narrative cannot be accepted as it stands, we must rewrite it so that it can continue to provide a foundation for Christian faith, and modify that faith accordingly. Thus, a plethora of 'lives of Jesus' have been produced throughout the nineteenth and twentieth centuries, and the stream shows little sign of drying up.

In the nineteenth and early twentieth centuries, most of the 'lives' reflected the characteristic emphases of liberal Protestantism. The miraculous and supernatural elements were de-emphasized or denied altogether. The focus of concern for Jesus himself was turned from the issue of who Jesus was to what Jesus taught. Jesus was presented primarily as an ethical teacher, whose message transcends his own time and culture, containing 'eternal truths about human life'.[19] From him we learn of the universal love of God, the intrinsic value of all persons as individuals, the need for humans to develop such qualities as humility and mercy.[20] In short, the message of Jesus

[19] Harry Emerson Fosdick, *The Man From Nazareth* (New York: Harper & Brothers, 1949), 244.

[20] Such readings are by no means limited to the 19th c. John Hick's recent *The Metaphor of God Incarnate* (London: SCM Press, 1993), while not a 'life of Jesus', contains a sketch of the 'historical Jesus' that is recognizably similar to the classical liberal portraits.

looked remarkably like the message of a liberal Protestant theologian.

The problem with this procedure has been aptly expressed by G. Tyrrell, who compares the efforts of A. Harnack, a representative liberal theologian, to that of a man who peers into a deep well but sees only his own face staring back at him.[21] Albert Schweitzer, in his justly famous book, *The Quest of the Historical Jesus*, expresses the same judgement Tyrrell passes on Harnack about the general attempt on the part of his contemporaries to discover the historical Jesus. If we discover the real historical Jesus, says Schweitzer, 'He will not be a Jesus Christ to whom the religion of the present can ascribe, according to its long-cherished custom, its own thoughts and ideas, as it did with the Jesus of its own making.'[22]

There are tremendous differences in the degree to which various attempts to write a life of Jesus take critical historical concerns seriously. In some, such as Ernest Renan's famous *Life of Jesus* that appeared in 1863, it is obvious that a serious concern for historical evidence is lacking.[23] Renan's portrait is an imaginative picture of a 'pale Galilean' whose early preachings were received enthusiastically amidst the beautiful streams and fields of Galilee, but who finally met a tragic end when he expected too much of his followers.

What is surprising, however, is that even the pictures of Jesus offered by scholars who energetically and conscientiously attempt to employ the most scrupulous historical canons too often appear to produce the same result: a Jesus who offers to the author and the contemporary world exactly what that author and world are looking for. As illustration, consider the recent work of John Dominic Crossan, *The Historical Jesus: The Life of a Mediterranean Jewish Peasant*.[24] Crossan's portrait is buttressed by an elaborate critical machinery, involving

[21] G. Tyrrell, *Christianity at the Cross-Roads* (London: Longmans, Green, & Co., 1909), 44. Quoted in I. Howard Marshall, *I Believe in the Historical Jesus* (Grand Rapids, Mich.: Wm. B. Eerdmans, 1977), 112–13.

[22] Albert Schweitzer, *The Quest of the Historical Jesus* (New York: Macmillan, 1948), 398–9.

[23] Ernst Renan, *The Life of Jesus* (New York: Random House, 1972). First published 1863.

[24] John Dominic Crossan, *The Historical Jesus: The Life of a Mediterranean Jewish Peasant* (San Francisco: Harper, 1991).

anthropological, historical, and documentary backing. Yet the Jesus offered by Crossan seems to be very much in touch with contemporary sensibilities; Jesus appears to be surprisingly politically correct. This Jesus has more than a touch of a radical who came of age in the 1960s; in scenes reminiscent of the Thanksgiving dinner in *Alice's Restaurant*, he parties with the poor in a most egalitarian manner, practising 'open commensality'.[25] Crossan's Jesus has a great deal of the feminist in him, and he has a great suspicion of civil and ecclesiastical authority, proclaiming an 'unbrokered kingdom of God'. It is true that, unlike earlier accounts that rationalistically soft-pedalled the miraculous, Crossan emphasizes that Jesus was an exorcist and magician of sorts,[26] but this change also appears to reflect the greater openness of our culture towards 'New Age' religious practices and the 'paranormal'. In any case, Crossan is careful not to claim that Jesus actually possessed genuine supernatural powers.

Whether supported by fancy historical methodology or not, truncated lives of Jesus still seem to tell more about the authors than about the historical Jesus. Liberation theologians give us Jesus as political revolutionary, feminists see Jesus as proto-feminist, and various academic portraits show us a Jesus who is politically correct. Such portraits can doubtless be worthwhile and illuminating, particularly in highlighting an aspect of the story that has been neglected, but they are invariably one-sided. This point is by now a commonplace insight, but that has not dissuaded scholars and non-scholars from continuing to produce personal versions of the 'real' historical Jesus.[27] John P. Meier, for instance, before embarking on his own quest for the historical Jesus, remarks that 'I never cease to be amazed at how present-day writers will first censure past critics for not being sufficiently self-critical and then proceed to engage

---

[25] See Crossan, *Historical Jesus*, 261–4.

[26] See ibid. 303–32.

[27] In addition to the scholarly books by Crossan cited above and the one by Meier discussed below, one might note the more popular recent work by A. N. Wilson, *Jesus* (London: Sinclair-Stevenson, 1992), or to cite a work that clearly borders on fantasy, Barbara Thiering's *Jesus the Man: A New Interpretation from the Dead Sea Scrolls* (London: Doubleday, 1992). For a thorough and convincing critique of both books see N. T. Wright, *Who Was Jesus?* (London: SPCK, 1992).

in an uncritical projection of their own ideas and agendas onto a portrait of the historical Jesus, hardly suppressing a gasp at how relevant he turns out to be.'[28]

I don't wish to conclude from this that responsible attempts to discover the historical truth about the matter are impossible and should not be attempted. I merely wish to note that the history of such attempts suggests very strongly that all 'selective' readings of the historical data, whether or not they are rooted in complex methodological procedures supposed to safeguard objectivity, are likely to be strongly influenced by the critic's own assumptions about what a religiously important figure should be like.

One problem with many of the revised versions of the narrative that have been developed, and the liberalized versions of Christian faith that accompany them, is that revising the narrative to make it credible to contemporary culture will also destroy any power the narrative might have to speak prophetically to that culture. It is probably no accident that the 'historical Jesus' people tend to create so often is a Jesus who offers us just what we want from him. Basil Mitchell speaks of an agnostic friend of his who says that the trouble with contemporary versions of Christianity is that they are not worth disbelieving in.[29] A Jesus who merely offers us ethical prescriptions that are platitudinous, or perhaps worse, simply reinforce our political and social prejudices, is hardly likely to be the Jesus who contains the solution to the problem of the meaning of human life and death. Such narratives are too thin to carry the metaphysical weight they are called upon to bear.

---

[28] John P. Meier, *A Marginal Jew: Rethinking the Historical Jesus* (New York: Doubleday, 1991), i. 5. Meier attempts to solve the problem of objectivity through the methodological device of a thought-experiment in which a Catholic, a Jew, a Protestant, and an agnostic engage in an 'unpapal conclave' to try to determine the historical facts. Thus after admitting that objectivity is impossible, Meier attempts to be objective through this device. However, why limit the conclave to these participants? Surely, we need conservative and liberal Catholics and Protestants, and why not add Hindus, Buddhists, and Muslims? Is there any reasonable hope that such a conclave would actually agree on anything?

[29] See Mitchell, *Theological Ping-Pong*, 35.

2.4. FREEING THE MEANING OF THE NARRATIVE FROM ITS HISTORICITY—SEPARATING THE TRUTH OF CHRISTIANITY FROM ITS HISTORICAL FOUNDATIONS

Perhaps the response that has the broadest appeal is one that frees the religious meaning of the narrative from its historicity, and thereby separates the questions of religious truth and historical truth. Rather than rooting Christian faith in the historical Jesus, one may try to free up religious faith from any concern with historical fact. Perhaps one can distinguish what is viewed as the true meaning of the incarnational narrative from its historical character, and find a way to establish or secure the truth of that meaning that is independent of history. This option does not necessarily have to deny the historical character of the narrative outright; it simply makes the question of historicity religiously irrelevant, or at least of no fundamental religious importance.

This response comes in two different forms. I shall call these the rationalist/moralist response and the romantic/existentialist response, respectively. Though there are large differences between these two categories, and even between different versions within each category, there is fundamental agreement that the religious meaning of the narrative can be separated from its historicity.

The foundation of the rationalist response is the view that ultimate religious truth must be knowable a priori or at least independently of any particular factual knowledge. The ultimate truths that religion claims to embody must have a timeless character.[30] Such a view of religious truth certainly fits many of the world religions nicely: the Hindu claim that *atman* is *brahman* or the Buddhist claim that desire is the ground of suffering seem to be the kinds of claims that must be true for all people at all times if they are true at all, and it is plausible that our access to such truths requires only the right kind of reflection on our nature. Traditional Christianity certainly does not appear to fit this view, but one can understand the

---

[30] See my essay, 'Empiricism, Rationalism, and the Possibility of Historical Religious Knowledge', in Evans and Merold Westphal (eds.), *Christian Perspectives on Religious Knowledge* (Grand Rapids, Mich.: Wm. B. Eerdmans, 1993), and the discussion of the issues in Ch. 8 below.

appeal of an attempt to make it fit this understanding of religious knowledge. Such a rationalism is clearly embedded in Lessing's famous 'ugly, broad ditch' metaphor. Lessing says that 'accidental truths of history can never be the ground of necessary truths of reason'.[31] It seems clear that the ultimate basis of Lessing's problem with historical religious knowledge is not the problem about empirical historical evidence that he himself cites, but rather his underlying sense that historical truths are just not the right kind of truth to bear the weight of ultimate religious concern.[32]

The most plausible kinds of timeless truths that might be knowable in this way for many Westerners are moral truths. Hence it is not surprising that this rationalist response often takes the form of reading the narrative as an embodiment or illustration of moral truths. Immanuel Kant's *Religion Within the Limits of Reason Alone* is one of the first and still one of the most distinguished of these attempts. In this work Kant gives a careful reinterpretation of the biblical narrative as a whole, from original sin to eschatology, but especially emphasizes the story of the 'Son of God'. For Kant, however, the Son of God represents an ideal of moral perfection, knowable a priori. Kant is willing to consider the idea that God might have granted humans a historical revelation of this ideal to 'speed up' the process of its dissemination. However, once the idea is understood, this revelation is dispensable. It may continue to serve as imaginative illustration of the ideal for some, but the validity of the ideal and the salvation that is dependent on a commitment to it cannot be dependent on historical faith.[33]

The romantic/existentialist version of this option frequently divorces the meaning of the narrative from its historicity by use of the category of myth. A classical expression of this response is found in D. F. Strauss's famous book, *The Life of Jesus*, the first edition of which was published in 1835. Strauss

---

[31] G. Lessing, 'On the Proof of the Spirit and of Power', in *Lessing's Theological Writings*, ed. and trans. Henry Chadwick (Stanford, Calif.: Stanford University Press, 1957), 53, 55.

[32] For more on this see Ch. 8, and Gordon E. Michalson, Jr., *Lessing's 'Ugly Ditch': A Study of Theology and History* (University Park, Penn.: Pennsylvania University State Press, 1985).

[33] See Immanuel Kant, *Religion Within the Limits of Reason Alone*, trans. Theodore M. Greene and Hoyt B. Hudson (New York: Harper & Row, 1960).

points out that orthodoxy had viewed the narrative as a history that contained supernatural events; liberalism, he says, had rejected the assumption that the supernatural events had occurred, but not the assumption that the narrative was historical. The revised 'lives of Jesus' that we discussed in the previous section stem from this viewpoint. Strauss himself wishes to consider the whole narrative from the viewpoint of 'myth'. The narrative should be viewed neither as reliable history, nor even as providing the raw materials for reliable history, but rather as expressing the faith of the Early Church in mythical form.[34]

Though most of the critical controversy surrounding the book focused on the way Strauss critically dissected the historical reliability of the narrative, he himself did not see the book as merely negative. Rather, he thought that clearing away a concern for historicity would open the door to a rediscovery of the religious truth of the myths themselves: 'it is essential religion which is here communicated under the form of a history; hence he who does not believe in the history as such, may yet appreciate the religious truths therein contained, equally with one who does also receive the history as such'.[35]

That Strauss's view is very much still alive can be seen in the prominence of the work of Joseph Campbell on myth, which has become well known because of the American television series, *Joseph Campbell and the Power of Myth*. Campbell views the incarnational narrative as a myth, and he views all the myths of the world as essentially variations on one story, which he calls the monomyth. The monomyth is a recounting of the story of redemption, the story of salvation, wherein each one of us can be the hero.[36] Obviously the historical narrative becomes completely unimportant on such a view.

Theologian Morton Kelsey has written a large number of books that attempt to understand the meaning of the incarnation as myth, employing, like Campbell, the categories of

---

[34] D. F. Strauss, *The Life of Jesus Critically Examined* (Philadelphia: Fortress Press, 1972), p. li.

[35] Strauss, *Life of Jesus*, 782.

[36] See Joseph Campbell, *The Hero With a Thousand Faces*, 2nd edn. (Princeton: Princeton University Press, 1968). Campbell is discussed at length in the next chapter.

Jungian psychology.[37] Unlike Campbell, Kelsey, who is an Episcopalian priest, attempts to recognize the importance of the historical character of the myth. In the end, however, the mythical significance of the narrative overwhelms its historicity, and it is difficult to see why this historicity really matters. That is, the truths expressed by the Christian myths and our response to those myths would look much the same whether the myths were historically enacted or not.

It is instructive to compare what might be termed the 're-mythologization' programme of people such as Campbell and Kelsey to Rudolf Bultmann's celebrated call for 'demythologization'. The two projects look antithetical, but it is not clear that they are really opposed, since Bultmann does not claim that the mythical stories have to be eliminated. Yet, whether opposed or not, both can be understood as versions of this same strategy. Bultmann, like Strauss, views the Gospel narratives as the mythical expressions of the faith of the Early Church. In calling for demythologizing the narrative, he does not wish to get back to the real, historical Jesus, but rather to reinterpret the narratives in terms of what he sees as their true meaning, employing the categories of existentialist philosophy. The consequence of this is that the historicity of the narrative is once more divorced from its religiously relevant meaning, just as is the case for Campbell. The main difference is that people such as Campbell are less confident that the meaning of the mythical narrative can be translated into philosophical terms; on their view the myth itself is the proper bearer of religious meaning.

Given the popularity of myth in contemporary culture, no one can deny that this fourth option continues to be attractive to many. Nor are rationalistic and moralistic versions of this response dead. Nevertheless, this option shares a difficulty with the previous response. We have noted how often those who revise the narrative have produced a 'Jesus' who reflects their own biases. However, those who view the narrative as a symbolic representation of some deeper religious truth may easily do something very similar. The rules of interpretation

---

[37] See e.g. Morton Kelsey, *Myth, History, and Faith* (Rockport, Mass.: Element, 1991).

are loose enough that it appears easy to generate just those 'truths' that we would like to hear. On the mythical option, indeed, this seems almost inevitable, for Jungians such as Campbell see the myth as a symbolic representation of truths about ourselves. We are the ultimate source of any 'revelation' gained.

Whatever problems the incarnational narrative presents, when understood as historical it poses a potential challenge to us, a revelation that does not simply stem from our own consciousness. Such a revelation might allow God to speak to us, and not simply allow us to hear our own voices. It is not therefore clear that it is altogether a gain to be done with the epistemological embarrassments of history by dividing the religious truth of the narrative from its historical truth. In the next chapter, I shall consider in more depth why the historicity of the incarnational narrative matters, in part by an examination of how well the category of 'myth' fits the story.

3

Why the Events Matter:
1. History, Meaning, and
Myth

THE English term 'history' can refer, as we have already noted, among other things, to an actual series of events, what in fact occurred, and also to the narrative or account that we construct about the events. In looking at the links between Christian faith and the historical character of its founding narrative, it is crucial to distinguish these two senses of 'history' and the different kinds of problems related to each. In this chapter and the next, I shall deal with the question as to why it matters that the events actually occurred.

It is important to see that this question is entirely distinct from the question as to whether the events did in fact occur. Regardless of one's answer to the factual question, one can reflect on the significance the events would have had if they had occurred, and the cost we might have to pay if forced to abandon belief in the historicity of the narrative.

Lessing, Kant, Bultmann, and Joseph Campbell in various ways force us to ask whether the historicity of the events really matters. What do we lose if we divorce the meaning of the narrative from its historicity? It is certainly not self-evident that the historicity of the narrative does matter.

Part of the answer given by traditional Christian faith to this problem lies in the doctrine of the atonement, and we will look at the possibilities that lie here in the next chapter. However, many Christian theologians, such as Duns Scotus and Austin Farrer, have held that the incarnation would have occurred even if the human race had not fallen and thus even if there had been no need for an atonement.[1] Whether this is so or not, it is certainly true that the atonement does not exhaust the meaning of the incarnation, and therefore does not exhaust the meaning of the historicity of the incarnation.

In the previous chapter I distinguished two strategies for divorcing the religious meaning of the narrative from its historicity, the rationalist/moralist option and the romantic/existentialist option. Both strategies claim that the religious functions of the narrative are independent of whether the events actually occurred. To this end both strategies sometimes characterize the narratives as mythical or at least as containing mythical elements. The difference between them lies chiefly in the degree of confidence they have as to whether the religious meaning in the myth can be translated into rational, philosophical categories. If such a translation is possible, then it looks as if the narrative can be successfully 'demythologized', as Kant attempted to do. If such translation is not possible, then we must rely on the power of the myth itself to carry us; advocates of this view say that in a scientific age religious faith requires a remythologization of our world. To see whether history is really essential for Christian faith, we must therefore turn our attention to the complex set of questions that are raised by the category of 'myth'.

3.1. SORTING OUT SENSES OF 'MYTH'

To make headway on the task of examining the implications of various proposals to demythologize or remythologize the incarnational narrative we must first sort out the different

---

[1] E. L. Mascall briefly discusses the controversy occasioned by the Scotist claim that God's incarnation would have occurred whether or not the human race had fallen, in *The Importance of Being Human* (New York: Columbia University Press, 1958), 92–3. Brian Hebblethwaite also mentions this claim as 'a Scotist thesis' in *The Incarnation* (Cambridge: Cambridge University Press, 1987), 56. In this work Hebblethwaite also gives (pp. 112–25) an interesting discussion of Austin Farrer's view of the incarnation, including Farrer's endorsement of the Scotist claim. See Austin Farrer, *Saving Belief* (London: Hodder & Stoughton, 1964), 111–12. For a comprehensive discussion of Scotus, see Allan B. Wolter, *The Philosophical Theology of John Duns Scotus* (Ithaca, NY: Cornell University Press, 1990).

senses of 'myth' that are rampant in the discussion. I cannot hope to give an exhaustive treatment of this concept, which is enormously complex and used in a wide variety of senses. Fortunately, for my purposes, it is not necessary to be exhaustive.

It appears to me that most authors agree that myths are for the most part narratives involving the actions of gods, other supernatural beings, and/or heroes who interact with gods and godlike beings and often have mysterious godlike powers themselves. Different conceptions of myth seem to me chiefly to stem from disagreements about two things: the purpose or function of myths, and the truth of myths. People disagree chiefly about why myths are invented, preserved, and savoured, and about whether myths are in some sense capable of being true. If myths can be true in some sense, disagreements also emerge about what kind of truth they can embody.

Let us look first at different views of the function of myths, with sidelong glances at the implications of various accounts of these functions for questions about truth. One popular account views myths as pre-scientific explanations. On this view, myths are essentially bad explanations of phenomena in the natural world. Before humans had plausible scientific explanations of natural phenomena such as the growth of crops and the fall of snow, they told fanciful stories that attributed these mysterious events to the agencies of gods. This particular view of the function of myth seems to imply that myths are false, since myths are seen as mistaken explanations. They are fanciful stories destined to be displaced by scientific knowledge. Essentially, this view of myth is that of Auguste Comte.[2]

Many sociologists, such as Durkheim, have developed a view of myth that stresses the way myths may function to reinforce the identity of a people, and 'explain' the ritual practices that give cohesion to the cultural group. Following this perspective,

---

[2] Comte viewed human intellectual progress as having three stages, the theological, metaphysical, and positivistic. Inquiry begins with mythological, or theological explanation, progresses to abstract, metaphysical accounts in terms of principles, and finally advances to empirically grounded laws that constitute positive science. See G. H. Lewes, *Comte's Philosophy of the Sciences* (London: G. Bell & Sons, 1904), for an account of Comte's view, which has been enormously influential. For example, the first part of B. F. Skinner's *Beyond Freedom and Dignity* (New York: Bantam Books, 1972) recapitulates Comte's view quite precisely.

some biblical scholars stress the way religious practices such as circumcision and the observance of the Sabbath may be explained and in part justified by the biblical stories of Genesis. Such a view seems less negative in its valuation of myth than Comte's, and does not obviously require that the stories in question be historically false. However, many theorists who accept such a view of the function of myth doubtless regard the historical truth of the stories as irrelevant to their function as myth.

A third account of the function of myths sees them as embodying psychological truth. While those who view myths solely as pre-scientific explanations see them as essentially false, and someone who views myths solely in terms of socio-logical function may see the truth of them as irrelevant, the psychological view regards the psychological truth of a myth as a key to its function. From a Freudian point of view the myth of Oedipus may be historically false, certainly to the extent that the tale embodies interaction between gods and humans. Nevertheless, the myth contains a type of truth; it expresses in a symbolic way a deep truth about the human psyche and its development. The appeal of the Oedipus myth is that it expresses in a dramatic narrative the longings of the developing infant boy to displace his father and marry his mother. We may imagine different versions of this view, depending on such things as the type of psychological insights embodied and whether those insights are capable of being expressed in a non-mythical form.

A fourth view of myth is that the function of myth is to express in a dramatic or narrative fashion some abstract meta-physical truth. As is the case for the psychological view, this account may hold that myths are historically false, but argue that they might possess a kind of metaphysical truth, because their real function is to express such metaphysical insights. Again we may imagine different versions of this view depend-ing on the metaphysics myths are supposed to express, and on whether the metaphysical truth embodied in myth can be given a non-mythical expression.

Of course, the above views of myth may be combined in various ways. Any of the views might hold that myths carry out important sociological functions as well as carrying out other functions. Someone who holds that the essential function of myth is to express psychological or metaphysical truth may also hold that myths may in some contexts serve as pre-scientific explanations. Or someone may hold, as many followers of Jung apparently do, that myths embody both psychological and metaphysical truth. I believe that the work of Joseph Campbell on myth embodies this perspective.[3] Such views are particularly plausible if one holds a metaphysical view such that human nature is in some way a microcosm that reflects the wider cosmos, or that the human self is in some way continuous with a higher reality, or even identical with that reality as in Advaita Vedanta Hinduism.

The crucial question for me is whether on any of these views of myth, some myths might embody historical truth. I think that in practice most theorists about myths do tend to think of them as historically false, whatever other kinds of truth they may include. This is not unreasonable, since in ordinary language it is often understood that the designation of some event as mythical implies that the event is not historical. If we pre-suppose a naturalistic view of the universe, and also assume that myths include reference to supernatural agents and events, then this implication seems inescapable. However, if naturalism is false—if God or gods exist and can act in the natural order—then there seems no necessary reason why a narrative with the structure and one or more of the functions of a myth might not be historically true or at least contain historical elements.

So we can imagine a sense of 'myth' in which to say of a narrative that it is mythical leaves open the possibility that it is historical. On this view a myth could be historically true, as well as possessing psychological and/or metaphysical truth and performing various sociological functions. It is this concept of myth that is implicit in some of C. S. Lewis's writings that we shall consider below, where Lewis discusses the incarnation of Christ as a myth which has been historically enacted without ceasing to be myth, and it is this sense that I shall assume in the following discussion.

---

[3] See Joseph Campbell, *The Hero With a Thousand Faces*, 2nd edn. (Princeton: Princeton University Press, 1968) for a good expression of Campbell's view.

This sense of myth has one significant argument in its favour; it begs the fewest questions and leaves open the most possibilities. For example, it would be less than ideal to *define* myth as only possessing psychological truth or only possessing metaphysical truth, or only carrying out sociological functions. Rather, we should leave it for inquiry to discern which of these functions myths possess or whether a myth might embody various kinds of insights. For similar reasons we should not define myth in such a manner that the question of whether a historical myth is possible is decided in advance. The Lewis concept of myth leaves open the possibility that myths may contain truths of all three kinds–psychological, metaphysical, and historical–though it does not require any particular myth to possess any truth.

The chief argument against this sense of myth is, I think, that it goes against common usage, in which myth does exclude history, and thus may lead to confusion. This is a real danger. Because of this, perhaps people who believe the incarnational narrative is historical but who still wish to describe it as a myth might do better to say that it resembles a myth in its structure and function. One could then say that the incarnational story is an historical narrative that possesses myth-like significance. However, no harm will come from violating popular usage so long as we are clear about how terms are being used. In my discussion, unless it is otherwise specified or made clear by context that some other sense is meant, I shall use the term 'myth' to refer to a narrative of the actions of gods and/or god-like heroes, which may carry out various sociological functions, but may also embody various kinds of truth, including historical truth.

By adopting this conventional definition, we can proceed to discuss the question as to whether the incarnational narrative can properly be claimed to belong to the genre of myth without assuming that a positive answer would imply that the story is unhistorical. As we shall see there is a lively debate about the plausibility of such a classification of this narrative, one that is independent of the debate about its historicity.

3.2. KIERKEGAARD VERSUS LEWIS ON CHRISTIANITY AND MYTH

The first question to be answered is whether the concept of myth can be applied to the Gospel narratives at all. If the answer is negative, then the case is quickly closed. The matter is of course hotly debated among theologians. Hans Frei has argued strenuously against people like Strauss that the category of myth is simply the wrong literary category to use in understanding the Gospels; they belong to the genre of realistic narrative.[4] Frei may well be right about the question of the literary form of the Gospels, at least for most of the materials in the Gospel narrative. Since I am neither a literary critic nor a biblical scholar, it is not for me to say. However, I suspect that even if he is, there is still a sense in which the biblical narratives may be spoken of as mythical or at least myth-like. I shall argue this by examining the positive assessment of the Gospels as myth found in C. S. Lewis. As a critical test, however, Lewis's views will be examined in relation to the apparently contrasting position of Søren Kierkegaard. Since Lewis and Kierkegaard agree about the historicity of the incarnational narrative, the nature of their apparent disagreement about its designation as myth stands out clearly.

In his book *Philosophical Fragments*, Kierkegaard has his pseudonym Johannes Climacus defend the uniqueness of the Christian story of the incarnation. Climacus does this by ironically pretending to 'invent' a story that is suspiciously similar to the Christian claim that God became a human being in order to make salvation possible for humans. The irony lies in the fact that the tale Climacus spins out turns out to be one that, according to Climacus himself, no human being could have invented.[5] In Climacus's version, the claim that God became a human being is 'the paradox', an offence to human thought that has no real parallel.[6] Climacus actually suggests that this uniqueness is an argument for the truth of Christianity; the

---

[4] See Hans Frei, *The Eclipse of Biblical Narrative* (New Haven: Yale University Press, 1974).
[5] Søren Kierkegaard, *Philosophical Fragments*, trans. Howard V. and Edna H. Hong (Princeton: Princeton University Press, 1985), 21–2.
[6] Ibid. 51–4.

Christian story must be a true revelation from God, because no human would or could make up such a story.[7] Furthermore, the historical character of the narrative is an essential element of its truth. Though the historical events in question are such that they cannot be *known* by being derivable from historical evidence, but are rather believed when the individual encounters the incarnate God and is transformed by the encounter, nevertheless the historicity of the incarnation is crucial for the salvation of the individual:

As is well known, Christianity is the only historical phenomenon that despite the historical—indeed, precisely by means of the historical—has wanted to be the single individual's point of departure for his eternal consciousness ... has wanted to base his happiness on his relation to something historical. No philosophy (for it is only for thought), no mythology (for it is only for the imagination), no historical knowledge (which is for memory) has ever had this idea—of which in this connection one can say with all multiple meanings that it did not arise in any human heart.[8]

The last part of this quote, an allusion to 1 Corinthians 2: 7–9, reveals Kierkegaard's chief concern here. To admit that the content of Christianity could have been developed by human philosophical thinking, or by poetic, imaginative construction, would compromise the need for an authoritative revelation. A religion founded on human mythology would be, for Kierkegaard, like a religion founded on human philosophy, a religion of 'immanence'. Christianity is, he thinks, a religion of 'transcendence', founded on a revelation from God that humans could not have constructed for themselves. So for Kierkegaard there are no mythological parallels to the story of Jesus of Nazareth, no significant parallels between Jesus Christ and pagan 'dying and rising gods'. It is important to point out, by the way, that this judgement of Kierkegaard's is not simply a reflection of ignorance. Kierkegaard was fascinated by mythology and well acquainted with both Greek and Nordic myths.
   A position that appears to be sharply at odds with Kierkegaard's claim about Christianity and myth is developed by

---

[7] Kierkegaard, *Philosophical Fragments*, 35–36.
[8] Ibid. 109.

C. S. Lewis in his provocative essay, 'Myth Became Fact'.[9] Lewis was, like Kierkegaard, fascinated by mythology, even as a child, and one of his best friends was the great mythologist J. R. R. Tolkien. Originally, Lewis, perhaps under the influence of Frazer's *The Golden Bough*, seems to have thought Christianity incredible because it was a myth; the Gospel was just one more ancient tale of a 'dying and rising god'.[10] His conversion was made possible when, with the help of friends, he was able to see Christianity as a historical myth, a true historical narrative that retains the character of mythology.[11]

What is that character? On Lewis's view, a myth is a story that captures universal, abstract truth in concrete form. 'In the enjoyment of a great myth we come nearest to experiencing as a concrete what can otherwise be understood only as an abstraction.'[12] Experience and understanding appear to be mutually exclusive; reflecting on repentance can't be done while repenting, nor can one study sexual pleasure while making love.[13] Myth is the partial solution to this dilemma, for myth is not, like propositional truth, merely abstract, nor is it, like direct experience, merely particular.[14]

Hence it is not too surprising that Lewis, unlike Kierkegaard, does not deny that there are parallels between Christianity and pagan mythology. 'We must not be nervous about 'parallels' and 'Pagan Christs': they *ought* to be there—it would be a stumbling block if they weren't.'[15] This does not mean for Lewis that the historical character of the Gospel is inessential or unimportant. To the contrary, it is an essential aspect of

[9] C. S. Lewis, 'Myth Became Fact', in *God in the Dock* (Grand Rapids, Mich.: Wm. B. Eerdmans, 1970), 63–7. Similar views about the relation of ancient pagan mythology to the Gospel can be found in Lewis's book *Miracles* (New York: Macmillan, 1947), 117–20, and 139 n.

[10] For Lewis's early dismissal of Christianity as 'mythology' see some of his letters to Arthur Greeves, found in *They Stand Together: The Letters of C. S. Lewis to Arthur Greeves (1914–1963)*, ed. Walter Hooper (New York: Macmillan, 1979), 134–8. Here Lewis says plainly that 'all religions, that is, all mythologies to give them their proper name are merely man's own invention—Christ as much as Loki'.

[11] For an account of the conversation Lewis had with J. R. R. Tolkien and Hugo Dyson that was instrumental for Lewis's conversion, see A. N. Wilson, *C. S. Lewis: A Biography* (New York: W. W. Norton & Co., 1990), 124–7.

[12] Lewis, 'Myth Became Fact', 66.

[13] Ibid. 65.

[14] Ibid. 66.

[15] Ibid. 67.

Christian faith to believe in a 'historical Person crucified (it is all in order) *under Pontius Pilate*'.[16] The Christian must believe that the events in the Gospel really happened, at a particular date. But the Christian must not only believe the events occurred, but 'receive the myth (fact though it has become) with the same imaginative embrace which we accord to all myths'.[17] As a myth, the Christian Gospel is addressed to us as savage, child, and poet, not merely to us as moralists, scholars, and philosophers: 'Christians also need to be reminded ... that what became Fact was a Myth, that it carries with it into the world of Fact all the properties of a myth'.[18]

3.3. IS THE GOSPEL STORY UNIQUE?

Who is right, here, Kierkegaard or Lewis? Is the Christian narrative unique, or does it have the character of myth, with pagan parallels?

It appears to me that there are at least two distinct issues here. First is the question as to whether the Christian story has the *character* and *function* of myth.[19] Does it, as Lewis claims, embody in a concrete and particular way abstract and universal truths, be they psychological or metaphysical? The second issue is the question as to whether the Christian story has parallels in other myths. Lewis claims both that the Gospel has the form of myth and that it has parallels in other myths, but these two claims are logically distinct.

Of the two the first seems to me to be by far the most important for Lewis. Though he says it would be a problem, 'a stumbling-block', if there weren't pagan parallels with Christ, I don't see how that problem could be a major one (though I will discuss the matter below). The really important thing is not that there are parallel myths, but that the Christian nar-

---

[16] Lewis, 'Myth Became Fact', 67.
[17] Ibid.
[18] Ibid.
[19] As we shall see, this first question is really not one but two questions. The final position of Lewis seems to be that the incarnational narrative has the function and some of the character of a myth, but not all. Specifically, Lewis claims that the incarnational narrative has a sober, history-like literary style that has no parallel in mythological literature.

rative itself has a certain character and significance. With respect to this issue, I don't see that Kierkegaard necessarily disagrees with Lewis. If Lewis, by calling the Gospel a myth, merely means to say that it has power to convey metaphysical and psychological truth in a concrete way, then I do not think Kierkegaard has any reason to object. After all, Kierkegaard's own pseudonym Climacus, in developing his supposed invention, characterizes the narrative as a *poetic* one.[20] Kierkegaard recognizes the story as one that reveals to us the truth about our own condition, the truth about the nature of God as the one who lovingly sacrifices himself for the sake of his forlorn creatures, and the truth about how we may be transformed and reconciled with this God.

Perhaps at this point Hans Frei might object to Lewis's view. Frei has argued strenuously against viewing the Gospel narratives as myth, partly because he does not wish to see the narrative merely as expressing or revealing some truths. For Frei, the narrative is one in which God's character is enacted, not merely expressed or revealed.

Frei certainly has a legitimate concern here. However, one can affirm that the incarnational narrative does reveal something to us about God—God's loving nature and our need for redemption, for example—while agreeing with Frei that this is not all that the narrative does. One way of expressing this point is to affirm that the narrative is irreplaceable; one could not substitute for the narrative a set of doctrinal propositions that the narrative merely 'illustrates'. Furthermore, the historicity of the narrative becomes crucial at just this point. One reason that it is vital to see the narrative as historical is precisely that it purports to be the story of what God has done in human history, not merely a story that reveals truths about God and human beings.

Nevertheless, all this is compatible with seeing the narrative as one that possesses poetic power, in the sense that it has universal meaning. In denying that the incarnational story is myth, Kierkegaard is denying that it is a human invention, not denying that the narrative possesses this kind of significance. There is no hint in Kierkegaard that the narrative could be

---

[20] See *Philosophical Fragments*, the title of ch. 2.

replaced with a system of abstract theological propositions. On the contrary, it is through engagement with the narrative that the hearer comes to know God in a concrete, particular way.

So I conclude Kierkegaard and Lewis agree on the most important issue: that the Gospel narrative has the form and function of myth, conceived as *Lewis* (but not Kierkegaard) understands myth. Their apparent disagreement stems from different understandings of what a 'myth' is. For Kierkegaard, a myth is by definition a product of the human imagination, so the incarnation, as God's story, enacted in history, is no myth. Lewis, on the other hand, with a different concept of myth that allows God to be the author of a historical myth, affirms the narrative as myth so as to highlight its universal significance and the irreplaceable character of the narrative form.

There still appears to be a disagreement over whether this story resembles other myths. Are there 'pagan parallels'? Is the story of Jesus as God incarnate, dying and rising from the dead, one that resembles the myths of Balder, or Osiris, or Attis?

I suspect that this question is thoroughly ambiguous, and the way we answer it will depend on how the question is clarified. If we mean, 'Are there any respects in which the story of Jesus resembles stories of Balder and other pagan rising and dying gods?' the answer will be certainly 'Yes', but that by itself is a trivial claim. There is a sense in which virtually everything resembles everything else. The interesting question is not whether the story of Jesus resembles the story of Balder in some respects, but rather concerns the significance of the similarities and dissimilarities. It should not be surprising that in certain contexts some of these similarities may strike us as significant and important, while the disanalogies seems less crucial, while in other contexts the disanalogies strike us as more profound, and the similarities as superficial. Whether two things are to be judged significantly alike depends partly on what features are important to us. As modes of inter-city transportation, cars and aeroplanes are interestingly similar; you can get from Chicago to Minneapolis in either. As ways of allowing humans to fly, cars aren't very similar to planes at all, despite the Beach Boys' fabled 'deuce coupe', which could have flown 'if she only had wings'.

I suspect Lewis and Kierkegaard make the apparently conflicting claims they do because they have different concerns. Specifically, Lewis wants to highlight the ways in which the Gospel narrative makes meaningful contact with the human condition. In stressing the mythical character of the Gospel, Lewis underlines the ways it speaks to us as humans. We have a need for psychological wholeness and healing, and a need to understand what kind of universe this is and our place in it. In so far as myths attempt to address these needs, the Gospel is pre-eminently myth, albeit historical myth, at least for Lewis. In so far as pagan myths address those same needs, it is not surprising that there should be parallels. If it is indeed a truth about the human condition that we cannot save ourselves and require a saviour, it is not surprising that pagans had what Lewis called 'queer dreams' about saviour-gods.[21] If it is indeed a truth about human life that its meaning can only be discovered when the selfish individual 'dies' and is reborn, then it is not surprising that stories of death and new life should be found in human consciousness. If we are primarily concerned with what we might call the existential power and metaphysical depth of the Christian story, then it is plausible that its character as myth will impress us, and that we will notice ways in which it resembles other myths.

Kierkegaard's concerns are different. He is not worried so much about the significance and power of the Christian narrative; that he takes for granted. At least, he thinks its power will be evident if we can recover the story as it really is, and cut through the familiarity and sentimentality that have made us immune to that power. Chiefly, I think, Kierkegaard is concerned with the issue of the authority of divine revelation, and another topic which he saw as closely related to divine authority, the epistemological implications of human sinfulness.

This may sound odd, since Kierkegaard is not popularly regarded as a thinker who was much concerned with the issue

---

[21] Though I know Lewis somewhere refers to pagan myths in this way, I cannot recall the reference.

of authority, despite the fact that he wrote a book on the subject. Nevertheless, his concern, I think, in denying that there are any significant pagan parallels to the Christian story was to emphasize the fact that in their sinfulness humans are unable to discover the truth about themselves and about God. However much we may obscurely desire God and sense a problem in our current condition, we lack both an adequate sense of what God is like, what it would be like to be properly related to him, and how far removed we are from having such an understanding of God and such a relationship to him. It is in the life, death, and resurrection of Jesus that God reveals these things to us, and they cannot be achieved through any myth of human devising. Our salvation depends on a revelation from God; if it could be achieved through an imaginative construction, then we would not be the fallen creatures we in fact are.

With these concerns we can easily understand why Kierkegaard should be more impressed with the differences between the Christian story and its alleged pagan parallels than the similarities. After all, Osiris, Adonis, Odin, and Balder are gods, not God. None of them has the character of the Christian God. None is an all-powerful, all-knowing, creator of the universe out of nothing, willing to sacrifice his own self out of profound love for the entire human race for the salvation of that race. A knowledge of these pagan stories does not make it any easier to understand how the God of Christian faith could become a specific human being, nor any easier to comprehend why God would do so. Such an action is as metaphysically incomprehensible to us as is the infinite God who is the agent, and such love is completely foreign to us. Stories of love, devotion, and sacrifice are not unknown to us as humans, but who can fathom such love, devotion, and sacrifice for the sake of those who are one's *enemies*, on the part of one who has no need at all for those whose love he is seeking? We can thus understand why Kierkegaard, in order to 'quicken the imagination', gives poetic analogies to the story, such as the fairy tale of the king who adopts a disguise to woo a peasant maiden, but insists in the end that the story nevertheless provides no valid analogy to the incarnation, because the differences between the king and the god are so profound. The way in

which the Christian story baffles both our metaphysical and
moral imaginations makes it 'the absolute paradox', something
no human would be capable of inventing.

   I do not think that Lewis would disagree with any of this.
Even though the story of God's work in Christ, in perfectly
answering our deepest needs, may have echoes in pagan myths,
this by no means entails that there aren't significant differences
between the Christian narrative and those myths. Lewis says
clearly, in a letter to his friend Arthur Greeves, that the incarnational narrative is 'God's myth' rather than being a myth of
human devising,[22] so Lewis would certainly agree with Kierkegaard that one could not replace the story of Jesus with a
tale about Osiris or Odin. Lewis does not say that the only
difference between the Christian story and the pagan myths is
simply that the Christian story happens to be historical. On the
contrary, in another essay, he clearly argues that the Christian
narrative has a completely different type of style from ancient
myths and legends:

I have been reading poems, romances, vision-literature, legends,
myths all my life. I know what they are like. I know that not one of
them is like this [the New Testament narrative]. Of this text there are
only two possible views. Either this is reportage—though it may no
doubt contain errors—pretty close up to the facts; nearly as close as
Boswell. Or else, some unknown writer in the second century,
without known predecessors or successors, suddenly anticipated the
whole technique of modern, novelistic, realistic narrative. If it is
untrue, it must be narrative of that kind. The reader who doesn't see
this simply has not learned to read.[23]

I do not at this point wish to defend the apologetic thrust of
this quotation; it may be argued that there are other genres
that Lewis does not consider. Rather, I wish to note that this
quote implies that when Lewis says that the incarnational
narrative has the form of myth, he does not mean that it
resembles ancient myths in terms of literary style. Here his
position is actually similar to that of Hans Frei, whose insist-
ence that the Gospel narratives are not myths rests heavily on

---

[22] Lewis writes to Greeves that 'it [Christianity] is God's myth where the others
are men's myths'. *They Stand Together*, 427.
[23] C. S. Lewis, 'Modern Theology and Biblical Criticism', in *Christian Reflections*
(London: Geoffrey Bles, 1967), 155.

the claim that as literature they are 'realistic narratives'. The opposition between Lewis and Frei is thus at least partly an illusion. When Lewis says that the narratives are mythical, he is not saying that as literature they resemble the myths of classical Greece and other cultures, but making a point about the *power* of the story. For Lewis, classifying the story as myth is not rooted in a judgement about the literary style of the New Testament; on this issue he agrees with Frei. It is rather a way of highlighting the way the story speaks to people at all times and places.

Nor does Lewis think the content of the Christian narrative can be found in any other mythical story, even if there are points of resemblance. Clearly, there are differences between these pagan stories and the Christian narrative as well, which is why Lewis says that 'modernist' Christians, who have given up belief in the historical reality of the Christian story, are still better off clinging to it and being nourished by it as myth, rather than simply cutting themselves off from Christianity altogether.[24] Not just any myth will do for Lewis.

I conclude then that the disagreement between Kierkegaard and Lewis is not as serious as it appears. Both would agree that the Christian narrative has the kind of poetic power myths possess. Both would agree that there are similarities as well as differences between the Christian narrative and pagan myths. Perhaps there is some disagreement over the relative significance of those similarities and differences, but this disagreement may be partially explained as a reflection of differing concerns in particular contexts. Certainly, some differences may remain, probably related to Lewis's acceptance of natural theology and Kierkegaard's rejection of such apologetic arguments, but I think that, given the appropriate occasion, we could go a long way towards resolving this disagreement as well. We cannot afford to sacrifice the concerns of either Lewis or Kierkegaard. The power and relevance of the Gospel to speak to the human condition must be exhibited, but we must not ignore the implications of human sinfulness.

I think therefore that we can concur with Lewis's view that the Christian narrative is a historical myth in Lewis's sense

[24] Lewis, 'Myth Become Fact', 67.

of myth, a 'myth become fact', while remaining sensitive to Kierkegaard's concerns. We can view the incarnational narrative as myth without thereby denying the uniqueness of the Christian story in its content or its realistic literary character, and also without implying that humans can dispense with divine revelation. The mythical character of the incarnational narrative is important, because it is part of the answer to the question as to why the story matters to twentieth-century people. However, the Christian story still claims to be unique. If Christianity is true, then its founding narrative is a myth of divine origin. Since it is a divine myth that contains the answer to the human dilemma, it resembles in some ways human myths that attempt answers to the fundamental problems of human life.[25] However, since Christianity teaches that humans are incapable of solving this dilemma on their own, it also necessarily holds that the divine myth is unique and irreplaceable.

3.4. DEMYTHOLOGIZING AND REMYTHOLOGIZING

Highlighting the mythical dimension of the incarnational narrative helps one to see one of the reasons that the narrative is important to people *now*. The Lewis claim highlights the power of the narrative to articulate the truth about God and the human condition in a concrete and particular way, though one must insist with Frei that this is by no means all the story does. The Lewis claim emphasizes the power of the narrative to articulate such truths without denying either its historical character or its unique status as irreplaceable divine revelation. One may object, and the objection has much to be said for it, that given the popular connotations of the term 'myth' it would be better to speak of the power and signficance of the narrative rather than to describe the narrative as myth. However, given

---

[25] Lewis himself is prepared to see the similarities between pagan and Christian stories to imply that God is at work revealing himself through the pagan mythologists as well, so they also are not purely human in their origin. The difference he saw was that the pagan stories 'are God expressing Himself through the minds of poets, using such images as He found there, while Christianity is God expressing Himself through what we call "real things" '. See *They Stand Together*, 427.

Lewis's definition of the term, his claim is defensible. What is important is not whether the term 'myth' is applied to the narrative, but understanding why the narrative has the power it does have.

We can now return to the question of historicity, our primary concern. If we view the incarnational narrative as myth in Lewis's sense, it does not have to be seen as unhistorical. But what value does an affirmation of its historicity have? What would be lost if we dropped any claims for historicity? These questions are raised by proposals both to demythologize and to remythologize the narrative.

Let us look at proposals to demythologize first. It seems to me that the Bultmannian programme of demythologizing the Gospel narrative partly reflects the concept of myth as a pre-scientific mode of explanation. According to this view, a myth is something a scientifically educated person cannot believe, leading to Bultmann's famous statement that 'it is impossible to use electrical light and the wireless and to avail ourselves of modern medical and surgical discoveries, and at the same time to believe in the New Testament world of spirits and miracles'.[26] However, Bultmann proposes to extract from the mythical husk of the Gospels a non-mythical core that expresses the existential meaning which is present in the New Testament but is sometimes obscured by the presuppositions of a discredited view of the natural world, a project that appears to view myths more in terms of their function in expressing a world-view or at least an attitude towards life.

It seems to me that this Bultmannian proposal not only assumes that myths are false explanations of phenomena in the natural world, but also manifests a commitment to a naturalistic view of how things are in the world. In other words, miracles don't occur, and there are no such entities as spirits. If the function of myth is to explain natural phenomena, and if the explanations given in myth require us to believe in entities that don't exist, then we must certainly demythologize the Gospel.

However, both of these two assumptions are questionable. The view that myths function mainly as pre-scientific expla-

---

[26] Rudolf Bultmann, *Kerygma and Myth* (New York: Harper & Row, 1961), 5.

nations is dubious in the light of the complexity of ways myths have been seen to function. So, even if Bultmann were right about the unhistorical character of references to miracles and spiritual agents, it would not follow that the Gospels need to be demythologized. In fact, it does not appear that Bultmann himself thinks this, since he also views the stories as concrete expressions of a particular life-view and evidently thinks that there is no need to reject the stories as stories. In preaching and common Christian life Bultmann seems to think the stories are still important as concrete bearers of metaphysical and/or psychological truth. The term 'demythologize' is misleading; what Bultmann really urges is simply that we recognize the unhistorical character of the stories, stories that can be theologically explicated, but not really replaced.

The assumption that stories about miracles and spirits are necessarily unhistorical is as dubious as the view of myth. There is a vast philosophical literature dealing with miracles and the plausibility of supernaturalism, and so it is impossible to be comprehensive in treating the issue. However, I will argue in Chapter 7 that there are no good philosophical arguments for denying the possibility of supernaturally caused events, nor do we have any good reasons to deny that such events could be known if they occurred.[27]

Bultmann here simply adopts without argument the outlook of what we might term the Enlightenment secular mind. Though this outlook is often honorifically designated as 'modern' and though it may be a common outlook among intellectuals, neither of those facts is weighty evidence for its truth. I believe that the typical conclusion of Enlightenment rationalism that religious belief is irrational rests on one or more of the following: (1) To be rational a belief must be based on evidence that is highly objective and certain; (2) science is the paradigm of a belief system that fulfils this requirement; (3) the evidential support for religious beliefs is completely unlike the evidential support that scientific beliefs possess. All of these assumptions are eminently dubious. Externalist, coherentist, and pragmatist epistemologies all agree in chal-

---

[27] For one philosophical attempt to argue for this view, see Richard Swinburne, *The Concept of Miracle* (London: Macmillan, 1970).

lenging the first. A major part of contemporary philosophy of science challenges the second, and a lot of interesting work in contemporary philosophy of religion challenges the third.[28] So I conclude that the 'modern' project of demythologizing the Gospel has little attraction.

But what of 'post-modern' suggestions that the Gospel needs remythologizing?[29] The answer depends largely on what sense of myth underlies the proposal. If the proposal is using 'myth' in the Lewis sense that allows for the possibility of historical myth, then it is one that *may* be helpful, depending on the significance accorded to history by the proposal. We have already seen that there is merit in calling attention to the mythical power of the Gospel narrative, the ways in which it expresses in a concrete and particular way the human situation in its universality, though it would be a mistake to limit the incarnational narrative solely to this function, thereby making its historical character inessential. If, however, myth is being taken in the common sense in which it precludes historicity, on the grounds that there are no supernatural agents and miracles, then I would object for exactly the same reasons advanced against demythologizers. The fact that myths may have socio-logical functions, or function as expressing metaphysical and psychological truths, does not entail that events that compose a mythical narrative could not actually occur.

[28] For contemporary epistemological challenges to classical foundationalism see William Alston, *Epistemic Justification* (Ithaca, NY: Cornell University Press, 1989) and Alvin Plantinga, *Warrant: The Current Debate* and *Warrant and Proper Function* (Oxford: Oxford University Press, 1993). A good introduction to the contemporary debate in philosophy of science can be found in Del Ratzsch, *Philosophy of Science* (Downer's Grove, Ill.: InterVarsity, 1986). For a strong argument that rationality in science and rationality in religious belief are analogous, see Michael C. Banner, *The Justification of Science and the Rationality of Religious Belief* (Oxford: Oxford University Press, 1990).

[29] One writer who has written a steady stream of books calling for such a re-mythologizing of Christianity is Morton Kelsey. Though closer to orthodox Christianity than Joseph Campbell, Kelsey mixes Christianity with Jungian psychology in a way that is reminiscent of Campbell. He argues constantly for stressing the mythical character of Christianity, and argues that this does not mean that it must be non-historical. However, the mythical character of the narrative is stressed in such a manner that the historical character begins to look non-essential; that is, the truths expressed by the Christian 'myths' and our response to those myths would look much the same whether the myths were historically enacted or not. This is the view that I criticize in the next section. See Kelsey's *Myth, History, and Faith* (Rockport, Mass.: Element, 1991).

3.5. THE ESSENTIAL HISTORICITY OF THE GOSPEL

A proposal to remythologize the Gospel must be scrutinized carefully, even if the proposer is operating with a sense of myth that allows that mythical narratives could be historically enacted. The crucial question concerns whether the Gospels are being understood in such a way that the mythical character of the narrative does all the work, with the historical character being merely an accidental feature. I shall argue that when this occurs, a great deal is lost.

Although a proposal to emphasize the mythical character of the Gospel may be perfectly in order so long as it is understood that the mythical significance of the narrative does not preclude historicity, one must emphasize the 'may' in this statement. There are ways of understanding the Gospel narrative which, though they do not eliminate the possibility of a historical enactment, nevertheless make history inessential to the whole business. We may imagine a theologian who is quick to soothe the 'literalist' or 'fundamentalist' or 'traditionalist' who is worried about the interpretation of the Gospel as myth: 'My dear ordinary Christian, you must not worry when I call the Gospel a myth; to call it a myth is merely to highlight the way it embodies universal meaning in a particular narrative. But as I use the term "myth", myths can be historical. So I don't deny that these events really happened.'

Our imaginary soothing theologian here, however, may not *affirm* that these events really happened either. That is, while giving his soothing speech, he may to himself be saying, 'Sure, it's possible the events really occurred. Anything is possible. But of course it really doesn't matter. What's really important is the myth itself, so I don't have to worry myself about embarrassing epistemological questions about the historical status of my beliefs, such as whether they are founded on evidence and, if so, whether the evidence is adequate. Nor do I have to get involved in messy disputes about whether miracles are really possible. If ordinary folks need to believe in such things, no real harm is done by letting them remain undisturbed, but we must not make such things an essential part of the faith.'

I believe that it is crucial for Christian faith to maintain not merely the possibility of the historicity of the incarnational narrative, but its actuality. We must understand the story in such a way that it is essential and not merely possible that it be historical. Why does history matter? From the point of view of orthodoxy, of course, it is sufficient to point out that this is part of the universal teaching of the Church, 'that which has been believed everywhere, always and by all'.[30] The Church is committed to the historical truth of the Gospel narratives, and cannot abandon history without abandoning the faith of the apostles and Church fathers.

However, such an appeal to authority will be unconvincing to many today, even many within the Church. Hence, it is necessary to ask *why* the Church has always maintained the historical character of its founding events. One might well answer by pointing out that this has been maintained simply because of a conviction that the narrative is historically *true*, surely the best reason of all for holding on to a conviction. The Church is committed to proclaiming that it is in fact through history that God has seen fit to make possible the salvation of the human race. Whether God could have brought about salvation in some other way not involving history is an interesting speculative question, but one does not have to answer it to have a conviction about how God in fact has chosen to save the human race.

However, this modesty about what possibilities God may or may not have had does not preclude some understanding of the reasons God may have had to operate as he did. That is, without denying that the primary reason for holding fast to the historical character of the founding narrative is simply that the narrative is in fact historically true, and without pretentiously claiming to prove the necessity of God's chosen

---

[30] Vincent of Lerins, *The Commonitories*, in The Fathers of the Church, vii (Washington, DC: The Catholic University of America Press, 1970), 270. Quoted in Richard Swinburne, *Revelation: From Metaphor to Analogy* (Oxford: Oxford University Press, 1992), 143. This phrase cannot of course be understood as literally what is believed by all people who have thought of themselves as Christians, for there are many today who fit this description who have not accepted the historical truth of the incarnational narrative. Rather, I understand the phrase 'everywhere, always, and by all' to refer to the teachings of the Early Church as embodied in the ecumenical creeds, and the teachings consistent with those early creeds and with each other of all the branches of the Church that remain committed to those creeds.

plan, we can try to understand the point or purpose of history in the economy of salvation. The fundamental reason why history seems to me to matter is simply this: *The historical character of the Gospel implies that salvation is made possible by the work of Christ.* If we understand the Gospel narrative as a non-historical myth, and think that salvation is made possible by the Gospel narrative, then we are saying that salvation is not something made possible by God's actions in history. The proposal to treat the Gospel narrative as a non-historical myth could be understood in various ways, each of which raises important problems. Two of these problems seem especially serious to me: (1) The elimination of historicity in favour of myth does not allow human sinfulness to be taken with real seriousness. (2) The elimination of historicity in favour of myth eliminates the possibility of an actual historical relationship with God. A look at two versions of the proposal to eliminate historicity will serve to illustrate how these problems arise.

1. If the narrative were a non-historical myth, then perhaps salvation would be made possible simply by the story itself. We might, for instance, see the Gospel story simply as providing a moral ideal to be emulated. This of course is the essence of the rationalist/moralist separation of the religious meaning of the narrative from its historicity. Inspired by the story, people strive to become Christ-like. Such a scenario seems to presuppose that human sinfulness is not as profound and pervasive as Christians have traditionally supposed, and as the evening news seems to confirm on a nightly basis. This view assumes that humans really do have the power to change themselves. As we shall discuss later, such an optimistic view of human nature certainly has psychological appeal, but it fits poorly with a realistic and accurate assessment of human behaviour. As the Cold War ended, there were dreams that a 'new world order' of peace would ensue. It has not taken long for such dreams to crumble in the face of ethnic strife all around the globe.

The traditional understanding of the incarnational narrative implies that there is a real gulf between God and humans, and that in becoming incarnate God actually steps across

this gulf and becomes one of us. No theory of the atonement has ever been universally accepted by the Church as
binding. However, *that* Jesus' life, death, and resurrection
are the means whereby God accomplished the atonement of
humans has never been doubted. Whether we understand
this atoning work as payment of a ransom, winning a victory
over Satan and the powers of evil, the payment of the just
penalty for sin, a priestly sacrifice, or regard all of the above
as capturing aspects of the reality of Christ's atonement, the
reality remains. If we treat the incarnational narrative simply
as a fictional illustration of a moral ideal, then there seems
to be nothing left of the atonement. I shall discuss theories
of atonement in the next chapter, but it is appropriate to
point out that the moralist interpretation of the narrative
really eliminates any need for atonement. Moreover, the
point being made here can be generalized. It does not apply
merely to the passion and resurrection, but to the narrative
as a whole. That narrative is a story about what God has
done to bridge the moral gulf between humans and God, so
as to make possible a real relationship. If we treat the
incarnational narrative simply as a fictional illustration of a
moral ideal, then one can hardly regard this gulf as having
been bridged.

2. Another alternative, if the Gospel narrative is non-
historical myth, is to see it as an illustration or communication of a timeless, metaphysical truth. Someone might attempt
to hold on to the reality of the atonement by viewing the
narrative as expressing some deep truth about the nature of
God, or perhaps as a symbol of an action God performs in
a timeless, eternal way. On this view, the historical events
are not decisive, and one should not see salvation as a
historical achievement. Rather, the narrative simply tells us
something true about the timeless character of God. Whether
or not Jesus really died and rose again, it remains true that
God eternally forgives and atones for human sin, and is
victorious over sin and death. The story of Jesus is important,
but whether the events occurred or not it remains true that
Jesus is 'the lamb slain before the foundation of the world',
a scriptural passage that is understood to teach that the

atonement refers to some eternal fact about God, and not something God accomplished through particular temporal actions.[31]

This proposal is much more appealing than the first, because it is grounded in something true: the historical reality of Christ's atoning work undoubtedly reflects the eternal character of God. It is precisely because God is essentially loving, compassionate, ready to forgive and re-create, that he acted as he did in Christ. Nevertheless, if we merely see the incarnational narrative as a story which symbolizes or communicates eternal truth without being historically true, much that is important would be lost from Christian faith.

Among the most important things would be this: The Church's proclamation is that salvation is not achieved through metaphysical insight but through a particular kind of relationship. Salvation is not merely recognizing some abstract truth about a timeless God but coming into relationship with God in the historically concrete person of Jesus of Nazareth. To be sure, one might claim, and I would agree, that knowing the metaphysical truth about God might enable me to have a relation of sorts with God. In so far as I understand God to be loving and forgiving, perhaps I could turn to him in repentance and faith.

However, such a relation with a timeless God could not have the interactive character of a relation with a God who has acted historically. Part of the value of history is of course that one can thereby in some way *see* that God is loving and forgiving; God doesn't just reveal this to us as propositional truth but concretely demonstrates it. However, the historicity of God's mighty saving acts is more than empirical evidence for a timeless truth. It is an enactment and embodiment of that truth; an

---

[31] For a theological treatment of Christ's saving work that tends in this direction, see Robert F. Capon, *Hunting the Divine Fox* (New York: Seabury Press, 1974), esp. 85–117. Capon criticizes the view that God's saving acts can be seen as 'transactions'. On his view, though every event in some sense is a happening, or transaction, the particular transactions we identify as saving events must be seen as sacramental communications of eternal realities. Relying on the doctrine of God's omnipresence, he argues, e.g., that God did not appear in Christ because to say that would be to imply that God was not already present. However, if the incarnation is in any sense unique then it must be true that God was doing something in Christ that He was not doing in other events.

identification with us that makes possible a different kind of relationship altogether.

An analogy may help here. Suppose I am in love with a woman and wish to marry her. Suppose she loves me in return. Should I not be content to know this wonderful truth that she holds this love for me? Why is it important to me that she actually marries me? The marriage is not merely assurance of the fact that she does love me; it is the actual establishment of our life together. It is not a mere symbol of her willingness to enter my life; it is the means whereby she does so. If her act in marrying me is one which involves great sacrifice and suffering on her part, then the relationship is deeper still. We could imagine, for example, that I am mired in poverty and despair, and that to marry me she must travel a great distance, both geographically and socially.

The analogy can be pushed still further. Suppose I lack the confidence to love her and relate to her as I ought. In such a case the mere knowledge of her love might not be enough to make a relation possible. If, however, she made the journey to come to me and identify with me in my misery, I might be moved and transformed in a way that would never be possible simply on the basis of an abstract knowledge of her love. In such a case I would experience her love historically. The analogy ultimately fails, of course, because the inability of humans to love God and the profound sufferings of God's journey to us have no true human analogues.

Hans Frei, in his polemic against understanding the narrative as myth, frequently says that 'the story is the meaning' rather than merely being simply an illustration of that meaning.[32] I believe that it is Frei's concern over the possibility that the narrative will simply be viewed as an 'illustration' that underlies his opposition to viewing the narrative as myth, and his concern here is well taken. However, Frei's opposition goes too far. One does not have to deny that the story expresses truths about God to see that this is not all that it does. A great deal would indeed be lost if historicity were abandoned and we were left with myth alone, but this does not mean that the myth-like elements of the narrative must be denied.

---

[32] Hans Frei, *Eclipse*, 280.

3.6. THE APPEAL OF NON-HISTORICAL MYTH

Having argued that the essential character of the Gospel would be lost or weakened by attempts to see it as non-historical myth, I should like to offer some reflections as to why attempts to do so are appealing to so many in our culture today. The popularity of myth itself is part of the story, of course, and this popularity is not hard to understand. If C. S. Lewis is right to say that myth conveys universal truth in an imaginative, concrete way, then myth is in many ways living water for a dry culture. We live in a culture that has undergone significant 'flattening'. Many people have no living religious faith and are detached from living religious communities, or indeed communities of any sort. Even those who are part of religious communities often find themselves in the same flattened world. Too often the mainline Church denominations offer only moralism, psychological platitudes, or political action. Evangelical Churches may offer the same, combined with worship experiences that have a thinness that mirrors the surrounding culture, instead of a profound encounter with a God who is holy and majestic. People who live in such communities often have no sense that the world is deep or profound, or that their lives have any depth of purpose. Rather, they see themselves simply as material pleasure-seekers, grasping whatever moments of enjoyment come their way. A litany of familiar complaints about contemporary Western culture can be cited at this point: work has become simply a means of earning money; marriages have become contractual relationships whose purpose is individual fulfilment and happiness; families are a burden for which the State should take responsibility. It is not hard to see why imaginative stories charged with metaphysical meaning offer relief in such a culture.

It is for these reasons that it is important to follow Lewis's advice and recover the myth-like dimensions of the Gospel narrative; its capacity to engage the imagination as well as the intellect. However, the appeal of myth by itself does not explain the appeal of divorcing Christian faith from history, and we must understand that appeal as well if we are to see the dangers in reducing the incarnational narrative to myth. Why is it that so many are attracted to Joseph Campbell's attempt to see the passion of Jesus as just another mythical expression of a universal truth?[33]

I am sure that I cannot give an exhaustive account of the reasons for this, but there are several factors that seem important to me. I shall briefly mention several of them, for the most part using the phenomenon of Joseph Campbell's work as my favoured illustration.

3.6.1. *The Appeal of Optimistic Anthropology*

I mentioned in discussing Kierkegaard that he defended the uniqueness of the story of the incarnation on the grounds that human sinfulness made it impossible for humans to discover the ultimate truth about their condition on their own. As Kierkegaard was well aware, this claim about human sinfulness is not one that goes down well with sinful human beings; if there is one thing sinful human beings do not like to hear, it is the truth about their sinfulness. Thus Kierkegaard, echoing St Paul, claims that a mark of authentic Christianity when it is preached will be the possibility of offence it poses.

Contrary to this offensiveness is any view that provides a flattering view of human nature, and Joseph Campbell's view of myth does just this. In *The Hero With a Thousand Faces*, Campbell regards all the myths of the world as essentially variations on one story, which he calls the monomyth. The monomyth is a recounting of the story of redemption, the story of salvation, for each one of us is the hero. We are our own saviours. The underlying message is that ultimate truth is indeed within our grasp. We have the truth and we can achieve salvation. A more flattering picture of the human self can hardly be imagined.

3.6.2. *The Abolition of Authority*

If we have the truth and can save ourselves, then we have no need of another saviour to whom we owe everything, including devotion and obedience. I think it should be stressed that the appeal here is not simply that the epistemological challenges

---

[33] See Campbell, *The Hero With a Thousand Faces*, 260.

of the Enlightenment concerning revelation claims no longer need to be faced. The deepest appeal is simply that I am thereby freed to become my own authority. For Campbell no particular version of the monomyth is definitive and final, and the correct reading of a myth is dictated by our own psychological insight. If the story of Jesus no longer speaks to one, take heart. There are plenty of other stories at hand. The individual does not answer to Church, creed, or Scripture but makes use of 'symbols' to the extent that he or she finds them enlightening. Thus the contemporary world helps itself to metaphysical meaning, and even ransacks biblical narratives, but never sees itself as responsible to any transcendent authority. Someone has said that myths contain 'all answers and no questions'. If we live only on non-historical myth, then there is a sense in which there is no one to question us, and we do not have to answer to anyone. The historical character of the Gospel narrative implies that there is a real person there to question us, and to whom we must answer.

3.6.3. *The Psychologizing of Culture*

It is characteristic of the advocates of mythologization today to make psychology the mouthpiece of metaphysics. The appeal of this is multifold. First, it fits with the general psychologization of Western culture, and the emphasis on the satisfaction of individual needs. Every problem becomes a psychological problem, and psychological problems are in turn laden with metaphysical depth: 'Every failure to cope with a life situation must be laid, in the end, to a restriction of consciousness.'[34] The therapist becomes the new high priest, the transmitter of sacred truth and mediator of healing insight. The new religion is virtually guaranteed to respond to my felt psychological needs. 'In the office of the modern psychoanalyst, the stages of the hero-adventure come to light again in the dreams and hallucinations of the patient.'[35] Of course, this psychologizing of ultimate truth fits well with the rejection of authority and optimistic anthropology mentioned above.

---

[34] Ibid. 121.
[35] Ibid.

My own psyche becomes the source of final truth.

3.6.4. *The Embracement of 'Pluralism'*

The rejection of authority and psychologizing of truth fits perfectly with the contemporary refusal to tolerate disagreement. I refer here to the response to religious diversity that often parades under the term 'pluralism'. Pluralism can mean many things, but too often it is used to imply that the various religions simply express the same truth through different systems. Campbell's claim about the monomyth is a perfect example of this: 'through various symbols the same redemption is revealed. "Truth is one", we read in the Vedas; "the sages call it by many names." '[36]

This pluralism is anything but a willingness to tolerate and respect honest disagreements, however. It is in fact an imperialistic attempt to decree that believers of all religious faiths must interpret their beliefs in the same way. Believers in monotheism, for example, are sternly rebuked:

This recognition of the secondary nature of the personality of whatever deity is worshiped is characteristic of most of the traditions of the world ... In Christianity, Mohammedanism, and Judaism, however, the personality of the divinity is taught to be final—which makes it comparatively difficult for the members of these communions to understand how one may go beyond the limitations of their own anthropomorphic divinity. The result has been, on the one hand, a general obfuscation of the symbols, and on the other, a god-ridden bigotry such as is unmatched elsewhere in the history of religion.[37]

In case his point is not clear enough, Campbell tells us elsewhere that the view that God revealed himself and moral truth to the ancient Hebrews in a special way is 'racism'.[38] If there is any racism here, it seems to be on Campbell's part. One might wonder whether the lack of respect shown here for the truth

---

[36] Campbell, *The Hero With a Thousand Faces*, 389–90.
[37] Ibid. 258–9 n.
[38] Joseph Campbell, 'Mythological Themes in Creative Literature and Art', in Campbell (ed.), *Myths, Dreams, and Religion* (New York: E. P. Dutton, 1970), 145–6.

claims of Judaism does not rest on a perhaps unwitting acceptance of anti-Semitic assumptions.

3.6.5. *The Appeal of the East*

A final source of appeal is revealed when Campbell tips his hand concerning monotheism. The monomyth has no 'correct', final interpretation, but the truth nevertheless resembles the insights of a particular brand of Hindu metaphysics.[39] Campbell persistently reads myths as expressing pantheistic or monistic insights: 'The two—the hero and his ultimate god, the seeker and the found—are thus understood as the outside and inside of a single self-mirrored mystery, which is identical with the mystery of the manifest world. The great deed of the supreme hero is to come to the knowledge of this unity in multiplicity and then to make it known.'[40] The supreme religious insight is to see that 'that font of life is the core of the individual, and within himself he will find it—if he can tear the coverings away'.[41] The appeal here is the perennial appeal of Hinduism and it doubtless encompasses all the factors touched on above. We have the ultimate flattering anthropology, a perspective that fuses psychology and metaphysics by identifying the self with God, and a perspective that claims to tolerantly encompass all other apparently disagreeing belief-systems.

It is worth noting in passing that the God of monism or pantheism, unlike the biblical God, is not a God that can challenge me or my culture morally. In fact, from such an exalted metaphysical perspective, the moral concerns of daily life take on a relative unimportance. As Campbell has it, moral virtue is only provisionally good, good as preparation. 'Virtue is but the pedagogical prelude to the culminating insight, which goes beyond all pairs of opposites.'[42] The ultimate good is a metaphysical merging of the self with the One, and that One

---

[39] It is worth noting that even theistic Hindus will not necessarily accept the way Campbell reads the myths. His own view reflects the classical 'Advaita Vedanta' tradition, which has been pervasive in Western scholarship about Hinduism, but is by no means representative of the faith of the average Hindu.

[40] Campbell, *The Hero With a Thousand Faces*, 40.

[41] Ibid. 191.

[42] Ibid. 44.

is not to be thought of as the personification of goodness, but as the absolute reality from which both good and evil flow.[43]

We see then that there are lots of reasons a mythological version of Christianity is appealing to our culture. At the same time we see how incongruent with biblical faith such a version of Christianity genuinely is. So much is lost that it is fair to say that what is left is hardly recognizable as Christianity at all. Thus, we must follow Lewis and highlight the imaginative power and significance of the Christian narrative, but we must not do so at the expense of its historical character.

3.7. CONCLUSIONS

There are good reasons, as I have noted, for avoiding the designation of the incarnational narrative as myth. Too many people will understand myth as ruling out history, and even those who do not think history is ruled out may see the historicity of the events as inessential and unimportant in relation to the mythical significance. In most contexts it would be better to stress the fact that God's saving acts constitute a narrative which possesses universal power and significance, without actually designating the story a myth.

However, if one is speaking in a context where the terminology will not be misunderstood, it is legitimate to speak of the incarnational narrative as a myth, following the example of C. S. Lewis, with the following proviso: the uniqueness of the narrative, its divine origin, and the essential significance of its historicity must all be maintained. Doing so will maintain the transcendence and authority of God's revelation and block any assumption that we humans are capable of gaining the truth about God and a right relationship to God through our own efforts. And we will also retain a clear sense that we are saved by what God has done for us, not simply by a story of our own making, or even of divine origin.

We still must confront the question of the historical truth of that story. Has God in fact become human so as to reconcile us to himself? Much of the power of the incarnational narrative

[43] Ibid.

is lost if we reinterpret it so it is no longer an account of what God has done for us and with us. Of course the power of the story is no guarantee of its truth. Nevertheless, a story with no power is a story with no interest.

A major part of the story of what God has done for us in the incarnation is articulated in the Christian doctrine of the atonement. That doctrine has, however, lost its force for many. Fully to understand why history matters, we must explore more deeply what God has done to make it possible for humans to be 'at-one' with himself, and we shall turn to that task in the next chapter.

4

Why the Events Matter:
2. God's Atoning Work

VIEWING the incarnational narrative as non-historical myth is a great loss. I argued in the previous chapter that without historicity, the narrative cannot be seen as a record of the divine actions whereby a historical relationship between humans and God is established. A myth which merely symbolically expresses some metaphysical/psychological truth cannot function in this way. Even viewing the narrative as a divine revelation about the nature of God would still amount to a loss, when compared with a record of historical actions, for there is a great difference between a story which reveals truth about someone, and an actual series of events which makes possible a relation with that someone.

One of the points I argued was that proposals to view the narrative as myth do not take seriously the problem traditionally described by theologians under the concept of human sinfulness. The depth of the human problem is not fully plumbed on such views, and as a result the difficulties in resolving the problem are not squarely faced. It is only when we see how difficult it is to establish a proper relation with God that the significance of the narrative that tells how such a relation is made possible gains its full power.

It is of course in the doctrine of atonement that the Christian faith has traditionally expressed its view of how Jesus made it possible for this relation to be healed. Classical theories of atonement are attempts to articulate how God's actions in history make possible salvation. However, one must admit that the idea that Jesus atoned for humans by his life, death, and resurrection is regarded by many as raising more difficulties than it solves.

I am not a theologian, and even if I were, it would be presumptuous to attempt to resolve all the theological controversies that swirl around the atonement. Much less can I hope to demonstrate the truth of the doctrine to the satisfaction of non-Christians. My task will be a more modest one: to show that the idea of the atonement is still powerful. I shall try to show that the need for atonement is still evident in human experience, and that versions of this doctrine are possible that are not vulnerable to standard, popular objections. In this way I hope to reinforce the point of the previous chapter. The incarnational narrative is a story which purports to tell what God has actually done to make salvation possible. One cannot show that the story is in fact historical by demonstrating its logical coherence and religious power. What one can hope to show is that the truth of its historicity is worth our attention.

In addition, as I shall point out in Chapter 10, evidentialist defences of the incarnational narrative depend crucially on estimates of the likelihood of a particular kind of divine revelation. If we have some good reason to think that God might reveal himself in a particular way, then one might well require less historical evidence in order to believe that God has so revealed himself. If the need for atonement is deeply embedded in human moral experience, then the plausibility of an alleged revelation that centres around such an atonement will certainly be higher than it would be if the idea of atonement made no sense to humans.

4.1. POPULAR OBJECTIONS TO THE ATONEMENT

The story of the atonement is the story of how God himself became a human being, lived and died among us, and rose again from the dead, so as to deal with the problem of human sinfulness and to reconcile us to himself. Obviously, such a story is vulnerable in any number of ways. It will make no sense to those who do not believe in God, for instance. That kind of objection could not be met without mounting a full-scale defence of theism, a task outside the scope of this work.[1]

I suspect that many people feel the atonement is problematic because they identify atonement with one particular theory of atonement, the theory of penal substitution, and understand even that theory in a rather distorted fashion. Popular presentations of Christian faith often present the idea of atonement in something like the following way:[2] Human beings have sinned against God and thereby incurred a debt that demands everlasting punishment. God is both just and merciful. In his mercy he wishes to forgive human beings and not punish them, but his justice does not allow this. God resolves this problem by becoming a human being himself, and suffering the pain and death of crucifixion, as a substitute for the punishment we humans deserve. Since God is infinitely good, his death is an adequate payment for the infinite debt sinful humans owe. Since the debt has now been paid, a just God can offer forgiveness. When we humans respond in faith to Jesus, then God accepts the sufferings of Jesus as payment for our sin.

Many Christians would accept the above as explaining how God atones for human sin in Jesus, and I wish to say that when the above story is properly interpreted and qualified, I think it does capture at least a significant part of the truth. However, there are grave difficulties with this sort of account as popularly understood, and though I do not think these difficulties are insoluble, they are formidable. These difficulties are well known, but a brief review of a few of them may be helpful.

First, the above story does not really seem to see God as forgiving sins. One could say that God releases us from a debt we owe, but it seems that God does not really forgive the debt, but extracts it from someone else. If one argues that God's justice does not allow God to forgive without punishing someone, the difficulties are increased. It is very unclear how it could be just to punish an innocent person in place of some

[1] That task has been admirably carried out, in very diverse ways, by Richard Swinburne, in *The Existence of God* (Oxford: Oxford University Press, 1979), and William Alston, *Perceiving God: The Epistemology of Religious Experience* (Ithaca, NY: Cornell University Press, 1991).

[2] This rather crude account of atonement and the difficulties it raises are recounted more clearly in a paper by Eleonore Stump, 'Atonement According to Aquinas', in *Philosophy and the Christian Faith*, ed. Thomas Morris (Notre Dame, Ind.: University of Notre Dame Press, 1988), 61–91, and my account is loosely modelled on hers.

other guilty individual, even if the innocent person undergoes the punishment willingly, since moral guilt does not seem the kind of thing that can be transferred to another. Furthermore, the above account is often presented in quantitative terms: all humans are infinitely guilty and deserving of everlasting punishment, yet the sufferings and death of one innocent individual are supposed to be equivalent to this infinite debt. However, it is quite unclear how such an equivalency is established. Moreover, it is far from clear how such a legal transaction in which the punishment of one individual is substituted for another is supposed to heal the breach between God and humans and establish the relationship between them that God intends.

The doctrine of the atonement, when understood in this way, far from making evident the significance of the historical character of the incarnational narrative, is often viewed as problematic in itself. Such a doctrine seems to imply that God is unwilling to forgive without exacting an appropriate pound of flesh, and perhaps worse, that God is willing to extract it from an innocent person if the guilty debtor cannot pay. Fortunately, such accounts of the atonement are not the only options for understanding God's atoning activities. There are a variety of theories of the atonement that have been developed historically, and quite a few that continue to have contemporary defenders. In fact, 'substitutionary theories', that employ legal metaphors such as those in the above 'popular' story, are quite defensible when properly understood. Before exploring some of the ways atonement might be understood, it is well to begin by reminding ourselves of some of those features of our moral and religious experience that suggest the need for something like the atonement.

4.2 THE NEED FOR ATONEMENT

Ultimately, a full understanding of the need for atonement requires a fully developed theological understanding of the self in its relations to others. For the atonement is ultimately the story of the healing of those relations, beginning with the most fundamental relation to God and working out to others.

However, I think that the moral experience of the non-religious person contains intimations of the need for something like an atonement. This is what we should expect if Christianity is true, for Christians believe that God is the creator of all persons, and that all persons therefore have intimations of God's reality and even dealings with God, though they may not recognize that it is God with whom they have dealings. Even apart from mature religious faith, ordinary moral experience contains elements that point beyond morality.

An understanding of the need for atonement must begin with an understanding of the role guilt plays in human life. We live of course in a society that tends to identify guilt with guilt feelings, and regards the latter as a bad thing that one should attempt to eliminate through therapy or other psychological techniques. (At least this is so for our *own* guilt; paradoxically, there is also a retributivist strand in contemporary culture that wants to come down hard on 'them', the guilty ones who are causing all the trouble.) To some degree this tendency to dismiss guilt is an understandable reaction in the case of those who have been socialized to have excessive and unreasonable feelings of guilt. However, morally sensitive people who have a realistic understanding of themselves and the world around them realize that there is such a thing as actually being guilty. Sometimes when I feel guilty, it is because I am guilty.

The phenomenon of guilt gets articulated in a host of images and metaphors. Some are drawn from civil society. When I have treated another badly, I feel as if I have incurred a debt to that person. Others are drawn from legal institutions. To be guilty is to have broken a law, to have become the sort of person who deserves punishment. Alternatively, guilt is understood in terms of purity and defilement; when I am guilty I have become unclean and in some way in need of cleansing. I want to be whole and clean, but see myself as broken and dirty.

Though there are many who stand ready to help us overcome all such 'negative emotions', the morally mature and sensitive person understands that there are times when such emotions are appropriate, and that a human life that has no place for them is a life that is shallow and does not take seriously the moral task of becoming a whole and decent human being. There is in fact a paradox that lies at the heart of the moral life, a paradox difficult to understand and express clearly. The people who are morally most mature and advanced—those who are, we might say, closest to sainthood—are often the people who struggle the most with feelings of guilt and moral inadequacy. The Mother Teresas of this world, far from feeling morally superior, often have a strong sense of their solidarity with ordinary, morally fallible human beings. If anything, they feel less comfortable with their moral progress than the ordinary person who might be inclined to look at his neighbour and judge that he is 'as good as or better than most folks'.

We might of course just say that these morally heroic people are simply neurotic, and that the feelings of guilt they struggle with are unreasonable and false. After all, if we judge by comparative human standards, such people have little to feel guilty about. However, the kind of person I have in mind here is precisely the kind of person who seems healthiest and least neurotic, and appears to have a most realistic self-understanding.

It is apparent that such people do not judge themselves by comparative human standards. They don't pat themselves on the back and say 'I'm a pretty great person; look how much more I do than the average Joe.' Such moral smugness and superiority, far from being the conquering of a neurosis, would be proof that the individual is really not a deeply moral, sensitive person after all. No, the person is not content to compare himself or herself to 'most people', but judges life by a higher standard. It is this higher standard that makes the person's moral achievements a reality, but paradoxically, also makes it necessary for the individual to struggle with guilt. Moral progress is accompanied, not by moral smugness and self-satisfaction, but by an increasing ability to live with a painful understanding that there is a gulf between what one has accomplished and the task, between what one has become and what one would like to be.

Kierkegaard speaks of this split between what one is and what one knows one should be as a wound, and says that it is the mark of the truly moral or ethical person to 'keep the wound open', and not bandage it with superficial palliatives.[3]

---

[3] See his *Concluding Unscientific Postscript*, trans. Howard V. and Edna H. Hong (Princeton: Princeton University Press, 1992), 85.

For it is living with that painful awareness that makes further moral growth possible.

A concrete example may help to illustrate the point. Compare two people living in North America with similar incomes and life situations. Let us call the first individual Kelly. Kelly lives to impress his colleagues by demonstrating his flair for fine clothes, his beautiful BMW, and his great popularity with the opposite sex. He knows that there are people in the world whose life situations are less fortunate—in other countries and even in his own. However, as much as possible he tries not to think about such people, though he would gladly perhaps attend a benefit concert to aid the starving, especially if the event promised to be a memorable evening and lots of famous and glamorous people would be there. Kelly does make a contribution to charity every now and then; in fact his accountant made him feel good the other day when he told him that his tax-deductible contributions last year were around 3 per cent—slightly above the average of the general population.

Kelly's co-worker Sara is much more affected by the poverty of those she knows about in her world. Like Kelly, she enjoys nice clothes, and she thinks it would doubtless be fun to own a BMW. However, she owns an old Toyota and she has for a number of years sent a substantial sum of money each month to a development agency that is working to end hunger in various regions of the world. She also volunteers one evening a week in a literacy programme, working with children from the centre of her city. Nevertheless, she is far from feeling morally complacent and self-satisfied. She decides to fast one day a month, and increase her contribution for world hunger. Even then, however, as she contemplates the enormity of the needs in a world full of starving people, she thinks that her level of sacrifice is hardly anything that she should feel is something special. After all, her life is a very comfortable one, when compared with the misery of those she is trying to help. When she thinks of what she is able to do, in fact, instead of feeling proud or superior, she sometimes feels discouraged and other times is tempted to smile or even laugh at her efforts. Nevertheless, despite her feelings of inadequacy she does not give up, and she feels it is good to do the little she does.

I would argue that Sara is morally superior to Kelly, and that one measure of her moral superiority is her keener sense of guilt. In other words, Sara is morally superior to Kelly, not just because she gives more money and time to others, but because she does not view what she does as completely adequate. She struggles with the question as to what she really owes her fellow human beings, and does not attempt to answer the question simply by comparing herself with the moral standards of contemporary society. At times she feels guilty. Though her guilt does not paralyse her, it does cause her seriously to examine her lifestyle at certain moments.

I would argue that guilt is therefore a real feature of the moral life. If we make our picture of Sara a little more complete, this will be even more evident. Sara is no plaster saint; she gets grouchy and impatient at times, especially with some of her relatives. She has said things to her mother that hurt her mother deeply, and that she later regretted very much. It isn't as if her mother didn't provoke her! Even so, Sara feels there have been times that she should have been more understanding of her mother. Relations with other people involve this kind of regret, for even the best of us at times hurt others, even, and perhaps especially, those we love. The person who feels she is always right, and that it is always the fault of the other person, is once more the person who is morally immature.

I conclude that guilt is a problem in the moral life, and that paradoxically, it is a greater problem, at least in terms of awareness, for the person who is morally sensitive and mature. How do we deal with the problem? I have already mentioned the superficial answer of the morally shallow individual: Just forget about it. Go to a therapist who will assure you that you are okay and that you are normal. Immerse yourself in the pursuit of trivial pleasures and you will soon cease to worry about the moral integrity of your life. Comfort yourself by making invidious comparisons with others. Justify your broken relationships by blaming it all on the others. Surely none of these techniques is worthy of serious consideration.

More serious answers involve the notions of asking forgiveness, making up for the past by what one does in the future, and redoubling one's efforts to become the person one should be. A case can be made that the solution to the problem of guilt lies in these kinds of moral efforts. I shall not here try to prove that humans cannot themselves 'atone' for their pasts. However, there is evidence that even the best human beings worry about the adequacy of this kind of solution.

First of all, we naturally worry about whether the future can really make up for the past. My guilt is a consequence of what I have done, and what has been done cannot be undone. Even if my future conduct is exemplary, am I not simply doing what I should be doing? Can I really create some kind of 'surplus' of good that somehow makes up for the past?

Secondly, we worry about whether such a moralistic solution is not merely a recipe for disastrously compounding our guilt. Perhaps by living exemplary lives in the future, we can make up for the past and heal our broken relationships, restore our sense of personal integrity and purity. But suppose we continue to fail? Suppose that our future efforts are pretty similar to our past ones, or only marginally better? In that case, we have redoubled our guilt. We feel guilty for the former past, and the more recent past, *and* guilty because of our failure to undo our past. The task we have taken on seems fraught with possibilities for disaster.

The problem of guilt is so great, and our worries about such solutions so serious, that some simply find the burden of the moral life intolerable. The great philosopher and psychologist William James saw this burden as the source of appeal of Absolute Idealism. The Idealist believes that whatever happens is somehow necessary to the Absolute and that all suffering and tragedy contributes to the good of the whole. This allows the believer to take what James called a 'moral holiday'.[4] James himself could not accept this vision of reality and held firmly to the importance of the moral life and its struggles. Nevertheless, James himself saw the burdensome character of this moral life, and urged the moral agent to simply 'take' a moral holiday from time to time, and quit worrying about such moral concerns, even without the theoretical justification offered by the Idealist.

Our need for 'moral holidays' illustrates the tension of

[4] See William James, *Pragmatism* (published with *The Meaning of Truth*) (Cambridge, Mass.: Harvard University Press, 1975), 41, 43, 56.

the moral life, a tension we are tempted to overcome by either relaxing the strenuousness of the moral ideal, or self-deceptively convincing ourselves that we have realized that ideal. And it is precisely this tension that the Christian story of the atonement addresses: the claim of the Church is that in the story of Jesus we see how our failures can be overcome without undermining the seriousness of the ideal.

An awareness of the problem of guilt is far from a demonstration of the need for the atonement in its theological sense. Much more needs to be said about the nature of the problem and the difficulties of alternative, humanistic solutions. However, I think one can at least say that what Christians claim the incarnational narrative offers is not remote from human experience. For what they claim is that the story of Jesus is the story of how God has acted to deal with the problem of guilt. It is the story of how broken relationships can be healed, how our sense of being debtors can be overcome, how we can understand ourselves as clean and whole again. Those are qualities that we humans need and that we want. Whether the story of Jesus in fact offers us these qualities is another issue, but if it does, one cannot claim that the story lacks relevance to our lives today.

When we move from the viewpoint of general moral experience to the viewpoint of the person who sees his or her life as lived before God, both the need for atonement and its possibility stand out yet more clearly. If God has created us to live in fellowship with him and with each other, then it makes sense to see the moral life as the calling he offers and demands from each one of us. In this context, the moral life takes on a new earnestness and intensity.[5] Our moral failings are not merely damaging mistakes; they are failures to realize our eternal destiny. They do not merely disrupt our relations with other human beings, but shatter our relationship with the eternal loving person who called us into being. We are guilty not merely of violating our own standards and of hurting our fellow humans; we have broken God's law and wounded the one who has given us our very lives. From such a perspective

[5] See my former colleague Charles Taliaferro's essay, 'The Intensity of Theism', *Sophia* 31/3 (1992) 61–73.

the need for atonement is much greater, but there is also greater possibility of help. We cannot easily believe that a God who created us and loves us will simply abandon us to our self-willed destruction. Rather, it is plausible to believe, or at least to hope, that God would do something to heal our relations to himself and each other. God would somehow work for at-one-ment. Christians believe that the incarnational narrative is in part the story of how God has done this.

4.3. THEORIES OF ATONEMENT AND THE REALITY OF ATONEMENT

How is the life, death, and resurrection of Jesus supposed to atone for sin? That is a question which the Church recognizes as legitimate and to which it has offered several good answers. Nevertheless, C. S. Lewis, with that down-to-earth wisdom he so often manifests, is quite right to affirm that 'a man can accept what Christ has done without knowing how it works'.[6] To be a Christian one must believe in the reality of the atone-ment, rather than some particular theory of how the atonement was achieved, for 'the thing itself is infinitely more important than any explanations the theologians have produced'.[7] The Christian Church has developed many different theoretical accounts of how Jesus atoned for human sin, but no particular theory has ever been enshrined in any of the ecumenically accepted creeds.

There are several possible reasons why this is so. First, we may simply be in the presence of mystery. I am no friend of those who cry 'mystery' to avoid intellectual difficulties. It is especially dubious to appeal to mystery when one is faced with apparent logical contradictions. Genuine intellectual problems must be faced, and hence if someone claims that the atonement contradicts our understanding of moral truths, then such an objection cannot be covered over by appeal to divine mystery (though we should be open to the possibility that what we thought were moral truths will need correction in light of the

---

[6] C. S. Lewis, *Mere Christianity* (New York: Macmillan, 1952), 58.
[7] Ibid. 57.

atonement). However, it is one thing to try to show that the atonement does not contradict what we know to be true; quite another to understand fully how God works. Though we must not be too quick to appeal to mystery, it would be arrogance to assume that finite, sinful humans can always understand the actions of God. To the degree that understanding is possible, it may be that it will also be partial, dependent on metaphors and analogies that cannot be literally applied to the subject in all respects.

Secondly, the reality of the atonement may be complex and multi-dimensional. The problem of guilt is complex and multi-dimensional, and so it is reasonable that the solution to the problem will have the same qualities. If our relation to God is to be healed, there may be need for changes both in ourselves and in God. We may need to be changed in our thinking, our willing, and our emotions. We may need a way of dealing with our past guilt, and also a way of reorienting our lives so as to avoid future guilt. If so, it is not surprising that no simple answer to the question of how atonement works can be given. More than one answer may be correct, and it is not safe to assume that the various theories are necessarily mutually exclusive rivals, even if we do not clearly see how they relate to one another. This is even more the case if the various answers we give turn out to be partially dependent on metaphor.

It is not surprising or embarrassing then that the universal witness of the Christian Church is that Christ's life, death, and resurrection is the story of how atonement was made possible, rather than to a particular theory of how this was accomplished. It is hardly unusual for a person to know by experience that something has truly happened that the person cannot fully explain. Every day I recognize the reality of the weather I experience with almost no ability on my part to understand the mechanisms that produce wind, thunder, hail, and snow. Every Christian who has experienced the atonement of Jesus is in a similar position. It is perfectly reasonable for someone to experience and affirm the reality of the atonement, and invite others to share in such an experience, even without a theoretical explanation.

4.4 MAKING SENSE OF THE STORY OF ATONEMENT

To say that one does not need a theoretical account of the atonement to experience and affirm its reality is by no means to admit that no plausible accounts can be given. On the contrary, recently there has been a surge of books and articles defending several plausible accounts.[8]

One of the most helpful books is *The Actuality of Atonement* by Colin Gunton.[9] Gunton incorporates both of the ideas advanced above about the limitations of theories of atonement. That is, he affirms both that the reality of God's atoning work is not completely transparent to human thinking, and that this reality is complex. Because of the former, our understanding of the atonement is dependent on metaphors; because of the latter we need a variety of metaphors that enrich and mutually qualify each other. His general perspective could be described as that of a 'critical realist' who wishes to avoid both a crude literalism that assumes human language can flatly describe God and God's doings, and a subjectivism that assumes that statements about God can only be 'symbols' to be evaluated pragmatically.

Gunton takes three of the traditional atonement theories as giving us insight into its reality. The traditional ransom theory saw the atonement as a victory over Satan and the powers of evil, in which humans who were in bondage to sin were liberated. Though Gunton says that one cannot accept the idea of a literal ransom justly paid to the devil, we can certainly

---

[8] In addition to the work of Colin Gunton discussed in the paragraph below, I would cite two recent theological works: Paul Fiddes, *Past Event and Present Salvation: A Study in the Christian Doctrine of the Atonement* (Louisville, Ky.: Westminster/John Knox Press, 1989); and Vernon White, *Atonement and Incarnation: An Essay in Universalism and Particularity* (Cambridge: Cambridge University Press, 1991). These two works are complementary in interesting ways. Fiddes's work, while recognizing that the atonement has both objective and subjective aspects, stresses the way that the atoning work of Christ makes contact with and impact upon our present lives. He draws upon Abelard's theory of atonement, which he argues has been misinterpreted as exclusively subjectivist. White, on the other hand, stresses the atonement as an objective event in the life of God himself, in which evil is taken on and reshaped for good. This occurred historically in the person of Jesus, but in doing so this experience is taken into the life of God and thus makes possible a recreative activity that involves the whole universe. I see these two accounts not necessarily as rivals, but as telling valuable complementary stories.

[9] Colin Gunton, *The Actuality of Atonement: A Study of Metaphor, Rationality, and the Christian Tradition* (Grand Rapids, Mich.: Wm. B. Eerdmans, 1989).

make good sense of the idea that human life is still in the grip of evil forces that are too strong for the individual to overcome. Jesus' life, death, and resurrection can be understood as an encounter with and victory over these forces, in which God fully experienced our painful enslavement and won a decisive battle over these forces.

Gunton treats substitutionary theories in a similar manner. He argues that we can certainly understand the notion that sin carries with it tragic and painful consequences, and understand Jesus' death as an act of God whereby God suffers those consequences, both as a representative of and substitute for sinful humans. The key here is to understand this act not in purely legal terms, as an external transaction, but as an action whereby God identifies with us and heals the relation between us. In raising Jesus God signifies that the barriers have been removed and that the consequences of sin have been dealt with in a satisfactory manner.

The life and death of Jesus can also be seen as a priestly sacrifice. The ancient cult in which the priest ritually offered to God on behalf of an offender a lamb or bullock so as to purify and cleanse the offender may seem remote from contemporary experience. However, a sense of uncleanness and a need to sacrifice something dear so as to purge oneself of that uncleanness are still very much a part of human life. We often feel better when we have fasted for world hunger, or when we have given away something we really wanted, not merely because of the good that our gift may do, but because we feel (however irrationally) that we have somehow cleansed or purified our souls. I have sometimes wondered if part of the appeal of a strenuous exercise workout may lie here; the pain of a long, hard run may be partly an unconscious effort to pay for our sins, and the clean feeling it produces may only partly be due to the hot shower that follows! We can therefore understand Christ metaphorically both as the priest who offers the sacrifice on our behalf and the lamb laid on the altar.

Richard Swinburne has recently offered a theory of atonement that relies heavily on this concept of sacrifice.[10] If we

---

[10] See Richard Swinburne, *Responsibility and Atonement* (Oxford: Oxford University Press, 1989).

take seriously the notion that we have wronged God, says Swinburne, then we will see ourselves as needing to repent, make reparations, and 'penance'. The latter term Swinburne uses in a somewhat unusual way, to denote the need of an offender to pay some penalty in addition to repairing the actual damage done. Since we humans are unable properly to repair the damage we have done, much less make extra amends, God has in his mercy given us the gift of the life and death of Jesus. When we are joined in baptism and faith to the life and death of Jesus, then we can offer back to God the gift he has given to us, as a sacrificial atonement, which substitutes for the punishment we would otherwise deserve (though Swinburne does not say that God would necessarily inflict such punishment).[11] When we join ourselves to Christ by partaking of communion, we 'plead' Christ's sacrifice as a substitute for the punishment we deserve.

Eleonore Stump, in a very striking paper, tells a story that captures nicely some of the moral features of our situation and how God's actions may be said to be an atonement.[12] She tells a story of a mother who has worked hard to create a beautiful garden. Suppose we imagine that her son has thoughtlessly or even maliciously damaged the garden, in open defiance of her instructions. Perhaps she will punish the son, who certainly seems to deserve it. However, she loves the son, and does not wish to do this, and it is not clear how such punishment would restore the damaged relationship with him that is a source of grief to her.

Alternatively, she could simply overlook the deed and forgive her son, but she has good reasons for not doing so. Such easy forgiveness not only trivializes the gravity of the wrong done; it too would do nothing to restore the relationship between herself and her son. After all, the seriousness of the offence lies not simply in the harm to the garden, but rather in the way the action bespeaks a wilful disregard for that in which

---

[11] Swinburne, *Responsibility and Atonement*, 162.

[12] See Stump, 'Atonement According to Aquinas', 61–91. Philosophers recently have been inventive in using the form of stories or parables to illustrate the nature of the atonement. In addition to the story by Stump discussed below, see Richard Purtill's parable in 'Justice, Mercy, Supererogation, and Atonement', in Thomas P. Flint (ed.), *Christian Philosophy* (Notre Dame, Ind.: University of Notre Dame Press, 1990), 37–50.

the mother has invested herself, and a disregard for the mother herself. Merely forgiving the offence without any repentance or restitution on the part of the offender would do nothing to heal this relationship, and it is this healing that is the goal of at-one-ment.

Of course the boy may not even wish to say he is sorry, and make amends, but even if this problem can be overcome, it would seem good for the mother to require some tangible action as an expression of the desire to heal the damage. No more fitting means to do this could be hit on than the repair of the damaged garden itself. However, suppose the boy is young and lacks the ability to do the work. Perhaps the boy has an older brother whom he could enlist to help him. If this occurs, then even if the work is actually done by the brother, the mother will still be pleased with the younger boy, if he truly allies his own will with the brother and co-operates in doing the work, even if the younger boy's efforts add little or nothing to restoring the flowers.

Stump then alters the imaginative story. Suppose there is no older brother, or indeed any third party who could help the young boy. In such a situation a mother who is truly loving might well get down on her hands and knees and do the work herself. She herself suffers the consequences of the boy's misbehaviour, and endures the painful work needed to repair the damage. One could say that she herself endures the 'punishment' the boy deserves. Such a tangible expression of the mother's love might well be just what is needed to crack open the boy's heart and move him to desire reconciliation. The young boy might 'help' by adding his halting efforts to hers and thereby appropriating the mother's efforts. Though she is really the one who has done the work, by his participation he has in a sense made that work his own.

Of course such a story fails if we interpret it as a strict allegory of the story of God's love for us in Christ. Nevertheless, it embodies many of the essential points that I think the story of Jesus contains. Like the boy, we humans have violated God's world and ignored God's instructions. Furthermore, it seems that while we may be in some distress, we have no clear, unified desire to make things right. While God could perhaps simply overlook or forgive our sins, to do so would ignore the damage in our relation to God. If God himself were to 'come into the garden', get down on his hands and knees, to speak, by becoming one of us, and himself experience and suffer the terrible consequences of our behaviour, then new possibilities emerge. Such love may move us to want our relation to God restored, and we can understand how, if we unite ourselves to Jesus, God might accept the suffering of Jesus as a substitute for the punishment we really deserve.

Of course such a sketch leaves very many questions un-answered. We want to know how the actions of God lead to changes in ourselves.[13] How is God's atoning work related to faith and repentance on our part? How can God help us without destroying our freedom?[14] We may speculate as to how the atoning work changes God himself. Was the suffering of God in human form somehow necessary in order for God to welcome us 'home' or were there other ways of overcoming this estrangement?[15] Christians disagree on such questions, and it is the job of theologians to answer them. However, I do not see how such disagreements could make belief in the reality of the atonement unreasonable. For what they show is that there are a plurality of ways of understanding that reality, and if one particular way of articulating the story is morally incredible, there are other ways of making sense of it.

The Christian churches give unanimous testimony to the reality of the atonement. The fact that no single theory of the atonement has won universal acceptance does not show that the story is one that lacks power and relevance today. It is rather confirmation of the fact that the work the Church claims

[13] In the remainder of the essay we have been discussing, Stump addresses the question as to how the atonement not only resolves the problem of past guilt, but makes it possible for God to transform our human nature so as to overcome future sin.

[14] See Eleonore Stump, 'Atonement and Justification', in Ronald J. Feenstra and Cornelius Plantinga (eds.), *Trinity, Incarnation, and Atonement* (Notre Dame, Ind.: University of Notre Dame Press, 1989), 178–209, for a very clear account of how God's atoning work might be the source of our faith and repentance without destroying our human free will.

[15] In another article, 'Aquinas on Atonement', in *Trinity, Incarnation, and Atonement*, Philip Quinn argues that we should see Jesus' sufferings not as a strict legal satisfaction of our debt, but rather as something God is moved to accept as satisfaction of our debt in an act of mercy. In this way, Quinn attempts to overcome various difficulties as to how the sufferings of Jesus could count as paying off a strict legal debt on the part of someone else.

God accomplished in Christ is both complex and mysterious. Whether true or not, the story remains one in which we are interested. It is a story that we may hope is true, for it offers new possibilities for restoring damaged humans and relationships.

5

Awareness of the Narrative:
Do We Need to Know?

AN event could be important, even if it were not important to know about it. In the previous two chapters I have argued that the historicity of the incarnational narrative is essential to its power and function. We saw in Chapter 3 that though it may be true that some of the power and relevance of the narrative for people today lies in the myth-like revelatory significance it possesses, much of the power of that narrative is lost if its historicity is denied. Chapter 4 explores the power and relevance of an atonement, and argues that if the narrative is a record of how God acted to make possible a relationship by atoning for human sin, then the events are obviously significant. If human salvation is dependent on those events, then salvation cannot be achieved if the events did not occur.

We must recall at this point the distinction between 'history' in the sense of a series of events and 'history' as a record of those events. One could view the previous two chapters as an argument for the history of the narrative in the first of these two senses, but not the second. That is, one could believe that the salvation of the human race does indeed depend upon the career of Jesus, but claim that this does not mean that it is crucial for anyone to be aware of this narrative. Rather, human salvation has been objectively accomplished by God, regardless of whether anyone knows about this.

Such a view may seem far-fetched, but there are in fact some strong pressures that tend to push Christians in this direction. To the degree that one stresses that salvation is the work of

God, and that it is objectively accomplished by what has happened in history, then our human response and participation in that work seem to diminish in importance. An excellent illustration of this can be found in Vernon White's fine book, *Atonement and Incarnation*.[1]

In this work, White argues for the objectivity both of the incarnation and Christ's atoning work. On his view, by becoming incarnate, God was able to incorporate the experience of being an individual into his own ontological reality. Such a participation in the human world not only gives 'moral authenticity' to God's redemptive work, but is also 'an experiential prerequisite for being able to achieve it in the rest of humanity, and for the rest of humanity to achieve it through him'.[2] Such an incarnation is not only revelatory of God's saving work, but constitutive of it.

The details of White's argument for this view do not interest me at the moment; rather I wish to focus on the implications he draws from his stress on the objective character of God's saving acts. White is a person who is not afraid to think deeply and consistently about his position, and he acknowledges that his view ultimately implies that what saves us is what God has done in Christ. Though those events were particular, historical occurrences, as cosmic events their significance goes far beyond Christianity as a particular religion. In the end, salvation would be possible even if Christianity as a religion had never existed, even if the knowledge of what God had done in Jesus had perished in the first century:

Does this then reduce the role and significance of the Christian Church to an inessential historical accident? Strictly speaking it is true that the logic of our position implies that, were there no historical knowledge of the Christ event and no human agency to transmit it, it would still have saving efficacy. Christ would still be applying his incarnational experience throughout all time and eternity to 'reconcile all things'—anonymously.[3]

White claims that these implications are not really embar-

---

[1] Vernon White, *Atonement and Incarnation: An Essay in Universalism and Particularity* (Cambridge: Cambridge University Press, 1991).

[2] Ibid. 40.

[3] Ibid. 113–14.

rassing. They free the Church from the 'absurd' claim that salvation depends on the effectiveness of the Church in proclaiming the Gospel.

White couples these claims with an embracement of the view that salvation is ultimately achieved universally, a position that coheres nicely with his view that our knowledge of the saving events is not essential. However, for anyone who finds universalism a dubious view, either on biblical or experiential grounds, matters may be more difficult. Most Christians have traditionally believed that salvation was something that one could achieve or fail to achieve, though they have usually coupled this claim with the view that the achievement is to be credited to God and not to ourselves. Nevertheless, the Christian view that salvation is dependent on what occurs in time gives human life a peculiar seriousness and intensity. The stakes are high, since the nature of my human existence has an eternal significance. Furthermore, a large segment of the Church, particularly the Western Church that has been so heavily influenced by Augustine, has traditionally held that this eternal salvation was something to be gained through that faith in the historical Jesus that the Church proclaims and invites.

Theories such as White's, that stress the objective nature of God's atonement and incarnation, and therefore minimize the importance of subjective appropriation, are logically coherent with theories of the atonement that view God's atoning work as understandable purely as an external, legal transaction. (I hasten to add that White does not accept such a theory of the atonement.) If God has paid the debt humans owe, then it would appear that humans owe no debt, whether they know that or not, and whether they know how God paid their debt or not. (This is not of course to say that advocates of such a view of the atonement, if there are any, would support White's type of view.) If one sees the atonement not simply as payment of a debt or the exaction of a legal punishment, but as a sacrifice offered to God on our behalf, this problem is less severe, since it is plausible to regard such an offering as an acceptable substitute for our deserved punishment in God's eyes only to the degree that we are somehow linked or united to Jesus. There are also ways in which theories that employ the metaphor of penal substitution can make sense of the idea that the substitution is acceptable only for those who are united to Christ. Advocates of a purely 'legal' or 'debt' view of the atonement usually argue that some subjective appropriation is necessary for the payment to be properly 'credited' to the individual.

Many plausible views of the atonement, then, require some kind of relation to Christ on the part of those for whom atonement has been provided, and many views of this relation require some kind of conscious awareness on the part of those who are thus related. This relation has been conceived in various ways; in being saved the sinner 'receives' and incorporates Christ into his or her life, or alternatively, the sinner is regarded as being incorporated into Christ by being made a part of Christ's mystical body, the Church. However this unity is understood, it is regarded as made possible by faith, obedience, and sacramental participation. We become one with Christ by faith in the power of his atonement, by serving him with love and trusting devotion, and by incorporating ourselves into his mystical body through baptism and the receiving of communion. If such a view is right, we can see why it is important for us to be aware of the narrative, for it is difficult to have faith in or be obedient to someone one does not know, and it is difficult to see how one could really participate in baptism and communion without some understanding of the narrative that underlies the symbols involved. 'How are they to believe in one of whom they have never heard?'[4]

However, this answer, if it is successful, creates a new difficulty, one that White correctly sees his own view as avoiding. Asserting that salvation is by faith, and that faith requires some information about the historical object of faith, seems to imply that those who have not heard about Jesus, and who consequently lack faith, are not saved, and cannot be saved without gaining this knowledge. It is at just this point that the problem of particularity becomes a serious difficulty.

The problem can be nicely illustrated from the writings of Kierkegaard, who has one of his pseudonyms embody the

---

[4] Romans 10: 14.

tension. In *Concluding Unscientific Postscript*, Kierkegaard's pseudonym Johannes Climacus asserts that the Christian believer cannot fully identify with all other human beings, but must regard those human beings who lack faith in the Jesus of history as outside the kingdom of God. 'The person who with the passion of his whole soul bases his happiness on one condition, which is the relation to something historical, obviously cannot at the same time regard this condition as nonsense.'[5] The believer not only does not regard this condition as nonsense, but necessarily holds that 'outside this condition there is no eternal happiness'.[6] This gives the Christian, according to Climacus, a superficial resemblance to someone who has received preferential treatment, a misunderstanding that in turn gives rise, he thinks, to the understandable but none the less mistaken doctrine of predestination.[7] 'The happiness linked to a historical condition excludes all who are outside the condition, and among those are the countless ones who are excluded through no fault of their own but by the accidental circumstance that Christianity has not yet been proclaimed to them.'[8]

Climacus himself recognizes this position as deeply problematic. As he puts it, it looks as if the Christian believer on this view 'lacks sympathy with' and does not recognize solidarity with the human race as a whole. He or she is forced to say that even close friends and family may be eternally excluded from God's kingdom. Climacus says that such an attitude appears as 'hate' to others, and this is how he exegetes Christ's saying that the true disciple must 'hate' his father and mother.[9]

However, the greatest difficulty with this position is that it appears to introduce a great injustice into God's dealings with the human race. The same pseudonym Climacus clearly affirms the underlying moral principle in an earlier book of Kierkegaard's: 'Would the god allow the power of time to decide

[5] Søren Kierkegaard, *Concluding Unscientific Postscript*, trans. Howard V. and Edna H. Hong (Princeton: Princeton University Press, 1992), 585–6.
[6] Ibid. 586.
[7] Ibid. 582.
[8] Ibid. 582–3.
[9] Ibid. 576.

whom he would grant his favor, or would it not be worthy of the god to make the reconciliation equally difficult for every human being at every time and place ...'.[10] It seems unjust to allow accidents of history and geography to decide the eternal destiny of an individual, yet if we claim that one's eternal destiny is determined by one's response to a historical event, it is hard to see how such a consequence can be avoided. It seems plausible that many people, both today and in the past, lack faith in Jesus because they have never had the opportunity to learn about him, or else they have only had the opportunity to learn about him in a distorted fashion.

There is another grave difficulty for Christians in holding that explicit knowledge of the incarnational story is necessary for salvation. It seems absurd to regard God's faithful followers from Old Testament times as excluded from God's kingdom. The heroes of faith surely include such people as Abraham, Moses, David, and Elijah, but of course such people had no explicit knowledge of the story of Jesus.

5.1. THE DILEMMA OF HISTORICAL PARTICULARITY

The difficulty Kierkegaard articulates can be put in the form of a logical dilemma. Either historical awareness of the incarnational narrative is necessary for salvation or it is not necessary. If it is necessary, then many people are excluded from the possibility of salvation for reasons that appear morally unacceptable. If it is not necessary, then one cannot view awareness of such a narrative as something that it is essential for humans to possess.

5.1.1. *Restrictivism*

Let us explore both horns of this dilemma. Grasping the first seems less than promising to me, but it has been argued that the implications of regarding such historical awareness as necessary are not morally unacceptable. John Sanders, in his

---

[10] Søren Kierkegaard, *Philosophical Fragments*, trans. Howard V. and Edna H. Hong (Princeton: Princeton University Press, 1985), 106.

fine book *No Other Name*, calls this position 'restrictivism'.[11] The moral acceptability of restrictivism basically rests on the claim that all human beings in fact deserve damnation. The fact that God graciously saves some implies no injustice to others. Can such a position be defended?

Richard Purtill (who is not a restrictivist) has defended a position in ethics he calls 'moderate retributionism'.[12] Moderate retributionism is the claim that though it is never just to punish a person more than the person deserves, it is permissible in some cases to punish a person less than the person deserves. If we claim that all human beings in fact deserve to forfeit salvation, then it might be argued that God, in saving some of those people and consequently punishing them less than they deserve, does no injustice to those who are not saved. They still receive what they deserve.

Of course many will not grant the premiss that all human beings deserve to forfeit salvation. But even if that is granted, it isn't clear that Purtill's principle will fully clear the advocate of restrictivism. For what moderate retributionism holds is not that a person may always punish less than is deserved, but rather that a person may do this in cases where there is a good reason to do so.

Suppose I am a high school teacher, and my class of students has violated a class rule against making racial slurs. A poster degrading a member of another race has been tacked to the bulletin board. Everyone in the class is guilty because all saw the poster and no one made any efforts to remove it or inform the proper authorities. I announce that as punishment everyone in the class must go to detention hall and write an essay on the damaging effects of racial slurs.

If I should decide to exempt a few students from the penalty, am I unfair to the rest of the class? I think the answer depends on whether I have a good reason for exercising mercy in such cases. If I exempt two students because their mother is seriously ill and they need to be with her, such an action would be reasonable. If I exempt a student on the grounds that she seems

[11] John Sanders, *No Other Name* (Grand Rapids, Mich.: Wm. B. Eerdmans, 1992).
[12] Richard L. Purtill, 'Justice, Mercy, Supererogation, and Atonement', in Thomas P. Flint (ed.), *Christian Philosophy* (Notre Dame, Ind.: University of Notre Dame Press, 1990), 40.

sincerely sorry, and has already on her own initiative made some extra efforts to apologize and set things right with the offended party, this too might be reasonable. However, if I simply exempted a group of students in a fairly arbitrary manner, or for some morally dubious reason (e.g. I like them or I consider them attractive), then the punished students could rightly accuse me of injustice in my treatment of them.

Suppose then that God chooses to save those humans who respond with faith to the news of God's saving actions. Does God thereby treat unjustly those who do not have an opportunity to respond?[13] The answer would depend on whether God's forgiveness of some people but not others is done for morally appropriate reasons. It would not do, I think, to say that God's reason for forgiving those people who respond in faith is simply that they did respond in faith, for in that case they would simply be taking advantage of an opportunity not extended to others, and we still have no good reason why they and not the others were extended that opportunity. It seems preposterous, as well as a contradiction to central Christian theological convictions, to say that those who received the opportunity were morally superior in some way to the others.

Probably the best response at this point is to fall back on the claim that God doubtless has a reason, but that it is not one we humans could be expected to understand. That at least seems more reasonable than the claim that the opportunity was simply extended to some and not to others as a result of an arbitrary act of will on the part of God. An appeal to divine inscrutability is not necessarily to be despised, for it is quite understandable that finite humans cannot expect to understand all the actions of an infinite God. However, such a move has its price, and the price in this case is a distancing of God from our moral conceptions. It becomes difficult to hold on to a firm

---

[13] Sanders notes that some argue that God knows who would have responded in faith to the Gospel, perhaps relying on 'middle knowledge', and that God sees to it that everyone who would have responded to the Gospel has an opportunity to do so. Thus on this view God does no injustice to those who have not heard, because they would not have responded even if they had heard. Aside from the dubiousness of 'middle knowledge', and its compatibility with free will, this line of thought strikes me as empirically most implausible. Can it be seriously maintained that none of the people in cultures that never heard the Gospel message would have responded positively? See Sanders, *No Other Name*, 151–75.

belief in the goodness of God, for in effect we are admitting that God acts in ways that appear to us to be preferential and unfair, even if we somehow continue to believe that in reality he does not do so.

Of course some are willing to pay this price, and even the greater one of holding that God simply cannot be judged by our human moral standards at all. Whatever God does is right, and if God elects to save some people and not others, he needs no reasons. His sovereign will is all the reason he needs. For many, however, such a God becomes one who cannot be worshipped and praised, a God who isn't worth believing in, because he cannot be counted on to work for goodness and justice.

5.1.2. *Wider Hope Theories*

The other horn of the dilemma seems more promising. Suppose we hold that historical awareness of God's saving actions is not essential for salvation. John Sanders calls views which allow for the salvation of those who lack conscious faith in Jesus 'wider hope' theories. The problem with wider hope theories, of course, is that they seem to imply that the good news of the Gospel is not so terribly important after all.

I believe that such problems are more soluble than those involved in the first horn of the dilemma. I shall work from the assumption that a loving, merciful God would welcome into his kingdom all those who would truly wish to be there, excluding only those who would exclude themselves and could thereby only be brought into the kingdom by coercion. Such an assumption by no means implies any kind of universalism. Since God's kingdom will reflect the character of God himself—it will be a kingdom characterized by love of the good, the true, and the just–it is easily imaginable that there will be those who have so corrupted their characters that they would find such a society a living horror. It is very hard for those who are cruel and full of hatred to be forced to endure the company of those who are truly kind and loving.

Moreover, the traditional Christian assumption is that all human beings to some degree or another fit this description of being people who love evil; all are sinners. In fact, it is precisely this assumption that gives the doctrine of the atonement as a historical act its force, as we saw in the last chapter. Simply to say that the 'righteous pagan' can be reconciled to God apart from a faithful response to that atonement seems either to deny that doctrine of universal sin, or else it so emphasizes the 'objective' power of the atonement that its link to actual human life, its power to change and transform us, seems undermined.

Can we maintain that awareness of God's historical incarnation is necessary for salvation and also hold that at least some of those who lack such historical knowledge are saved? Logically, one cannot hold that p is necessary for q, and also hold that q can be achieved without p. One must clear-headedly hold on to this logical truth and not allow sentiment to fuzzy up our thinking on such matters.

Nevertheless, though we cannot get around this logical truth, several moves are possible for the Christian at this point. First, one might recognize that though historical knowledge of the incarnation is not necessary for salvation, it is an effective means for obtaining salvation for those who hear the good news and respond in faith. Just because p is not necessary for q, it does not follow that p is not sufficient for obtaining q, and may be a crucial means for doing so. Thus, one may admit that salvation may be gained apart from historical faith while still regarding historically grounded faith as valuable.

Almost no Christian theologian today does in fact hold that explicit faith in Jesus in this life is necessary for salvation. To begin, there are the Old Testament believers mentioned already; it would appear that saving faith for them might involve some anticipation that God would atone for sin in some way—perhaps even a hope that God would act decisively in history in some way—but one could not claim that it was necessary for such people to believe in the actual story of Jesus.

There is also the case of infants and young children to consider. Though in medieval times it was not uncommon to maintain that unbaptized infants were damned, it is today a rare view. Even very conservative theologians typically hold today that those who die in infancy are not excluded from the kingdom of God, but such an admission logically implies that conscious faith in Jesus during earthly life is not strictly necessary for salvation.

This view that explicit faith in Jesus is not necessary for salvation has a long and honourable history within the Christian tradition. In various forms it has been held by Justin Martyr, John Wesley, A. H. Strong, William Shedd, and in our century by such theologians as Karl Rahner, Gabriel Fackre, George Lindbeck, and Lesslie Newbigin.[14] Vatican II explicitly endorsed the idea that those who 'do not know the Gospel of Christ or his Church' also, 'can attain to everlasting salvation'.[15] Such people are sometimes viewed as having 'implicit faith' or as being 'anonymous Christians'.

Such a view does indeed imply that salvation can be gained apart from any knowledge of the historical career of Jesus. But this does not imply that salvation gained in such a manner is independent of the work of Christ. One may still maintain that Christ's atoning work is objectively necessary for their salvation. Nor does this imply that such people have no subjective awareness of Jesus the Christ. After all, it is part of the narrative itself to maintain that Jesus is identical with the Son of God, the second person of the Trinity. Such a Jesus is the Word, by whom all things were created and who comes into the world to 'enlighten everyone'.[16] Such a Christ may reveal himself to other people in other forms. Thus such people may have an awareness of Christ, even if they are not aware of his historical existence as Jesus. The faith they have which makes salvation possible may still be faith in Christ, even if they do not know that it is Jesus the Christ who is the object of their faith. Thus, some knowledge of Christ may be necessary for salvation, even if knowledge of the story of Christ's life on earth is not.

In *No Other Name* Sanders employs a helpful classificatory terminology to describe a variety of wider hope views. One

---

[14] One of the real merits of Sanders's *No Other Name* is that he includes an extensive bibliography and historical review of theologians who have held the various positions with respect to the possibility of salvation outside the Church. Sanders discusses all these figures and many more, in several parts of his work. See 137–49, 159–64, 195–214, and 249–64. The book as a whole is replete with numerous historical references and illustrations.

[15] *Lumen Gentium* 16 (*Dogmatic Constitution of the Church*) *The Documents of Vatican II*, ed. Walter M. Abbott (New York: Herder & Herder, 1966), 35.

[16] John 1: 9. Other translations say that Jesus is the light who enlightens every person who comes into the world.

view, similar to the idea outlined in the previous paragraph, he terms 'inclusivism'.[17] Inclusivists see human beings as justified by their faithful response to God, while seeing the content of faith as varying, depending on the nature of the revelation they have received. Such a view provides a plausible account of Old Testament believers, who obviously did not have conscious faith in Jesus, but nevertheless are said in the New Testament to be justified by faith.

An alternative view, which Sanders terms 'eschatological evangelism', is to affirm that while it is true that faith in the historical Jesus is necessary for salvation, it is not necessary to acquire such faith *in this life*.[18] One might say that the 'righteous pagan' may not yet be in the kingdom of God but will eventually be part of that kingdom. Perhaps after death God grants to all those who have not had an opportunity to make an informed choice in this life a clarifying experience, in which they become aware of who Jesus really is, and can therefore respond or fail to respond in faith. Such a moment of clarification would be vital, not only for all those who have never heard the good news, but for all who have heard in a distorted fashion, or who have been blocked from a faithful response by other sociological factors for which they cannot be held culpable.

To summarize, there are two options if one chooses to embrace the second horn of the dilemma. One may hold with inclusivists that historical knowledge of the incarnation is not strictly necessary for salvation, but argue that it is none the less very valuable. Alternatively, one may accept the view of eschatological evangelism that such historical knowledge is strictly necessary ultimately to obtain salvation, but that it is not necessary to have such knowledge in this life.

These views could also be combined in various ways. One might hold that the revelation after death comes only to those

---

[17] Sanders, *No Other Name*, 215–80.

[18] See ibid. 177–214. A different view, popular among Catholics, which has similar implications to the eschatological evangelism view, is that a moment of revelation and decision occurs for everyone at the moment of death. See ibid. 172–3. I find this view less than plausible, if this moment is regarded as preceding death, since at this time people are often in great pain and hardly seem capable of making an informed decision. If the moment is after death, then this position seems identical to the eschatological evangelism position.

who have responded in faith to whatever insight was granted them in this life. This view would preserve the generally held view that the individual's destiny is 'sealed at death' and also allow one to continue to hold that explicit faith in Jesus is necessary for salvation.

5.2. HOW EGALITARIAN IS GOD?

The original dilemma arose because of a conviction that God loves all human persons and would not treat some humans unfairly or unjustly. The two positions just developed attempt to relieve God of the accusation of unfairness by showing how people who don't have a fair chance to acquire a knowledge of God's historical saving acts might none the less obtain salvation. Nevertheless, a little reflection shows that in such a situation there is still inequality. If it is a great good to have historical awareness of God's incarnation, then those who do not have such knowledge in this life lack a great good. If some of these people will ultimately obtain this good by coming to know about these events after death, then they have nevertheless not enjoyed the benefits of conscious membership of God's kingdom in this life. So far as I can see, belief that salvation is linked to knowledge of a historical revelation is incompatible with a belief that there is a strict equality between human beings with respect to such a good.

If we look at the biblical account of God's revelatory and saving activity, not only in the Gospels but throughout the Bible, God does not appear to be a strict egalitarian. The concept of election is a central biblical notion. Though God is said to love all his creatures, from beginning to end God is selective and particular in his dealings with individuals and nations. As Newbigin puts it, 'the point of view of the Bible is that God chose Abel and not Cain, Isaac and not Ishmael, Jacob and not Esau, David and not his elder brothers'.[19] In the New Testament, Jesus chose a select group to be his disciples, and Paul maintains that the salvation of the Gentiles and

[19] Lesslie Newbigin, *The Gospel in a Pluralist Society* (Grand Rapids, Mich.: Wm. B. Eerdmans, 1989), 81.

(temporary) exclusion of most of the Jewish people must be understood in the light of God's election.

To link the particularity of God's saving acts to the doctrine of election may appear to make a bad situation yet more desperate. Nevertheless, I make the association simply to underscore the fact that traditional Christian faith is irrevocably tied to a view of God that sees God treating people in very different ways. God is not seen as a strict egalitarian in his dealings with humans. Rather than deny this, we must face the fact squarely and try to understand why God might deal with humans in such a manner, and whether doing so implies any unfairness or injustice on God's part.

I should like to deal with the second part of this task first. What would it mean for God to act in a strictly egalitarian manner? Would it mean that all human persons are entitled to equal amounts of every kind of goodness? Should God have created all humans with equal capacities for intelligence, musical creativity, and emotional empathy? Should God guarantee that all humans have equally good educations and equal amounts of nurturing love? If someone enjoys less of one kind of goodness should God compensate by ensuring the person enjoys more of some other good? Should God have created all humans to have an equal life-span?

As soon as such questions are posed, it is obvious that God is not strictly egalitarian in his dealings with humans, even if no historical revelation has occurred. It follows from this that no theist who continues to believe in the goodness of God can accept the claim that God has a moral duty to treat humans in such an egalitarian manner.

Nor is it difficult to come up with plausible reasons why God should reject a policy of strict egalitarianism. If God wished to create individuals who are truly unique, then it would seem necessary for humans to differ in their natural endowments. If all humans were equally musically talented, then we could never marvel at the existence of a Mozart. Nor could God guarantee that humans would have equal educations and family situations and still give humans the freedom to make their own choices about their lives and their relationships. Strict equality could only be achieved by God if he drastically reduced the individuality and uniqueness of individuals and similarly reduced the scope of human freedom. The human race would then resemble a group of robotic clones.

Quite independent of any question of historical saving acts, we see therefore that God must be understood by the theist as valuing and respecting the uniqueness and relative autonomy of human beings. Perhaps such a creation policy would be unnecessary for a group of beings who are essentially complete as individuals, and therefore do not need each other, but we can see it as making sense for a race of creatures who are intended to live in relationships with each other. Newbigin stresses the fact that God chose to create a race of beings who depend upon each other.[20] Because no individual is perfectly endowed with intelligence, physical strength, and emotional resiliency, we need each other. Because we are free and responsible creatures, we are vulnerable to each other. Our historical choices shape the character of our relationships, and thus our choices have consequences for others. All too often those consequences have been tragic. In choosing to create such a race of relational, historically responsible creatures, God necessarily chooses not to be a strict egalitarian.

The inequalities in human life are certainly troubling and I do not mean to underestimate the difficulties involved in the problem of differential human suffering. I only wish to insist that there are no special difficulties, no new problems, introduced by God's historical saving acts, or by asserting that it is good for us to know about such acts.

Not every kind of inequality towards humans on God's part is morally tolerable. I should find it impossible to believe in the goodness of God if it were the case that God simply loved some human beings and not others, and arranged for some to have an opportunity to enjoy eternal communion with himself, while making this impossible for others for no good reason. However, if there are good reasons for God's creating a race of interdependent, responsible beings, then we have reason to believe that these beings will be endowed by God with many kinds of different capacities, and born into a world where their social relations will create many kinds of further inequalities.

So far as I can see, linking human salvation to historical

---

[20] Newbigin, *The Gospel in a Pluralist Society*, 82–3.

information certainly leads to inequalities, but the inequalities do not seem more problematic than the disparities that already exist in human intelligence, happiness, health, moral and religious sensitivity, and so on. Furthermore, linking salvation to historical information would appear justified, if it is, for the same reasons that other kinds of inequalities might be justified. If we were religiously self-enclosed monads, essentially perfect individuals, we would certainly need no such historical revelation. We would be in the position that classical Hinduism affirms we are in: the divine truth is present within every person, and therefore every person is essentially religiously self-sufficient. If salvation depends on historical information, then it shares the general character of our historical existence. The fact that we must be told the good news means that our salvation is dependent on what others do, and upon the nature of our relationships with others. Salvation is grounded in a historical community that is the bearer of this good news.

All this is quite compatible with God providentially involving himself in the process so as to prevent any ultimate unfairness, either by providing some way that individuals who are 'innocently ignorant' might obtain the benefits of God's saving acts apart from conscious faith, or by ensuring that such people have a clarifying experience that makes possible an informed choice after death. Or perhaps God could do both of these things, as I, in fact, believe he does. Such actions would reveal God's deep and persistent love for all his human creatures, without undermining or destroying their nature as individually unique, historical, relational beings.

5.3. ELECTION AND PARTICULARITY

The term 'election' is still troublesome; to many it suggests the idea that God 'plays favourites', so to speak. However, the fact that God chose to work for the salvation of the human race through particular nations, individuals, and events, does not have to carry any such implications. Though the language of favouritism is certainly present in the Bible in places, the overall message about God's intentions requires us to view such passages as metaphorical, as a communication of God's purposes in ways that accommodate our finite and limited human understanding.

In the Old Testament, Israel is certainly regarded as God's chosen people, and in the New Testament, the Church is certainly regarded as a new, elect people of God. However, in both cases it is a mistake to see this election as the granting of special privileges or rights over against God. Again, Lesslie Newbigin puts the matter well:

It is indeed true that in many moving passages of the Old Testament we are told of God's undying love for Israel, of his commitment to its cause. Yet this love and commitment are to Israel as the instrument of God's purpose of love for all the nations, and when Israel interprets God's love as a license to do as it pleases chastisement follows.[21]

God's calling is then a call to carry out a special task, one with a universal meaning for the entire human race, not a granting of special privileges. Nor is it the case, as Newbigin again points out, that carrying out this task earns some special standing with God, for God's grace is offered freely and unconditionally.[22]

Most fundamentally, what must be stressed is that Christianity proclaims that it is Jesus the Christ who is foundationally God's elected one. From the Christian viewpoint, Jesus is the centrepiece of world history. Israel is elected by God to prepare for the coming of God's elect. The Church is created as God's elect, a covenant people in so far as it is united with Jesus.

Though I have attempted to avoid Christological controversies, I wonder whether part of the uneasiness some feel over having salvation depend upon a particular individual is not relieved by a 'high' Christology. If one views Jesus as a mere human being who is somehow selected or 'adopted' by God, one might well wonder why this individual is selected rather than another, though I would maintain that such a worry can ultimately be resolved by appealing to the universal purposes of God in so electing Jesus, and the necessary inequality involved in taking human historical particularity seriously. However, if the human person Jesus is identical with the second person of the Trinity, then we can make even better sense of

---

[21] Newbigin, *The Gospel in a Pluralist Society*, 84.
[22] Ibid. 85.

the notion that Jesus was the elect of God from all eternity. For God's election in this case is not an arbitrary selection of one human being rather than another. Rather, Jesus as God is realizing God's own eternal resolution to act to redeem his fallen race.

I conclude that we can take seriously the idea that the historical knowledge of Jesus is of tremendous value without holding that those who are blocked from conscious faith are permanently excluded from God's kingdom. To lack such knowledge can be a real loss, for it is tragic for someone to fail to enjoy in a conscious manner the benefits of citizenship in God's kingdom, even for those who are part of that kingdom without realizing it, or who ultimately will become part of that kingdom. Such loss entails genuine inequality, but this inequality is inherent in a race of historical, interdependent creatures. If it is good for God to have created such creatures, then it is fitting that their redemption should share in the conditions of historicity as well. The tragedy, the loss, and the inequality do not have to be seen as ultimate and final, however, for a God for whom all things are possible.

6

Is the Incarnation Logically Possible?

I HAVE argued, in Chapters 3 and 4, that the historicity of the incarnational narrative matters. In Chapter 3 I argued that from the point of view of Christian faith, regarding the narrative as non-historical myth or moral illustration is a genuine, perhaps essential loss. In Chapter 4 I argued that it still makes sense to view the salvation of humans as dependent in part on the occurrence of historical events. In Chapter 5 I argued that knowledge of these events is extremely valuable and important to obtain salvation, even if it is not essential to have such knowledge in this life.

However, none of these arguments will have much weight if the events did not occur, or if they did, but it is impossible for us to have knowledge (or at least justified true belief) about them. If either of those conditions hold, then it would appear that one should either reject Christianity or else make peace with the loss of the historicity of the narrative, however great this loss may be. To show that it is unnecessary to take either of these options I need to show that the events did occur and that we can know or justifiably believe that they did occur. For practical purposes, the two tasks cannot be sharply distinguished, since to show that the events occurred would be to give us such knowledge or justified belief or else it would show that we already know or are entitled to believe that they occurred.

Showing that such knowledge is possible is no easy task. In fact, I believe that much of the appeal of understanding the incarnational narrative as non-historical myth rests on the conviction that the task is impossible. No matter how great the loss, if we have no other alternative, then we must make the best of things. Nevertheless, I believe that the task can be done, and that the widespread assumption that it cannot be accomplished rests on modernist epistemologies that have been discredited. To show this is the burden of the rest of this book.

I shall eventually provide two positive accounts of how such knowledge is possible. These accounts are often taken as alternative, rival theories, but I shall try to show how they can be viewed as complementary stories. Before providing these accounts, however, there is much preliminary work to be done. There are substantial arguments that such knowledge is not even *possible*. Some of these arguments centre around the notion of special actions of God in history. It is evident, I think, that the incarnational narrative as traditionally understood includes such actions. In the next chapter, I shall examine a cluster of objections to such actions on the part of God. The first argument I will examine is an argument that such special acts of God are problematic. Either such acts are impossible, or else they are epistemologically unrecognizable. Yet another objection that will be examined in Chapter 7 is the claim that belief in such special acts is religiously or theologically objectionable.

A variation on the epistemological objection to special acts of God is the claim that such acts cannot be recognized by one who is committed to critical, historical investigation. This kind of argument, which rests on the nature of historical knowledge and critical historical method, will be considered in Chapter 8. If the incarnational narrative necessarily includes such divine actions, then the argument claims that we cannot have *historical* knowledge of it.

The other type of argument against the possibility of such knowledge, that will be considered in the remainder of this chapter, rests on the claim that the fundamental concept embedded in the narrative is logically incoherent. If the incarnational narrative embodies logical contradictions at central points then it cannot be a true, historical account. The defender of knowledge of the incarnational narrative must show that the narrative is logically coherent, or at least that we are justified in believing that is coherent.

6.1. FUNCTIONAL AND ONTOLOGICAL VERSIONS OF INCARNATION

I have so far in this book attempted to steer away from Christological controversies, intramural debates among Christians concerning the proper interpretation of the incarnational narrative. Of course for orthodoxy the doctrinal implications of the narrative concerning the person of Jesus were spelled out at Nicea and Chalcedon. Very roughly, Jesus is understood as both fully human and fully divine, and yet a fully unified individual. The human individual Jesus of Nazareth is asserted to be identical with the second person of the Trinity. Though Jesus has both a divine and human nature, and though these natures are not diluted or fused, he remains a single person.

Such a traditional 'high' or 'maximal' Christology is by no means universally accepted today. Some would urge that the divinity of Jesus be affirmed in functional rather than ontological terms. In other words, we can affirm that Jesus was God in the sense of being the locus of divine action, without making any claims about the *being* of Jesus. Jesus was ontologically a human being whose life became the 'place' where God could act decisively to redeem the human race. A classical example of such a Christology can be found in D. M. Baillie's *God Was in Christ*.[1] Although such Christologies as Baillie's do not capture all that the traditional doctrine asserts, they are still 'high' by some standards—relatively high, we might say—in that they view Jesus as divine in a unique sense that no other human person shares. They still want to view Jesus as the focal point of human history, the one who not only reveals God to us but acts to make salvation possible.

Though my own sympathies lie with Brian Hebblethwaite's argument that the functions of Jesus as agent of our salvation can only be carried out if there is a sense in which Jesus is

[1] D. M. Baillie, *God Was In Christ* (London: Faber & Faber, 1948).

ontologically God,[2] I shall not try to settle the controversy between functional and ontological versions of the doctrine of incarnation. Even the functional versions involve the kinds of historical particularity that this book attempts to defend. Someone who holds that Jesus is to be thought of as God because of what God has done and is doing through Jesus may still hold that what God has done in Jesus is unique, that it is essential for our salvation, and that it is important for us to know about what God has done if we are to be full conscious participants in the kingdom of God.

Nevertheless, in this chapter I propose to consider whether the doctrine of the incarnation is logically coherent when it is understood in the traditional, ontological manner. My reason for doing so is simple. If it can be shown that the doctrine of the incarnation taken in the full and robust ontological sense is logically coherent, or at least that there are good reasons to believe that it is coherent, then it seems likely that weaker versions of the doctrine are coherent. If it turns out to be the case that one can coherently assert that Jesus is identical in substance with God then it is likely that the weaker claim that God acts in Jesus in a special manner is coherent as well, since that weaker claim would appear to avoid the metaphysical problems inherent in the stronger doctrine. (I say only that this is likely, not certain, since it is always possible that weaker versions might introduce some new internal inconsistency.) Of course it is possible that weaker versions of the doctrine might be coherent even if the traditional view is not, so all would not necessarily be lost even if my attempt fails. If my argument succeeds, however, we can safely conclude that there is no logical impossibility in the idea of God becoming incarnate in Jesus in at least *one* sense, and it seems likely, though not certain, that weaker versions of the doctrine are coherent as well.

I shall be relatively brief in this chapter, since there have recently been able defences of the coherence of the Chalcedonian doctrine of the incarnation. I shall rely heavily on the work of Thomas Morris in *The Logic of God Incarnate*,

---

[2] Brian Hebblethwaite, *The Incarnation* (Cambridge: Cambridge University Press, 1987), 21–6 and 69–70.

though, unlike Morris, I incline towards a kenotic version of the orthodox view.[3]

6.2. ACCUSATIONS OF INCOHERENCE

The Chalcedonian doctrine of the incarnation is frequently accused of being logically incoherent. Fortunately or unfortunately, accusations in this case are more plentiful than careful arguments for the claim. A well-known statement by John Hick is typical:

... orthodoxy insisted upon the two natures, human and divine, coinhering in the one historical Jesus Christ. But orthodoxy has never been able to give this idea any content. It remains a form of words without assignable meaning. For to say, without explanation, that the historical Jesus of Nazareth was also God is as devoid of meaning as to say that this circle drawn with a pencil on paper is also a square.[4]

It is perhaps not altogether clear what Hick means by this. He surely does not mean merely that the doctrine is ambiguous, capable of more than one interpretation, for though there is a sense in which an ambiguous doctrine needs to have its meaning developed or clarified, such doctrines are far from being devoid of meaning.

Perhaps Hick means to say that the doctrine of incarnation is strictly meaningless, a string of words that amounts to nonsense, such as 'the slithy toves did gyre and gimbel' from *Jabberwocky*, or the standard example of a meaningless string

---

[3] See Thomas V. Morris, *The Logic of God Incarnate* (Ithaca, NY: Cornell University Press, 1986). David Brown has also published a defence of the logical coherence of the doctrine of the Incarnation, in *The Divine Trinity* (London: Duckworth, 1985). Brown, like Morris, distinguishes between a kenotic version of the theory and a more traditional version, and argues that both are logically coherent. Morris argues for the superiority of the traditional view, while Brown says that the two views are evenly matched and he cannot decide between them. Unfortunately, Brown states the kenotic theory in a confusing way, and, I think, in a manner that makes it indefensible. For a clear, defensible version of the kenotic theory, see Ronald J. Feenstra, 'Reconsidering Kenotic Christology', in *Trinity, Incarnation, and Atonement*, ed. Ronald J. Feenstra and Cornelius Plantinga (Notre Dame, Ind.: University of Notre Dame Press, 1989), 128–52.

[4] John Hick, 'Jesus and the World Religions', in Hick (ed.), *The Myth of God Incarnate* (London: SCM Press, 1977), 178.

from analytic philosophy: 'Green is or'. If so, his claim seems most implausible, for a string of meaningless words could not possibly inspire a spirited debate that has endured for more than 1500 years about the meaning and truth of the statement expressed by the string.

Most likely, the best clue to Hick's intent is found in the comparison he draws to the claim that a drawn circle is also a square. This claim seems logically incoherent, and the state of affairs expressed by the proposition 'This circle is also a square' seems metaphysically impossible. Perhaps Hick means that 'being divine' and 'being human' are logically mutually exclusive predicates, like 'being a square' and 'being a circle' and thus the proposition that a single individual exemplifies both predicates is incoherent. Thus any attempt to articulate the doctrine of the incarnation will inevitably involve logical contradictions.

If this is what Hick means to claim, then he has expressed himself unfortunately, since a logically incoherent statement is not devoid of semantic content. It is just because we do understand the expression 'a circle that is a square' that we judge the proposition 'this circle is a square' to be incoherent and the state of affairs described to be metaphysically impossible. Nevertheless, the charge made is a serious one.

Hick does not provide any argument for the accusation, and he has in fact recently retreated from the claim that the doctrine of the incarnation is logically incoherent, in favour of the weaker charge that no one has successfully stated a coherent version of the doctrine that is also religiously satisfying.[5] Others have given the kind of argument, however, that probably underlies Hick's earlier statement. For example, A. D. Smith has argued that as a human being, Jesus faced and underwent death, and that death involves the possibility of annihilation. However, it is an essential property of God that God exists necessarily; God cannot die or be annihilated. If Jesus is God, he cannot be annihilated. If Jesus is human, he can be annihilated. But it is incoherent to affirm that it is both possible and not possible for Jesus to be annihilated.[6]

---

[5] John Hick, *The Metaphor of God Incarnate* (London: SCM Press, 1993), 3–4.
[6] A. D. Smith, 'God's Death', *Theology*, 80 (July, 1977), 262–8.

The particular argument Smith gives here may not be too convincing, since it depends on tricky modal properties (possibly being subject to annihilation), and on debatable claims about the meaning of death.[7] (Is it really true that death must necessarily be identified with annihilation, so that if a person enjoys life after death this implies the person did not really die?) Nevertheless, we can see in his argument a pattern or form of argument that seems impressive, at least initially. Being divine seems to require certain properties, such as being omnipotent, omniscient, and omnipresent. We normally think of human beings as lacking such properties, and many perhaps see it is as an essential aspect of human nature or the human condition that humans are finite in their knowledge and power, limited in place, and so on. If we accept the metaphysical principle of the indiscernibility of identicals (roughly, that *a* and *b* must have identical properties if they are identical), then we cannot affirm that Jesus as God has some property or properties that Jesus as a human lacks.

This is not merely an esoteric point of logic, but the basic reason why it is so hard to conceive of God becoming a human being. It is profoundly difficult to understand how a particular human being, one who eats, sleeps, gets tired, appears limited in knowledge and so on, can at the same time have such divine properties as being all-powerful, being completely self-sufficient, and being omniscient. Kierkegaard expresses the difficulty well: 'Look, there he stands—the god. Where? There. Can you not see him? He is the god, and yet he has no place where he can lay his head.'[8] It cannot be denied that the idea of God incarnate is at least problematic and mysterious. It is perhaps impossible for humans in this life to understand clearly. However, does this lack of comprehension provide a basis for concluding that the doctrine is logically incoherent?

---

[7] For a good reply to Smith, see Morris, *Logic of God Incarnate*, 56–62.
[8] Søren Kierkegaard, *Philosophical Fragments* (Princeton: Princeton University Press, 1985), 32.

6.3. HOW MUCH DO WE KNOW ABOUT GOD AND HUMAN NATURE?

That the incarnation is difficult, perhaps even impossible, for humans to understand seems undeniable to me. What I want to maintain, however, is that this fact lends no support to the claim that the doctrine is logically incoherent. A modest degree of agnosticism about our understanding of the incarnation is more of a problem for those who claim that the doctrine is incoherent than it is for believers.

Kierkegaard expresses this agnosticism about our understanding of the incarnation very powerfully in his characterization of God in human form as the 'absolute paradox'. Kierkegaard is often interpreted as meaning by this that the incarnation is a logical contradiction. I have argued in other places that this interpretation is mistaken.[9] In saying that the incarnation is a paradox, Kierkegaard affirms that human understanding cannot comprehend how it is possible for God to have become human and that it is not possible for sinful humans to believe that it has occurred apart from divine assistance, but he does not mean that it is or can be known to be a logical contradiction.

One reason why this is so is simply that Kierkegaard holds what I should describe as a modest agnosticism about our knowledge of God and of human nature. Specifically, he holds that apart from God's revelation, we lack a correct and deep understanding both about God and about human nature. We neither know God nor ourselves as we need to.[10] Yet to know that 'the god-man' is a logical contradiction, we would have to have a fair degree of clarity about both concepts, just as we need to be relatively clear about what is a square and what is a circle in order to recognize their logical incompatibility. Of course this lack of understanding of the concept of God does not have to be absolute. Indeed, this agnosticism about the concept cannot be absolute; if we knew nothing about God

---

[9] See my *Passionate Reason: Making Sense of Kierkegaard's* Philosophical Fragments (Bloomington, Ind.: Indiana University Press, 1992), 96–107. See also my *Kierkegaard's* Fragments and Postscript: *The Religious Philosophy of Johannes Climacus* (Atlantic Highlands, NJ: Humanities Press, 1983), 212–19.

[10] This is what I take to be the main message of ch. 3 of *Philosophical Fragments*.

and humans then the concept of the 'god-man' would have no meaning whatsoever for us.

The same kind of modest agnosticism about our understanding of God's nature is found in Brian Hebblethwaite:

> To suppose that God can and does relate himself to us and make himself known to us in this particular way, over and above the intimations of his reality and nature which religion in general provides, does, of course, imply that it is *possible* for him to do so. But who are we to say that the nature of God almighty, the infinite and eternal ground of our being, is such as to render this impossible? . . . We have no basis at all for saying that God *cannot* be such as to be able, without ceasing to be God, to unite his creation to himself first in an incarnate life, and then in and through our response to the risen and ascended one.[11]

John Hick has objected to Hebblethwaite here on the grounds that if we are genuinely agnostic about the divine nature, so that we cannot know that an incarnation is impossible, then we cannot know that it is possible either.[12]

This objection is misguided. We must remember that the agnosticism Hebblethwaite endorses here is only what I have termed a modest one. He is not claiming that it is impossible for us to come to know that the incarnation is possible. He is merely claiming that we do not know enough about God's nature a priori to say whether such a thing is possible or not. Such an assertion is quite consistent with the claim that a posteriori we can know that it is possible for God to do this. Since whatever is actual is also possible, it follows that if we have good reason to believe that the incarnation has occurred, we also have good reason to believe it is possible for God almighty to become incarnate. This is in no way inconsistent with the claim that if God had not done so, we would have had no way of determining whether such a thing is possible or not.

We might of course have intuitions about such a thing. We might be inclined to think such a thing is impossible. Hebblethwaite's point is simply that we do not know enough

[11] Hebblethwaite, *Incarnation*, 24–5.
[12] John Hick, Letter to the Editor, *Theology*, 80 (May, 1977), 205. Quoted in Morris, *Logic of God Incarnate*, 73–4.

a priori about God to trust such intuitions. The claim that the incarnation is a surprise to human reason, that it goes against our natural expectations about what God could and would do, is hardly a problem for Christian theology, since it has been insisted that this is the case since New Testament days. ' "What no eye has seen, nor ear heard, nor the human heart conceived, what God has prepared for those who love him"—these things God has revealed to us through the Spirit; for the Spirit searches everything, even the depths of God ... no one comprehends what is truly God's except the Spirit of God."[13] It is a fundamental tenet of Christian faith that much of our knowledge of God is made possible by God's self-revelation, and that this revelation occurred definitively in Jesus Christ. Such a position is not only consistent with, but supports, a modest agnosticism about our a priori knowledge of God. Of course one cannot maintain that we know *nothing* about God prior to any special revelation, for we must know something about the meaning of the terms 'God' and 'human being' in order to understand the Christian claim. To know that this claim is logically impossible, however, we would need a clear understanding of which properties are essential to being God and which are essential for being human, and it is very doubtful that we have the reliable a priori knowledge of the divine nature that we would need in order to have precise a priori knowledge about God's essential properties.

6.4. COHERENCE AND THE BURDEN OF PROOF

It might seem necessary, or at least advantageous, to be able to demonstrate the logical coherence of the incarnation, and yet the modest agnosticism of Kierkegaard and Hebblethwaite would preclude this, or at least preclude our being able to do this a priori. Do we not need to show that the incarnation is logically possible in order to be able to determine if it has actually occurred? Such a requirement would be quite unreasonable. A proof of coherence or non-contradictoriness is often extraordinarily difficult to achieve. This is true even of

---

[13] I Corinthians 2: 9–11.

pure mathematics, as Peter Geach has noted, where one would think such a proof would be achievable, if anywhere.[14]

Richard Swinburne has given very detailed attention to the whole question of the coherence of the concept of God, in his book *The Coherence of Theism*.[15] In this work he rebuts many detailed arguments for the incoherence of the classical theistic attributes. In the end, however, he concludes that no direct proof of the coherence of the concept of God can be offered. The best that the theist can hope for is to argue for the truth of the claim that the theistic God exists, for if we know God actually exists, then we can safely conclude that the claim that he does is coherent.[16] Swinburne argues that this result should not be unsettling for the theist, for it is in accord with the traditional view that our human ability to comprehend God's nature is quite limited. However, if it is unreasonable to expect a logical proof of the coherence of the claim that God exists, it is certainly unreasonable to expect such a proof of the coherence of the claim that God became incarnate.

Apart from empirical evidence for the truth of the Christian doctrine, one might try to defend its logical coherence by producing models or at least analogies, which are themselves clearly coherent, and by trying to show that the claim that God became incarnate or could become incarnate is entailed by other clearly coherent propositions. The former task is an ancient and honourable one in Christian theology, but I doubt that any analogies will definitively settle the matter. Doubts can always be raised about the closeness of the analogy, and indeed the Christian herself will insist that all strictly earthly analogies will be limited. (It seems true that all analogies are limited to some degree; otherwise they would provide more than an analogy.) If a really close analogy is provided, doubts could be raised about the coherence of the analogue itself, or its proper description. Similar doubts can be raised about the coherence of the propositions that are supposed to entail the

[14] Peter Geach, *God and the Soul* (London: Routledge & Kegan Paul, 1969), 106–7.

[15] Richard Swinburne, *The Coherence of Theism* (Oxford: Oxford University Press, 1977).

[16] Ibid. 295–6.

possibility of an incarnation, or about whether the entailments in fact hold.

This is why recent defences of the coherence of the doctrine of the incarnation, such as that of Morris, have largely taken the form of rebuttals of arguments that the doctrine is incoherent. It would of course be very damaging if someone could produce a good argument that the incarnation is logically impossible, for in that case we would have a strong reason for discounting empirical evidence that the incarnation actually occurred. However, if we have no good reasons to believe that the doctrine is incoherent, and if I am right in claiming that in this case we are not justified in trusting what we might term our pre-reflective intuitions that the doctrine is incoherent, I would claim that we are justified in believing it is coherent. The burden of proof, in other words, seems to me to be on those that claim the doctrine is incoherent.

Why is this the case? One reason is that I think we are entitled to presume that any doctrine that is widely believed to be true is coherent. This is the case even if the doctrine in question is in fact false. I am not of course suggesting that it is impossible for an incoherent claim to be widely accepted. Rather, I mean that in cases of widely accepted beliefs, one should probably assume the doctrine is coherent unless there are good reasons to think otherwise.

An example will illustrate the point. A belief in reincarnation is of course pervasive in Hinduism and Buddhism. Such a belief is commonly criticized as not merely false but logically incoherent. It would be, I think, important for believers in reincarnation to rebut such arguments. If we have strong arguments for the incoherence of the doctrine, then the burden of proof would shift to those who maintain coherence. However, if believers can successfully rebut these arguments, then it seems quite reasonable for them to maintain the coherence of the doctrine of reincarnation, even if they cannot demonstrate that coherence positively. If a belief is held by millions of people over many centuries, it seems arrogant and presumptuous to claim that such a belief is incoherent without good reason. In the absence of such reasons, the belief is entitled to be provisionally judged as coherent.

There is another reason for this policy, and it is that to do otherwise would 'block the road of enquiry'. If we judge a belief coherent, then we will have reasons to look for evidence for and against its truth, while a judgement that a belief is incoherent makes such inquiry unnecessary. So a presumption that the doctrine of reincarnation is coherent gives us a reason for considering what kind of evidence could be found for and against the belief, and for actually seeking out such evidence.

If it is actually possible to seek out such evidence, then this provides an additional reason to judge a widely held belief provisionally coherent. The fact that we can debate whether certain types of experiences provide evidence for reincarnation or not is a point in favour of its coherence. Since a judgement that a belief is coherent is simply a judgement that the belief is possibly true, it follows that if we can conceive of conditions that point to its truth then we have reasons to think the doctrine is coherent. Furthermore, if we can look for and examine evidence, then the doctrine must be clear enough to be understandable in some sense.

In succeeding chapters I will discuss the case that can be made for the truth of the doctrine of the incarnation. The fact that such a discussion can occur is itself a reason to accept the doctrine as coherent. Hence, I conclude that the burden of proof lies on those who claim the doctrine of the incarnation is incoherent. If no good case can be made, then it is in order to assume the doctrine is coherent, and try to determine how to decide if it is true and whether it is true. Of course this presumption is only valid if there are in fact no good arguments that the doctrine is incoherent, and so the believer is by no means exempted from the task of examining and responding to such arguments.

6.5 REBUTTING ARGUMENTS FOR INCOHERENCE: THE WORK OF MORRIS

As I have already noted, most arguments for the claim that the incarnation is logically impossible rest on the principle of the indiscernibility of identicals. It is alleged that the same individual cannot be divine and human because it is essential for a divine being to have qualities such as omnipotence, omniscience, and omnipresence, while it is essential for human beings to lack such properties, or to have others, such as being contingent, that a divine being necessarily lacks.

Thomas Morris has offered a vigorous rebuttal of such arguments in *The Logic of God Incarnate*. Like David Brown's *The Divine Trinity*, Morris defends the logical coherence of both traditional and 'kenotic' accounts of the doctrine of the incarnation, though, for reasons I will later discuss and criticize, he prefers the traditional account. The difference between the two accounts lies in a disagreement about what properties are essential to God and also a disagreement as to what properties Jesus as a human being actually possesses. The traditional view holds that God is necessarily omnipotent, omniscient, omnipresent, morally perfect, and so on, while the kenotic view holds that, for at least some of the traditional theistic attributes, it is essential only that a being have such properties as 'being-omnipotent except when one freely chooses to relinquish this power'. The kenotic view thus allows for the possibility that Jesus, though a divine being, may actually have 'emptied himself', and divested himself of such properties as omnipotence and omniscience *simpliciter*. On this view, it is logically coherent to affirm that Jesus was divine, and yet that Jesus was not omnipotent, because a divine being is not necessarily omnipotent at all times.

Though Morris claims that the kenotic view is coherent, he himself defends a version of the traditional position that he calls the 'two-minds' view of the incarnation. He rebuts charges of incoherence by making several important metaphysical distinctions. First, he distinguishes between an individual nature and a 'kind-nature' or essence. Nothing can have more than one individual nature, but it is possible for an individual to belong to more than one natural kind. In response to the objection that divine and human natures have incompatible properties, Morris proposes that we distinguish between common and even universal properties and truly essential properties. It may be common for human beings to be created, contingent, limited in knowledge and power, and so on. Perhaps all human beings except Jesus have these properties. However, we don't know a priori that these properties are essential to being human. They may be essential to being *merely* human, but it is possible for Jesus to be *fully* human without being merely human. If God has in fact become human, then this provides a good a posteriori reason for concluding that one can be fully human without being merely human. It may be that my *individual* nature is such that it is part of *my* essence to be created and finite, and the individual natures of other humans may be similarly finite, but it does not follow from this that these properties are essential to the human kind-nature.

What is necessary to be fully human? Morris says that it is plausible to think that whatever has a human body, at some time or other, and also has a human mind is rightly regarded as fully human. Jesus clearly had a human body, and according to Morris, also a human mind, and hence is fully human.

But how can Jesus be omniscient and yet have a human mind, a mind which learns from sensory experience, thinks through arguments, makes new discoveries, and so on? Here is where Morris proposes the 'two-minds' theory. Jesus had both a human and a divine mind. His divine mind remains fully omniscient, but his human mind is subject to the ordinary limitations of human thought. The two minds are related to each other in an 'asymmetric accessing relationship'. The divine mind has full access to everything in the human mind, but not vice versa. The two-minds theory not only helps Morris show the logical coherence of the doctrine of incarnation, but also suggests how the biblical picture of Jesus as a human who was finite in knowledge can be accommodated.

It has been objected that Morris does not recognize that the divine mind of Jesus as omniscient would have the same degree of access to all human minds, and thus the unique relation of Jesus' divine mind to his human mind has not been explained.[17] This objection is telling against the original formulation of Morris, but I think the problem can be solved. The objection points out that more needs to be said about the *kind* of access the divine mind of Jesus has to his human mind. On my view, the access involved must include what philosophers sometimes call a 'token-reflexive' dimension, so that the divine mind of Jesus is aware not only of the content of his human mind, but

---

[17] The objection is raised by Hick, e.g. in *Metaphor of God Incarnate*, 47–60.

is aware of that human mind as *his* (God's son's) human mind. This is analogous to the way in which I am aware of the contents of my own mind, but also aware of them *as* the contents of *my* own mind. This latter awareness is not reducible to the former.

If it is objected that the reference to Jesus' human mind as his own is circular, since it presupposes the unique relation between the second person of the Trinity and Jesus' human mind that is the point at issue, I would say that this points to the fact that every person's relation to his or her mind is basic and irreducible. In order for it to be truly the case that I have a unique awareness of my mind as mine, it must be a fact that I do have this relation to my mind. The awareness does not constitute the 'ownership' relation but necessarily presupposes it. I could not truly be aware of my mind as mine unless it was mine. Any analysis of a person's relation to his or her own conscious mind will therefore have a circular character, and there is no reason to expect things will be different in the case of the mind of the human Son of God.

Can an individual person really have two minds? Morris argues that this is quite conceivable. He gives various analogies, including a complex computer system, the relation between the conscious and unconscious mind, hypnosis, the case of a commissurotomy where the individual person appears to have two distinct consciousnesses, and the case of multiple personality. The latter analogy is particularly interesting, in that there are cases of multiple personality in which there is an 'executive' personality that is aware of all that the other personalities do, and has the power to 'switch' and control the personalities, while being unknown to the other personalities. Yet in such cases, where there is a unified pattern of activities and co-ordinated purposes, there are strong arguments for still maintaining that these distinct personalities belong to one person.[18] Such a view certainly makes it appear that a single person can resemble a social organization more than we might have been inclined to think, but careful analysis shows that even ordinary people who do not suffer from multiple per-

[18] See David Benner and C. Stephen Evans, 'Unity and Multiplicity in Hypnosis, Commissurotomy, and Multiple Personality Disorder', *Journal of Mind and Behavior* 5/4: (Autumn 1984), 423–31.

sonalities are less unified than we might think. All of us have some ability to 'dissociate' part of our minds. The difference between a multiple personality and a 'normal' person is one of degree and not kind. So it does appear that it is possible for one person to have two distinct minds that are asymmetrically related in the way Morris suggests.

Of course Morris is not saying that Jesus as a human being suffered from a multiple personality disorder. Because of the asymmetry between the two minds, Jesus' human mind is not aware of the divine mind and thus is not in itself 'multiple'. Still, one might think that it would be damaging to employ a disorder such as multiple personality as an analogy for the incarnation. After all, such conditions are viewed as forms of mental illness. However, Morris argues that using this model for the incarnation is not damaging because there are two significant differences between the case of the incarnation and multiple personality. In cases of multiple personality, there is an element of involuntariness and also some degree of dys-functionality. However, in the case of the incarnation, Christ, as the second person of the Trinity, is a completely voluntary agent. The possession of the two minds in this case is not dysfunctional; it is not the result of some psychological trauma, but an appropriate, perhaps even necessary, arrangement to achieve the ends of human redemption.

6.6 KENOTIC THEORIES

I think that Morris has given a convincing argument that we have no strong reasons to doubt the logical coherence of his two-minds account of the incarnation. However, I do not think his reasons for rejecting the alternative kenotic theory, the view that holds that in becoming human God the Son emptied himself or voluntarily relinquished such properties as omni-potence and omniscience, are strong. The kenotic theory seems preferable to me on grounds of simplicity; it does not require the somewhat exotic, even if coherent, suggestion that Jesus has two minds while remaining a single person.

Morris ultimately rejects the kenotic version of the doctrine, on the grounds that it conflicts with his 'Anselmian intuitions'.

Building on Anselm's conception of God as 'a being than which none greater can be conceived', Anselmian theology views it as legitimate to ascribe to God whatever perfections we can conceive to be consistently co-exemplified. Since Morris thinks it is more perfect for a being to be omnipotent and omniscient than to have those qualities 'unless freely choosing to relinquish them', he opts for a more traditional view that ascribes the unqualified versions of these properties to God.

I believe that Morris's objections can be answered if we place the kenotic theory of the incarnation in the context of the doctrine of the Trinity. Christians believe in one God in three persons. The human being Jesus is claimed to be identical with the second person of the Trinity, not with God as a whole. As Ronald Feenstra notes, even if Morris's Anselmian intuitions are sound, surely they apply only to God as a whole, not to the individual persons of the Trinity.[19] We have no reliable a priori intuitions about what properties are essentially possessed by the distinct persons of the Trinity, for the simple reason that the doctrine of the Trinity is known on the basis of special revelation if it is known at all. We have no rational intuitions that God is three in one at all, and hence our trustworthy intuitions about what the persons of the Trinity can and cannot do are limited. Hence, even if one agrees with Morris that God as a unified whole is essentially omnipotent and omniscient, it does not follow that each person of the Trinity must exemplify these properties.

The kenotic theory is often regarded as rebutted by a famous rhetorical question posed by William Temple: 'What was happening to the rest of the universe during the period of our Lord's earthly life?'[20] Temple's implication was clearly that while Jesus as human has divested himself of his omnipotence and omniscience, he cannot exercise his creative power in conserving and providentially ordering the universe. However, there is no reason to think that the universe would lack for care in such a situation, since the creative power of God could still be exercised by the Father and the Spirit, and even the earthly Jesus could still share in their work through his unity

---

[19] Feenstra, 'Reconsidering Kenotic Christology', 143.
[20] William Temple, *Christus Veritas* (London: Macmillan, 1924), 142. Quoted in Hebblethwaite, *Incarnation*, 68.

with the Father and the Spirit.[21] So even someone who shares Morris's faith in Anselmian intuitions about God may still accept a kenotic theory.

It is in any case not clear to me that Morris's Anselmian intuitions are correct in this case. Morris thinks that it is more perfect for a being to be omnipotent than to be omnipotent-unless-freely-choosing-to-relinquish-omnipotence. However, philosophers in recent years have shown how terribly difficult it is to develop a clear and coherent account of omnipotence. Richard Swinburne, for one, has argued that being omnipotent entails being able to relinquish omnipotence.[22] If this is correct, then omnipotence that cannot be relinquished is impossible and hence cannot be exemplified by anyone. It is not clear to me in any case that a being who lacks the power to voluntarily restrict himself is necessarily superior to one who has this power.

Whether I am right or not about this, I think that disputes of this nature, along with the modest agnosticism defended above, cast some doubt on the reliability of such Anselmian intuitions. Even if it is correct that God is necessarily the most perfect being it is logically possible to be, our intuitions about what is perfect may not be altogether trustworthy. As Morris himself suggests, it is entirely in order for such a priori intuitions to be corrected by empirical evidence. We might well suppose that a perfect being would not or even could not 'dirty himself' by entering the created order as an embodied human being, but that supposition may say more about our epistemic limitations than about what is truly possible for God.

Some other objections that are made to kenotic theology are theological rather than logical in nature. Some argue that Jesus is now ascended and glorified, and thus has resumed the full range of traditional divine attributes. The objection is that if kenotic self-divestiture is necessary for humanness, then this

---

[21] It is clear from these remarks, I think, that a plausible version of the kenotic theory depends on what is sometimes termed a social version of the doctrine of the Trinity, in which Father, Son, and Spirit are regarded as truly distinct centres of consciousness. Since I regard Social Trinitarianism as the most plausible version of this doctrine, I do not perceive this to be a problem. For a spirited defence of Social Trinitarianism, see Cornelius Plantinga, 'Social Trinity and Tritheism', in *Trinity, Incarnation, and Atonement*.

[22] Swinburne, *Coherence of Theism*, 149–61.

would imply that Jesus is no longer human, which goes against the traditional Christian teaching that Jesus continues to fully share our humanness.

This objection is easily answered. First of all, it is not obvious that the ascension and glorification of Jesus require that he now possess omniscience and omnipotence. One can surely imagine that Jesus retains his humanness in a glorified form, a form that is promised to all who share in his resurrected life eventually, without necessarily being omnipotent and omniscient. As a human being Jesus might continue to exhibit perfect obedience and trust in the Father, an obedience and trust that is rewarded by the Father with glorification and intimate personal union. Such a view of the glorification of Jesus actually has significant theological advantages, for it maintains a close identification between his current state and our own promised future. Or, if Jesus does possess such qualities it is not obvious that he must possess them on his own, independently of his relation to the Father. One might think of his omniscience and omnipotence as gifts from the Father, a reward for his suffering obedience that by no means obliterates his humanness.

Alternatively, one could follow a suggestion made by Ronald Feenstra, and distinguish between the kenosis or self-emptying of Jesus and his incarnation.[23] Perhaps kenosis is not a necessary condition for incarnation; after all, Thomas Morris has argued convincingly that God could become incarnate without any kenosis. Perhaps kenosis is simply the particular way in which God chose to become incarnate. If that is the case, then the kenosis could cease at the time of the glorification of Jesus, but Jesus could continue to be fully incarnate as a human being, retaining his sense of what it is like to be a limited human being by his memories of his earthly life. The Father might reward his obedience and humility with a restoration of all the powers and glories which he relinquished in being born as a baby.

I conclude that the notion of a kenotic incarnation of God the Son appears to be coherent, as does a non-kenotic incarnation. I find the kenotic theory more plausible, partly because of the great moral and spiritual power involved in the idea that

[23] See Ronald Feenstra again, 'Reconsidering Kenotic Christology', 148.

God identified so fully with the human condition, with all its limitations. Such a view also seems simpler to me than the 'two-minds' view, and seems to be a view that can more naturally and easily accommodate the historical portrait of Jesus provided in the Gospels. Though we obviously cannot really imagine *how* God could become a human being, and divest himself of some of the traditional divine attributes, we have no good reason to think this is impossible. It is of course quite another matter to say that the story is not only possible but actual.

7

Miracles: Their Possibility
and Knowability

THE incarnational narrative, as I have defined it, is a narrative about the earthly career of the Son of God and thus is dependent on the coherence of some concept of God becoming incarnate. In the last chapter I argued that even if incarnation is understood in a robust, traditional sense, there are no good reasons for thinking that such a concept is logically incoherent or metaphysically impossible. Such an argument, however, even if successful is far from establishing the possibility that the narrative as a whole is historically true; it merely removes one objection. There are many other reasons for doubting whether the events depicted in such a narrative could possibly occur.

7.1. SPECIAL ACTS OF GOD

Some of these reasons cluster around the concept of a 'special act of God', the idea of God acting in a special manner in some particular time and place. This notion of a special act of God is a term that gets its meaning by contrast; such acts must somehow be distinguished from God's activity in creating and conserving the universe. If Christian theism is true then in some sense God is active in every event; nothing that occurs would occur apart from his creative power. Some have taken this to imply that everything that occurs is God's doing; every particular act is an act of God.[1] I believe that the doctrines of creation and divine conservation can be understood in a way that does not imply this. In particular, if God creates genuinely free agents and conserves them in existence, it seems to me that their free actions must in some sense be attributable to them and not to God, even though God is responsible for their existence and their powers. Since such agents interact with the physical world in complex ways, if this view is correct, it is clearly going to be the case that there are also many events in the natural world that are not properly regarded as solely acts of God.

Even with regard to what might be regarded as events whose causes lie wholly within the physical world, one might argue that not every event is an act of God in the sense that God intends that particular action to occur. If we believe, as we surely must, that God creates and conserves the natural world as having certain general characteristics, such as are discovered and expressed in the laws of natural science, then one might argue that God simply wills for the material world to manifest those general characteristics, and does not necessarily intend every particular outcome of their workings. Of course, depending on the extent of divine foreknowledge, God must surely recognize and permit the particular outcomes that are the consequences of the general created character of the natural order, subject to the widespread exceptions that must be made for human agency, but that does not necessarily mean that God designed the natural order simply with those particular ends in view. Hence, although theists must certainly see God as acting pervasively in the world through creation and conservation, they do not have to see every particular event in the natural world as intended by God.

Whether this claim is plausible or not, one can distinguish special acts of God from God's general activity in creating and conserving the universe, however far-reaching the latter sort of activity may be. Such a distinction is often made by thinking of divine special action as involving some kind of intervention,

[1] Thomas Aquinas, e.g., held such a view. See his discussions in *Summa Theologiae*, I, q. 103 a. 5 and a. 7, and q. 105 a. 4 and a. 5. Also in *Summa contra Gentiles*, 3. 64, 72, 74, 89, 90. A recent defence of this claim can be found in Vernon White, *The Fall of a Sparrow* (Exeter: Paternoster Press, 1985).

or interference, as theologians inclined to reject such views often prejudicially term such divine activity. Actually, neither term is helpful. The term 'interference' seems to imply that the universe is an autonomous mechanism, and that any special divine actions would somehow subvert the smooth operation of such a machine. There is no reason for the Christian theist to concede either claim. From the point of view of theism, the world is not autonomous, but exhibits whatever characteristics it has, including its natural regularities, because of God's creative intentions. Moreover, there is no reason to think that any special actions on the part of God would necessarily subvert God's purposes in creation. Such actions might well be directed harmoniously and co-operatively with the divinely ordained natural regularities towards those same ends. Even the term 'intervention' is misleading, in that it seems to imply the picture of God acting in a world from which God is normally absent.[2]

However, there are a variety of ways of making such a distinction, and not all involve such a quasi-deistic concept of intervention. For that matter a concept of divine special acts can be developed that does not require any special form of divine causal power. Even someone who holds that God's general activity is all-pervasive might make a distinction between God's general and special activity by holding that special acts of God are those actions of God that have a special importance in the overall divine plan. Assuming, for instance, that God is atemporal, one might hold that God has eternally willed the outcome of every event, but still hold that some of those events are special in the sense that they occupy a pivotal position in the whole scheme of things. Alternatively, one might hold, as William Alston maintains, that some acts might be termed special acts of God on the grounds that these acts

---

[2] I believe it is because of the unfortunate connotations of this concept of 'intervention' that N. T. Wright rejects the distinction between the 'natural and the supernatural'. See his *The New Testament and the People of God* (London: SPCK, 1992), 5, 10, 92, 97. However, merely because the distinction between the natural and the supernatural has often been drawn in unfortunate, implicitly deistic ways, does not mean that some distinction between God's normal activity in the natural world and more special activity does not need to be drawn. David Brown has understood this well, though he continues to use the term 'intervention', which, as I note in the text, seems a slightly misleading term, though it is often a convenient one, and I sometimes use it myself. See his *The Divine Trinity* (London: Gerald Duckworth, 1985).

are those in which God's purposes are more evidently fulfilled or clearly discerned, at least from the perspective of us humans.[3]

We might term such conceptions of divine special actions 'weak' conceptions, in that they do not involve any notion of special divine causality. A special act of God in a strong sense might then be understood as requiring some specific divine intention and exercise of causal power, distinct from that involved in creation and conservation, though we should be careful not to think of such exercises of divine power as deistic intrusions. Henceforth, I shall use 'special act of God' in this strong sense unless it is otherwise made clear. Such a special exercise of divine power is an important element in one traditional concept of miracle,[4] and thus special acts of God in the strong sense are closely linked to this concept of miracle, even if the two concepts are not identical.

What exactly is the relation between miracles and special acts in the strong sense? If one requires a miracle, in addition to being a specially caused divine action, to be an event that functions as a 'sign', perhaps involving something that inspires wonder on the part of the recipient, then the class of special acts is clearly broader than the class of miracles. God could, for example, causally produce a thought in the mind of an individual which no one would suspect of being miraculous in character and which would not function as religiously significant. For that matter, effects in the physical world could be directly produced by God that would be similarly, for all practical purposes, undetectable. If God were to save an airliner from crashing by fusing a hidden bolt that was about to crack, there is no reason why anyone would necessarily suspect that any divine causality was active in the matter.

Nevertheless, there is clearly one sense in which such events would be miraculous, in that they involve outcomes, in the one case the occurrence of a thought and in the other the safe arrival of an airliner, that would not have occurred in the normal course of nature. For that reason, I myself think that

---

[3] See William Alston, 'God's Action in the World', in *Divine Nature and Human Language* (Ithaca, NY: Cornell University Press, 1989), 217–21.

[4] I discuss below a different conception of miracle that does not require any special divine causality.

the cause of clarity is best served by simply identifying special acts of God in the strong sense with miracles, understood as events that would not have occurred in the normal course of nature, but occur because of a special divine intention and exercise of divine causal power. One can then go on to distinguish conceptually miracles that are undetectable from miracles that function religiously as signs.

Many religious believers regularly pray for God to guide them in making some decision, or to help them accomplish some task, and they often regard such prayers as being fulfilled. Does this mean they believe miracles, at least in my sense, occur very frequently? Perhaps, though not necessarily. Some might think of these answers to prayer as grounded in the natural order which God has eternally willed in the light of his foreknowledge and providential care, and in that case no special act in the strong sense would be necessary. But I see no great problem in allowing for the possibility that miracles as special acts might be much more common than some might think. Such miraculous acts might not be *obvious* miracles, since they involve outcomes that might for all we know have come about by purely natural means, but they might nevertheless be the result of a special divine causality.

Some people might not wish to describe such a wide class of events as miraculous, and would deny that undetectable, or at least not obviously recognizable, special acts of God are miracles. For them, a miracle must be religiously significant and also be in some sense recognizable and 'obvious'. If one prefers to reserve the term 'miracle' for this narrower subclass of miracles in my sense, I would have no objection. There may be a point in restricting the term 'miracle' to special acts of God that have a particular kind of importance, leaving out any special acts of God in daily life that are not easily recognizable as special acts. But then some other term will be needed for the broader category. My point is that we do have a concept of a type of action of God in which something occurs that would not have occurred in the normal course of things. I propose to call such special acts of God 'miracles'.

It is evident that the very idea of incarnation involves a special action in at least the weak sense. Would an incarnation require a special action in the strong sense? Is God becoming human not itself a miracle? This is denied by some theologians, even ones who wish to uphold a traditional Chalcedonian view.[5] Fortunately, this is not a question that I need to resolve, for I do not wish to inquire merely about the possibility of some incarnational story being true, but about the possibility that the Christian incarnational narrative is true. Regardless of whether or not incarnation itself is or involves a special action of God in the strong sense, it appears undeniable to me that the particular narrative that the Church has presented does involve such actions.

The Jesus presented in the Gospels, and proclaimed from the pulpits, is a Jesus born of a virgin, who performs miraculous healings, exhibits supernatural knowledge, and is finally raised from the dead and exalted into heaven. It is of course possible, as we saw in Chapter 2, to rewrite the narrative and attempt to purge the miraculous elements. But such a rewritten narrative is certainly a different story. One might argue with respect to any particular miracle recounted as performed by Jesus that the miracle has no great intrinsic theological significance. (The resurrection of Jesus might be an exception to this claim, although the resurrection is not generally viewed as a miracle performed by Jesus, but by God the Father.) However, one cannot reasonably argue that the miracles of Jesus as a whole are an insignificant feature of the narrative, or that all such stories could be deleted from the narrative without altering our understanding of the character and status of Jesus.

If miracles are or require special acts of God, and if the Christian incarnational narrative includes miracles, then the particular incarnational narrative that Christianity offers is logically linked to special acts of God. Attempts to tell *this* story without miracles are doomed to failure, though of course one can, as we have seen, try to replace this story with one of a different character. To defend the incarnational narrative it is necessary, therefore, to defend the claim that miracles could occur, and that they could be known to occur.

In the remainder of this chapter, I shall defend the claim that such divine acts are possible, and that it is possible to know they have occurred. I shall also consider the question as to whether acceptance of miracles leads to any special theological or religious problems, as is sometimes claimed by contemporary theologians. In the next chapter, I shall look at the question as to whether there are any special problems involved in coming to know that such events have occurred in the *past*. Do the procedures that are required for obtaining historical knowledge make it impossible to know that God has acted specially in the past?

7.2 COULD GOD PERFORM MIRACLES?

Miracles can be seen as a metaphysical, epistemological, or theological problem. That is, one can worry about whether miracles as events can occur, about whether such events could be known or rationally believed to occur, and about whether belief in such events would be religiously or theologically objectionable in some way. I shall deal with these three problems as distinct difficulties, beginning with metaphysical questions, since if miracles cannot occur, there is little point in trying to determine whether we know that they occur, or whether it would be religiously problematic to accept them.

Let me begin by discussing the concept of miracle again. I have defined a miracle as an event that is the result of a special divine intention and exercise of causal power that is distinct from the intention and power God manifests in creating and conserving the universe. There are of course concepts of miracle that do not involve such special divine activity. Paul Tillich, for instance, defines a miracle as an event that is astonishing, that is somehow revelatory of the ground or power of being, and that is received in an ecstatic experience, but he specifically claims that such events should not be understood as outside the normal course of nature.[6] I see no need to deny that miracles in Tillich's sense are possible. Even if we replace Tillich's Ground of Being, which does not seem capable of performing a miracle in the sense of a special act, with a concept of God as personal agent, it is certainly plausible to think that

---

[6] Paul Tillich, *Systematic Theology*, i (London: Nisbet, 1953), 130.

God could produce events that have revelatory or religious value through the medium of natural processes in the way that Tillich envisions. Such events would be special acts in what I have termed the weak sense. All I wish to say is that they are not miracles in the sense that I am discussing.

The alternative to a Tillichian type of definition of miracle is often thought to be what might be called a 'Hume-type' definition, after David Hume's statement that a miracle is '*a transgression of a law of nature by a particular volition of the Deity, or by the interposition of some invisible agent*'.[7] Hume's definition is often employed by both enemies of miracles and friends, such as Richard Swinburne,[8] and I have in the past used a similar definition myself.[9] I now have three reservations about Hume-type definitions.

First, this concept of miracle is anachronistic when applied to the first century, when the modern concept of a law of nature was unknown. This objection is not fatal, since it is arguable that first-century people did possess the concept of natural regularities that were rooted in natural powers, and understood a miracle as the production of an effect that exceeded the powers of any natural agent and that therefore could not have been expected to occur in the normal course of nature.[10] One might claim that this first-century concept is at

---

[7] See David Hume, *An Enquiry Concerning Human Understanding* (Indianapolis: Hackett Publishing Co., 1977), 77 n.

[8] See Richard Swinburne, *The Concept of Miracle* (London: Macmillan, 1970), 13.

[9] See my *Philosophy of Religion: Thinking About Faith* (Downer's Grove, Ill.: InterVarsity Press, 1985), 107–110.

[10] Strictly speaking, I suspect that even this account of 'natural powers' is somewhat anachronistic when applied to ancient Israel because Jewish culture of that era probably did not think of 'nature' at all in the modern sense of a more or less autonomous sphere of reality to be sharply distinguished from the supernatural realm. This modern concept of nature is a dubious one that I do not wish to endorse. However, the notion of 'natural powers' can be understood without appeal to any such idea of nature. Nature can be understood as the constant outcome of God's creative activity and not an autonomous sphere of reality. The natures and natural powers of objects in the world can be understood as the normal outcome of that creative activity, with miracles being understood as an expression of some special intention. Thus miracles are not to be distinguished from other natural events by saying that God is active in the former but not in the latter but rather by the manner of God's activity. I believe that it is clear than ancient peoples, including the Israelites, possessed this concept of the natural powers of objects. For example, they clearly understood that in the normal course of events, dead people could not be restored to life without a special exercise of divine power.

least a functional analogue of the more modern concept of a law of nature, and that roughly the same idea is being expressed. Still, even if that is so, it would seem better to stick to the older conception, expressible in terms of natural powers and regularities.

The second reason for not employing the Humean definition is that the term 'transgression' (others speak of 'violation') of a law of nature is seriously misleading. A transgression or violation of a law sounds like an ethically improper action, but we are not considering the violation of some legal or ethical norm, but simply the occurrence of a special divine action that is distinct from God's normal creative activity. Of course one can raise ethical questions about the goodness or wisdom of such an action, but the answers to those questions will be determined by the nature of the actions themselves. In acting specially, what intentions is God implementing? No conclusions about the character of such actions can be derived merely from the fact that they are distinct from God's normal creative actions. One might perhaps properly speak of an exception to what would normally occur, given the laws of nature, but not of violation. Since God, if theism is true, must be seen as the author of such natural laws, it is difficult to see why such an exception could not be made by God, or why it would necessarily be wrong for God to do so.

Finally, however, it does not seem to be the case that miracles even require exceptions to natural laws. The Hume-type definition should be avoided because it is not clear that special divine causation necessarily requires any 'violation' of natural laws. William Alston has argued that the only laws of nature we have any basis for accepting are laws that specify what must occur on the assumption that the event is the product of a 'closed system'.[11] That is, scientifically discovered laws of nature do not specify what must occur absolutely or unqualifiedly, but rather specify what must (or will, on some interpretations) occur *unless* some other force unanticipated by the law intervenes. Thus a man who steps off a cliff will fall to the earth, unless he is snagged by a hook dangled from a helicopter, or is blown back by an incredibly powerful gust of

[11] Alston, 'God's Action in the World', 212.

wind, or is blown up by an explosive before he reaches the ground, and so on. So, as Alston notes, and as C. S. Lewis had clearly seen before him, 'since the laws we work with make (implicit or explicit) provision for interference by outside forces unanticipated by the law, it can hardly be claimed that the law will be violated if a divine force intervenes'.[12] The miraculous event is exceptional in the sense that something happens that would not have occurred in the normal course of nature, and one could say that the event constitutes an exception to what one would expect on the assumption that only natural forces are operating. So a sense can be given to the claim that a miracle involves an 'exception' to a law of nature, and I shall so speak about miracles at times. Strictly speaking, however, such a miracle does not require any 'suspension' or 'violation' of laws of nature.

What grounds are there for claiming that miracles are impossible? Well, one could rule out the possibility of such divine activity if one knew or had good grounds for believing that God does not exist, or that God either cannot act in this way or has good reasons for never doing so. I shall not here attempt to defend the reasonableness of belief in God, though there are plenty of philosophical defences of such belief around.[13] I take it as patently obvious that unless God exists, the idea that the Christian story is true is a non-starter. Similarly, if God is a Tillichian Ground of Being rather than a personal agent, then it is obvious that such a narrative cannot be true.

Sometimes the idea that God is a personal agent is stigmatized as a view that sees God as overly 'anthropomorphic', merely a 'being alongside other beings'. It is quite possible, however, to understand God as a distinct being, in the sense of being a centre for personal agency that is not identical with other centres of personal agency, without implying an overly anthropomorphic view of God. God is of course different from human personal agents in many ways. They are his crea-

---

[12] Alston, 'God's Action in the World', 212.

[13] In addition to the works of Swinburne and Alston mentioned earlier as defences of theism, see also Alvin Plantinga and Nicholas Wolterstorff (eds.), *Faith and Rationality* (Notre Dame, Ind.: University of Notre Dame Press, 1983) for a defence of the rationality of belief in God.

tures; he is their creator. They are finite; he is infinite. But such differences do not imply that God cannot be like human agents in some respects. Or more properly, since humans are regarded as created in God's image, it does not imply that humans cannot resemble God in some respects. The claim that a God who is a personal agent would thereby be placed on the level of finite creatures needs argument; its truth is far from obvious and in fact to me it seems obviously false.

In any case, in this book I am simply assuming the reasonableness of a theistic view of God as an all-powerful personal agent who creates and conserves the world. Moreover, if God does exist as a personal agent, and if God is the ground of the natural order, including its natural processes, it is difficult to see why the activity of God must be limited to his activity in maintaining those natural processes. It is of course possible that though God could act specially in the natural order, he has good reasons not to do so and never does. Such claims are essentially theological and I will deal with them in a later section of this chapter, after discussing epistemological objections to miracles.

What other grounds might there be for denying the possibility of miracles? It is often alleged that a belief that miracles occur is incompatible with modern science. John Macquarrie, for instance, says that 'the traditional conception of miracle is irreconcilable with our modern understanding of both science and history'.[14] Regrettably, theologians who assert this seem remarkably reluctant to specify the character of the problem. As we have just seen, in discussing the inappropriateness of describing miracles as violations of natural laws, there seems to be no difficulty in conceiving of miracles while robustly affirming scientific laws. Since a miracle by definition involves the activity of a causal power unanticipated by the relevant scientific law, and the scientific law only states what must happen if no outside power intervenes, then miracles cannot contravene scientific laws.

One can say, of course, that a miracle involves an outcome different from that which would occur in the normal course

---

[14] John Macquarrie, *Principles of Christian Theology*, 2nd edn. (New York: Charles Scribner's Sons, 1977), 248.

of nature; otherwise the miracle would not involve special divine power, and therefore in some sense there is an 'exception' to the laws of nature. If one claims that the only forces operating that are envisaged as overriding the force of the law and thus making it inapplicable are other natural ones, then one might even make a case for saying the law has been 'violated'. However, I do not see, apart from a philosophical commitment to the denial that anything besides nature exists, why the causal forces that might make a law inapplicable must be limited to natural events. Moreover, since God, if he exists, is the author of the laws of nature, there is reason to think that such exceptions to laws of nature are real possibilities. For such an event to occur, God merely has to manifest a causal power distinct and different from his normal creative activity.

Some philosophers have argued that the very concept of a law of nature implies that there cannot be exceptions to such laws.[15] On this view the claim that there cannot be an exception to a law of nature is a conceptual truth, for a law of nature is simply a description of a universal pattern. If the pattern is not universal, then we do not have a true law of nature. Thus, if a miracle is an exception to a law of nature, then we know a priori that there cannot be a miracle.

This argument commits the same sin that critics of the ontological argument for God's existence allege infects Anselm's attempted proof, namely, trying to decide what is true in the real world by the manner in which we define our terms. Surely we cannot decide whether or not there are any exceptions to the normal regularities of nature by how we choose to define such concepts as 'law of nature'. If someone insists that a true law of nature must be exceptionless, then the theist who believes in miracles may concede that terms may be defined as one likes, and simply point out that one can then simply redefine the term 'miracle' accordingly. If laws of nature must be exceptionless, then we need a concept such as 'quasi-laws of nature', which refers to natural regularities which hold except in those cases where God chooses to work a miracle. It will then be a factual question whether or not the regularities

---

[15] For a good example of this type of argument, see Alastair McKinnon, ' "Miracle" and "Paradox" ', *American Philosophical Quarterly*, 4 (October 1967), 308–14.

we observe in nature are 'laws' in the strict sense insisted upon, and therefore there are no miracles, or whether there are miracles, and therefore at least some of the natural regularities we observe are merely 'quasi-laws'. For both normal practical and scientific contexts, it will make very little difference which is the case, though of course it might make a great difference for those exceptional situations where a recognizable miracle is alleged to have occurred. (By definition, there could be no practical difference for science in the case of what I earlier called an undetectable or unrecognizable miracle.) Whether miracles are metaphysically possible depends on whether the laws (or quasi-laws) of nature depend on God or not, and if so, whether or not God might ever have reasons to make exceptions to such laws, not on how humans choose to define terms such as 'law of nature'.

7.3. CAN A MIRACLE BE CONCEIVED?

Gordon Kaufman has argued that we cannot believe that miracles as special acts of God occur, because we cannot even conceive of such an event.[16] Accounts of miracles on this view are not so much false as unintelligible.

Such a claim has more than a trace of similarity to the now discredited claim of the logical positivists that the proposition that God exists is not false but unintelligible. It is difficult to see how a belief, such as that miracles have occurred, that has been accepted or rejected for centuries and has sparked volumes of acute philosophical argument pro and con, could be meaningless. Nevertheless, since Kaufman is a respected theologian, and his argument has had some influence, it is worth briefly looking at the accusation.

What argument does Kaufman give for the astounding claim that, speaking of particular events that are caused by God, we have an 'inability to conceive *these events themselves*'?[17] The

---

[16] See Gordon Kaufman, 'On the Meaning of "Act of God"', in Owen C. Thomas (ed.), *God's Activity in the World* (Chico, Calif.: Scholar's Press, 1983), 137–61. This article is also included as part of Kaufman's book, *God the Problem* (Cambridge, Mass.: Harvard University Press, 1972).

[17] Kaufman, 'Meaning of "Act of God"', 145. Italics his.

argument is not easy to discern, particularly since Kaufman blends this claim with a quite different thesis, namely that historians would never be justified in accepting a miracle claim. (This latter claim will be examined in the next chapter, which deals with the procedures and assumptions of the historian.) Nevertheless, the argument appears to be something like this. Kaufman says we have no choice but to adopt what he terms 'the modern view', in which events are not conceived as isolated happenings. On this modern view, 'all events are so interrelated and interconnected in many complex ways that to think or to describe any particular event always involves us in reference to those events which preceded it as necessary conditions for its occurring ... and to those ever widening circles of events which it will condition and shape in a variety of ways'.[18] The problem with 'acts of God', says Kaufman, is that they have their origin 'directly or immediately in the divine will and action rather than in the context of preceding and coincident finite events'.[19] However, says Kaufman, 'an "event" without finite antecedents is no event at all and cannot be clearly conceived; "experience" with tears and breaks destroying its continuity and unity could not even be experienced'.[20]

It is tempting to respond to such a claim that something cannot be conceived by simply saying that it is possible to conceive such a thing; I at least have no particular trouble conceiving of the possibility, for example, that a friend of mine who has terminal cancer could be miraculously healed by a special act of God. Perhaps my hope is in vain; it may even be foolish, but it certainly appears conceivable. However, more can be said. It is worth pointing out that if Kaufman is correct, then human free will, in the strong libertarian sense, is also unintelligible, for libertarians also believe that there are 'breaks' in the causal nexus in the sense that genuinely free acts occur.[21] When I act freely, though there are certainly antecedents to my action, nothing about the past made this action

---

[18] Kaufman, 'Meaning of "Act of God"', 145.
[19] Ibid. 147.
[20] Ibid.
[21] This argument against Kaufman is made nicely by Frank G. Kirkpatrick, in 'Understanding an Act of God', in Thomas (ed.), *God's Activity in the World*, 176.

necessary. When a miracle occurs in human history, there are natural antecedent events to the miracle as well. What makes the miracle a miracle is that it cannot be regarded as completely causally explained by those natural antecedent events. Some of them may be necessary, but even together they are not sufficient. Rather, the miraculous event must be attributed to a divine agent, at least in part. In an analogous way, if humans have what libertarians call 'contra-causal freedom', then no event or set of events in the past is sufficient to explain the event, though there are doubtless past conditions that are necessary. Rather, something genuinely new has come into being, something rather like the 'absolute beginning point' that Kaufman denies could occur within nature or history.[22] There is of course the difference that in the case of human action, the cause of the act is a human and not a divine agent, and in some sense humans are certainly part of nature. Nevertheless, agent causality, even in its human form, embodies just the sort of 'rift' in the causal chain that Kaufman claims is inconceivable. Perhaps libertarianism is false, but it certainly does not appear to be inconceivable.

Kaufman claims that he is not assuming a deterministic picture of the universe, but anything less than an all-embracing determinism must allow for the possibility that events are not completely determined by previous natural events, and if this is possible to conceive, it seems possible to think of such events as originating in some non-natural cause, if there are any non-natural realities. It is worth pointing out that Kaufman's argument, assuming it does imply some kind of determinism, would have the strange consequence that quantum mechanics, on one interpretation at least, would be unintelligible. Whether this scientific theory be true or not, there are certainly many scientists and philosophers who seem to think one can conceive of an indeterminism involving 'breaks' in the causal chain, at least at the subatomic level.[23]

Kaufman seems to picture the whole of nature and history as one tightly interlocking causal whole. Every event is the

---

[22] Kaufman, 147.
[23] I do not mean to imply that quantum physics makes miracles possible or likely, just that it undermines Kaufman's view of the natural order as necessarily conceived as a closed system.

'focal point in a web that reaches in all directions beyond it indefinitely'.[24] Whether this be the correct picture of nature and history or not, it is surely extravagant to claim that such a robust metaphysical monism is embodied in our very *concept* of an event. If this is the truth about the world, it is not a truth that can simply be deduced from the concept of an event. If there are other realities outside our physical universe, whether they be God, gods, fairies, or creatures from an alternative universe, I for one have no difficulty conceiving of the possibility that they might causally contribute to the stream of human history. If one insists on being a metaphysical monist, such realities could even be added to the web in which Kaufman believes.

In an endnote, Kaufman tries to illustrate his claim that miraculous events are inconceivable by arguing that we can form no conception of a virgin birth. However, his argument for this is purely an argument that we don't know how God would in fact carry out such an act: 'Are we to suppose that at some point a male sperm appeared within Mary's womb, there fertilizing an egg? If so, how are we to think of this?'[25] Kaufman's point seems to be that such an event is scientifically inexplicable. But of course this is patently obvious. If the event were scientifically explicable, it would not be a miracle. Why shouldn't we think that at some point a male sperm appeared within Mary's womb, or for that matter, that the egg was simply transformed into a fertilized egg without a male sperm, or any one of a hundred other possibilities? If one asks *how* this occurred, the answer is of course that it occurred because God willed it to occur and exercised the appropriate divine power to that end. Such an answer may be false, as may all belief in miracles, but it is hardly inconceivable. It is in fact difficult to see how any theologian who purports to believe in creation could find such an act inconceivable, because the question as to how God created the heavens and the earth must clearly be answered in the same kind of way: God simply willed the universe to be and exercised the appropriate divine power to that end.

[24] Kaufman, 'Meaning of "Act of God"', 147.
[25] Ibid. 159.

7.4. IS IT POSSIBLE TO HAVE GOOD EVIDENCE FOR MIRACLES?

Perhaps the critic of miracles will have more success with epistemological than with metaphysical arguments. It is commonly argued that the amount of evidence one would require to believe in a miracle is so high that it is difficult, perhaps even impossible, ever to satisfy such a heavy burden of proof.[26] This type of argument goes back to and even precedes Hume's famous objections to miracles, which are also epistemological in character. Here my discussion must be even more sketchy than in the last section, since the philosophical literature dealing with Hume-type arguments against belief in miracles is enormous. Hume's own main argument against miracles revolves around the concept of probability. Probability is a notoriously difficult concept to analyse, and it is not completely obvious what kind of probability Hume has in mind. It seems most likely that Hume is talking about *epistemic* probability, the probability of an event's occurrence given what is known about the event and the situation. Essentially, he claims that since a miracle involves a 'violation' of a law of nature, miracles are highly unlikely events. (I will here ignore the inappropriateness of this description of miracles as violations, since it has already been discussed and plays no important role in the argument.) Laws of nature for Hume are descriptions of the normal course of experience. Hume himself says that a 'firm and unalterable experience' has established these laws, and that our experience is uniformly against miracles.[27] Strictly speaking, this is a question-begging claim; if we really knew that our experience of natural regularities was 'unalterable' then we would know that miracles could not occur, and we would be back to the metaphysical type argument just considered. However, such a claim would contradict Hume's own views about the nature of experience and our knowledge of laws of nature, so we should probably regard this as a slip on his part. In any case his argument does not require such a view.

---

[26] Van Harvey, *The Historian and the Believer* (New York: Macmillan, 1966), 87.
[27] Hume, *Concerning Human Understanding*, 76, 77.

Hume is not really entitled to say that our experience is completely uniform that miracles have not occurred, since that begs the question at issue, which is whether anyone has experienced a miracle. So probably we should interpret Hume as saying that in the overwhelming majority of cases, perhaps all the cases other than the putative miracle that is under consideration, our experience is that nature is uniform. Since he thinks we estimate probability on the basis of past experience, it follows that the prior probability of a miracle is extremely low. For Hume, this means that the evidence on behalf of a miracle would have to be extremely powerful to warrant belief in the miracle, evidence of such force that 'its falsehood would be more miraculous, than the fact, which it endeavours to establish'.[28]

Are Hume's claims about the probability of miracles correct? Estimates of prior probability are very tricky, since they are usually made relative to some body of background knowledge. If we know that a box contains 9,999 white marbles and one black marble, then we know the probability of drawing a black marble on any particular draw is rather low. On the other hand, if we draw a great many marbles, then the probability of drawing a black marble sometime or other becomes increasingly high. Similarly, if miracles are very rare events, then the probability of a miracle at any particular place and time may be very low, while the probability of a miracle occurring at some time or other might be much higher.

The number of people in the world who are Olympic swimmers is quite small compared with the total population of the world. Hence, if all we know about a particular person is that she is a member of the human race, the probability that she will be an Olympic swimmer is extremely small. If we know that this person attends a college known for producing many Olympic swimmers, the probability is somewhat higher, and if we know the person is a member of the swim team at that college, the probability may actually become quite high. If we see the person swim in a pool and by consulting our watches determine that she is swimming at a world-class rate of speed, the probability may become still higher. The point is that

[28] Hume, *Concerning Human Understanding*, 77.

in estimating probability, we bring to bear all the relevant knowledge we have, and not just our knowledge of the frequency with which events of the type occur. The difficulty with estimating the prior probability of a miracle lies in determining what relevant background knowledge we have.

Clearly, it will be relevant if someone has some knowledge or well-founded beliefs about the existence of God and God's character and purposes. If I know that God does not exist, or that if he does, he is the sort of being who would not act in a way that would involve an exception to a natural regularity, then I have good grounds for estimating the prior probability of a miracle as very low. On the other hand, if I believe that God exists, miracles would be somewhat more probable. If I believe that God loves and has concern for his creation, and especially for the human race, and that this creation, particularly the human race, has gone terribly wrong, then it seems to me that it is not too improbable to believe that God would take some action to restore that creation and that fallen humanity.

It also seems plausible to hold that this action would involve some kind of communication from God, and special communication from God, even apart from accompanying miracles to authenticate that communication, looks very much like a special action. In other words, though the probability of a miracle occurring at any particular moment in history may be very low, the probability of a miracle occurring at some time or other might be a good deal higher for a person who has the appropriate background beliefs. If I believe that it is fairly likely, or at least not too unlikely, that God would at some point want to communicate with his creatures, then it is natural to look with care at the possible candidates for such a revelatory intervention. The number of plausible accounts of such a revelation are not really so great, and hence it seems mistaken to say that all or any of them must have extremely small antecedent likelihood for everyone.

A miracle that was part of a plausible narrative, perhaps including other miracles, and that involves such a restoration and communication from God would be much more probable than a miracle that was an isolated occurrence, serving no discernible divine purpose. Exactly what the prior probability of a miracle such as the resurrection of Jesus may be if this is correct is probably impossible to say, since we have no way of quantifying such matters, but Hume is surely wrong in his dogmatic claim that the probability must be vanishingly low. Hence, although it certainly seems plausible to say that one ought to treat miracle claims with a certain degree of initial scepticism, it is by no means the case that this initial scepticism must always be insurmountable. Whether that is so will depend on the overall plausibility of the narrative, which will in turn be shaped by beliefs about the existence and character of God, the human condition and human relations to God, and the character of the narrative as a whole.

In any case, we can clearly see that our initial presumption against exceptions to natural regularities cannot be so total as to prevent empirical testing of laws of nature. It must be possible for observers to recognize and give credible testimony that an exception to what is thought to be a law of nature has occurred. If this were not possible, then it would be impossible to test laws of nature, and almost all working scientists agree that such testability is an important characteristic of genuine scientific laws. If we followed Hume's policy, we would in effect always reject an observation of an apparent counterinstance to a law of nature, on the grounds that its prior probability is too low, but this would make scientific progress impossible.

So it must be possible to believe on reasonable grounds that an exception to what is currently accepted as a law of nature has occurred. The opponent of miracles will probably object at this point that though such a case might be an exception to what is accepted as a law of nature, it may not be an exception to the true laws of nature.[29] Presumably, in the case of a scientific advance in understanding, it is just this situation that obtains. Event E appears to be an exception to accepted law of nature L_1, which then leads us to revise L_1 in favour of L_2.

---

[29] An argument to this effect can be found in Patrick Nowell-Smith, 'Miracles', Antony Flew and Alasdair MacIntyre (eds.), *New Essays in Philosophical Theology*, (New York: Macmillan, 1955), 243–53. Nowell-Smith argues that our inability to say that some future natural law will not explain the event in effect makes it impossible to define the concept of the supernatural as something to be distinguished from the natural order.

I have already argued that we do not in fact have to understand a miracle as an exception to a law of nature. But let us waive this response, and assume for the moment that miracles should be characterized in this way, since they do involve an outcome that is different from what we would expect if only known scientific factors were at work. One might say that a miracle is something that appears to be an exception to a law of nature, even if it is not ultimately. So we do have a problem of distinguishing genuine miracles from counter-instances to accepted laws of nature that simply show that those accepted laws are not in fact true laws. In the case where we have an apparent counter-instance to an accepted law of nature, it is always possible that it is the second type of counter-instance that has occurred, and thus that we do not have an exception to a genuine law of nature.

Richard Swinburne has suggested that we decide whether or not this is the situation by determining whether the apparent counter-instance is a repeatable or non-repeatable instance.[30] In a case where the counter-instance is repeated when the circumstances are similar, then the reasonable conclusion to draw is that the accepted law of nature should be revised to accommodate the counter-instance. However, in a case where the counter-instance seems to be a 'one-time' occurrence, then it would not appear reasonable to revise the accepted law of nature, and it would seem we have a genuine candidate for a miracle. We should continue to accept the relevant law as genuine, and *if* we have good reason to believe God's power is involved, hold that the relevant conditions for satisfying the law did not hold because of this additional factor that the law did not anticipate.

We could always, of course, revise our laws of nature in an *ad hoc* manner so that they would be exceptionless, but we simply do not think of laws of nature in this way. No physicist would take seriously as a proposal for a basic law of nature a regularity that holds at all times except, let us say, for one place in Palestine in AD 30.

Of course, the judgement about which kind of case we have is a fallible one, a fact that Swinburne himself emphasizes.

---

[30] See Swinburne, *Concept of Miracle*, 23–32.

Thus, we have no sure-fire way of making the determination, and Swinburne's suggestion may need to be supplemented in doubtful cases by other criteria. Clearly, for example, the character of the alleged miracle, the religious context in which it appears, and the purposes it serves will all be relevant to making the determination. Even so, our judgements will be fallible. Thus, we might judge an event to be a non-repeatable counter-instance and thus an exception to a law of nature, when in fact it is not. However, the possibility of error goes both ways. It is also possible a genuine miracle might occur and be unrecognized. (I have in fact suggested that there might be a whole class of unrecognizable miracles that do not involve any obvious exception to natural powers.) Unless we know a priori that miracles are impossible or extremely improbable, we have no basis for asserting that it will always be more probable that the event could be scientifically explained if we had more accurate knowledge of the laws of nature. The mere abstract possibility that an event could be explained by some yet-to-be-discovered law of nature is no reason to believe that it actually can be so explained, any more than the abstract possibility that all my perceptual experience of the external world might be illusory is a reason to believe that the external world does not exist.

7.5. MUST WE BE METHODOLOGICAL NATURALISTS?

Perhaps the most plausible form of the epistemological objection to miracles is what might be called the objection from methodology. One might concede that miracles are metaphysically possible, and even grant that in principle they could be known to have occurred, but argue that the methods followed by reasonable people never, or almost never, in fact lead to belief in a miracle. The reason this is so is that we have a natural and reasonable preference for naturalistic explanations. We normally look for natural causes, and if we don't discover any plausible ones, the reasonable policy is not to invoke the activity of God, but to assume that some unknown natural causes are at work. William Alston, while not ruling out belief in miracles as a 'live possibility', seems to endorse this kind of methodological naturalism:

We can be justified in dismissing the possibility of a naturalistic explanation only if we have (a) a complete description of the particular case and (b) a complete inventory of natural causes of that sort of occurrence. Armed with that, we might be able to show that there were no available natural causes that could have produced that result. But when are we in a position to do that?[31]

A version of this argument from methodology will be considered and criticized in the next chapter, where I look at the objections to special acts of God from the methods of 'critical history'. However, several points need to be made here.

First, there is a sense in which a moderate version of this methodological naturalism might be acceptable to the believer in miracles. The believer in miracles does not wish to endorse gullible superstition. She may agree that miracles are strange and surprising things, and, particularly if she is inclined to think that genuine miracles are highly unusual and that God's ordinary providential care and answers to prayer can be understood without resort to the kind of 'undetectable' miracle that I earlier discussed, she will agree that some degree of initial scepticism is reasonable when faced with miracle claims. This is particularly true of miracle stories which are not embedded in the kind of context that, I argued above, would be necessary to give such claims plausibility. So the believer in miracles does not deny that there is some presumption in favour of natural explanations. She merely denies that this presumption is so strong that it will always outweigh the evidence in favour of a miracle. The amount of evidence that would be required will vary, I think, depending on the intrinsic plausibility and apparent religious significance of the miracle. If my contention above that there is some likelihood that God would act in human history at some point to communicate with and redeem his fallen creatures is reasonable, and if there are only a handful of plausible narratives where this is alleged to have taken place, then when considering these particular narratives, the general presumption that might be operative most of the time with

---

[31] Alston, 'God's Action in the World', 214.

respect to a preference for natural explanations could reasonably be weakened.

The requirements that Alston puts on the believer in miracles here seem much too strong. Why should we only consider a supernatural explanation of an event in cases where we have a complete description of the case, as well as complete knowledge of what natural causes there are for that kind of occurrence? Certainly, it would appear that we need to know enough about the case to know that there is no plausible natural account available, and enough about the natural world to know what plausible natural explanations there might be. However, we surely know enough about the natural order to know that it is most unlikely that there could be any natural explanation for a person who has been dead for three days being restored to life, or for a person walking across the surface of a lake, or for water instantaneously being turned into wine. To say that the postulation of some completely unknown natural cause is always more probable than the ascription of such an event to supernatural causality simply on the grounds that we cannot say that such a natural cause is impossible is in effect to say that we must think of the world as if naturalism were *true*. Such a strong version of methodological naturalism is only reasonable if we are metaphysical naturalists.

It might appear that believers in those 'ordinary' not-so-obvious miracles I discussed earlier have much less stringent standards. However, such believers might make a distinction between events that must be believed to be miracles, such as those involved with the incarnational narrative, and other miracles they are inclined to accept. These other miracles might be regarded as events which God *may* have brought about through special power, and the believer may incline to the view that love for God requires that one adopt the proper attitude of gratitude for those events which God has brought about, even if it is only a possibility that the means whereby they were brought about involved special divine power.

If an alleged miracle is part of a plausible narrative in which the purposes of God as we have come to know God are fulfilled, then it is by no means obvious that attributing such an event to God's action is always less probable than simply saying there is some natural explanation, though we have no idea what it is. For in the latter case we have not really offered an explanation at all. Clearly, it is more plausible to attribute some miracles to God's handiwork than others, but if this is so, then it seems clear that such explanations have explanatory value, as in other cases of personal explanation.[32]

The miracles that are embedded in the incarnational narrative appear to serve several valuable religious functions, including functioning as signs that God is indeed acting decisively for human redemption, as well as symbolically expressing the mercy and compassion of God that Jesus as Son of God embodies. Though I do not myself think that the presumption in favour of natural explanations rules out belief in miracles in other times and places, including today, it would appear particularly true that for the case of the story of Jesus, a presumption that would make it impossible to accept the miracles that are an essential part of the story should be rejected.

7.6. ARE MIRACLES THEOLOGICALLY OBJECTIONABLE?

Alvin Plantinga has wittily said that some theologians view proofs of God's existence the same way they do faith-healing. They say it can't be done, but even if it can, it shouldn't be.[33] Whether this accurately describes theologians' attitudes towards proofs of God's existence or not, the attitude towards faith-healing certainly does exist, and is often generalized towards miracles in general. Even if God could do miracles, such theologians think that he should not do so. There may then be theological or religious objections to belief in miracles. Even if miracles are metaphysically possible, and even if they could be known if they occurred, if we know God is the kind of being who would not perform a miracle, or believe that God has good reasons for never performing a miracle, then we may dismiss any real possibility that miracles occur.

What exactly are the theological objections to miracles? One

---

[32] See Swinburne, *Concept of Miracle*, 53–7, for a good discussion of the role of personal explanations in miracle accounts.

[33] A. Plantinga, 'Reason and Belief in God', in *Faith and Rationality*, 63.

kind of objection can, I think, be quickly dismissed. This is the claim that a God who does miracles would be a God who is merely a 'being among other beings', an excessively anthropomorphic deity. I have already briefly answered this objection.[34] Clearly a God who is a personal agent and not merely a 'ground of being' must be capable of specific acts with specific intentions. To deny that God is capable of such actions is simply to deny God's personal character. To say that God acts in the created world is by no means to imply that God is a creature within that world.[35] An infinite cause can have finite effects, and must, if God is to create any finite objects.

Two other types of objection may be worth more attention. The first deals with the question of whether a miracle would somehow undermine the structure of the created order. Often this objection is cryptically expressed, rather than clearly articulated. Thus, Paul Tillich says that the kind of miracle we have been considering would 'destroy the structure of being'.[36] Other theologians express objections to special acts of God as deeds that would 'violate' God's own creation or amount to 'interference' in the natural order of things.

What may lie behind such statements is Hume's concept of a miracle as a 'violation' of a law of nature. We have already seen that it would be incorrect to describe such an alteration of God's normal creative activity as a 'violation', and even further, that there is no need to think that a miracle as a special act of God involves any overturning of laws of nature, which express only what must occur if certain initial conditions obtain, and do not apply when those conditions do not obtain, as clearly they will not in a case involving the additional factor of special divine activity.

It is difficult to see what more there is to this type of objection, but perhaps there is something. Suppose we think of the natural world as embodying God-given structures; the things that God has made have particular *natures*. Brian

---

[34] See above, s. 7.2.

[35] I believe that many theologians deny this because they are influenced by Kant's claim that the concept of causality is a construct of the human understanding that can only legitimately be applied within the world of appearances. Space does not permit a thorough criticism of such a view, but it seems incompatible with the doctrine of creation as most Christians, Jews, and Muslims have understood that doctrine.

[36] Tillich, *Systematic Theology*, i. 129.

Hebblethwaite speaks of such 'God-given structures of creation, and their necessary role in setting creatures at a distance from their creator and providing a stable environment for their lives'.[37] Maurice Wiles, drawing on some words from Hebblethwaite, suggests that God's omnipotence might be 'self-limited (logically) by the nature of what he has made',[38] just as God limits himself by giving free will to human nature. The suggestion that this is a logical limit seems too strong to me, for it can hardly be logically impossible for God to alter the contingent nature of what he has freely created. But perhaps it would somehow be wrong for God to do this; perhaps it would involve a kind of self-negation on his part, a failure to respect the integrity of his own creation. Austin Farrer speaks of created things as 'running themselves in their own way'. What God wills is for the created things to 'be themselves' and act in accordance with their natures.[39] If God performs a miracle, would he thereby not allow his creations to be themselves?

The first thing that must be said here is a reminder that there is a sense in which none of God's creation simply does its own thing. It is easy to slide back into an implicit deism in which we think of the created order as truly independent of God. The truth is, however, that if theism is true, then the autonomy of the created order, while real, is only relative. Everything is what it is only because of God's continuous creative activity; nothing outside of God is anything 'all by itself'. Since created objects receive whatever 'nature' they have continuously from God, it is misleading to think of God as 'violating their autonomy' if God were to alter that nature. They would be neither more nor less dependent on God if that were to occur, and God cannot be reasonably thought to have some kind of 'obligation' not to alter their behaviour.

However, there is no reason to think miracles must always involve an alteration in the nature of created objects. To say this is to embrace an analogue of the idea that miracles are

---

[37] Brian Hebblethwaite, *Evil, Suffering, and Religion* (London: Sheldon Press, 1976), 92–3.

[38] Maurice Wiles, *God's Action in the World* (London: SCM Press, 1986), 67.

[39] See Austin Farrer, *Saving Belief* (Hodder and Stoughton, 1964), 52; and *A Science of God?* (Geoffrey Bles, 1966), 87–8.

violations of laws of nature. In some cases God may simply change one thing into another, water into wine for instance, and that may look like a change in the nature of the water. But it is more correct to say that in this case the water has ceased to exist as water. As long as it is water, it has the nature of water, and when it has become wine, it has the nature of wine, and is no longer water.

But in other cases no change in the nature of anything is required. What occurs in this kind of miracle is not that an element in the natural world is deformed and no longer acts in accordance with its nature. Rather, what happens is that a new factor is added to the situation. The outcome is not what we would 'naturally' expect, not because some finite object has been distorted, but because God is also at work in the situation. In any case, if a miracle is a beneficent one, there is no reason to think that a change in a natural object would have to be a 'violation' or 'deformation' of it, rather than an enhancement or improvement. Assuming I like wine, I may well regard changing water into wine as an improvement, especially if the wine is good wine. A miracle might be just what allows some created object to express in a more perfect form its true character, just as an exceptional or unusual action may be one that most clearly expresses the personality or character of a human agent.

If a virgin becomes pregnant because of God's activity, her nature as a woman is not altered. Let us suppose that the miracle occurs because God creates a sperm and thereby causes an egg to be fertilized. The sperm in this case is a special creation of God but once created, it retains its nature as sperm, and throughout the process, natural objects retain their natural character. Wombs are wombs, and pregnancy is pregnancy. In a case of miracle, the effects may be different, not because objects have acquired strange, new, 'unnatural' natural properties, but because there is an additional power at work in the situation.

There is one final theological objection to miracles that concerns theodicy and the problem of evil. Theologians as diverse as Maurice Wiles and Brian Hebblethwaite agree that if God acts in the world by direct intervention, one could legitimately wonder why God does not act more frequently, particularly to prevent such terrible evils as Auschwitz.[40] Frank Dilley, in a well-known and influential article, raises the problem with refreshing clarity and bluntness:

it [belief that God sometimes intervenes in human history] makes God responsible for every preventable natural evil. If God could send an east wind to rescue the people of Israel, then he could have sent one to melt the iceberg that sank the Titanic, and he could have sent a disease germ to destroy Hitler as he sent a plague to rout the armies of Sennacherib. It would take very little interference to make the world considerably better.[41]

There are I think various ideas embodied in such comments. One worry may be that if God does miracles on some occasions but not on others, he may be treating some people unfairly. Suppose for example, that two children are dying of cancer, and one is miraculously healed. Has God been unfair to the other child?

I can hardly expect to treat the huge subject of the problem of evil and theodicy here, but I will try to say something about the narrower problem as to whether a God who works miracles makes the problem of evil any more difficult than it is, without presuming to solve the difficulty. The heart of this narrower issue, which was addressed in Chapter 5, concerns how egalitarian God must be. I argued in that chapter that though we certainly can believe that God loves all human beings, and indeed all of his creation, we have no basis for thinking that God is under some obligation to assure complete equality for all human persons with respect to the temporal conditions of life. Given the kind of world God has evidently chosen to create, it is hard to see how any theist could find such a claim plausible. Nor is it at all plausible to think that any human person has some kind of claim or right to have a miracle performed. I therefore cannot see how any human could properly charge God with unfairness for not performing a miracle on behalf of some specific person or group.

Of course it will often, perhaps almost always, be the case

[40] See Wiles, *God's Action in the World*, 66–7, where he approvingly quotes Hebblethwaite, *Evil, Suffering, and God*, 92–3.
[41] Frank Dilley, 'Does the "God Who Acts" Really Act?', in Thomas (ed.), *God's Activity in the World*, 54–5.

that we as humans will be ignorant of the reasons why God sometimes acts miraculously and sometimes does not. Does this mean God's actions are arbitrary? That hardly follows. God's actions may sometimes appear arbitrary, but the claim that they are in fact arbitrary could only reasonably be made by someone in a position to know and critically evaluate God's creative plans and purposes. But it is almost universally agreed by believers in special acts of God that God's ways are mysterious and inscrutable. Certainly, God must have reasons for acting miraculously at some times and not at others, and we may well speculate as to what those might be. It is thought sometimes that miracles are performed in connection with the lives of notable saints, or to further significantly the spread of the Gospel. Most significantly, many Christians who are doubtful about most other miracles may be inclined to think that the 'salvation history' of the Jewish people, culminating in the life of Jesus, was so important to the whole human race that it might appropriately be accompanied by miracles. However, the main message of Job has often been taken to be that it is rash for any human to presume to claim an understanding of the purposes and means by which God governs the cosmos, and that lesson still seems to be one worth taking to heart.

One may well *ask* why God did not prevent Auschwitz, or for that matter, thousands of other acts of human cruelty, dating back to the dawn of time. Perhaps an answer can be given in terms of God's honouring of human freedom, or perhaps not. It seems to me that there is nothing wrong with simply admitting that we do not really know why God sometimes acts in special ways and sometimes does not. We should also recall that since miracles can be unrecognized, we actually do not know how much God has intervened in the course of human history.[42] Perhaps we should agree with one of the characters in Woody Allen's movie, *Hannah and Her Sisters*, who remarks that she is not surprised that such things as the Holocaust occur, but is surprised that they do not occur more often. We do not really know how much or how little God

[42] I should like to remind the reader that the language of intervention is really misleading. In using it, I do *not* mean to imply that God is normally absent from his creation. Rather, 'intervention' here simply means 'special action'.

might intervene in human history. Such ignorance is hardly a reason for claiming that God could not act in history at all.

Another idea that lies behind the charge that special acts of God are a problem for theodicy seems to be this. An important part of a Christian theodicy is an explanation of natural evil; at least a significant part of natural evil can be explained as a consequence of God's policy of creating the world with natural laws or regularities, which in turn lead occasionally to natural disasters and ills, but which also make possible a stable world in which the consequences of actions are predictable. A world in which God sometimes intervenes would appear to be a world which is not strictly governed by such natural laws. If God can intervene on a few occasions, why should he not intervene much more frequently?

That is a fair question, but once more I am not sure that an answer can or need be given. We need perhaps to be reminded of our finitude and of the hubris involved in a claim to understand why and how God creates and conserves the natural order of things. But in this case an answer to the question that is fairly plausible does suggest itself. Suppose that the kind of theodicy that justifies natural evils as the necessary price for a stable natural order, and which is thereby supposed to create a difficulty for miracles, is successful. (In reality, I am by no means sure that such a theodicy is successful; even Wiles doubts whether such a theodicy succeeds in the end.[43]) Suppose also that God has strong reasons for intervening in the natural order on a few occasions. In such a situation God would have good reasons for limiting those miraculous occasions; he would have precisely the same reasons for not doing *more* miracles than he does that people such as Wiles allege he has for not doing *any* at all.

In other words, though it may be reasonable to think that God has good reasons for generally structuring the world to operate by way of natural regularities, this does not imply that such a policy must be absolute. God might still have overriding reasons for doing miracles in special cases. Consider the analogy of a wise parent. Such a parent may provide rules for

---

[43] See Wiles, *God's Action in the World*, 67, where he admits that such a theodicy is at least seriously incomplete.

children and be generally consistent in applying and enforcing such rules, and still make exceptions in exceptional circumstances. The same considerations that lead the parent to introduce the general rules in the first place would lead the parent to limit the number of exceptions.

The same value that Wiles and Hebblethwaite see in the policy of creating the world to run on general laws can be cited as an explanation of why these miraculous interventions are not more frequent. God could certainly do an occasional miracle without undermining the stable and predictable character of the natural order; to suggest otherwise is a wild exaggeration. If the miracles are such as not to be recognizable, even more could be done without this disturbing the general structure of the natural order that we must assume to act. However, if obvious miracles were frequent, then such a stable order would certainly be undermined. Hence, if God has good reasons to intervene selectively in human affairs, and if Wiles and others are correct to stress the value of natural laws, then God would equally have good reasons to limit those interventions.

In any case, it is difficult to see how it could be good for theodicy to say that God never intervenes in human history for good. If God has the power to intervene, and I have argued this is a metaphysical possibility, then if God never employs this power, this would seem to be a graver difficulty for theodicy than if he employed it only selectively. A God who never acts in human history would be like a person who declines a specific request to help a person in need by explaining that he never helps anyone, hardly a praiseworthy example of love and compassion.

Most significantly of all, and this brings the point of this discussion back to the incarnational narrative, the denial of special acts of God in history would fatally undermine the best Christian response to the problem of evil. Though there are many philosophical attempts at theodicy, and I by no means wish to say these are without value, I believe that Alvin Plantinga is right to stress the difference between a theodicy and a philosophical defence against the problem of evil. A theodicy attempts to explain why God allows evil, and it is an ambitious undertaking. A defence argues, more modestly, that God has reasons for allowing evil, and we are justified in believing in

God's goodness, even if we do not know what God's reasons are.

The story of Jesus as suffering Son of God provides a crucial basis for such a defence. For although the story by no means gives us a philosophical explanation for evil, if the story is true, it can be taken as assurance that God cares about evil, and will act ultimately to redeem the greatest evil and bring about good. This story is not merely a claim that God cares about evil and suffering, but a concrete manifestation of that care. God himself chooses to suffer with his creation, and then triumphs through that suffering. The person who accepts the narrative may be no closer to a theodicy, but she may have good reason to trust in God's goodness, because she has come to know God in a deeper way. The tremendous religious power of the narrative depends largely on the claim that it is not merely a myth or illustration of a philosophical doctrine. It is rather the historical enactment of the creator's story in making himself one with his beleaguered creation. Unless God acted decisively and specially in Jesus, the strongest Christian answer to the problem of evil, the answer of Jesus on the cross, is undermined.

8

Critical History and the Supernatural

WE have no good reason to believe that it is metaphysically impossible for God to become a human being, and a narrative containing accounts of miracles that recounts such an incarnation cannot be claimed to be false merely because of its supernatural elements. Or so I have argued. One might concede both of these contentions, and accept that God could in theory become a human being and that miraculous events could be known to occur, while still holding that it is very difficult, if not impossible, to know that the founding Christian narrative is true, on the grounds that the incarnational narrative is not the kind of story that could be *historically* known. After all, it is one thing to admit that if a miracle occurred in my own experience, or to someone I know well, it might be believable; quite another thing to say that miraculous events that occurred in ancient times could be reliably known.

This kind of problem goes back at least as far as 'Lessing's ditch'. I refer here of course to Gotthold Ephraim Lessing, the German dramatist, critic, and aesthetician (1729–81). Lessing is known for a seminal essay in which he raised the issue as to how he could make the transition from historical beliefs to religious knowledge as a barrier to becoming a Christian: 'That, then, is the ugly, broad ditch which I cannot get across, however often and however earnestly I have tried to make the leap.'[1] Lessing's ditch is not one ditch, but several

---

[1] G. Lessing, 'On the Proof of the Spirit and of Power', in *Lessing's Theological*

ditches confusedly rolled together, as Gordon E. Michalson has convincingly shown in a recent book.[2] The truth is that for Lessing, religious knowledge must be of 'eternal truths of Reason', and historical knowledge is not the kind of thing suited to be the proper object of religious belief. The problem for Lessing lies, not in the quality of historical evidence available, but in the empirical, contingent character of historical knowledge.

8.1. RATIONALISM ABOUT RELIGIOUS KNOWLEDGE

Before dealing with the problem of whether historical knowledge can come to terms with miraculous events, I shall first try to show how epistemological objections to historical religious knowledge that appear to stem from scruples about the empirical evidence for that knowledge sometimes rest on covert rationalist assumptions, as is the case for Lessing. Only when we set this type of rationalism aside can we tackle the genuinely historical problems that are present.

In this discussion, I shall not use the terms 'empiricist' and 'rationalist' to refer to precisely defined epistemological positions, but somewhat loosely to refer to general tendencies to conceive of religious knowledge in particular ways. An empiricist conception of religious knowledge is roughly one that regards at least some of our significant religious knowledge as derived from experience. For example, someone who claims to have observed a miracle performed by God is making a claim to know something religiously significant on the basis of experience. Typically, the empiricist regards at least some, though probably not all, religious truths as contingent in nature. (Though I do not assume that necessary truths cannot

Writings, ed. and trans. Henry Chadwick (Stanford, Calif.: Stanford University Press, 1957), 55.

[2] Gordon E. Michalson, Jr., *Lessing's 'Ugly Ditch': A Study of Theology and History* (University Park, Penn.: Pennsylvania State Press, 1985). Michalson distinguishes between the temporal ditch, the metaphysical ditch, and the ditch of appropriation, each of which in turn comes in various versions. While I found his work illuminating and helpful, I find it more useful for my purposes to employ a somewhat different taxonomy of the types of problems that beset religious knowledge seen as historical knowledge.

be learned from experience.) The claims that 'God called Abram to leave Ur', or that 'God delivered Israel from Egypt', or 'God raised Jesus of Nazareth from the dead', would all be examples of such logically contingent religious propositions. Any philosopher or theologian who regards Christianity as subject to partial empirical confirmation or disconfirmation through historical evidence would serve as an example of someone who holds such an empiricist conception of religious knowledge. Bishop Butler, Richard Swinburne, and Michael Martin all regard Christianity in this way.[3]

A rationalist conception of religious knowledge, on the other hand, is one that views religious knowledge in the following way: the paradigm of religious knowledge is a 'timeless eternal truth'. Religious truths are either necessary truths or else resemble necessary truths in important ways. Knowledge of these truths is not dependent on ordinary experience, but is gained through a process of reflection. As theologians sometimes use the word 'rationalist' for any philosophical position that sees religious knowledge as needing rational justification, it is important to note that the word 'rationalist' here carries as its contrast 'empiricist', not 'fideist'.

For the rationalist in my sense, religious truths are either self-evident, or else they are truths that are 'recollected' (using the term in a way reminiscent of but broader than Plato's concept of recollection). Recollection in this sense is a type of reflection on universal structures of the world, human life, or experience. For the rationalist, religious truths are not necessarily simple or obvious; gaining such truth may involve an arduous process of reflection. However, once the truth is 'seen', it is also seen that this is a truth which is unaffected by empirical evidence of the ordinary sort. Claims that 'finite egos are only apparently distinct from the Absolute and are in fact identical with the Absolute', or that 'the true being of the human person lies in the person's *potentiality to be*', or 'God is not a being, but the ground of possibility of being', would all be examples of religious knowledge conceived in a rationalist manner. All

[3] See Joseph Butler's *Analogy of Religion* (Oxford: Clarendon Press, 1896), Richard Swinburne's *Revelation: From Metaphor to Analogy* (Oxford: Clarendon Press, 1992), and Michael Martin's *The Case Against Christianity* (Philadelphia: Temple University Press, 1991).

these propositions have the following characteristics: If true they are necessarily true or else they are I what shall call inescapably true. An inescapable truth is one that is necessarily true given the structure of human nature. Since the features of human nature in question may not be logically necessary, religious truths of this type are not strictly necessary in the logical sense, but they resemble necessary truths in being truths that could not be altered by ordinary particular events. They could not be altered unless human beings were altered to become radically different kinds of beings. Their truth could not depend on whether particular events have occurred, and though a particular experience or set of experiences could be the occasion for someone's coming to realize their truth, they do not seem to be the kind of truths one would normally learn through observation.

It might be thought that such a rationalistic conception of religious knowledge would not be widely held. Certainly, I believe that not many theologians would describe their view of religious knowledge as rationalistic; they might indeed be surprised to hear someone else thus describe them. Nevertheless, I think that such a rationalistic perspective is fairly widespread.

I shall briefly mention three philosophical examples of rationalist conceptions of religious knowledge: Kant, Wittgenstein, and Hegel, corresponding to three distinct types of rationalism. In his *Religion Within the Limits of Reason Alone* Kant says very explicitly that '[w]e need, therefore, no empirical example to make the idea of a person morally well-pleasing to God our archetype; this idea as an archetype is already present in our reason'.[4]

Ludwig Wittgenstein, in his early work *Tractatus Logico-*

---

[4] Immanuel Kant, *Religion Within the Limits of Reason Alone*, trans. Theodore Greene and Hoyt Hudson (New York: Harper & Row, 1960), 56. Someone might argue that Kant is not really a religious rationalist in my sense, because though he thinks there is much religious truth that is known in the rationalist manner, he also is open to the possibility of a historical revelation that, at least for some people, has essential importance. As a strict historical claim, this objection may be correct, and Kant may not be a strict rationalist. Nevertheless, Kant's work in *Religion Within the Limits of Reason Alone* was part of a series of historical influences that tended to minimize the importance of historical revelation. It is my own judgement that the overall thrust of Kant's work does indeed reduce the significance of historical revelation by viewing it simply as a vehicle for the 'pure religion of reason'.

Philosophicus, appears to view ethical and religious knowledge as a mystical knowledge that is in some way similar to the truths of logic: strictly speaking, such propositions say nothing, though in a mystical way they may 'show' us something of great importance. 'If there is any value that does have value, it must lie outside the whole sphere of what happens and is the case. For all that happens and is the case is accidental.'[5] The same thing is said about God: 'God does not reveal himself *in* the world.'[6]

Hegel's conception of religion as the more immediate knowledge of the absolute reality that is conceptually grasped in philosophy illustrates a third type of rationalism: 'The object of religion as well as of philosophy is eternal truth in its objectivity, God and nothing but God, and the explication of God. Philosophy is not a wisdom of the world, but is knowledge of what is not of the world; it is not knowledge which concerns external mass, or empirical existence and life, but is knowledge of that which is eternal.'[7]

Kant, Wittgenstein, and Hegel are of course philosophers and not theologians, but it is significant that they have all had an enormous influence on theology. They represent, I think, three possible strands of religious rationalism. (Other strands may be possible as well, but I see these as prominent.) One strand, represented by Kant, attempts to reduce religious truth to moral truths, knowable by reason. So if someone objects that we have no reliable historical knowledge of Jesus as an object of faith, one may simply reply that what is really important are the moral possibilities embodied in Jesus' life. Theologian Don Cupitt, in responding to the charge that our critical-historical knowledge of Jesus is limited, takes exactly this stance:

[T]he core of a religion does not lie in the biography or personality of the founder, but in the specifically religious values to which, according to tradition, he bore witness. By these values I mean

    [5] Ludwig Wittgenstein, *Tractatus Logico-Philosophicus* (New York: Humanities Press, 1961), 6.41 (p. 145).
    [6] Ibid. 6.432 (p. 149).
    [7] *G. W. F. Hegel On Art, Religion, and Philosophy* (New York: Harper & Row, 1970), 145. (Taken from a translation of *Lectures on the Philosophy of Religion*, by E. B. Speirs and J. Burdon Sanderson.)

possible determinations of the human spirit whereby it relates itself to the ultimate goal of existence ...

How can we depend upon the uncertainties of historical tradition for knowledge of, and our power to attain, a history-transcending truth?[8]

The second type of rationalistic impulse, illustrated by Wittgenstein, lies in seeing religious truth as mystical rather than moral, some type of truth that really cannot be expressed in human language at all. Paul Tillich's claims about 'the God beyond the God of theism', who is not a being but the Ground of Being or Being-itself, might be an example of this tendency.[9]

This second type may resemble and shade over into the third type, illustrated by Hegel, which I would describe as metaphysical/speculative rationalism, for here religious truth is identified with speculative truths derived from reflection on the human condition. Besides neo-Hegelian theologians, many of the claims of Buddhism and Hinduism could serve as examples of this metaphysical/speculative rationalism. For rationalists in general, there is a tendency to transform the historical materials of a religious tradition into archetypes with a universal validity, or mythology with a universal meaning, or illustrations of necessary moral truths.

I have claimed that a strongly negative claim about historical religious knowledge often rests on a rationalist conception of religious knowledge. Empiricist conceptions of religious knowledge, on the other hand, except for extreme and implausible versions of empiricism, are open in principle to such knowledge. It is certainly in keeping with the spirit of empiricism that one should say that whether or not we have any historical religious knowledge is a question for experience to decide; we cannot say a priori that such a thing is impossible. Furthermore, it seems plausible that someone who says that such knowledge is in principle impossible must root that claim, at least ultimately, in an a priori conception of the nature of religious knowledge or of historical knowledge or both.

Not all Christian theologians have been clear about where

---

[8] Don Cupitt, 'A Final Comment', in John Hick (ed.), *The Myth of God Incarnate*, (London: SCM Press, 1977), 205.
[9] See Paul Tillich, *The Courage To Be* (New Haven: Yale University Press, 1952), 184–90.

they stand on these issues. I think the reason for this is that though theologians find the type of perspective of Kant or Wittgenstein attractive, as Christian theologians they wish in some way to maintain the importance of history, and thus there is a tendency to be either unclear about whether faith includes belief in historical propositions, or to be downright inconsistent on this issue. Van Harvey, for example, criticizes Rudolf Bultmann at just this point. He maintains that Bultmann's theological position ought to lead him to regard historical claims about Jesus as unimportant:

> As I have argued in the preceding chapter, this reference to a decisive act of God in Jesus Christ seems gratuitous within the framework of Bultmann's theology. For him, Jesus is merely the historical cause (*das Dass*), which initiates faith. The figure of Jesus does not inform in any way the content (*das Was*) of faith. Moreover, this reference to Jesus not only seems unnecessary but contradictory, since it is impossible to reconcile with Bultmann's basic premise that faith is a possibility for man as man.[10]

To use my language, Harvey accuses Bultmann of illegitimately dragging in empirical content when his operative understanding of religious knowledge is rationalist.

I believe, however, that *critics* of historical religious knowledge may easily make a similar mistake, with Lessing as a prime example.[11] They raise objections to historical religious knowledge that are apparently empirical in nature, and thus should presuppose an empiricist conception of religious knowledge that is open in principle to such historical knowledge. When we look more deeply, however, we find that these empirical objections are a smokescreen for covert rationalist presuppositions. Legitimate empirical problems then lend unwarranted support for the covert rationalism; alternatively, the covert rationalism is employed to portray the empirical difficulties as being insuperable, impossible to overcome, instead of simply being difficulties. If we wish to give historical

---

[10] Van A. Harvey, *The Historian and the Believer* (New York: Macmillan, 1966), 165.
[11] For a fuller discussion of all these points see my 'Empiricism, Rationalism, and the Possibility of Historical Religious Knowledge', in C. Stephen Evans and Merold Westphal (eds.), *Christian Perspectives on Religious Knowledge* (Grand Rapids, Mich.: Wm. B. Eerdmans, 1993).

religious knowledge a fair chance, we must put aside such rationalistic assumptions about the character of religious knowledge.

The claim that it is impossible for anyone to experience God or God's activity does not look as though it follows from any plausible version of empiricism. Rather, it reflects a priori convictions about the character of the divine and the relation of the divine to the natural world. Someone who insists that empirical religious knowledge is impossible seems to know a priori that religious knowledge has as its subject matter something that could not appear in space and time, or something that could not be recognized if it did. However, such an a priori conviction does not stem from the genuinely empirical spirit, but reflects a rationalist mind-set. Why should we assume that whatever religious knowledge takes as its object must be timeless, eternal, or wholly other in such a way that it can't manifest itself in the natural world at all?[12] While it may be a genuinely empiricist claim to say that empirical religious knowledge is difficult to attain or can only be attained under certain conditions, empiricism provides no real support for the thesis that empirical religious knowledge is impossible. Once more we appear to have a dogmatic rationalist claim that is not self-evident or necessarily true, one that Christianity has traditionally rejected, and which therefore stands in need of argument.

8.2. CAN THE RATIONALIST CONCEPTION OF RELIGIOUS KNOWLEDGE BE DEFENDED?

Perhaps some support is provided for the rationalist conception of religious knowledge by what might be termed the *problem of particularity*. If religious knowledge is tied to historical events, then it will necessarily be tied to particular events at a particular place and time, known to some people perhaps, but not to others, who unfortunately were blocked from this knowledge by the accidents of history and geogra-

[12] See ibid. for an extended argument against the Kantian claim that experience of God is impossible.

phy. If religious knowledge concerns some timeless inner truth then it would be equally available to all human beings, at least in principle, and it might be argued that such equality is what we would expect from God if God is good. This version of the problem of particularity is closely linked with the problem of whether God must be egalitarian in his dealings with humans, dealt with in Chapter 5.

I argued there that the problem of particularity should not be conflated with the problem of the ultimate status of those who are non-Christians, and I shall briefly summarize the argument. That the problems are logically distinct can be seen by pointing out that a belief that ultimate religious truth is partly historical in character does not entail any particular view of the ultimate status of non-Christians. One may hold that the final truth about God is revealed in a particular historical narrative, and embrace universalism. Or, one may say that at death people may receive a clarification that allows them to make a genuine decision. Or, one might say that some follow Christ in this life without realizing it is Christ whom they are following. However, my point here is not to argue for such soteriological theories, but to point out that the question of whether religious knowledge might be historical must be distinguished from the question of the ultimate fate of those who do not respond to that revelation in this life for 'accidental' reasons. The two questions are logically distinct.

One other clarification is in order here. The possibility of a historical revelation and thus of historical religious knowledge must be distinguished from the question of the exclusivity of such a revelation. The claim that God has revealed himself in the history of the Jewish people and in Jesus of Nazareth is not equivalent to the claim that God has revealed himself solely through this history. Of course some Christians, mistakenly in my opinion, have wished to assert such exclusivity, but that is a separate, additional claim. Exclusivity is even stronger than a claim of finality and supremacy, which many more Christians have wished to assert in some sense, but finality and supremacy are also logically distinct from the simple claim that historical religious knowledge has been provided. This is illustrated by the work of John Hick, whose position seems to be that God has revealed himself in a variety of places and times through a variety of 'prophets', and that these multiple revelations are roughly equal in religious truth.[13] Once the possibility of historical religious knowledge is granted, the questions as to the relations that various claimants to be historical religious knowledge have to each other come to the fore, and it certainly must be considered whether one set of such claims could have some sort of superiority over others. However, that discussion is logically distinct from and should not preclude the primary discussion as to whether historical religious knowledge is possible at all.

Once the questions of the 'fate of the heathen' and of exclusivity and revelational superiority are laid to one side, the problem of particularity is somewhat clearer, but not necessarily solved. One might still wonder why God should reveal himself at one place rather than another, one time rather than another, to one people rather than another. The proper answer to such musings is, I suspect, to confess that we don't know why God should do these things. However, I don't see why we should know. If God is indeed a personal being, then it seems reasonable that his actions, like those of all other persons we know, should have specificity. Perhaps it makes sense to say that God might be expected to act in particular ways at particular times. But I don't see why we humans should expect to know why God performed *this* particular action at *this* particular place and time.

The rationalist view that ultimate religious truth is a timeless truth in some sense equally available to all human beings does have a certain attractiveness. However, I wonder if it does not owe that attractiveness to the flattering picture it presupposes of human nature. To use the language of Kierkegaard in *Philosophical Fragments*, this picture is essentially one that sees human beings as possessing the Truth in some Socratic/Platonic sense. Kierkegaard, reflecting on the *Phaedo*, says that the Platonic doctrine of recollection implies the immortality and thus divinity of the soul, and that recollection is simply knowledge of the god.[14] Such a view implies that even

---

[13] See John Hick, *God and the Universe of Faiths* (New York: St Martin's Press, 1973), and many of his later publications.

[14] See the discussion of recollection in *The Concept of Irony* (Bloomington, Ind.: Indiana University Press, 1968), 96 ff., and also S. Kierkegaard, *Philosophical Frag-*

if ultimate religious Truth is not consciously recognized by
everyone, every human being possesses the essential ability to
grasp that Truth. Here human beings and ultimate reality are
seen as being on good terms, as having a natural affinity.
According to Kierkegaard, Christianity, with its doctrine of
sin, presupposes that human beings lack this Truth. We not
only lack a conscious understanding of the Truth, but even
lack the ability to gain such an understanding if we must
rely solely on our natural resources. That is precisely why a
historical revelation is necessary. If God cannot accurately be
known in our 'inner consciousness' then God must break in
on that consciousness. We need God to break in on us from
'outside' that consciousness, Kierkegaard thinks. We need to
know God as God really is, not as we imagine him or want
him to be. Human history has the right kind of 'objectivity'
about it. What has happened in history has happened, whether
I like it or not. In other words, though Kierkegaard is far from
claiming to know why God became incarnate in first-century
Palestine rather than second-century North America, he does
think that the claim that God has appeared in a *particular* time
and place makes sense, given the Christian picture of human
nature.

Of course it is obvious that human beings can and do interpret historical events, and so even a historical revelation allows
plenty of room for people to try to make God in their own
image. To this end one may call as evidence the plethora of
'lives of Jesus' in which Jesus always seems to embody just
those qualities the author admires. Still, if God has really
appeared in human history, there is a sense in which God is
really *outside* our preconceptions. God is really *other*, to use a
currently fashionable category. Moreover, that otherness may
show itself in the shock of recognition manifested in the testimony of those who encountered God in Jesus, a shock that
continues to be felt as others encounter God through that
testimony.

Kierkegaard thinks that this Christian picture will naturally
be perceived by humans as offensive, at least until they have

ments, trans. Howard V. and Edna Hong (Princeton: Princeton University Press,
1985), 87.

been transformed by God's revelation and have responded to that revelation in faith. After all, if we think we 'have God within us' then the Christian picture is a kind of insult. It is a challenge to our pride and self-sufficiency. If Kierkegaard is right about this, then the natural attractiveness of the rationalist picture of religious knowledge may not stem from the truth of that picture, but from its psychological appeal. In this respect the common charge that religious belief is rooted in wish-fulfilment may be less applicable to Christian belief than to some other religious beliefs. It is probably for this reason that Kierkegaard claims that a lack of concern for truth is one of the biggest reasons people do not become Christians; most people, he says, would rather believe what is comforting and flattering than what is true, and the Christian picture of human nature and the human task is anything but comforting and flattering.[15]

I conclude that though the claim that God has revealed himself in history may be surprising and even upsetting, we have no real good reason to think that such a revelation is impossible. Particularity may be troublesome, but it should not be thought to rule out a historical revelation unless we have some good reason to think the rationalist conception of religious knowledge is true. The 'problem of particularity' is a problem that *rests on* a rationalist conception of religious knowledge; it will only be regarded as a severe problem by people who already accept the rationalist conception of religious knowledge, together with its underlying optimistic view of human nature.[16] It therefore cannot settle the question of whether religious knowledge can be historical and particular by providing support for that rationalist conception. The rationalist conception of religious knowledge does not appear intuitively obvious or self-evident. It stands in need of argu-

---

[15] See *The Sickness Unto Death* (Princeton: Princeton University Press, 1980), 42–3. This edition, like the others in the *Kierkegaard's Writings* edition, contains in the margins the pagination of the *Samlede Værker*, 1st edn.

[16] One might question whether a religious rationalist necessarily has such an optimistic view of human nature; the rationalist might think that if we had any religious knowledge it would be through pure reason, but we have none. However, if the rationalist is not a sceptic and affirms that some religious knowledge is possible, then the optimistic view of human capacities seems to be presupposed. I owe this point to Bruce Langtry.

ment. Perhaps there are good arguments for it I have not considered. If so, they need to be brought to the table and examined. In the meantime, I conclude that we have no good reason to rule out the possibility of historical religious knowledge.

8.3. HANS FREI AND THE CHARACTER OF THE BIBLICAL NARRATIVE

Of course someone who is not a religious rationalist may still wonder whether a historical narrative with religious significance could ever be known to be historically true, if that narrative is one that contains miracles. In *The Eclipse of Biblical Narrative*, Hans Frei tells the story of how what he terms the 'realistic character of Biblical narrative' came to be 'ignored, or—even more fascinating—its presence or distinctiveness came to be denied for lack of a "method" to isolate it'.[17] As Frei tells the tale, the realistic or 'history-like' character of biblical narrative is an obvious feature of the text, so much so that it is 'acknowledged by all hands to be there'.[18] Nevertheless, because commentators tended to assume that meaning consists of ostensive reference, they mistakenly thought that such a history-like narrative could only be meaningful if it referred to actual historical events.[19] However, the many supernatural elements in the narrative made it increasingly difficult and finally impossible to believe in the historical truth of the narrative, for 'it is taken for granted that modern historians will look with a jaundiced eye on appeal to miracle as an explanatory account of events'.[20] In the end, Frei maintains, the history-like character of the narrative was either ignored or denied. Since commentators could recognize the history-like character of the text only by thinking of it as actual history,

[17] Hans Frei, *The Eclipse of Biblical Narrative* (New Haven: Yale University Press, 1974), 10.
[18] Ibid. 10.
[19] I myself find it hard to believe that Frei is correct in thinking that so many people could confuse meaning with reference or think that what fails to refer historically would thereby lack meaning, but the faultiness of his diagnosis of the cause of the problem does not affect the correctness of his description of what occurred.
[20] Frei, *Eclipse of Biblical Narrative*, 14.

they increasingly ignored that character. On Frei's account, the alternative overlooked was that of 'realistic narrative', the type of narrative embodied in the modern realistic novel. Treating the Gospels as 'realistic narratives' involves a more neutral standpoint; while Frei does not himself deny the possibility that at least central elements in the narrative are historical, one can accept their realistic character without assuming historicity.

Frei's work in calling the attention of scholars to the actual character of the New Testament narratives seems to me to be profoundly important and correct. A narrative may indeed have a history-like or realistic character without being historical. Modern realistic fiction is a concrete demonstration of that. So Frei is right to say that the question of whether a narrative has a history-like character and thus a 'literal' meaning must be distinguished from the question of whether a narrative is historically reliable. However, as Frei certainly recognized, a narrative intended as history and not fiction is also 'history-like'. So it is quite consistent with Frei's view to say that, having established that a narrative is history-like, one should go on and attempt to establish whether the narrative is intended as history, and if it is, whether the historical narrative is a reliable one.

In the remainder of this chapter I wish to discuss the assumption that seems to make it necessary for many people to regard the narratives found in the New Testament concerning Jesus of Nazareth as fundamentally historically untrue: the assumption that critical historical judgement rules out taking seriously accounts of events that involve miracles or supernatural agency. If miracles can occur as part of history, and if it is possible to have good historical evidence that miracles have occurred, then there seems to be no good a priori reason for denying the intended historical character of the New Testament narrative. If the narrative is history-like, one possible explanation of this fact is that it was written as history. Of course the dismissal of the narrative as historically untrue also remains an option. However, I wish to show that those who are in some way committed to the truthfulness of the New Testament narrative are not forced by this commitment to deny its narrative character as history. The possibility remains that it is true history. It is of course not *mere* history; it is a narrative fraught with theological significance. However, I have already argued in Chapters 3 and 4 that it is a mistake to think that this significance can be neatly separated from the narrative, understood as historical.

8.4. THE ASSUMPTIONS OF THE 'CRITICAL HISTORIAN'

Why, precisely, do 'modern historians' or those who wish to emulate them find it impossible to take seriously as history a narrative with such supernatural elements? Why, to use Frei's words, should it be that 'historical accounting' demands a narrative 'whose connections may be rendered without recourse to supernatural agency'?[21] Though it is often assumed and frequently asserted that a 'modern, critical' approach to the narrative must exclude the supernatural, attempts to explicitly argue for such a view are more rare. In the late nineteenth century, philosopher F. H. Bradley provided such an argument.[22] Perhaps the best-known theologian to make such an argument was Ernst Troeltsch, the important turn-of-the-century German scholar. Among contemporary theologians, Van Harvey, who makes no secret of his debt to Troeltsch, has repeated and reformulated Troeltsch's position.[23] I shall give an exposition of the views of Troeltsch and Harvey, and in so doing critically examine the reasons they give for their view

---

[21] Frei, *Eclipse of Biblical Narrative*, 14.

[22] F. H. Bradley, *The Presuppositions of Critical History* (Oxford: J. Parker & Co., 1874); repr. in *The Presuppositions of Critical History*, ed. Lionel Rubinoff (Chicago: Quadrangle Books, 1968), 75–147.

[23] The fullest statement of Van Harvey's position is found in his book *The Historian and the Believer* (New York: Macmillan, 1966). A more contemporary statement of his position is found in an essay 'New Testament Scholarship and Christian Belief', in *Jesus: History and Myth* (Buffalo: Prometheus Books, 1986), 193–200. A concise statement of Troeltsch's views can be found in his essay, 'Historiography', *Encyclopaedia of Religion and Ethics*, ed. James Hastings (New York: Charles Scribner's Sons, 1922), 716–23. Harvey himself cites Troeltsch's *Gesammelte Schriften* (Tübingen: J. C. B. Mohr, 1913), ii. 729–53, repeatedly in *The Historian and the Believer*.

that taking miracles and supernatural agency seriously involves a 'pre-critical' view of history.[24]

Both Troeltsch and Harvey are quite clear that the problem with traditional Christian approaches to the Gospel narrative does not arise from particular historical findings, but from the *method* to which the modern historian is committed.[25] Thus, the issues to be faced do not concern the evidence for or against some particular miracle; rather they concern the general principles historians should follow. As is so often the case, this discussion of 'methodology' is really a discussion of philosophical issues, and hence requires no special training as a biblical scholar or historian to be understood.

Both Troeltsch and Harvey make several crucial assumptions that are questionable, but which I shall not examine until later chapters. First of all, they both assume that historical knowledge about the incarnational narrative must be derived from what they call critical history. One response to their contentions, one that will be developed later, would be to argue that whether 'critical historians' can obtain knowledge of the

---

[24] Some of the arguments that follow are similar to arguments developed by William J. Abraham in his fine book *Divine Revelation and the Limits of Historical Criticism* (Oxford: Oxford University Press, 1982). Abraham argues that critical historical judgement does not always preclude an acceptance of miracles. However, Abraham goes further than I am willing to in accepting the validity of the principles of Troeltsch that I wish to criticize, and then arguing that the religious believer can give a 'rebuttal' that overcomes the negative conclusions that historical research would otherwise give rise to. In what follows I wish to challenge the prima-facie validity of those very principles. I should also like to note that although Van Harvey's book (1966) may seem somewhat dated, the methodology he defends is still embedded in the practices of a great many biblical scholars. I do find it remarkable that there are not more recent, explicit defences of this position. One might think that this means that biblical scholars and theologians are abandoning such a negative view of miracles. Superficially, this may appear to be the case, in that recent accounts of the historical Jesus, such as those of Crossan and Meier, do stress the fact that miracle stories seem to be early elements in the tradition, rather than late accretions. However, a careful look at Crossan will show that the miracles that are allowed as having actually occurred are miracles of healing and exorcism that are explicable through psychosomatic or other natural means. In Meier's case, all the historian can do is affirm that the earliest followers of Jesus *believed* that Jesus performed miracles; the historian is not allowed to make any judgement as to whether the miracles actually occurred. The fact that there are so few explicit defences of the Troeltsch–Harvey type of position is not really evidence that the view has been abandoned. Rather, it seems to me that this is due to the fact that the view is so widely held as to appear to its proponents as simply being 'common sense' that needs no defence.

[25] Harvey, *Historian and Believer*, 4–5.

incarnational narrative is unimportant, because there are other ways of deriving the necessary knowledge. Secondly, both assume, I think, an internalist, evidentialist account of all historical knowledge. That is, both assume that if I am to know something about the past, I must know it on the basis of evidence of which I am aware or at least of which I could become aware. This ignores the possibility that at least some historical knowledge or justified beliefs may be the result of belief-forming processes that do not require evidential inference. On an 'externalist' account of historical knowledge, beliefs formed by such processes might constitute knowledge even if I am not aware of any evidence for the belief.[26] This possibility has real relevance to the case of historical religious knowledge, and I shall look carefully at it in Chapter 11, since some theologians, such as John Calvin, have attributed our knowledge of the truth of the biblical narrative to the internal operation of the Holy Spirit, and while this could be construed evidentially, it might also be understood as involving belief-formation in a non-evidential manner.

Finally, Harvey and Troeltsch seem to assume a kind of 'ethic of belief' or 'morality of knowledge' that implies that we have intellectual duties not to hold historical beliefs without the right kind of evidence. The topic of what are our intellectual duties is a fascinating one, and I shall address it in the next chapter. Here I only wish to point out that in most cases we don't have voluntary control over our beliefs, and thus our duties can't be construed simply as duties to acquire or refrain from holding certain beliefs, but more plausibly as duties to cultivate certain kinds of intellectual habits. For the sake of argument in this chapter, I will accept the general idea that with respect to historical beliefs we have some intellectual duties to cultivate the kinds of habits a good historian would have, whatever those might turn out to be, and the assumption that our historical knowledge is best understood as based on evidence. Though I don't believe Harvey has clearly laid out a plausible ethic of belief to back up his charge that holding

---

[26] For a good account of the difference between internalist 'evidentialist' epistemologies and 'reliabilist' externalist epistemologies see William Alston, *Epistemic Justification: Essays in the Theory of Knowledge* (Ithaca, NY: Cornell University Press, 1989). These issues are discussed much more fully in Chs. 9 and 11.

Christian beliefs in the face of modern critical history involves intellectual dishonesty, I shall have to look, in the next chapter, at the question as to what epistemic duties there might be.

According to Troeltsch, there are three principles of critical historical investigation that cause problems for the traditional Christian. There is first the *principle of criticism*.[27] Essentially, this is a claim that historical judgements are always provisional, corrigible, and approximative. Such judgements are always more or less probable, based on the evidence available for them. Secondly, there is the *principle of analogy*.[28] This principle is a kind of assumption of uniformity, in that it is assumed that our present experience is not radically different from the experiences of humans in the past. The same kinds of causal laws and natural processes operative today were operative in the past. Thirdly, there is the *principle of correlation*.[29] This is essentially an assumption about causality, that holds that one must always understand a historical event in the context of its natural antecedents and consequences. Historical events must be understood in terms of their natural historical contexts.

Harvey essentially takes over Troeltsch's three principles, reinterprets them so as to eliminate certain obvious objections, and places them in the context of more contemporary discussions of evidence and epistemology. Harvey's own account of the 'morality of knowledge' involves four aspects: (1) the radical autonomy of the historian,[30] (2) the responsibility of the historian to employ arguments and cite evidence that can be rationally assessed,[31] (3) the need of the historian to exercise 'sound and balanced judgment',[32] and (4) the need to use 'critically interpreted experience as the background against which

---

[27] Troeltsch does not cite this principle in a clear form in his essay 'Historiography', but it is perhaps implicit in his claim that modern historians take a 'purely scientific attitude to historical fact'. See p. 718. Van Harvey cites Troeltsch's *Gesammelte Schriften* ii, 729–53, as the basis of his discussion of the principle of criticism.

[28] Troeltsch states this idea in 'Historiography', 718: 'On the analogy of the events known to us we seek by conjecture and sympathetic understanding to explain and reconstruct the past.'

[29] Ibid. 'The sole task of history in its specifically theoretical aspect is to explain every movement, process, state, and nexus of things by reference to the web of its causal relations.'

[30] Harvey, *Historian and Believer*, 39–42.

[31] Ibid. 43–64.

[32] Ibid.

sound judgments are made about the past'.[33] When expressed in summary form, the last three of these sound platitudinous, but when developed by Harvey they are filled in with a 'Troeltsch-like' content that gives them more critical punch.

Harvey himself says the first three of his principles go together. while the fourth is logically more independent.[34] I agree with this claim; in fact, it appears to me that suitably interpreted versions of the first three principles, without the fourth, would probably not get Harvey the conclusions he wishes. Nevertheless, all his principles bristle with difficulties. I shall try to show that each of the first three principles is ambiguous in the following way: each has what I shall call a platitudinous interpretation, which gives the principle its plausibility, but which has no controversial implications for traditional Christian beliefs. Each allows for a more radical reading, which does conflict with traditional Christian beliefs about the supernatural. However, I will argue that the principles Harvey espouses are implausible as principles binding on all reasonable historians when interpreted in this more radical way.

1. The *autonomy* of the historian is understood by Harvey in terms of the Enlightenment ideal as articulated by Kant: 'Dare to use your own reason'. This is understood as the rejection of all authority; the only authority that exists for the critical historian is the authority that he confers on his sources.[35] Harvey quotes Collingwood with approval: 'In so far as an historian accepts the testimony of an authority and treats it as historical truth he obviously forfeits the name of historian.'[36] Harvey himself says, 'If the historian permits his authorities to stand uncriticized, he abdicates his role as critical historian. He is no longer a seeker of knowledge but a mediator of past belief; not a thinker but a transmitter of tradition.'[37] All this is justified by appealing to the historically conditioned nature of witnesses and authorities: 'What a witness thinks he

---

[33] Harvey, *Historian and Believer*, 38. The discussion of this principle occupies much of 68–99.
[34] Ibid. 38.
[35] Ibid. 42.
[36] Ibid. 40.
[37] Ibid. 42.

sees is in large part filtered through the prism of his own individual mode of perception and conception which, in turn, is heavily influenced by the modes of thought of the culture of which he is a part. Men are historical creatures, and their judgments reflect the "world" that they bring with them and to which they appeal in support of those judgments.'[38]

Ironically, Harvey seems to think that 'critical historians' are immune from this historical predicament and thus stand apart from the common run of humankind. He doesn't see that the 'critical historian' he puts forward as an ideal may similarly be a product of historical circumstances.[39] Thus he is uncritical of the assumptions of this 'enlightened' thinker. As we shall see when we examine Harvey's fourth principle, the 'modern, critical' historian is hardly innocent of philosophical assumptions that may reflect his historical situation, and which colour the way he views ancient witnesses.

Harvey would probably defend himself here by noting the dangers of historical relativism. He rightly deplores this relativism and affirms the possibility of 'self-transcendence' on the part of the historian.[40] Thus, reliable historical knowledge is possible, he thinks. However, Harvey does not seem to notice that if 'self-transcendence' is possible on the part of historians, it is likely that the people historians study must be capable of this self-transcendence as well.

Understood in one sense, the claim that historians must be 'autonomous' seems quite uncontroversial. If someone is making a historical investigation, then she must determine what sources are reliable, what inferences to draw from the available evidence, and so on. The historian must certainly recognize general truths about the human condition, such as that humans are sometimes mistaken and deceived, and that sources are sometimes untrustworthy. It would be unreasonable for a historian to take a particular source as an absolute, unchallengeable authority. Rather, the authority of a source is

---

[38] Ibid. 41–2.

[39] For a brilliant argument that the scholarly community of historical, biblical critics constitutes just such a historically conditioned community, that essentially operates similarly to religious interpretative communities, see Jon D. Levenson, *The Hebrew Bible, the Old Testament, and Historical Criticism: Jews and Christians in Biblical Studies* (Philadelphia: Westminster-John Knox Press, 1993).

[40] Harvey, *Historian and Believer*, 221.

the sort of thing that is open to question, and for which evidence is often appropriately sought.

However, it appears to me that Harvey does not wish to interpret his principle of autonomy simply as entailing such innocent platitudes. Rather, his claims seem to embody what C. A. J. Coady calls the 'reductionist thesis' about the evidential value of testimony.[41] This is the claim that testimony is not, like observation and perhaps memory, an independent source of epistemic warrant or justification. Rather, we should accept testimony only if we have evidence that testimony is reliable. Testimony, by itself, carries little or no epistemic weight; we regard it as good evidence only when we have evidence that warrants us in accepting the testimony.

Such a claim about testimony can be found in Locke and Hume, but despite this illustrious heritage, Coady shows that such a thesis is quite impossible to defend. The difficulty is simple yet profound: unless testimony as such carries some epistemic weight, some presumption in its favour, we cannot possibly have any evidence that testimony is reliable. For any such evidential case for testimony must be communal in character; one could not possibly show the reliability of testimony in general simply by examining one's own experience. Rather, one must examine the testimony of humans generally, and critically examine that testimony. But one can only learn about other people's testimony, and examine its reliability, by taking the word of a lot of other people. Any investigation of the reliability of human testimony must certainly depend on the more general reliability of human experience. However, without some acceptance of testimony, one could know nothing about the experience of others or its reliability. Testimony, then, like memory and observation, must be accepted as a basic and independent source of prima-facie epistemic warrant.

Obviously, just as is the case for observation and memory, testimonial claims constitute only prima-facie evidence. They can be and often are overridden. Nevertheless, one cannot reasonably regard testimony *per se* as inherently dubious,

---

[41] C. A. J. Coady, *Testimony* (Oxford: Oxford University Press, 1992), 79–100. Coady himself defends a view of testimony that bears some similarity to that of Thomas Reid.

though of course one could well have reasons for doubting certain kinds of testimony.

If we follow Coady in this view of testimony, then we cannot follow Harvey in thinking that the autonomous historian is one who necessarily takes a superior and suspicious attitudes towards all historical sources. Harvey seems to think that people who leave us narratives about the past are generally incapable of getting things right; their accounts are always coloured by the biases that derive from their historical situation. This is especially true of people of ancient times, with the notable exception of the Greeks. Harvey here reflects a standard attitude of 'modern man', one that is especially clear in his hero Troeltsch, who speaks quite disparagingly of ancient peoples in whom 'there is not the slightest trace of a desire for real knowledge or of a critical spirit'.[42] We learn from the accounts of such people by reading *through* their stories and reconstructing what really happened on the basis of our superior understanding of the situation.

This concept of autonomy seems overblown to me, as does the exaggerated sense of superiority to ancient peoples. This kind of autonomy is inconsistent with the fundamental importance historians do in fact accord testimony. Autonomy in this sense trips over the same kind of problem that plagues a certain type of 'evidentialist' in epistemology generally. This kind of evidentialist says I should not believe a proposition unless I have objectively certain evidence for that proposition. The problem immediately arises of course as to whether I have evidence for my evidence. To stop a regress, it appears that I must have some evidence that either requires no evidence or that I am willing to accept without evidence. If I don't have enough evidence of the former sort, then it appears I am stuck with the latter.

Harvey says I can accept no authority without critical examination of that authority that gives me a basis for certifying that authority as reliable. Coady's argument against the reductionist view of testimony already undermines this claim. It is further undermined by an argument of Coady against R. G. Collingwood's well-known critique of testimony as

[42] Troeltsch, 'Historiography', 717.

providing historical evidence. Collingwood, who clearly influenced Harvey at this point, contrasts what he calls scientific, critical history with a pre-critical history that he terms disparagingly 'scissors and paste' history.[43] The difference between the two rests largely on the modern historians' refusal to take testimony as having any independent evidential force, according to Collingwood.

Collingwood is quite right to say there are significant differences between the critical practices of modern, academic historians and those of earlier times, and doubtless there have been advances in historical method, including the ways in which testimony is assessed. Certainly, contemporary historians don't simply accept the word of earlier authorities, though it is doubtful that the best historians of the past behaved in this way either.

Still, Collingwood's view is at best a gross exaggeration. The key critical point is simply that no plausible account of actual historical practice can be given in which some testimony is not regarded as having non-derivative evidential weight. Testimony is of course subject to doubt, and dubious testimony is in need of corroboration, which may sometimes consist in part of non-testimonial evidence. However, in most cases, if not all, the evidence needed to confirm testimony will consist partly of other testimony. It is thus not possible to do history if one adopts such a sceptical attitude towards all testimony as Collingwood suggests. I can't, for example, rely on things such as the number and independence of witnesses unless I can put some basic credence in testimony.

Actually, it appears to me that Harvey is mistaken in the picture he accepts (perhaps unconsciously) of the historian as a godlike being who *bestows* authority on certain fortunate sources. I doubt that it is possible for historians to bestow authority or confer it. Surely, the normal procedure is for a historian to *recognize* an authority as reliable. In many cases it is through evidence that the historian comes to recognize this reliability, but it is unlikely that such reliability could ever be recognized if the historian did not generally accept a lot of evidence, including testimonial evidence, as trustworthy

<hr>

[43] See Coady's discussion of Collingwood in *Testimony*, 233–48.

without any special corroboration. It is true that knowledge of the historical circumstances of a historical source may give a historian insight into ways that source may be unreliable, and thus sometimes the historian is rightly suspicious of sources. But this suspicion must be balanced by the suspicion of the historian towards her own biases. A source may see things wrongly because of bias, but it is also possible that a source sees things rightly, but the historian may be blocked from realizing this because of *her* bias. Blanket, wholesale scepticism about the accounts of ancient peoples is surely as unreasonable as gullible acceptance of all accounts. Whether an account is fanciful and whether an ancient author had a sense of what it means to tell a true story are matters to be determined by the nature of the text itself, and the evidence we have that bears on its story, and not simply determined on the basis of sweeping and dubious claims about the supposed 'mind' of ancient peoples.

2. The second and third principles of Harvey seem to be essentially linked together. Harvey says that the historian is committed to publicly assessable evidence for claims made and that 'sound judgment' must be employed in assessing that evidence.[44]

As stated these principles look perfectly formal, and also perfectly platitudinous. To flesh out his principles, Harvey borrows a model from early work by Stephen Toulmin. A historical conclusion is founded on data which are linked with the conclusion on the basis of a warrant.[45] Warrants are essentially licensed argument-forms. Conclusions can be challenged by denying the relevance or applicability of the data and warrants to the conclusion or by challenging the warrant itself. These challenges, called rebuttals, are in turn met by giving reasons to accept the warrants, which are called backings.

However, all of this still looks perfectly formal and even platitudinous. It seems unlikely that inferences to supernatural explanations can be excluded by such formal machinery. Why, for example, should the following kind of warrant be excluded: 'Since exceptions to laws of nature can only be explained by

---

[44] Harvey, *Historian and Believer*, 38.
[45] Ibid. 49–54.

the work of God, any event involving such an exception must be due to divine agency'? If I accept this principle, then if my data involves an event that I have good reason to believe is an exception to a law of nature, such as a resurrection of a person from the dead, then I would have rational warrant for believing that God was part of the cause of the event.

Perhaps to exclude such a case, Harvey might want to understand the 'publicly assessable' part of his principles as requiring warrants that are acceptable to all historians, including secular historians. A warrant principle such as the one above would then be excluded as not 'public' since it is not accepted by those committed to the assumptions that are embedded in modern-day thinking, assumptions that are in practice naturalistic. In such a case, the principles of Harvey cease to be purely formal and platitudinous, but it is not at all clear that the principles are now obligatory for all reasonable historians. Why, the religious believer may ask, should the unbeliever have the authority to decide which warrants are proper and which are not?

If Harvey attempts to argue that the only warrants acceptable as licensing reasonable inferences are ones that are acceptable to all historians, then I am afraid that proper warrants may be hard to come by. For historians typically disagree about such things as what conclusions are supported by a particular body of data. It seems that something akin to a classical foundationalist epistemology, to be discussed at greater length in the following chapter, has seeped into Harvey's thought, if he takes this line, for the requirement that warrants be acceptable to all historians seems strikingly akin to the characteristic foundationalist principle that the foundations of our knowledge generally must be acceptable to 'all sane, rational beings'.

Actually, it is not clear that Harvey would claim that legitimate warrants must be acceptable to all historians. He is much concerned to refute historical scepticism, which he sees as a refuge to the traditional theologian who wishes to evade Harvey's relentless attack. As Harvey sees it, the person who is generally sceptical about knowledge of the past can use this scepticism in the following way: since we don't ever really know what happened in the past, the religious believer is as entitled to her unjustified beliefs as anyone else.[46] Harvey argues that historical scepticism is usually the result of setting up one kind of warrant as an ideal, and despairing when historical judgements cannot all be grounded in that way. Instead, Harvey says one must look at the actual warrants used by historians, and not try to impose some uniform ideal.[47] However, if that is so, why should not Christian historians, and others open to supernatural explanations, employ the forms of warrant that seem reasonable to them? Personal explanations, that is, explanations that attribute an event to the actions of persons acting for reasons, are commonly given by sensible, rational people. If God exists, and if God is personal, then there is no obvious reason why such explanations should be rejected in advance, particularly if we can know something about God and God's character such that one might understand some of the reasons God might have for performing certain kinds of actions.

3. Because of the problems we have seen with Harvey's first three principles, I believe that the crucial principle that Harvey advances is the fourth one: the need to use 'critically interpreted judgment' in order to understand the past. It is here that the influence of Troeltsch can be seen most clearly. Harvey's first three principles seem to flesh out to some extent Troeltsch's first principle, the 'principle of criticism'. His fourth principle seems to embody both Troeltsch's other two principles, the principle of correlation (the idea that past events must be understood with reference to a natural causal network) and the principle of analogy (the idea that human experience has a certain uniformity such that present-day conclusions can be extended to the past). That is, Harvey seems to understand 'critically interpreted judgment' in a particular way. Understood in one way, the claim that the historian should employ critically interpreted judgement once more sounds quite innocent and unobjectionable. However, Harvey understands this principle to imply that historians must apply his first three criteria in a way that is 'informed by the new way of looking

---

[46] Harvey discusses this type of strategy ibid. 204–42.
[47] Ibid. 47–8.

at the world created by the sciences'.[48] Concretely, this means that on the basis of our present experience of the natural world as governed by scientific laws, we rule out all causes other than natural causes.

He characterizes this requirement in a number of ways. The new thinking that is required of the historian is thinking which is rooted in 'what we now call the common-sense view of the world'; autonomous thinking is 'thinking in terms of the new world-picture'; rational assessment is 'appealing to the known structures of present experience'.[49]

Harvey does not accept the positivistic ideal that historical knowledge consists of or even is grounded in laws of nature; he agrees that our warrants for historical beliefs are more like 'truisms' or probabilistic generalizations than true laws.[50] Nevertheless, Harvey argues that 'history presupposes all the sciences' in the sense that certain events and certain explanations are ruled out as impossible. Thus, the laws of natural science play a negative function by ruling out certain things, even if they do not positively justify our historical assertions.[51] Nor does the new physics change this situation: 'Nature, to be sure, may be far more refractory to mathematical description at the subatomic level than hitherto believed, but this does not warrant a return to the credulity once characteristic of a majority of the human race.'[52]

Harvey says that miracles may be logically possible, but to be a serious candidate as a historical explanation something must be a 'relevant possibility, a likely candidate to account for certain data'.[53] Since an alleged miracle 'contradicts our present knowledge in a specific scientific field' it is always in tension with well-established warrants. Hence 'the burden of evidence and argument suddenly falls on the one who alleges the report to be true' and Harvey thinks that it is extremely difficult to meet this obligation.[54]

However, all these claims made by Harvey seem philo-

[48] Harvey, *The Historian and the Believer*, 68.
[49] Ibid.
[50] Ibid. 82.
[51] Ibid. 77.
[52] Ibid. 76.
[53] Ibid. 86.
[54] Ibid. 87.

sophical in character, and all of them, like most philosophical claims, seem eminently disputable. In fact, I have in the last chapter provided strong philosophical arguments against all of them. It is not clear, therefore, why a historian who did not share Harvey's philosophical biases would be disqualified as a 'critical historian'. Harvey's procedure is in effect a commitment to a kind of 'methodological naturalism' in history, but if I am right in claiming that it is Harvey's dubious metaphysical naturalism, or equally dubious epistemological assumptions about miracles, that underlie this methodological naturalism, then there seems no reason at all to think that a responsible, critical historian must follow Harvey.[55]

Harvey finds it morally questionable for people to interject what he calls 'faith claims' into historical matters; to interject faith into historical inquiry is to set aside the warrants and backings, to forget the 'common sense' which the historian must presuppose to make any claims at all. It raises questions about the corruption of the believing scholar's personal integrity. What Harvey does not recognize is that the 'common sense' procedures, assessments, and arguments of the community of historical biblical scholars is not a neutral framework, but itself embodies faith commitments. So it is not necessarily a 'corruption' or loss of integrity for someone to bring faith commitments to bear on historical inquiry. In fact one might argue that it is more honest to pursue such issues with a self-conscious awareness of one's commitments than to claim to be free of such commitments altogether.

8.5. TROELTSCH'S PRINCIPLES OF CORRELATION AND ANALOGY

Perhaps it is worth looking briefly at two of the principles of Troeltsch to see if they might lend some support to Harvey's rejection of the miraculous as historically credible. Troeltsch held, it will be recalled, that the historian necessarily follows

[55] For a powerful discussion and critique of arguments in favour of methodological naturalism, see a so-far unpublished paper of Alvin Plantinga, 'Methodological Naturalism'.

the principles of analogy and correlation. The principle of analogy is a claim that judgements about the past presuppose that our contemporary experience is not radically dissimilar from past experience, and the principle of correlation is a claim that historical understanding involves placing an event in a network of causal antecedents and consequents.

It is difficult to state the principle of analogy in a manner that is both clear and plausible. As proponents of 'modern, critical history', such as Harvey, would be the first to maintain, the world-views of people of diverse cultures and ages can be profoundly different, and so it is not at all obvious that their experience of the world cannot be profoundly different as well. Nevertheless, if one can state a plausible version of this principle, it is not obvious that it leads to negative conclusions about the possibility of miracles.

Put crudely, I believe that Troeltsch's principle of analogy is supposed to work something like this: 'Since we don't observe miracles occurring today, we can't reasonably believe they occurred in the past either.' Now, as it stands, this inference seems dubious. The hypothetical proposition (if miracles don't occur today, they could not have occurred in the past) may well be false. I see no reason to think it is true, since many religious believers have thought that God would only perform miracles in quite unusual circumstances. If one believed that the incarnation of Jesus was a historical event that made possible the redemption of humanity and the whole created order, one might reasonably believe that miracles might accompany that event even if they do not occur today.

However, even if the inference were sound, the antecedent proposition is questionable. That is, Troeltsch and his followers such as Harvey simply assume without argument that miracles do not occur today. However fashionable such a belief may be among secular intellectuals and among religious people intimidated by secular thought-forms, it is not shared by millions of people, including many highly educated people. Though I don't see why anyone should accept Troeltsch's principle of analogy, someone might well do so, and reason as follows: 'Since miracles occur today, in some special circumstances at least, it is likely that they occurred in the past as well, perhaps in similar circumstances.' Even people who have no direct experience of miracles today might well think that Troeltsch's principle is innocent if they have experiences of God, experiences with a living God who reveals himself as the kind of being who *could* perform a miracle. Perhaps Troeltsch's principle reveals a kind of sociological truth: people who have no experience of miracles and no experience of the kind of God who could perform miracles find it hard to believe in miracles. Our culture may be such that there are many people who satisfy this description, though there are many more who do not, but from this sociological principle no valid inferences can be made about whether miracles truly occur and can be rationally accepted.

Troeltsch's other principle, the principle of correlation, seems ambiguous. If we mean by this principle simply that events must be understood in relation to the actual causal forces and effects that surround them, then it seems plausible enough. However, the religious believer will claim that it is possible that God, who is actively at work in all of creation, is one of those causal powers (as well as being the ultimate creative source of all the other beings exerting causal power). Unless Troeltsch knows a priori that naturalism is true and there is no God, or that God never exercises causal power in the natural world except in accordance with natural laws, then he has no reason to exclude the possibility that the activity of God can be located in the causal network in terms of which an event must be understood.

Troeltsch's methodological claim here may well be rooted in the Kantian or quasi-Kantian claim that neither God nor the effects of God's action can be empirically observed, because human knowledge is limited to the realm of appearances and cannot reach the transcendent realm of metaphysics. However, it seems hardly plausible that one must be committed to Kantian philosophy to be counted a critical historian. It is hard to see why non-Kantian Christians should agree that the historian is limited in this way. The Kantian picture certainly seems to fit poorly with the biblical picture of a God who is intimately involved with history. Though the motivation for such a Kantian claim may be a pious attempt to preserve God's transcendence, I see no good reason why an experience of God, much less an experience of the effects of God's activity, would imply that God is a finite object within the spatio-temporal order, or merely an 'appearance'. The claim that only such finite objects could be experienced is not a neutral claim but a controverted piece of philosophy, and the view that God's activity in the world could never be recognized looks very much like covert naturalism.[56]

8.6. THE SOCIOLOGY OF KNOWLEDGE AND APPEALS TO AUTHORITY

In the end I suspect that Harvey and others who share his view will be unmoved by arguments such as I have put forward. For Harvey, defences of miracles are difficult to take seriously; such thinking violates 'what we now call the common-sense view of the world'.[57] Such claims go hand in hand with sweeping claims about what it is possible for the 'modern mind' to believe.[58] Defences of miracles are defences of a lost cause, roughly akin to putting forward arguments in favour of a flat earth. Those such as myself who put forward such arguments are viewed with wonderment; we are living fossils, 'pre-critical' thinkers who have somehow survived into the late twentieth century, oblivious to the securely established conclusions of Hume and Kant.

There is a deep irony here, for the mind-set of the 'critical' thinker I have just described is anything but critical. In fact, what we have here is an unacknowledged, and perhaps unconscious, appeal to authority, the anonymous authority of the 'modern mind'. Such an appeal is doubly ironical, for one of the accusations Harvey and his type bring against de-

[56] Or possibly a reversion to the rationalism discussed at the beginning of this chapter. For an example of a historian who seems to accept the quasi-Kantian claims under discussion, see Martin Marty, *History and Historical Understanding* (Grand Rapids, Mich.: Wm. B. Eerdmans, 1984), 41–54.

[57] Harvey, *Historian and Believer*, 68.

[58] It is dismaying to discover the frequency with which theologians, and occasionally philosophers, appeal to this alleged sociological or psychological truth. See e.g. in Owen Thomas (ed.), *God's Activity in the World* (Chico, Calif.: Scholar's Press, 1983), the essays by Langdon Gilkey (p. 31), Frank Dilley (p. 54), Rudolph Bultmann (p. 64), Gordon Kaufman (pp. 140–1). Also see William Alston's crisp rejoinder to this way of thinking in his essay, 'God's Action in the World', in *Divine Nature and Human Language*, 210.

fenders of the reliability of the biblical narrative is that such defenders uncritically accept the authority of the Bible. Nevertheless, those who find biblical miracles plausible are somehow unreasonable because they do not accede to the supposed common sense that 'we' all are supposed to share.

Though I am not a fan of everything in post-modern writers, one thing that post-modernism has usefully taught us to do when someone talks about 'we' is to ask 'Who is this 'we'?' Does this 'we' include the poor? Does it include women? Does it include non-Westerners and minorities of colour within the West? Since traditional religious beliefs, including belief in the supernatural, are more common among the poor, among women, minorities, and in the Christian Church in Asia, Africa, and Latin America (though not always more common among the self-appointed advocates of those groups), these questions are quite relevant. Nor of course, for that matter, is there any shortage of white, Western, educated males who believe in the supernatural, if one simply looks around at the actual world. It seems to me that theologians who are truly 'critical' will begin to ask critical questions about their own inherited intellectual baggage, and will be much less quick to assume that the taken-for-granted assumptions of many secular Western intellectuals over the past two hundred years form a necessary part of 'common sense'. Though there is much that is bizarre that is being put forward under the banner of 'post-modernism', surely one thing that this intellectual movement should cause us to do is to re-examine the 'modern' intellectual assumptions about the supernatural that we have inherited from the Enlightenment.

Deciding whether belief in miracles is reasonable on the basis of what 'most intellectuals' in the West over the past two hundred years have thought is only a bit more reasonable than deciding who to vote for on the basis of who is leading in the opinion polls. Though an appeal to authority can be reasonable, it is not reasonable to appeal to authority to ignore an argument that challenges the grounds upon which an authority's judgement is based. Thus, if the opinions of many Western intellectuals are rooted in dubious philosophical assumptions, an argument that points this out cannot be rebutted simply by appealing to the authority of the intellectuals in question.

Often the names of philosophers are cited by theologians in this connection: Hume, Kant, Marx, Feuerbach, and Nietzsche are frequently invoked. However, if this is to be more than the invocation of sacred mantras the specific arguments of the philosophers in question must be brought into the arena and defended, and this is all too frequently not done. So, when Hans Frei informs us that however dubious Karl Marx's views about the historical Jesus may have been, he was essentially correct in saying that the criticism of historical religion in Germany was a finished task,[59] we must ask whether this is a historical, sociological report or something more than this. If Frei means by this merely that most intellectuals in Germany from this period on ceased to worry very much about the truth of historic Christianity, he may well be correct, but the crucial question is 'So what?' Were these intellectuals right to ignore these questions? Were the philosophical assumptions that made it necessary for them to ignore the possibility that the biblical narrative was truly historical good assumptions? The truly critical thinker, the one with the philosopher's spirit, is willing to ask such questions and ask them in a fresh spirit, without necessarily seeking to answer them 'as the age demands', as the past age did, or as the present age tends to do.

I conclude that Van Harvey has by no means given any good reasons why the 'critical historian' should rule out the possibility that supernatural, miracle-filled narratives are historically true. If Hans Frei is right in insisting that the New Testament narratives have a 'realistic, history-like' character, then they should be considered as possibly historical. We may of course reject the historical truth of the biblical narratives. However, those who wish to affirm the biblical narratives as true are not automatically forced to reject their historical character in order to save the truth of the text. It is much too hasty to reject the historicity of a narrative simply on the ground that the narrative contains an account of miracles.

[59] Hans Frei, *Eclipse of Biblical Narrative*, 224–32. Though it is not completely clear how Frei himself wants us to take his comments here, it is fair to say that at various points Frei does engage in the kind of illegitimate appeal to sociological thinking I criticize here, in which options are dismissed on the grounds that they are not taken seriously any more by intellectuals of a certain group.

9

Epistemology and the Ethics of Belief

IN the last three chapters I have argued that we have no good reasons to doubt the possible historical truth and knowability of the incarnational narrative. Contrary to the claims of some critics, we have no good reasons to believe the central concept of the narrative, that of a human being who is also God, is logically incoherent and thus we have no good reasons to think the narrative embodies a logically contradictory claim (Ch. 6). The supernatural elements in the narrative are not a decisive barrier to accepting it, since there are no good reasons to believe that miracles are not possible, nor do we have any good reasons for thinking that miracles are unknowable (Ch. 7). There are no methodological constraints that in principle would bar a 'critical historian' from accepting such a narrative, and in fact much of the resistance to the narrative stems from covert rationalistic assumptions about religious knowledge (Ch. 8).

Nevertheless, these arguments have been negative in character, with the aim of showing only that it is possible to have knowledge of such a narrative. It is now time to look at the positive accounts that might be given of how such knowledge could be actual. To this end we must turn to some basic epistemological questions. I suggested in the first chapter that one of the factors that created difficulties for the historicity of the incarnational narrative was the widespread embracement of Enlightenment epistemological thinking, the epistemologies of modernity. To have a real chance of surmounting the difficulties we must have some sense of what problems there are with the epistemologies of modernity, and what viable options we can see for understanding knowledge and reasonable belief today.

It hardly needs saying that the issues to be dealt with in this chapter are enormously complex, and that it is too much to ask for a comprehensive defence of the epistemological perspective that will be sketched. What I will try to do is to present an outline of a view that has already been developed and defended in some detail in the contemporary epistemological discussion, a discussion that has been original and enlightening, despite the pronouncements of some that we have come to the 'end of epistemology'. I will certainly try to highlight the strengths of the kind of epistemology sketched and briefly indicate how it may overcome certain problems, but I cannot hope to give a definitive response to every possible objection, much less present a positive case that will be convincing to all its critics. (Though one of the strengths of the epistemology defended is that it does not require that such a task be carried out before one is entitled to accept the view.)

9.1. THE TASK OF EPISTEMOLOGY

Before sketching an epistemological view, it is important to be clear about what epistemology is, and this in turn requires clarity about the aims of epistemology. A good deal of modern epistemology has been driven by what John Dewey called 'the quest for certainty'.[1] Specifically, epistemology has often been seen as an attempt to refute *scepticism*, the denial that knowledge is possible at all. This relation to scepticism has sometimes taken a positive form, as in Descartes's claim that the path to certainty lies through a vigorous attempt to overturn all one's previous opinions, and build the house of knowledge afresh on secure foundations. Sometimes the relation to scepticism has been less confident and full of anxiety, as in the recurrent attempts in the history of philosophy, frequently with little success, to show that knowledge of the external

---

[1] John Dewey, *The Quest for Certainty* (New York: G. P. Putnam's Sons, 1929).

world or of other minds is possible, or that inductive inference is justifiable.

Epistemology in this ambitious sense begins by taking very seriously the question as to whether humans can know anything. It aims to show that knowledge is possible by refuting the sceptic, producing an account of knowledge and justified belief that will give us assurances that at least some of what we think we know is indeed genuine knowledge.

Though a concern with scepticism has by no means vanished, in recent years a more modest conception of the task of epistemology has become prominent, in which one begins with the assumption that knowledge is possible, indeed that it is actual. On this conception of epistemology, the aim of theory of knowledge is not to refute the sceptic, but to reflect on the knowledge we have so as to become clearer about the nature of knowledge and how it is obtained. In the course of such reflection, one may well gain insight into what is wrong with scepticism, but the aim is not to produce a refutation of scepticism that would be convincing to the sceptic. One begins by more or less assuming that the sceptic must be wrong; after all, we do know things. The interesting question is rather why the sceptic is wrong.

On this alternative, modest view, epistemology takes itself to be, as Roderick Chisholm has said, an inductive enterprise, though here induction must be understood in a very broad sense. It begins by assuming we know some things and attempts to develop criteria of knowledge from reflecting on these cases.[2] One might, for example, begin with cases of knowledge and cases of propositions that are not known, and attempt to determine principles that distinguish the two types of case. Of course the examples one begins with might be faulty; after formulation of principles one might well come back and question some of them. Nevertheless, there is no escape from the riskiness inherent in the procedure, and the

---

[2] See Alvin Plantinga's discussion of this kind of inductive procedure in 'Reason and Belief in God', in Alvin Plantinga and Nicholas Wolterstorff (eds.) *Faith and Rationality* (Notre Dame, Ind.: University of Notre Dame Press, 1983), 75–8. Plantinga here draws on the work of Roderick Chisholm, *The Problem of the Criterion* (Milwaukee: Marquette University Press, 1973), 14 ff. For an introductory treatment by Chisholm, see his *Theory of Knowledge*, 2nd. edn. (Englewood Cliffs, NJ: Prentice-Hall, 1977), esp. 120–34.

general assumption is that we could not possibly come to know what knowledge is unless we already had some actual examples of knowledge.

It would be pointless to attempt to determine which of these two conceptions of epistemology, which I will call the ambitious and modest conceptions respectively, is correct. They are two entirely different enterprises, and there is no reason to think they are incompatible in principle. Nevertheless, it is epistemology in the modest sense that will be my concern, for several reasons.

First, it is my conviction that the modest type of epistemology is simply a more interesting enterprise. Ambitious epistemology has had a good trial, and there is very little general agreement as to how to solve its problems. Numerous attempts to show that we are not brains in vats or the dream of an evil deity have been attempted; scads of arguments have been developed to show that the people around me have minds and are not robots, that the world is more than five minutes old, and that past experience provides a reliable basis for generalizations about the future. Little consensus exists as to which, if any, of these arguments are successful.

Fortunately for the ambitious epistemologist, humans take little notice of these epistemological failures. Most of us have little interest, outside the philosopher's classroom, in such arguments, or the problems the arguments attempt to answer. We may find the problems interesting in the sense that thinking about such issues helps us understand what we know better, but we do not worry seriously about whether my colleagues are robots, or whether Martians have captured me and placed my amputated brain in an electrically stimulated vat.

To summarize, the conclusions of David Hume—who was by no means the complete sceptic some textbooks make him out to be—about scepticism seem to me to be eminently reasonable. Hume claimed that total scepticism is unattainable, but if it were achievable, it would be incurable.[3] No one can in fact be a complete sceptic, but if someone could, there would be no way of overcoming the condition.

---

[3] See David Hume, *An Enquiry Concerning Human Understanding* (Indianapolis: Hackett Publishing Co., 1977), 103.

Hence a good case can be made for putting aside the attempt to refute scepticism. The problem of scepticism may well be of great interest, and there is much to be learned from considering the question of how we have the knowledge that the sceptic denies, but there is little profit in taking his anxieties in earnest.

Whether the above claims about scepticism be sound or not, there is another reason for restricting our attention to modest epistemology. What I wish to determine is whether there are any special reasons for being sceptical about historical religious claims. If there are any such reasons, they can only be obscured by any general sceptical thesis. It hardly seems promising to attempt to convince someone who is not sure that anyone really knows that the world is more than five minutes old that we can know that God delivered the ancient Israelites from Egypt through the prophet Moses.

One strategy for defending religious beliefs rests on a type of scepticism. This strategy, termed by Terence Penelhum 'skeptical fideism', argues that since none of our beliefs has adequate rational foundation, religious beliefs are no worse off than any others.[4] Regardless of the merits of such a strategy, it is not the line I propose to take. Rather, I want to assume that ordinary human beings do indeed know things, and that we can make progress towards understanding what knowledge is, and ask about the prospects for historical religious knowledge on such an assumption.

The aims of the modest epistemologist are then to reflect on such concepts as knowledge, belief, justification, and truth, with an eye towards clarifying what they are. Epistemology, is not, as Quine suggests, simply a branch of empirical psychology, for its standpoint is primarily normative and evaluative. However, it does assume that we know things prior to doing any epistemology, and thus is not completely independent of empirical knowledge. It cannot proceed independently of what we know about the world and about our own powers and nature.

---

[4] See Terence Penelhum, *God and Skepticism* (Dordrecht: D. Reidel, 1983).

9.2. CLASSICAL FOUNDATIONALISM

I agree with Nicholas Wolterstorff that classical modern epistemology was born out of the cultural anxiety that accompanied the fracturing of the medieval tradition.[5] The political and religious controversies of the Reformation and of the period that followed seemed to show that the appeal to traditional authority was not adequate to arrive at truth. We of course continue to live in such a 'fractured' intellectual world, so it will not be surprising if the factors that created modern epistemology are still present to make similar views attractive to us. As Wolterstorff tells the story, John Locke is the key figure in this development; Descartes, while important, is a transitional figure who still believes in the possibility of *scientia* in the medieval sense. It is Locke who comes to the conclusion that, though knowledge is extremely important in providing the foundations of our intellectual life, the area of knowledge in the medieval sense of a direct perception of truth is 'short and scanty'. Thus for Locke it is crucial to understand the standards for rational belief.

By and large Locke takes an 'evidentialist' view of belief; that is, he says that all beliefs need to be based on evidence. There is a terminological difficulty in characterizing Locke's view of belief and the need for evidence, for Locke tends to follow the medieval practice of regarding knowledge and belief as mutually exclusive attitudes; what I know I do not therefore believe.[6] Contemporary philosophers, on the other hand, tend to regard knowledge as a special kind of belief. Hence, though

[5] See Nicholas Wolterstorff, 'Tradition, Insight, and Constraint', in *Proceedings and Addresses of the American Philosophical Association*, 66/3 (1992), 43–57. Also see his *John Locke's Ethic of Belief: When Tradition Fractures* (forthcoming: Cambridge University Press).

[6] John Locke, *An Essay Concerning Human Understanding*, ed. Peter H. Nidditch (Oxford: Oxford University Press, 1975), 4, 14, 1 (p. 652). The terminological difference between contemporary philosophers on the one hand and medieval and early modern philosophers on the other that is here discussed is an interesting one that deserves more attention than it has received. Though I shall follow contemporary usage, I do not hereby mean to imply that there are no substantive issues embedded in these terminological decisions, nor am I defending contemporary usage, though it may well be defensible. I simply wish to use the language contemporary philosophers will understand.

Locke says all beliefs must be rooted in evidence, he does not mean that all beliefs in the contemporary sense must be based on inferential evidence, for things that are known by direct intuition are not inferentially based in this way. For beliefs that fall short of knowledge in this sense, however, evidence is required.

Locke says that if we follow our 'duty' with respect to our beliefs, then belief 'cannot be afforded to anything, but upon good reason'.[7] Not only must we base our beliefs on evidence; we must also proportion the 'firmness' of our belief to the quality of the evidence. Our epistemic duty is to examine all the 'grounds of probability', and then proportion our degree of belief to the degree of probability the evidence gives the proposition in question.[8] As Wolterstorff makes clear, despite his universalistic rhetoric, Locke actually does not seem to think that the circumstances of life make it possible for most people to follow this practice for all beliefs, but Locke still holds it forth as an ideal. Everyone has enough leisure on Sundays and holidays to 'do one's best' to arrive at reasonable beliefs in matters of religion and morals, and intellectuals with more leisure have correspondingly greater duties.

Such an evidentialist 'ethic of belief' lacks punch until it is specified what is to count as evidence and what standard of evidence is required. Locke's own ethic of belief does give us this specificity, and it is here we can see a close relation to what has become known as 'classical foundationalism'. Though the amount of knowledge we have is scanty, Locke thinks we must make whatever facts we do know our evidential base for determining the probability of our other beliefs. Some of our beliefs may rest on other beliefs, but the total structure of belief must rest on facts that are known with certainty if our epistemological house is to be in order. Different classical foundationalists have different requirements for this foundational status. Descartes requires indubitability; truth of the foundational propositions must be 'clear and distinct'. Plantinga characterizes modern foundationalists in general as

---

[7] Ibid. 4. 17. 24 (p. 687).
[8] Ibid. 4. 15. 5 (p. 656).

holding that basic propositions must either be self-evident, incorrigible, or evident to the senses.[9]

Classical foundationalism in this sense requires at least three things. We must have access to a body of highly certain facts that is sufficient to be the foundation of our beliefs. We must be able properly to determine what evidential support these facts lend to our other beliefs. Finally, we must also have the ability to regulate our beliefs so as to conform to the evidence. It is very dubious that any of these conditions hold.

Though there is little consensus in contemporary epistemological discussions, there is general agreement that classical foundationalism cannot work. First of all, it is dubious that we have access to an adequate body of facts that are known with certainty. If there are any propositions other than logical and mathematical truths, and propositions such as 'I exist' or 'I am conscious' that can be known with certainty, the best candidates are probably propositions about the content of experience, such as 'I am having a sensation of redness.' (Or, in Chisholm's terminology, 'I am being appeared to redly.') Nevertheless, even in this sort of case, concepts from our public language are being employed. At least the possibility of a misdescription of the experience seems possible, and it is difficult to distinguish a case of substantive error from a case where the experience is wrongly described.

Whatever one thinks about the status of such propositions, it is hard to claim that they would provide an adequate basis for our scientific and everyday beliefs, even if they were completely certain. Attempts to show that one can move from such propositions about our own sense experiences to propositions about the external world have been notably unsuccessful. Furthermore, the lessons learned from philosophy of science seem to show that even if we had a significant body of particular facts known in the foregoing ways, there would still be grave difficulties in moving from these facts to scientific theories. Scientific laws have a universal form; they say what will always occur if certain conditions hold, and it is hard to see how any group of finite facts could make such universal propositions

---

[9] See Plantinga, 'Reason and Belief in God', 59. 'Incorrigibility' is a weaker notion than 'infallibility'. An incorrigible belief could be mistaken, but is regarded as so certain that if we were mistaken in holding it, the mistake could not be corrected.

probable. It is now commonplace to recognize that scientific theories are underdetermined by the facts and that such aesthetic criteria as simplicity must be invoked to justify the acceptance of one theory over another theory when both are equally adequate to explain the facts. Hence, even if we waive the problem of the external world and allow the foundationalist to begin with observed facts about the public world, as Locke wishes to do, it is not clear that the body of facts is sufficient to account for our knowledge.

Finally, it does not appear that we have the kind of voluntary control over our beliefs that Locke's 'ethic of belief' appears to demand from us. For the most part (many philosophers would say always) our beliefs are not things we can directly decide upon. The typical case is that we simply find ourselves believing or disbelieving a proposition. The most we can do, except perhaps in unusual cases, to control our beliefs would appear to be to work towards developing good habits of belief formation, or indirectly to shape our beliefs through decisions to consider certain types of evidence, or associate with those likely to influence us, and other such indirect means.

9.3. REALISM AND ANTI-REALISM

For these and other reasons classical foundationalism is now virtually abandoned, at least in theory. (I shall try to show in a later chapter that in practice some biblical scholars who profess to reject classical foundationalism nevertheless seem to employ something like it as an ideal.) However, it is much more difficult to say what should take its place.

One option is to reject the realistic conception of truth that the classical tradition presupposes. There are currently many fashionable forms of 'anti-realism' that unite in rejecting the idea that the truth of a proposition is determined by how the world is. Such views reject the idea that truth is fixed by a reality that is independent of how we humans think and talk. Such conceptions of truth have had their proponents in theology. Some theologians, inspired by Wittgenstein, or perhaps by their own readings of Wittgenstein, have proposed that to say that it is true that God exists is to make a comment about the use of the proposition 'God exists' within the religious community; to say that God is real is to make a 'grammatical remark', a notation that within the religious community the term 'God' is used as a term that denotes a reality,[10] rather than to make a claim about an objective reality.

It will not be possible for me to treat the question of the viability of such an anti-realist conception of truth in general, or religious truth in particular. The issues are too complex and far-reaching to be resolvable in any brief account. Rather, I simply want to bypass this whole controversy. The justification for doing so is simply that, regardless of the viability of such a conception of truth, it is not the kind of truth I am interested in finding, and I think I am representative here of most ordinary religious believers as well as unbelievers. I want to discuss questions such as whether the man Jesus of Nazareth was really divine, was born of a virgin, taught certain things, performed some miracles, was crucified and raised from the dead. In doing so, I wish to know the truth in a realistic sense: Was he really born of a virgin? Did he really rise from the dead? I am not so interested in the question as to whether the Church, in its liturgy and teachings, treats these propositions as true, except in so far as this may help me to discover their truth in a realistic sense. To say that such claims are 'true' in the sense that those who make them find their lives transformed is similarly uninteresting, except in so far as such claims may bear on the question of the objective truth of the matter. I want to know whether the Church is rooting its teachings and liturgy in what really happened, and whether or not people whose lives have been transformed by faith in Jesus have in some way been transformed by a falsehood, or are rooted in an objective reality.

Anti-realist philosophers have of course produced arguments that truth in the realistic sense is impossible, and those arguments have led to critical responses from realists.[11] I shall

---

[10] See D. Z. Phillips, *Faith and Philosophical Enquiry* (London: Routledge, 1970), and George Lindbeck, *The Nature of Doctrine* (Philadelphia: Westminster, 1984). Phillips does not like the way Lindbeck develops this line of thought and criticizes him harshly in *Faith After Foundationalism* (London: Routledge, 1988), 195–211.

[11] See William P. Alston, 'Yes, Virginia, There Is a Real World', in *Proceedings and Addresses of the American Philosophical Association*, 52/6 (August 1979), 779–808. Also see Alvin Plantinga, 'How to Be an Anti-Realist', ibid. 56/1 (Sept. 1982), 47–70.

here assume that some of those responses are cogent and proceed to work with a basic, common-sense level of realism, one that does not presuppose any fancy ontology, but simply says with Aristotle, that 'it is because the actual thing exists or does not exist that the statement is said to be true or false'.[12]

9.4. KNOWLEDGE, JUSTIFICATION, AND WARRANT

Almost all contemporary epistemologists reject the conception of knowledge as direct insight into the truth employed by Locke in favour of an account that sees knowledge as a species of true belief that is justified or warranted in some way. If we assume we have some handle on what it means for a belief to be true, then the question of knowledge centres heavily on what kind of justification is required to transform a true belief into knowledge.

Actually, it is becoming increasingly clear that 'justification' is itself an unclear term for whatever it is that converts true belief into knowledge. In an important essay, William Alston has made a distinction between 'deontological' conceptions of justification and other conceptions.[13] Justification appears to have as its natural home an ethical or quasi-ethical framework. It is linked to such concepts as intellectual duties and rights. In the deontological sense, a belief is justified when, in Locke's language, I have 'done my best' to fulfil my intellectual duties. I am justified in this sense in believing a proposition if I have done all that I could reasonably be expected to do to determine its truth, and in Locke's case of course this means I have discovered good evidence for the belief.

There are actually a number of different versions of the deontological conception of justification, depending on how my duties are conceived. Do I need to conform to what is

---

Both these publications were APA presidential addresses for the Central Division (previously called the Western Division).

[12] Aristotle, *Categories*, 5. 10–19. *Complete Works of Aristotle*, i, ed. Jonathan Barnes (Princeton: Princeton University Press, 1984), 8.

[13] William Alston, 'Concepts of Epistemic Justification', in *Epistemic Justification: Essays in the Theory of Knowledge* (Ithaca: Cornell University Press, 1989). See also 'The Deontological Conception of Justification', ibid.

objectively my intellectual duty, for example, or is it enough if I live up to what I believe to be my intellectual obligations? There are doubtless several important concepts of justification that lurk in this area, but regardless of how the deontological conception is developed, Alston argues vigorously that it is not justification in this sense that transforms true belief into knowledge. First of all, such a conception of justification pre-supposes too much voluntary control over our beliefs. Since ought implies can, if to be justified in believing a proposition *p* implies that I must believe *p* only if I have dutifully found the right kind of evidence, it follows that, if I cannot govern my beliefs in the appropriate way, I cannot reasonably be regarded as obligated to do so. A reasonable ethic of belief cannot then demand of me that I directly control my beliefs; it can only ask of me that I attempt to develop good epistemic habits and practices.

Secondly, and perhaps even more importantly, justification in this deontological sense does not have the right kind of relationship to truth. It is possible to have fulfilled one's intellectual obligations in an exemplary way and yet to be woefully lacking in knowledge, due to circumstances beyond one's control. Philosophers are here fond of exotic, science-fiction examples: If I am really a brain in a vat being electrically stimulated by Andromedans, my beliefs may be intellectually spotless in terms of duty-fulfilment, while systematically false. In such a situation, even if I accidentally, as it were, acquire a true belief, the belief will not be knowledge, though I am fully justified in holding it.

Perhaps a slightly less exotic example can be given by turning to imaginative anthropology. Suppose I am a teenager brought up in a remote culture in the fourth century. Being unusually concerned for truth and conscientious in my intellectual life, I have done all that is in my power to investigate the truth about my culture's beliefs, many of which consist of primitive cosmological theories. Like any other person, of course, including people in twentieth-century culture, I am somewhat dependent on the testimony of others, particularly those I have good grounds for regarding as authorities. I believe, for example, that the sun is a burning ball of oil, a couple of miles wide, that travels across the sky a few miles above the ground.

My chief ground for this belief is that it was taught by Shomo, the most eminent scientist my culture has produced, who had ruthlessly criticized earlier religious views of the sun as a god. Suppose that I accept all of Shomo's theories, and that 90 per cent of them are false. Oddly enough, Shomo's account of the moon turns out to be substantially correct. Even more oddly, however, Shomo's reasons for his beliefs about the moon are religious in character. Unable to quite free himself from earlier religious thinking, Shomo teaches that the moon is a large piece of matter that orbits the earth, on the grounds that this was taught by the sacred oracle, Moono. In such a situation, my beliefs about the moon may be completely justified, deontologically, and true, but they do not amount to knowledge. The problem this case illustrates is that there does not seem to be any necessary link between being justified in the deontological sense and truth. In the imagined case, the belief is both true and deontologically justified, but there seems no link between its being justified and its being true.

Because of our lack of direct, voluntary control over our beliefs, and because of this failure of deontological justification to connect strongly with truth, Alston suggests that there is a different kind of justification that is important, epistemologically. He calls this an 'evaluative' rather than a deontological sense. To say that a belief is justified in this sense is to say that 'it is a good thing from the epistemic point of view'.[14] The epistemic point of view itself is a matter of looking at our beliefs from the point of view of their truth and falsity, and so the epistemic goodness in question is linked to the likelihood of the belief's being true. This leads Alston to understand epistemic justification as a matter of a belief's being based on an adequate 'truth-conducive' ground, a ground that makes the truth of the belief objectively likely, along with its being the case that the subject has no overriding reasons to believe otherwise.[15] For example, I see a computer disk lying on my desk, and form the belief that there is a disk present. The ground is my experience; if it turns out to be the case that normally when I have such an experience, the belief that it

[14] Ibid. 97.
[15] Ibid. 105.

grounds is true, then the belief is justified, provided I have no overriders, such as any reason to suspect that my vision is abnormal.

Alston makes a simple but extremely important point about justification, that will have some importance for us in future chapters. If my belief is based on an adequate truth-conducive ground, along with the absence of overriders, then it is justified. This is so, whether or not I am able to justify the belief to someone else. Being justified in believing something is not identical with being able to justify a belief.[16] Furthermore, my knowledge that the disk is on the table must not be confused with the higher level knowledge *that* I know this. It is one thing to know 'the disk is on the table'; quite another to know 'I know the disk is on the table.'

Alston confesses in a footnote that he worries about the aptness of the term 'justification' to designate his evaluative, non-deontological concept, and Alvin Plantinga has developed this worry into a full-fledged epistemological distinction. In his recent book, *Warrant: The Current Debate*, Plantinga argues that the term 'justification' has its proper home with respect to our intellectual duties, and, like Alston, he argues vigorously that when construed deontologically in this way, justification is not what must be added to true belief to produce knowledge.[17] Simply doing our intellectual duty does not necessarily put us in a position to know something. So Plantinga chooses to term whatever it is that does produce this positive epistemic quality, 'warrant'. From his point of view then, warrant and justification are two different qualities and it is warrant that is most directly linked with knowledge.

After reviewing and criticizing a series of other attempts to analyse this elusive positive epistemic quality in *Warrant: The Current Debate*, Plantinga gives his own account of the matter in the sequel, *Warrant and Proper Function*.[18] Plantinga sees warrant as linked to the notion of proper function. The root

---

[16] Alston makes the point frequently. See e.g. 'Has Foundationalism Been Refuted?', ibid. 43–7.

[17] Alvin Plantinga, *Warrant: The Current Debate* (Oxford: Oxford University Press, 1993). See chs. 1 and 2 particularly.

[18] Alvina Plantinga, *Warrant and Proper Function* (Oxford: Oxford University Press, 1993).

idea is roughly that our beliefs are warranted when they are produced by our human cognitive faculties, when those faculties are aimed at truth, and when they are working effectively and properly in circumstances similar to those in which they were designed to function.[19]

One of the most notable characteristics of this view lies in the fact that it implies that it is possible for one of my beliefs to possess warrant without my being able to provide much in the way of argument or evidence for it, just as Alston's view implies that one of my beliefs can be justified without my being able to justify it. It is perfectly conceivable that true beliefs might be reliably produced in me, through my senses, my memory, or other basic cognitive faculties which were designed to produce true beliefs, without it being the case that I can provide much in the way of evidence for them. Both Alston's evaluative concept of justification and Plantinga's concept of warrant include a strong 'objective' component. In the final analysis, what gives a belief its positive epistemic status is not my ability to justify it, or know that it is justified. It is rather the fact that the belief is objectively rooted in something that makes it likely to be true. In Alston's case this is a ground or reason, which does not have to be a belief but could be an experience or psychological state of the person. In Plantinga's case it is the fact that the belief is produced by a certain kind of process, a process designed to produce true beliefs, that conveys warrant to it. This raises an important question about the extent to which the factors that give a belief this positive epistemic status must be accessible to the person in question, a question that is debated under the rubric of 'externalism'.

---

[19] *Warrant and Proper Function* spells out a more detailed definition: 'to a first approximation, we may say that a belief B has warrant for S if and only if the relevant segments (the segments involved in the production of B) are functioning properly in a cognitive environment sufficiently similar to that for which S's faculties are designed; and the modules of the design plan governing the production of B are (1) aimed at truth, and (2) such that there is a high objective probability that a belief formed in accordance with those modules (in that sort of cognitive environment) is true' (p. 19).

9.5. EXTERNALISM AND INTERNALISM

A great many philosophers have supposed that qualities such as Alston's evaluative type of justification or Plantinga's warrant are not sufficient to be the crucial component that must be added to true belief to produce knowledge. They have supposed that really to be justified in holding a belief it is not enough to have formed a belief on an objectively adequate basis, or for a belief to have been formed by a cognitive mechanism functioning properly in the right kind of circumstances. Surely, if I am to be justified in believing, or if I am to have the kind of 'warrant' that makes a true belief knowledge, I must know or at least have good reason to believe that the ground for my belief is adequate, or that the cognitive mechanism is reliable and functioning properly. In practice, this means that I must be able to tell, simply by 'reflecting on my own state of mind', to use the kind of phrase that Chisholm employs, that I am justified in this manner.[20]

On this kind of epistemology, commonly called 'internalism', we must be able to tell, simply by reflecting on our own psychological states, what is required for justification and whether beliefs are justified. The idea is not simply that I might be able to come to know these things after some research; if I am now justified in my beliefs then I must be aware or easily be capable of becoming aware of them right now. Alston details a number of powerful reasons for rejecting internalism, regardless of its initial appeal.

The first problem is that our powers as armchair psychologists do not seem to be as great as internalism requires. The tremendous disagreement among internalist philosophers themselves as to what it is that justifies various beliefs suggests that the conclusions we can reach just by reflection on such matters are somewhat arbitrary and indeterminate.[21]

The second great problem is that if internalism is correct, then the amount of knowledge we can plausibly be said to possess turns out to be quite small. For a very small number

---

[20] See Roderick Chisholm, *Theory of Knowledge*, 3rd edn. (Englewood Cliff, NJ: Prentice-Hall, 1989), 7.

[21] William Alston, 'Knowledge of God', in Marcus Hester (ed.), *Faith, Reason, and Skepticism* (Philadelphia: Temple University Press), 17–21.

of our beliefs there is some appeal in affirming that we can tell just by thinking about it that they are justified. However, though the internalist may dispute this, it seems to me that the number of beliefs for which this is so is limited to beliefs about one's own conscious states, simple propositions of logic and mathematics, and other self-evident truths. Such a set of beliefs provides a manifestly inadequate basis for ordinary perceptual and scientific beliefs. Hence, if internalism is accepted, we will have to concede that we know and are justified in believing far less than we in fact take for granted in our daily lives.

Thirdly, the internalist view is guilty of arbitrariness. The power of reason, understood as rational reflection, is taken uncritically as a reliable source of justification. All other human cognitive powers, such as perception and memory, must somehow justify themselves to reflection. But why assume reflection is reliable, if no other powers can be trusted as reliable? If we demand justification for human cognitive powers, why not a justification for reflection itself? A famous passage from Thomas Reid makes this point very effectively:

The skeptic asks me, Why do you believe the existence of the external object which you perceive? This belief, sir, is none of my manu-facture; it came from the mint of Nature; it bears her image and superscription; and, if it is not right the fault is not mine: I even took it upon trust, and without suspicion. Reason, says the sceptic, is the only judge of truth, and you ought to throw off every opinion and every belief that is not grounded on reason. Why, sir, should I believe the faculty of reason more than that of perception?—they came both out of the same shop, and were made by the same artist; and if he puts one piece of false ware into my hands, what should hinder him from putting another?[22]

Finally, internalism shares a failing with deontological con-ceptions of justification. Even if it should be the case that it is intuitively evident that a belief is justified, it does not follow logically that the belief is likely to be true. There may be some kind of link between being intuitively evident to a human being and being true, but it certainly does not seem intuitively

---

[22] Thomas Reid, *An Inquiry into the Human Mind* (Chicago: University of Chicago Press, 1970), 82. Originally published (1764) as *An Inquiry into the Human Mind on the Principles of Common Sense*.

evident that there is such a link. Hence the internalist type of justification does not give us what is needed for knowledge.[23]

The appeal of internalism may lie in the confusion between being justified in holding a belief and being able to justify a belief, which, we noted above, must be clearly distinguished. It is quite plausible to hold that I must know that my reasons or grounds for a belief are good, or that my cognitive powers are functioning properly and reliable, if I am called upon to *show* that the belief is justified. It is equally plausible that such knowledge is required to know *that* I am justified or *that* I know. But it does not follow that this is necessary simply to be justified or warranted.

Externalism, which is simply the denial of the internalist claim that I must be able to tell by reflection that my belief is justified in order to be justified, does not deny the value of knowing that I know. Nor does it deny the value of knowing that my justification for my belief is strong, or knowing that my cognitive faculties are working properly. However, it denies that I can generally know these things simply by reflection, and it denies that I have to know them in order simply to know something or to be justified or warranted in believing a proposition.

One consequence of externalism (critics call it a problem, but externalists just think it is the way things are) is that attempts to show that we are justified in our beliefs (in Alston's sense), or that we have warrant (in Plantinga's sense), have a kind of circular character. A belief is justified if it is based on a truth-conducive ground, or warranted if it is the product of a reliable, well-functioning cognitive faculty operating in normal circumstances. How can we tell if a ground is reliable, or if our cognitive capacities are functioning properly? With respect to perception, we might simply investigate cases of beliefs formed as a result of perceptual input, and see how reliable the mechanism is. Or, alternatively, we might turn to neurophysiology and physics to give us a theoretical account of how our perceptual mechanism works. However, in both cases, we will obviously have to rely on the very perceptual mechanisms we are trying to certify to do the certifying.

[23] Alston, 'Knowledge of God', 24.

This is not formal, logical circularity. The justification does not have to consist of an argument which explicitly assumes its conclusion. Rather, the circularity seems to be more informal in character. In order to show that our perceptual mechanisms are reliable, we must assume, practically and implicitly, that at least a good many of our perceptual judgements are reliable. From the externalist standpoint, some people may consider this fact regrettable, but it is an inescapable feature of the human condition. The presence of such circularity is a mark of what could be called a *basic* source of human knowledge.[24] Basic sources are simply those sources whose reliability cannot be investigated or established without at least practical trust in them.

It is important to recognize that this circularity does not affect being justified in believing some proposition, or being warranted, but only showing that I am justified or warranted. Thus, when I try to show that I am justified in a belief I may bump up against the circularity problem, but that does not mean that I am not in fact justified. This difference between being justified and showing that one is justified in some cases is linked to the level distinction between knowing and knowing that one knows. For one way of knowing that one knows is to show (someone else or oneself) that one is justified in the belief in question. It is conceivable therefore that if I can't show that my belief is justified, that in some cases (and only in some cases) I won't know that I know, but my failure to know that I know p does not entail that I do not know p.

Externalism does not have the weaknesses of internalism, though of course it may have others.[25] It does not rely on

---

[24] See Alston, 'Epistemic Circularity', in *Epistemic Justification*, 326.

[25] Of course there are many other problems with various forms of externalism that I have not discussed. One well-known example is the problem of generality that arises for reliabilism; roughly, the problem is determining the level of generality at which types of belief-forming processes must be specified if they are to provide warrant for beliefs. A particular belief can be seen as a token which is the outcome of many different such processes at various levels of generality. Belief-forming processes of great generality, such as vision, do not appear to be highly reliable, but it is difficult to specify more specific classes of such processes. Analogous problems arise for some other types of externalism. Though I shall not attempt to resolve this problem in general, in Ch. 11 I do try to say something about the relevant process for the formation of true beliefs about the incarnational narrative. In general, it is obviously not possible for me to deal with all the difficulties externalist theories face. Such

subjective reflection to determine when a belief is justified or what constitutes justification. It does not arbitrarily accept one of our human faculties as reliable while doubting the others. It makes sense of the fact that we actually do know a lot of things: science, history, and ordinary perceptual beliefs do not live under an illegitimate pedigree, for we can understand the reliable mechanisms that give rise to various kinds of knowledge. It is consistent with the fact that we think that how a belief is acquired and maintained is crucial in determining its epistemic status, so that a belief that is accepted for bad reasons is not justified. Most important of all, it links justification (or warrant) with truth, so that we can understand why it is that a true belief that is appropriately justified or warranted is regarded as knowledge. We know in such a case because we do not hold the true belief merely by accident; it was acquired through a mechanism that is designed to get at truth and that normally does lead to truth (Plantinga), or held on the basis of a ground that is strongly supportive of truth (Alston).

For all these reasons, I shall assume that a broadly externalist account is correct in investigating the epistemological status of historical religious claims, though I shall also pay attention to how matters look from an internalist standpoint, especially when looking at what I shall term the evidentialist account. (I say 'broadly externalist account' because I shall not try to settle the debate as to which particular version of externalism, such as Alston's or Plantinga's, is best.[26]) No special religious assumptions motivate this choice. It is true that such externalists as Plantinga and Alston are Christian philosophers, and Plantinga has developed a particular version of externalism that seems to fit well with theism.[27] However, externalism was

theories are relatively new, and are still being developed. I certainly don't claim in this brief treatment to have established the correctness of this approach, but I think I have given strong reasons why externalism should be given a fair try. It is a promising approach whose implications for religious beliefs, as well as many other types of beliefs, have not yet been fully worked out.

[26] Because I wish to develop my account without assuming one particular version of externalism, I shall often put points in more than one way; for example, alternating between Plantinga's language of warrant and Alston's language of justification.

[27] It should be noted that William Alston is not a *pure* externalist. He calls his own theory 'an internalist externalism', because he is inclined to think that in the normal case at least, a subject must have some awareness of the truth-conducive ground of a belief. However, Alston is best viewed as an externalist, because he does not require

developed and defended by many secular philosophers, such as Alvin Goldman, Fred Dretske, and Robert Nozick, with no religious axes to grind.[28] It was, in fact, developed as a form of 'naturalistic' epistemology, which desires to see human knowing as a natural phenomenon. Hence, just as the botanist presupposes the existence of the plants she wants to explain, it is proper for the epistemologist to begin with the assumption that there is knowledge.

9.6. FOUNDATIONALISM AND COHERENTISM

The adoption of externalism clears the way for a return to a type of foundationalism. The major alternative to foundationalism is coherentism, which understands justification in a 'holistic' fashion; on this view an individual's beliefs are interconnected in a systematic way, and the justification of a belief lies in its coherence with all one's other beliefs.[29] The demise of classical foundationalism has made coherentism a popular view. If there are no absolutely certain facts to serve as the foundation for our knowledge, and if what we take to be a 'fact' is to some degree shaped by our other beliefs, then why not understand justification in this holistic way?

While it is certainly plausible to think there is a holistic dimension to justification, particularly for showing that one is justified, a pure coherentist theory is subject to powerful and well-known objections. First of all, it would seem that there must be many belief systems that are equally coherent, and it seems strange to regard all such systems as equally justified in

that the subject be aware *that* the ground is adequate; what is crucial is that the ground in fact is adequate. See several of the essays in Alston's *Epistemic Justification*, particularly 'Internalism and Externalism in Epistemology', and 'An Internalist Externalism'.

[28] See Fred I. Dretske, *Knowledge and the Flow of Information* (Cambridge, Mass.: MIT Press, 1981); Robert Nozick, *Philosophical Explanations* (Cambridge, Mass.: Harvard University Press, 1981); and Alvin Goldman, *Epistemology and Cognition* (Cambridge, Mass.: Harvard University Press, 1986).

[29] Keith Lehrer is probably the most prominent defender of coherentism. For a clear defence of such a view, see his *Theory of Knowledge* (London: Routledge, 1990). Also see Laurence Bonjour, *The Structure of Empirical Knowledge* (Cambridge, Mass.: Harvard University Press, 1985).

the evaluative sense. Juan the Cuban Marxist, Ahmad the Libyan Muslim, and Nigel the English Christian might have equally coherent belief systems, but those systems cannot all be equally true, and it is hard to see how they could be equally justified or warranted in the sense of these terms in which they imply *knowledge* is possessed. It might be plausible to regard these various belief systems of different individuals as equally justified in a deontological sense, but we have already seen the weakness of such a deontological sense of justification.

The second problem is closely linked to the first. Because indefinitely many incompatible belief systems can be seen as coherent, it is hard to see how coherence can have the kind of relation to truth that is desirable in an epistemology. Of course one can jettison any realistic conception of truth and simply define truth in terms of coherence, as idealist philosophers tended to do, but we have already rejected any attempt to make sense of truth that is non-realistic in character.

The third problem with coherentism is perhaps the most basic; what we are justified in believing depends to some degree upon my relation to the external world, and not simply on the internal coherence of my beliefs. To take an example similar to one employed by Alvin Plantinga, imagine a person who is at the opera, call him Jerry, experiencing the sounds and sights of *La Bohème*, and who has a corresponding set of beliefs. Imagine that at this point Jerry's beliefs are coherent. The next day Jerry goes mountain climbing. His brain malfunctions in a bizarre way, and while climbing a peak, suddenly he gets a realistic 'flashback' such that he has exactly the system of beliefs and experiences he had the evening before. Since the beliefs were coherent then, they must still be coherent, but it hardly seems plausible to think that Jerry now has a well-justified system of beliefs. The problem does not lie in the coherence of the beliefs, but in the fact that Jerry does not have the right kind of causal relationship to the external world.[30]

Even if coherentism did not face such daunting problems, there is another reason why I shall not attempt to root my account of historical religious knowledge on such a view. That

---

[30] Bonjour acknowledges the force of this objection, and thus agrees that no pure coherentist theory can work. He proposes instead to add to coherentism an account of what he calls spontaneously formed beliefs. See Bonjour, particularly pp. 106–56.

is simply that coherentism makes the job too easy.[31] Because of the inherently subjective character of coherentist justification, it would not be difficult to show that on coherentist criteria many Christian believers are justified in believing historical propositions about Jesus. It might of course be very difficult for these individuals to persuade other people with different belief systems to accept such views, but such apologetic difficulties would seem to be a consequence of coherentism generally, unrelated to the particular claims in question.

Fortunately, there are other alternatives to classical foundationalism than coherentism. Specifically, it is possible to regard some of our beliefs as *basic* in the sense that they are not grounded in other beliefs, without regarding those beliefs as infallible or incorrigible.[32] There does appear to be a difference between our beliefs in the 'directness' with which they are related to our experience. Some of my beliefs are formed in a fairly direct manner; I see a book lying on my desk and form a justified belief that there is a copy of William Alston's *Epistemic Justification* on my desk. In this case the relation of the belief to my experience seems fairly direct. In other cases a belief clearly seems to involve some kind of inference from other beliefs. I receive a letter from a friend inquiring about job possibilities, and I form the justified belief that he would like to change positions. The fact that corresponds to this belief does not seem to be the kind of thing that I could directly perceive; certainly I have not on this occasion perceived it. Rather, it is something that I infer from other beliefs I have.

Since basic beliefs on this kind of account are not infallible or incorrigible, the justification they receive is only prima facie. Thus the justification given by my experience to the belief that William Alston's book is on my desk could be overridden or defeated in various ways. For example, if I know that William Alston wrote no such book, I may suspect that I am hallucinating. Thus, in forming the belief I implicitly assume

---

[31] For a powerful critique of the possibilities of coherentism for religious epistemology, see Alvin Plantinga, 'Coherentism and the Evidentialist Objection to Belief in God', in Robert Audi and W.J. Wainwright (eds.), *Rationality, Religious Belief, and Moral Commitment* (Ithaca, NY: Cornell University Press, 1986).

[32] For a classic exposition of this type of foundationalism, see Alston, 'Two Types of Foundationalism', and 'Has Foundationalism Been Refuted', repr. in *Epistemic Justification*. The term 'incorrigible' is defined above in n. 9.

that my faculties are operating normally and in fairly normal circumstances. Or if I know that a Hollywood film crew has been using my home as a movie set, and they have employed quite a number of fake books that have only covers but no writing, then the experience of seeing the apparent book will not justify the belief in question.

If another person challenges the belief and I wish to show that my belief is justified, then I may need to be able to show that such conditions do not hold. In that case, a coherentist dimension, of at least a local, contextual sort, will likely make up part of the case. However, it is important to see that on an externalist viewpoint, I do not have to know such things in order to be justified in my belief. What is important is that my belief be based on a ground that is in fact adequate (Alston) or be produced by properly functioning faculties in the right kind of circumstances (Plantinga), not that I be able to show that the ground is adequate or that my faculties are properly functioning, desirable as those things may be.

Foundationalism allows then for what may be called direct, or unmediated, justification, as well as indirect or mediated justification. I shall therefore, in the next two chapters, look at attempts to show that historical religious knowledge is possible in both of these ways. In Chapter 10, I will look at traditional evidentialist apologetics, an attempt to show that we have good evidence for the incarnational narrative, including its historical components. In Chapter 11, I will examine the case that this knowledge could be, in some sense, basic, by looking at theological claims about the internal testimony of the Holy Spirit.

9.7. EPISTEMOLOGICAL VIRTUES

While I have argued that the deontological concept of justification is not the concept that is linked to knowledge, that does not mean that it does not capture something of importance to our epistemic lives. The Lockean ethic of belief may not be viable, but that does not mean that there are no intellectual responsibilities.

Since we do not have direct voluntary control over our beliefs generally, it does not make sense to affirm that we have duties to govern our individual beliefs, much less apportion the strength of our beliefs to the strength of the evidence, as Locke taught. Besides the difficulty that we do not usually have direct control over our beliefs, the Lockean ethic also is undermined by the type of foundationalism we have adopted, which holds that some of our beliefs are basic and are not rooted in evidence, if by 'evidence' we mean something propositional in character that can be the basis of an argument or inference.

So what might an alternative to such a Lockean ethic of belief look like? Initially, perhaps we could characterize our intellectual responsibilities as duties to cultivate what might be called good epistemological habits. I lack both ability and space to develop a full account of these, but I will try to highlight a few basic points.[33]

Even our basic beliefs, on this view, are fallible and corrigible, and so we should try to develop the habit of reflecting on and checking our beliefs when we have defeaters for them. A basic belief that is justified is normally only prima facie justified, and one kind of epistemological fault would be a tendency to ignore or discount contrary evidence. Humans are of course particularly prone to doing this when they have a strong desire to believe something, and so a virtuous epistemic agent works at developing a special carefulness with respect to such cases. Balancing this 'wish-fulfilment' is the lesser noticed fault of 'fear-fulfilment', in which people believe what they most dread, skewing the evidence because they 'know' things will always turn out for the worse. Good news can be nearly as hard for some people to accept as bad news is for most of us.

An interesting case here involves what has been called peer disagreement. To what extent should we doubt our beliefs if we find our epistemic peers, people who appear to be equally competent and in a similar position to ourselves, come to different beliefs than we do? Certainly, this situation is far

[33] For a fuller account of a 'virtue' approach to epistemology, see Jay Wood's *Introduction to Epistemology: A Virtues Perspective* (Downer's Grove, Ill.: Inter-Varsity Press, forthcoming). See also Linda Zagzebski, 'Religious Knowledge and the Virtues of the Mind', in her *Rational Faith: Catholic Responses to Reformed Epistemology* (Notre Dame, Ind.: University of Notre Dame Press, 1993).

from unusual, particularly with respect to matters of morals, religion, and politics, but it is by no means absent in the scholarly life generally. Disagreement in the humanities is the rule, and is far from uncommon in the social sciences; even natural scientists with the same evidence find themselves on the opposite sides of some fences. What should we do in such a situation, besides concluding that at least one party is mistaken?

It seems to me that the reasonable position here is to avoid two extremes. One extreme is to despair and become sceptical. Since disagreement exists, the sceptic says, no one really knows anything. Or the sceptic might think we must try the path of classical foundationalism again, and try to discover some Shangri La of hard facts that will vanquish such disagreements once and for all, the failure of the quest eventually precipitating a deeper scepticism. Such a view does not, I think, come to terms with human finitude, not to mention the perversity that Christianity calls sin. Given the kind of creatures we are, disagreements about many issues seem inevitable, but that is no reason to give up the quest for truth. First of all, we can see cases in the past where those who held a controverted view were eventually vindicated. Secondly, many of the beliefs that are most controversial are ones that have very profound implications for human life, and it is hard to see how taking some view about them can be avoided.

The other extreme attitude is the individual who simply ignores the disagreement, dogmatically assuming that his way of thinking is in secure possession of the truth. Such a view is equally ill at ease with our human finitude; it fails to recognize the possibility of error and the important role that criticism from others plays in exposing error.

Hence it seems to me that the virtuous knower walks a tight-rope here. It is on the one hand generally good to take the criticisms of the other seriously, to reflect again and try to see things from the viewpoint of the other, understanding the counter-arguments as sympathetically as possible. Of course no one can take all criticisms seriously. Life is short, and no reputable scientist wastes much time refuting the claims of the flat-earth society. Some criticisms are just written off as beyond the pale. However, there is risk in dismissing the outlandish critic, and there is merit in a general willingness to rethink what is regarded as settled, provided the critic has something interesting to say.

On the other hand, having listened to the critic, it seems to me that the responsible knower also has a duty to try to come to some convictions, at least concerning those matters where life itself may not allow the luxury of suspended judgement. One must avoid the 'If I were someone else' syndrome. It is true that if I had been a Chinese student during the Cultural Revolution, I probably would have been a fervent defender of Chairman Mao, but how is that fact relevant to my actual intellectual life? I am not a Chinese student living during the Cultural Revolution. I am an actual person with a specific history and set of experiences, and it seems to me that I have some responsibility to try to form my beliefs in a way that does justice to my particular view on the world. I should attempt to own my beliefs, and take responsibility for them, particularly to the extent that I have reflected upon them critically.

Such an epistemic ideal seems to me an ideal, not a universal duty. None of us can become critically reflective about all our beliefs, and many people, as Locke saw clearly, live in situations that make epistemological virtue a luxury item. Nor is it always possible for humans to attain convictions about important matters. Sometimes we can do no better than admit we don't know. Such a humble confession of ignorance must not be confused, however, with the dogmatic claims of a type of 'agnostic' who says that no one has any knowledge about the matter. None the less, however relatively unimportant the intellectual virtues may be in some circumstances, that does not mean that they do not have significance for those who are blessed or burdened with education and reflective powers.

In so far as our beliefs are the product of our human cognitive capacities, it would seem that a virtuous knower would cultivate and certainly try not to damage those capacities. This would include such obvious things as not overindulging in alcohol or other drugs that might impair the mind, as well as seeking to educate oneself about matters of importance. A virtuous knower would also make an attempt to monitor the output of those capacities, to determine which of them are more reliable, and which less reliable, and the circumstances that bear upon the reliability of them. In short, we might say that a virtuous knower is someone who appreciates the methods and techniques we have for gaining knowledge.

A virtuous knower is willing to develop the requisite skills and discipline needed in the quest for knowledge, and humbly recognizes her intellectual limits where she lacks such skills. Humility turns out to be one of the prime intellectual virtues, involving both a recognition of the limitations imposed by our finitude as well as those limitations that are rooted in our personal powers and history.

I shall now proceed in the next three chapters to examine two accounts as to how historical, religious knowledge can be possessed. After doing so, in the concluding two chapters I shall ask if someone who takes herself to have such knowledge can be an epistemically virtuous person.

10

The Incarnational Narrative as Historical: Evidence for Belief

⁂

I T is time to ask how knowledge of the incarnational narrative might be acquired. I wish to examine two distinct theological traditions that give rather different answers to the question as to how Christians gain this historical knowledge. One story, that I shall examine in the next chapter, gives great emphasis to the internal testimony of the Holy Spirit.[1] The claim that belief in the incarnational story is justified because of internal testimony of the Spirit is sometimes regarded with suspicion. After all, the witness of the Spirit appears to be somewhat subjective. How can I know when the Spirit is witnessing and to what the Spirit is witnessing? One might think that we would do better to root our beliefs in something more objective.

So I shall first examine a story that puts the central focus on objective evidence, and regards the knowledge of the incarnational story as based on other things we know or believe. It

[1] One could call the account that emphasizes the witness of the Spirit a 'non-evidentialist' account since it does not *require* evidence for knowledge; the knowledge may be basic in character. However, this would be misleading since, as we shall see, consideration of evidence is also one form the work of the Spirit may take. Hence I shall call the account in this chapter the 'evidentialist' account, and that in the next chapter the 'Reformed' account. The evidentialist account *can* be a rival of the Reformed account when the evidentialist approach is taken as including a commitment to internalism. However, since externalism can also appeal to evidence, and the evidentialist case can be made on externalist grounds, the real opposition is between internalism and the externalism in terms of which I shall interpret the Reformed account.

is commonly claimed that all historical beliefs must be based on evidence, and so it is not surprising that there is a long tradition of Christian apologetics that attempts to show that there is indeed good evidence for Christian beliefs about the life, death, and resurrection of Jesus. I shall call this tradition that of evidentialist apologetics, or simply the evidentialist approach.

Philosophically speaking, the evidentialist approach has often been characterized by at least an implicit acceptance of epistemological internalism. The reason for this is straightforward. The apologist reasons that evidence is no good to me if I am not aware of it, and surely I must know the evidence is good evidence if I am reasonably to rely upon it. It is these internally available factors that are important, thinks the typical evidentialist.

The evidentialist who takes this internalist route says that for me to know a proposition several things must be the case: (1) First of all, of course, the proposition must be true. (2) I must have good evidence for the proposition. (3) My belief in the proposition must be based on that evidence. (4) I must be aware of that evidence, and aware that my belief is based on that evidence, or at least be capable of becoming aware of this on reflection. (5) Finally, I must be aware that the evidence for the proposition is good evidence. Since many of the evidentialist cases that have been developed seem implicitly to accept these internalist constraints, I shall examine the cases partly with respect to such criteria.

However, it is possible for an evidentialist apologetic to be developed that is not committed to internalism. After all, the practice of making inferences upon the basis of good evidence can be seen as a reliable, truth-conducive process. Reliably generated beliefs may be direct but they are often mediated. So externalists do not have to ignore inferential evidence. If we keep this possibility in mind as we look at the evidentialist apologetics, it will help us recognize that some of the difficulties that are alleged to accompany evidentialist apologetics may be difficulties that plague internalism generally, rather than weaknesses in the Christian evidential case. The fact that externalist epistemologies have space for evidentially grounded beliefs will also help us to see how the evidentialist account may be complementary to and indeed form part of the account given in the next chapter.

10.1. CLASSICAL EXAMPLES OF THE TWO-STAGE STRATEGY

Historical examples of evidentialist apologetics can be multiplied, but within the many types of apologetic arguments one type of argument has had special prominence. This is a type of argument that one might term the two-stage strategy. The first phase of such an argument consists mainly of natural theology, in which one attempts to show the reasonableness of believing in a God with at least some of the characteristics of the God of Christian faith, including perhaps the possibility of God performing miracles. Having established God's existence, the second phase of this strategy attempts to show that the events recorded in the Bible, and in many cases the Bible itself, are a true revelation of God and God's activities in making salvation possible. Frequently, this second phase of the strategy makes use of miracles as evidence of the genuineness of the revelation, particularly the miracle of the resurrection of Christ, which is often seen as functioning so as to validate the special status of Jesus, certifying his teachings and his claims about himself.

Thomas Aquinas provides a classical example. Aquinas says that some of the basic claims of Christian faith can be rationally demonstrated and therefore known, at least by some people, via such arguments as his own famous 'five ways'. Many important beliefs, though, including some about Jesus with historical content, are grasped only through faith. Faith is not mere conjecture, belief without evidence, or opinion, belief without conclusive evidence. For Aquinas, faith is basically believing a proposition on the basis of an authority. He says plainly that in order for such faith to be reasonable, and not foolish, one must have reasons for trusting the authority. Christian beliefs (including incarnational beliefs) are accepted on the grounds that they are revealed by God, the most trustworthy authority conceivable.

It is of course important to have good reasons for thinking that the revelation in question indeed comes from God.

Though Aquinas certainly thinks of this divine revelation as coming through Moses and the prophets, and supremely in the life, death, and resurrection of Jesus, he thinks that it has been embodied for us in the Bible and in the teachings of the Church. Here we find truths which unaided human reason cannot grasp (as well as some it could), 'secrets of divine Wisdom' that God has chosen to reveal to us.[2]

Historical apologetical arguments of the type we are to see in abundance in the eighteenth century do not play a prominent role in Aquinas, but he sees a need for some rational basis for putting our trust in the authority of the Bible. The 'divine Wisdom', he says, 'reveals its own presence, as well as the truth of its teaching and inspiration, by fitting arguments.'[3] Here I think he has in mind what will later be termed 'internal arguments'; these are arguments that the scriptural text itself points to its divinely inspired origins.

This cannot be the whole story, however. Since some of the truths contained in Scripture exceed the power of human reason it follows that reason cannot fully confirm those truths merely by an examination of their character. Hence it is fitting that confirmation be offered by 'works that surpass the ability of all nature', such as 'the wonderful cures of illnesses' and 'the raising of the dead'.[4] Most remarkable of all to Aquinas is the marvellous way in which simple people are brought to grasp and accept truths that are quite contrary to our natural human desires, even though they suffer persecution for so doing.

These arguments are underscored in a critique of the rival revelatory claims of Muhammad. Aquinas scores Muhammad for a failure 'to bring forth any signs produced in a supernatural way, which alone fittingly gives witness to divine inspiration; for a visible action that can be only divine reveals an invisibly inspired teacher of truth'.[5] In contrast to Christianity, Aquinas says that Muhammad produced converts through force of

---

[2] Thomas Aquinas, *Summa Contra Gentiles*, 1. 6. 1, trans. Anton C. Pegis (Garden City, NY: Doubleday & Co., 1955), 71.
[3] Aquinas, 1. 6. 1 (p. 71).
[4] Ibid. 1. 6. 1 (p. 72).
[5] Ibid. 1. 6. 4 (p. 73).

arms, and by propounding doctrines that human beings are naturally eager to believe anyway.[6]

We have here the two-phase strategy that has been employed time and time again in the history of Christian thought. Aquinas offers rational arguments for some basic religious truths, but most of the crucial beliefs of Christians, those that distinguish Christians from Muslims and Jews, for instance, are grasped through a revelation. That the Christian revelation is a genuine revelation is shown partly by an examination of its character, but miraculous signs play a crucial confirmatory role in its acceptance.

Cases with similar structures, though of course with interestingly different content in the arguments, can be found in Joseph Butler and William Paley in the eighteenth century. Butler's famous *Analogy of Religion*, published in 1736, has substantially the same structure as does the argument of Aquinas, though the first-stage arguments for belief in a 'moral government of the world by God' are quite different from the Thomistic arguments. For his case for specifically Christian beliefs, Butler relies on a number of arguments, particularly the 'fit' between the practical, ethical needs of humans and the 'solution' offered by Christianity, but he also places heavy emphasis on the miracles accompanying the giving of the Christian revelation. 'As revelation is itself miraculous, all pretence to it must necessarily imply some pretence of miracles.'[7]

The same general strategy of natural arguments for belief in God, followed by specific arguments for the inspired character of the Christian revelation, is found in William Paley. Paley is of course famous for his version of the argument that the design found in the natural order is evidence for God's reality, but in Paley's *A View of the Evidences of Christianity* (1794),

---

[6] I do not endorse here Aquinas's critique of Islam, nor am I unaware that forced conversions took place in Christendom and that television evangelists have been known to propound as Christian doctrines views that have a natural psychological appeal. ('Believe and you will become healthy and wealthy.') The point is not that Aquinas had a fully accurate and sympathetic understanding of Islam, but that he understood the need for rational grounds for choosing between rival claimants to be revelations from God. He also gives plausible criteria for making such a choice, as can be seen in that they cut against certain versions of Christianity as well.

[7] Bishop Joseph Butler, *Analogy of Religion* (New York: E. P. Dutton, 1906), 203.

we find even greater stress on the role of miracles in establishing the genuineness of a revelation: 'Now in what way can a revelation be made, but by miracles? In none which we are able to conceive.'[8]

A twentieth-century version of this two-stage strategy can be found in the writings of C. S. Lewis, particularly his popular *Mere Christianity*.[9] For the first phase of his argument, Lewis employed a form of the moral argument for God's existence; he also wrote a book defending the reasonableness of belief in miracles.[10] For the second phase, Lewis focused on the claims to divinity that are implicit and explicit in the Gospel narratives. Jesus, for example, claimed the power to forgive sins, which is the prerogative of God alone. Jesus taught with a unique authority, 'not as the scribes and pharisees'. Jesus represents himself as having a particularly intimate relation with God. In his triumphal entry into Jerusalem, the cleansing of the Temple, and last meal with his disciples, he evidenced a clear view that his own person was closely connected to the coming kingdom of God. The argument is that such claims, if not true, can only be put forward by an evil person or a lunatic, and yet Jesus clearly was not either.[11] Such an argument is prominent in a good deal of popular Christian apologetics.[12] One might call it the trilemma argument; given the testimony of the New Testament, Jesus was either divine, a bad person, or insane. He obviously was not evil or insane; therefore he was divine.

The arguments of Butler and Paley, as well as that of Lewis, are today widely thought to be outdated in that they rely on a view of the Bible that predates most modern 'critical' scholarship. Basically, they assume the four Gospels are at least prima facie reliable historical documents, representing the tes-

---

[8] William Paley, *A View of The Evidences of Christianity* (New York: Robert Carter & Bros., 1854), 20–1.

[9] C. S. Lewis, *Mere Christianity* (London: Collins, 1952).

[10] C. S. Lewis, *Miracles* (London: G. Bles, 1947).

[11] Lewis, *Mere Christianity*, 51–3.

[12] One of the clearest and most powerful presentations of the argument can be found in imaginative literary form in Peter Kreeft, *Between Heaven and Hell* (Downer's Grove, Ill.: InterVarsity Press, 1982). This book is a fictional dialogue between C. S. Lewis, John F. Kennedy, and Aldous Huxley, shortly after their deaths. (All three died on the same day.)

timony of eyewitnesses and those who were conversant with eyewitnesses. Most contemporary New Testament scholars today of course take a much more sceptical view of these documents. It is therefore clear that any contemporary version of this strategy that hopes to be successful must take account of this scholarship in some way.

10.2. SWINBURNE'S CONTEMPORARY EVIDENTIALIST APOLOGETIC

Recently, Richard Swinburne of Oxford has offered a defence of Christianity which self-consciously follows the structure of Butler and Paley, yet updates the argument to take account of contemporary critical scholarship on the New Testament. In his book, *Revelation: From Metaphor to Analogy*, Swinburne argues that we have good reason to hold that Christianity is true, including its historical claims, because it is the result of a propositional revelation from God. Christianity, he says, is unique among the major religions in that it not only claims to have a revelation but claims that it is to be believed because it has been authoritatively revealed.[13] Other religions either do not claim to base their truth on a revelation from God, or else base their claim that their revelation is genuine on our ability to confirm the truthfulness of the revelation on grounds that are independent of the revelation itself. Judaism and Islam might seem to be exceptions, but they are not 'serious candidates', according to Swinburne, because they do not claim that their revelations are authenticated by a major miracle, which is, according to Swinburne, a crucial test of such a revelation.[14]

Swinburne's evidentialist case is distinguished, I think, by the following features:

1. The whole case is couched in terms of probabilities. This is appropriate for Swinburne, since he analyses a belief that *p*

---

[13] Richard Swinburne, *Revelation: From Metaphor to Analogy* (Oxford: Oxford University Press, 1992), 95.
[14] Ibid. 94.

simply as a belief that p is more probable than not, or at least more probable than any alternative belief.[15]

2. The first phase of the argument is provided by his own cumulative case argument for theism. This is an argument that views many of the classical theistic arguments as providing at least weak support for belief in God when properly formulated. Though none of these arguments taken alone, or even collectively, proves God's existence, they increase the probability that God exists to the point where a person who has had experience of God is reasonable to trust the experience.[16]

Swinburne has also given a response to Humean arguments against miracles, providing a rigorous defence both of the possibility of miracles, and the possibility that we could have good evidence for miracles.[17]

3. The case is conducted against a background of claims about what is antecedently probable. For example, he says it is a priori quite probable that if there is a God then God would reveal to us what we need to know to obtain salvation. Furthermore, he thinks that it would be good if this revelation were 'not too evident',[18] so that those who are committed to the goals of the revelation can manifest their commitment to those goals at a time when the success of these goals is not certain.[19] The revelation would be likely to occur only once, or at least to occur only once decisively, since it would probably involve an atonement and 'atonements are costly',[20] and one would do for the entire human race.

4. Essentially, Swinburne deals with the problem of modern sceptical claims about the New Testament by simply accepting them, at least initially. Evidentially, the Bible must be considered at two different points in the case, and regarded in two different ways. From the viewpoint of the secular historian, Swinburne says we can only have a 'somewhat vague con-

---

[15] See Swinburne's discussion of belief in *Faith and Reason* (Oxford: Oxford University Press, 1981), 3–32.

[16] See Richard Swinburne, *The Existence of God* (Oxford: Oxford University Press, 1979).

[17] See Richard Swinburne, *The Concept of Miracle* (London: Macmillan, 1970).

[18] Swinburne, *Revelation*, 74.

[19] Ibid. 75.

[20] Ibid. 76.

clusion as to the general tenor of Christ's message'.[21] However, even given the sceptical results of modern biblical scholarship, which do not allow us to view the Gospels as a whole as reliable if we have no authoritative reasons to accept them and have to treat them simply as historical data, he thinks we can have some confidence that we know at least some of Jesus' actions, since actions can be remembered more easily than words.[22] Such biblical scholars as E. P. Sanders have tried to show that even on a critical, historical view of the Gospels, it is reasonable to believe that Jesus had a group of twelve special followers, that he ate a final commemorative meal with these followers, and that he went willingly to his death. Swinburne thinks it reasonable to understand these actions as having a particular kind of significance. Specifically, Swinburne says that we can reasonably judge that Jesus founded a Church by appointing those twelve apostles and by instituting the ceremony of the Eucharist. He also argues that, if the historical data is approached with the right kind of presupposition that is open to the possibility of the miraculous, then it is reasonable to believe that Jesus voluntarily suffered crucifixion, and that he was finally raised by God from the dead. The resurrection is crucial in authenticating that 'through Jesus, God was speaking'.[23] 'For bringing to life a prophet crucified for saying certain things is *par excellence* vindicating that message, declaring it to be true.'[24]

5. Given the scanty character of our knowledge of that message according to the results of ordinary historical inquiry, Swinburne regards the Church that Jesus founded as crucial:

Unless there is some sort of evidence ... that Christ founded a Church to whom he entrusted the propagation of his message, and unless there is evidence ... that the Church's interpretation of that message is likely to be correct, we would have to rely on the fairly slender amount of evidence for which there is good historical support in the New Testament as to what that message was.[25]

---

[21] Ibid. 106.
[22] Here Swinburne seems to rely on the kinds of views that have been ably defended by E. P. Sanders in *Jesus and Judaism* (London: SCM Press, 1985).
[23] Swinburne, *Revelation*, 110.
[24] Ibid. 111.
[25] Ibid. 109–10.

It isn't that important that we know initially much about that message so long as there is a Church to give a subsequent declaration as to what the message is.

Swinburne concludes that the overall case for Christianity he has constructed is strong, but by no means indisputable. The net result seems to be that Christian belief is reasonable, but the force claimed for the overall argument is modest: 'But if traditional doctrines have some, perhaps not very great, prior probability then the evidence of the Church founded on the Resurrection teaching them may well increase their probability until they became more probable than not (i.e. have posterior probability on that evidence of more than 1/2).'[26]

10.3. PROBLEMS WITH EVIDENTIALIST ACCOUNTS

I should like to discuss four kinds of problems that arise for evidentialist accounts of this two-stage type. It is important for me to stress that I am here outlining problem areas, not purporting to defeat the project. Ultimately, in fact, I shall argue that these problems are far from fatal to the enterprise, when that enterprise is properly understood. However, the issues raised seem to me to be genuine difficulties, and to be difficulties that any contemporary evidentialist account of the two-stage type must face in some manner. One of my purposes in calling attention to the problems is to help us to understand better the attractiveness of a non-evidentialist account that may not face the same difficulties, though of course it may face different ones.

10.3.1. *Philosophical Prologomena*

First, let us look at the philosophical first stage of such an evidentialist case. It is immediately obvious that such arguments rest heavily on both the prospects for natural theology and the philosophical case for miracles. Personally, I think that there is genuine force in a cumulative case argument for God's existence of the type Swinburne provides. It is a case that

[26] Swinburne, *Revelation*, 213.

highlights the ways certain features of general human experience, such as our sense of contingency and sense of purposiveness, seem to point towards God in a non-coercive way. When these considerations are linked both to religious experience and reflection on the depth of human religious needs, a case that I find powerful emerges, though I would prefer to speak in terms of plausibility rather than probability.

A similar comment can be made about miracles. Swinburne, for example, has given a defence of the idea that miracles as exceptions to laws of nature due to God's special activity can be recognized and accepted as what he calls 'non-repeatable counter-exceptions to laws of nature'. I have already discussed this issue and registered my agreement with Swinburne in Chapter 7.

However, both in the case of natural theology and miracles, my estimates here would not be shared by many philosophers or even many theologians. Despite the efforts of Swinburne and others, there has been no notable conversion to philosophical defences of theism nor any notable decrease in scepticism about miracles. Furthermore, the overall evidentialist case can be no stronger than its philosophical first stage.

I think these facts are significant. They do not show that arguments such as Swinburne's are not sound, nor even that they will not be rationally convincing to some. What these facts do indicate, I think, is that we must ask ourselves to whom are these arguments convincing and why. The evidentialist offers a case that is supposed to be based on objective evidence, evidence that would be generally accepted. Such a case is supposed to show that Christians do know what they claim to know. It appears in the end, however, that the claim that this objective evidence is objectively good evidence is not itself a claim that is generally accepted.

The Christian evidentialist must be prepared to say that some things are so, even though these claims are disputed and regarded as inadequately supported by sceptics. There is, we might say, a subjective dimension to the claimed objective case. In speaking of a subjective dimension to the case, I mean simply that at a certain point in the discussion, perhaps when defending the claim that the evidence is good evidence or points a certain way, the evidentialist must be prepared to say,

'This is how I see things,' or 'This I claim to be true,' even though these claims will be disputed by lots of other apparently rational people. Evidentialism provides no escape from this sort of subjectivity.

On my view these facts stem from basic features in the human epistemological situation, and I do not wish to say that those who rely on the witness of the Spirit, the approach to be discussed in the next chapter, are in any better position. However, since the testimony of the Spirit is sometimes criticized for its 'subjective' character, it is worthwhile to note that evidentialism also requires controversial claims. My point is that although the evidentialist is no worse off than someone who relies on the supposedly subjective 'witness of the Spirit', he may be no better off either. There is no escape from the situation of disagreement which troubles people who have convictions about such matters.

Since the subjectivity present in the evidentialist case here is rooted in the human condition, it is not, I think, a fatal problem for evidentialist apologetics. It would be a fatal problem only if we were wedded to classical foundationalism or one of its Enlightenment cousins. The evidentialist is no worse off than any other philosopher making a philosophical claim. One cannot dismiss an argument such as Swinburne's simply because parts of it are disputable. Every such case is found to be disputable and less than fully convincing by someone. To reject the evidentialist case because of this subjective dimension is unreasonable, therefore. It amounts to holding the arguments to a standard no philosophical argument can meet and which other arguments are not expected to meet.[27]

From a certain type of internalist viewpoint, it may seem necessary for the evidentialist apologist to show that the evidence can be recognized by anyone as good evidence. However, even a modest internalism may require only that the knower recognize the evidence as good evidence, rather than requiring that everyone else be able to do so. And from an externalist viewpoint, the question is simply whether the grounds of the belief *are* objectively adequate. Is the evidence

---

[27] This is not uncommon in philosophy of religion, however. Theistic arguments, e.g. may be written off as failures merely because a particular premise is 'disputable'.

that provides the basis for belief in God and for belief in authenticating miracles adequate in the sense that it is truth-conducive? If so, then the person who reasons from those grounds will be epistemically in a strong position and justified in William Alston's evaluative sense in forming the beliefs in question.[28] Though Swinburne is not himself an externalist, there is no reason why an externalist might not appeal to his type of argument.

10.3.2. *Antecedent Probabilities*

The evidentialist case for the reasonableness of accepting a particular revelation is heavily dependent on a number of antecedent probabilities. This is dramatically clear in the case of Swinburne. The probability of a revelation's being a true revelation from God depends on such things as the probability of God's existence, the probability that God would give the human race a revelation, and the probability that this revelation would have a particular character; for example, that it would occur decisively only once and that it would contain an atonement.

Now some of these propositions are ones that are defended in the philosophical first stage. Swinburne, for example, has offered an elaborate argument for the reasonableness of accepting the existence of God, and he has given an account of the moral situation of the human race that is supposed to make more evident the need for an atonement. However, a close inspection of these arguments in turn reveals that they depend heavily on other estimates of prior probability.

Though arguments such as Swinburne's may be detailed and rigorous, the rigour may sometimes tempt us to ignore the fact that they can be no stronger than the estimates of probability that lie at their foundation. These estimates in some cases seem quite subjective. It appears likely to Swinburne that if God reveals himself, the revelation will include an atonement, will occur only in one culture and time, and will have a less than perfectly clear character. To many others, however, these things appear much less likely or even appear to be unlikely. How are

---

[28] For an explanation of Alston's concept, see s. 9.4.

we to determine whose estimates of prior probability are more reasonable? Should each person simply go with her own intuitions? If that is right, does it not seem plausible that those intuitions are shaped by our prior beliefs? Is it accidental that Swinburne, who is a Christian, finds it probable that a revelation should occur that strongly resembles the Christian revelation?

Once more we find that the evidentialist appeal to objective evidence is heavily dependent on convictions that certainly are not shared by all the reasonable people who consider the issues. This does not show, I think, that the intuitions appealed to by the evidentialist case are unreasonable. I find them reasonable myself, though some more than others. Even if God's existence cannot be rigorously proved, if belief that God exists and has created humans is reasonable, then it surely is reasonable to be 'on the lookout' for some revelation from God to his creation. This is particularly true if that creation is fallen and my contention in Chapter 5 that there is a deep human need for atonement is correct. In such a case an alleged revelation that contained such an atonement would be particularly worthy of consideration; its antecedent probability would be far from negligible.

My point, therefore, is not that Swinburne's case is weak because it relies on such judgements of probability. To many people, including myself, the case appears to be strong. But honesty does demand that it be admitted that there is again a subjective dimension to the objective case, a dimension that makes the epistemological standpoint from which one examines that evidence crucial. An Enlightenment foundationalism that demands foundational evidence that is completely certain and completely objective, accessible to all sane, rational beings, certainly will find the evidentialist case wanting. However, since in the previous chapter we found such an epistemology to be itself wanting, this by no means rules out such evidentialist arguments as having any value. Swinburne himself, who is committed to a form of internalism, doubtless would acknowledge what I am calling the subjective character of the argument, and doubtless has ways of accepting it without embarrassment. But it is noteworthy, I think, that an externalist epistemology can appropriate the argument of Swinburne without regarding this subjectivity as devastating, since such an epistemology allows that I may be justified, even if I cannot successfully justify a belief to the satisfaction of others.

10.3.3. *Biblical Scholarship*

A third problem area concerns the sceptical conclusions of contemporary New Testament scholars. The actual historical evidence for the incarnational narrative is largely taken from the New Testament. If the New Testament is historically unreliable with respect to the basic character of the teachings of Jesus and the events of his life, then the actual historical evidence for the Church's narrative looks very weak.

We have looked briefly at Swinburne's response to this problem. Though Swinburne finds it reasonable later on to accept the Church's judgement that the Bible is, properly interpreted, inspired by God, and even infallible (though his understanding of infallibility is quite different from that of many believers), he realizes that appeal to such a view of the Bible as a premise would make his evidential case appear circular. So he begins with a consideration of the Bible as an 'ordinary historical document', and on this basis he concedes that the records of the Gospels are a patchwork of traditions which have been added to and reshaped by later editors for both apologetic and liturgical reasons. They often reflect the needs of the Early Christian Church rather than the unbiased testimony of eyewitnesses.

Swinburne's strategy makes good sense as apologetics. He does not want his argument to rest on claims about the New Testament that are no longer acceptable to scholars. He therefore wishes to accept, at this stage of the argument, what is regarded as the best scholarly conclusions about the New Testament, even though these scholarly conclusions are clearly not sympathetic to traditional Christian teachings. One might say that he wishes to base his argument on evidence that is as objective as possible, evidence that would be admitted as solid by at least a majority of scholars, regardless of their personal convictions.

However, there are limits as to how much scepticism he can allow. In the end, Swinburne realizes his case depends on historical claims that would not be accepted by everyone. For example, if one followed the extreme view of G. A. Wells, who thinks it is doubtful that Jesus even existed, one could hardly conclude that one had good evidence that Jesus was God's revelation to humans.[29] To take a less extreme and therefore more plausible example, respected scholar John Dominic Crossan argues that, though Jesus obviously would have had a last meal with his followers, there was no meal that was thought of as the last one at the time and in which Jesus instituted the eucharistic practice. Instead, the story about the last supper is a retrojection into history of a eucharistic practice that the 'Christ cult' had developed, a cult that is somewhat removed from the historical Jesus.[30] This contention of Crossan's is sharply at odds with Swinburne's view that in instituting the Eucharist Jesus was founding the Church.

So Swinburne recognizes he cannot totally avoid getting involved in controversies about the reliability of the New Testament records. But his strategy makes sense in that the less controversial is the historical part of his case, the more widespread is the audience that might find it convincing. Nevertheless, the strategy also contains risks; one is that the historical scepticism that Swinburne concedes might overwhelm the historical basis he still needs. There are grounds for concern on this score.

Swinburne, following some of the work of E. P. Sanders, argues that deeds are more likely to be remembered than words, and that therefore we may have more reliable information about Jesus' actions than Jesus' teachings. This may be the case, though to me it seems doubtful; some biblical scholars claim that Jesus' teachings may well have been orally preserved with a high degree of accuracy, in the same way that other rabbinical teachings of the period were transmitted by their disciples, though others do not agree that the disciples of Jesus could have preserved his words with such accuracy.[31] It also

[29] See G. A. Wells, 'The Historicity of Jesus', in R. Joseph Hoffman and Gerald A. Larue (eds.), *Jesus in History and Myth* (Buffalo: Prometheus Books, 1986), 27–45.

[30] John Dominic Crossan, *The Historical Jesus: The Life of a Mediterranean Jewish Peasant* (San Francisco: HarperCollins, 1991), 360–7.

[31] See the work of the Swedish scholars Harald Riesenfeld and Birger Gerhardsson for an account of how carefully controlled rabbinic traditions could faithfully preserve accounts of a rabbi's teachings, and an argument that something of this nature occurred

seems likely that the kind of memory of the deeds in question—such as the last supper—that is required must include words, since the deeds must be remembered as falling under a certain sort of description, e.g. the institution of a memorial meal.[32]

However, even if it is the case that deeds are more easily remembered than words, it is also the case that it would be no more difficult for the Early Christian Church to create stories about actions of Jesus than to create accounts of his teachings. In other words, if the Early Church created sayings of Jesus because of its polemical and liturgical needs, it seems equally possible to have done this for actions. Certainly, even if historical actions lie at the basis of various stories, the *interpretations* of those actions may have been shaped and coloured by the needs of the communities responsible for the stories.

A major difficulty for Swinburne's account is that it requires us to have reliable knowledge of just those features of actions that are most difficult for the historian to recreate: knowledge of the motives and intentions of the agent. It is not enough for Swinburne to know that Jesus chose twelve disciples; *we need to know that Jesus did so with the intention of founding a Church*. Many scholars might agree that the number twelve is significant, symbolizing in some way the restoration of Israel, but this does not clearly imply an intention to found a Church authorized to preserve the teachings of Jesus. It is not enough to know that Jesus ate a ceremonial meal with his followers; *we need to know that the purpose of this meal was to institute a memorial ritual*. It is not enough to know that Jesus was executed; *we need to know that Jesus suffered a voluntary death*. If the New Testament documents are largely created by the Early Church for liturgical and polemical purposes, then it is difficult to see how we can claim to have reliable knowledge of such things, for surely nothing would be easier than for the community to attribute motives and intentions to Jesus'

for the teachings of Jesus as well. See Harald Riesenfeld, *The Gospel Tradition and its Beginnings* (London: A. R. Mowbray, 1957), and Birger Gerhardsson, *Tradition and Transmission in Early Christianity* (Lund: C. W. K. Gleerup, 1964). Their work is discussed by I. Howard Marshall, *I Believe in the Historical Jesus* (Grand Rapids, Mich.: Wm. B. Eerdmans, 1977), 195.

[32] This point was suggested to me in a letter by Paul Helm. In a personal note, Swinburne replied that he accepts the claim that at least some words connected with the actions, such as 'This is my body', would have to be remembered.

actions that correspond to the current needs of the Church. In short, if the New Testament critics who are sceptical about the major outlines of the Gospels are correct, then it is hard to see how Swinburne can have the reliable knowledge he needs about the events in question.

The same question arises about the resurrection of Jesus. Swinburne here puts a fair amount of weight on the empty tomb narratives. After all, it is supremely the miracle of the resurrection that constitutes the 'vindicating miracle' that Jesus is God's revelation, and the evidence for the resurrection is crucial. It is noteworthy, however, that the same New Testament critics that Swinburne accepts for the most part with respect to the Gospels, following the same principles with respect to the interpretation of the Gospels, commonly see the empty tomb narratives as late, unhistorical accretions to the stories about the resurrection.[33] It is often claimed, for example, that Paul is unaware of these empty tomb stories, and that they are best understood as attempts to make sense of the fact that the location of Jesus' tomb was lost.

It isn't clear why Swinburne thinks this historical evidence for the resurrection should be taken seriously, since the same biblical scholarship he accepts for most of the rest of the Gospels has dismissed the empty tomb narratives as late and unhistorical. Swinburne might well reply here that the claim that the empty tomb narratives are late and unreliable is disputed by other New Testament scholars.[34] Doubtless this is so; there is hardly any conclusion about the New Testament that is not so disputed by scholars. One could perhaps even argue

---

[33] See e.g. Werner Georg Kümmel, *The Theology of the New Testament*, trans. John Steely (New York: Abingdon Press, 1973), 98–9; and Hugh Anderson, *Jesus and Christian Origins* (New York: Oxford University Press, 1964), 192–5. Both are cited in James A. Keller, 'Contemporary Christian Doubts About the Resurrection', in *Faith and Philosophy*, 5/1 (1988), 57. A more recent example of scepticism about the empty tomb narratives can be found in Gerd Luedemann, *The Resurrection of Jesus: History, Experience, Theology*, trans. John Bowden (Minneapolis: Augsburg Fortress Press, 1995). Though Luedemann claims that something really did happen that gave rise to the Easter tradition, he is pretty vague about what that something was, and doubts that it had anything to do with the empty tomb tradition.

[34] The support for the genuineness of the empty tomb tradition is well summarized in Stephen Davis, *Risen Indeed: Making Sense of the Resurrection* (Grand Rapids, Mich.: Wm. B. Eerdmans, 1993), ch. 4, though Davis is a philosopher and not a New Testament scholar himself.

that the tide is currently running in this more conservative direction of taking the empty tomb narratives seriously. But the disagreement remains. Why not simply conclude, then, that we can't really know the truth here, and that we can have only an uncertain opinion, as Swinburne does for most of the material in the Gospels?

Or would Swinburne object that these sceptical critics see those empty tomb reports as late only because such critics presuppose the improbability of the miracle? Swinburne, however, argues that the prior probability of the resurrection is not low. However, much of the rejection of the rest of the New Testament as historically reliable is based on the same kind of naturalistic presupposition, and so if Swinburne's possible reply about the resurrection is cogent, then we should not be so pessimistic about the remainder. Here the argument of Chapter 8, that historical scholars do not necessarily have to rule out miracles and the supernatural as explanations of events, should be recalled.[35]

What conclusion is to be drawn from these points? I do not wish to say that Swinburne is wrong to think that we have good evidence for Christian claims to revelation. Rather, I wish to make the following points. First of all, if someone finds Swinburne's historical conclusions to be reasonable, and they provide enough backing for his crucial claims about the person of Jesus and the Church with its teaching, well and good. However, if someone finds the historical case deficient, the fault may not lie in the evidence, but rather in the excessively sceptical reading of that evidence. In other words, if the historical basis of the case is attacked, one possible response is to view the concessions made to the more sceptical forms of historical criticism as only made *for the sake of argument*.[36] If Swinburne's view turns out to be historically weak, one way of strengthening it is to challenge the more extreme and sceptical claims of New Testament critics, a task that I undertake in a provisional and doubtless inadequate manner in Chapter 14.

However, even if Swinburne's argument is strong as it stands, it is worth pointing out that his case will be significantly

[35] Also see the argument in s. 14.2.
[36] I do not claim that Swinburne views the historical claims he makes in this light; I am only saying that it would be open to him to do this.

strengthened if the historical part of the case is strengthened. For example, our knowledge of the purposes of the last supper would be greatly enhanced if we had some reason to think that the writers of the Gospels had reliable information about those purposes. For an evidential case, it would be very valuable if we had good reason to believe that the Gospel writers had some reliable knowledge of the interpretative context for understanding the life and teachings of Jesus.

If, for example, Matthew was actually written by Matthew or a follower of Matthew who had access to eyewitnesses, or at least reliable knowledge of eyewitness-rooted traditions, and if we have reason to think Matthew or his follower cared about historical reliability, then it is far more plausible to think that the main outlines of his narratives about the last supper and the resurrection are credible than would be the case if Matthew is the work of some nameless editor who merely compiled a mass of traditions, some of which may go back to actual events, but many of which are the result of folk tales and legends that arise in a community about an important religious figure.[37] Or, to take a case intermediate between apostolic authorship and late editorship by someone with no reliable knowledge, it would be advantageous for an evidentialist case if the author of Matthew were part of a community that could reasonably be thought to have preserved some authentic knowledge of the life of Jesus.

This example is purely hypothetical, of course. On the standard 'two-source' theory of the Gospels, Matthew is regarded by many as relying for his knowledge of the passion narrative mainly on Mark, with the changes Matthew makes being explicable by his theological and polemical purposes, rather than any concern for historical truth. I do not claim that an evidential case such as Swinburne's depends on establishing apostolic authorship for Matthew or any other Gospel. My point simply is that such questions are quite relevant to such a case, and that if one had good reasons to doubt the standard 'two-source' view as stated above, and take seriously some apostolic connection to Matthew, one would have a much

[37] See Robert M. Price, 'Is There a Place for Historical Criticism?' in *Religious Studies* 27/3 (1991), 371–88.

stronger evidential case.[38] Furthermore, there are many first-rate biblical scholars who regard the dominant 'two-source' view of the Synoptics as based on shaky evidence and burdened with major unsolved problems.[39] Vigorous arguments have been made to support early dates for all the Gospels, dates that would necessarily put their composition back to a period in which the memories of eyewitnesses would have been available and in which oral traditions would have been fresh.[40] The evidentialist may therefore find it worthwhile to give a critical examination to sceptical claims made by some biblical scholars.

Such a critical look at biblical scholarship does not require anything like a question-begging assumption of inspiration or infallibility. What is required is rather hard thinking about what is meant by the claim that the Bible must be treated as 'an ordinary historical document' and must be investigated by 'ordinary historical methods'. The evidentialist should look closely at what those methods presuppose, implicitly or explicitly, about what is to count as evidence, what kinds of events can occur, and how to determine the meaning of what has occurred.

There is apologetical value in accepting, for the sake of argument, the conclusions of one's opponents. If I can get my opponent to see that some belief I wish to defend follows from her own premises, then I have been successful. So one can see the value of accepting, for the sake of argument, fairly sceptical

[38] For a good example of such criticism of the two-source theory, see William Farmer's recent work, *The Gospel of Jesus: The Pastoral Relevance of the Synoptic Problem* (Louisville, Ky.: Westminster/John Knox Press, 1994), as well as his earlier *Jesus and the Gospel: Tradition, Scripture, and Canon* (Philadelphia: Fortress Press, 1982). Also see Hans-Joachim Schulz, *Die apostolische Herkunft der Evangelien* (QD 145; Freiburg: Herder, 1993), which is a work that presents the views of theologians of Eastern Christianity who are trained in liturgical history. Another work that vigorously dissents from the standard two-source theory and that contains a sustained, strong argument for early dating of the Synoptics is John Wenham, *Redating Matthew, Mark and Luke: A Fresh Assault on the Synoptic Problem* (Downer's Grove, Ill.: InterVarsity Press, 1992).

[39] Besides the work of Farmer and Wenham just cited, see e.g. B. C. Butler, *The Originality of St Matthew* (Cambridge: Cambridge University Press, 1951); P. Parker, *The Gospel Before Mark* (Chicago: University of Chicago Press, 1953); and E. P. Sanders, *The Tendencies of the Synoptic Tradition* (Cambridge: Cambridge University Press, 1969). Though these books are far from recent, that simply means the problems with the two-source hypothesis have now been recognized for some time.

[40] See John A. T. Robinson, *Redating the New Testament* (London: SCM Press, 1976).

accounts of the New Testament. One can then argue, 'See, even on your account of the historical status of the New Testament, the conclusions I wish to defend can be derived'. However, once we have put aside Enlightenment epistemologies that demand an evidential base of highly certain facts, we must recognize that this argumentative technique implies no general necessity to accept the views of one's opponents about such matters.

A dramatic way of putting this point is to say that rational historical inquiry about the Bible does not require anything like the 'unpapal enclave' that is envisioned by John Meier. Meier supposes that an objective historical picture of what happened in first-century Palestine would be the outcome of what might be agreed upon if a Protestant, a Catholic, a Jew, and an agnostic were imprisoned in the Harvard Divinity Library and fed bread and water until they produced a report.[41] Why should the Christian join such a conclave or take the report as authoritative?

Of course, as we have just noted, one might join such a conclave for apologetic reasons. One can imagine an argument that might be presented to someone on the basis of the report of the conclave: 'See, even on your own truncated view of the evidence, one can learn enough about Jesus to see he is God's messenger.' However, such an argument must be seen for what it is, an *ad hominem* concession for the sake of the argument. Historical inquiry is not limited to such a perspective.

Of course, the sceptic may dismiss the scholarship of someone whose assumptions differ from her own, but that may well happen anyway. A strong evidentialist case may then vigorously contest the philosophical and literary assumptions of much historical criticism of the Bible, while of course maintaining the greatest respect for genuine historical learning. Historical inquiry in general is philosophically loaded; inquiry into events such as the resurrection of Jesus is particularly so. I shall leave this issue for now, but we will return to the philosophically loaded character of contemporary biblical scholarship in Chapters 13 and 14.

---

[41] See John P. Meier, *A Marginal Jew: Rethinking the Historical Jesus*, i (New York: Doubleday, 1991), 1.

Whether the evidentialist tries to make do with a minimal amount of historical evidence or tries to show that there are good grounds for many beliefs about Jesus, the case will necessarily be entangled in disagreements over such historical judgements. Once more, therefore, the case offered by the evidentialist is disputable. Appeals to historical evidence can no more escape the realm of subjective commitment than can philosophical argument. But once more this will be seen as a fatal and devastating problem only if we assume something akin to classical foundationalism in our epistemology.

10.3.4. *Probability and Passionate Conviction and Commitment*

The last problem area I wish to discuss concerns what might be called the incommensurability between the type of commitment called for in living Christian faith and the kind of probability which an evidential case such as Swinburne's provides.

As we have seen, Swinburne's evidential case is very complicated. To be successful it requires, among other things, good arguments for the existence of God, and for at least some of God's characteristics, a good argument for the possibility of miracles, a convincing account of how miracles may be supported by evidence, critical arguments that the historical documents in question have some degree of reliability, and some good reason for thinking that some particular Church or group of Churches constitutes the Church founded by God as the preserver and interpreter of the revelation. Can we be confident that we have correctly evaluated such a complicated case, relying as it does on a multitude of tricky and controversial claims and assumptions?

It is particularly difficult to see how such a case could provide justification for the ordinary believer. Swinburne's case is quite diverse in its contents. Parts are philosophical, parts are theological, and parts involve critical historical judgements about the New Testament. It would be a rare layperson who would have the knowledge and competence to make an informed judgement about even one of these areas, much less about all of them. One might of course retreat to the view that it is not necessary for laypeople to examine this case for themselves. Rather, they should rely on the authority of those within the Christian community who are experts.

Stephen Wykstra has defended what he calls 'sensible evidentialism', that regards the need for evidence as satisfiable by the community, rather than by the individual.[42] On this sort of view, those who are members of the Christian community may rely on others in the community to process the evidential case. But of course other 'experts', non-Christian philosophers and biblical scholars, for example, will disagree radically. Why should the Christian community's experts be believed in this case? Where experts disagree, most intelligent laypeople will feel some obligation to examine matters for themselves. Perhaps those who are already members of the Christian community will have reasons for putting their trust in their own community's experts, but it is doubtful that these reasons would be compelling for those not members of the community. That does not mean that the members of the community are not justified in their belief, on Wykstra's kind of view, but if the situation is as I described some of the appeal of evidentialism is lost. For now the evidence, for most members of the community, is not a basis for belief that is independent of one's commitment to the community.

To conclude, it would seem that we could at best only regard an evidentialist case such as Swinburne's as offering some degree of probability for some people for its conclusions, and even for them those conclusions must be held in a tentative manner, subject to further revision in the light of new critical arguments. At least this seems to be the case if we accept the kind of 'ethic of belief' recommended by most internalists, who say that belief must be proportioned to the evidence available to a person, as Locke recommended. And in fact, as we have seen, Swinburne makes only modest claims for the kind of belief his case makes viable.[43]

Many people see a gap between this kind of tentative assent

---

[42] See Stephen J. Wykstra, 'Toward a Sensible Evidentialism: On the Notion of "Needing Evidence"', repr. in William L. Rowe and William J. Wainwright (eds.), *Philosophy of Religion*, 2nd edn. (San Diego: Harcourt Brace Jovanovich, 1989), 426–37.
[43] Richard Swinburne, *Revelation*, 213.

and the firmness and conviction called for by genuine religious faith, especially a religion such as Christianity, which asks of believers that they make a total commitment of themselves. The Christian knows that she may be asked to put her commitment to Christ above everything else; such a commitment may look like 'hate' to other family members whose ties are now relativized.[44] It may require acts that appear imprudent and even crazy from the viewpoint of 'common sense', such as giving away all one's possessions to the poor and even sacrificing one's own life.

Can this kind of passionate, all-or-nothing, costly commitment be rooted in a tentative judgement of probability? Robert Adams and C. S. Lewis have argued such commitments can be grounded in evidence that is merely probable.[45] Swinburne himself responds to this problem by distinguishing between belief and faith. The key element in faith is not belief, but trust, and trust in God is understood as a willingness to act on the assumption that God exists and that God is good, when there is some reason to doubt that this is the case.[46] Trust therefore is not only compatible with a less-than-certain belief; it positively requires it. The Christian does not necessarily believe that Jesus was raised from the dead, but is willing to act as if she believed it.[47]

Trust is certainly a key ingredient in faith, but it seems questionable, however, to say that trust requires some degree of doubt. Surely, I can trust an individual about whom I have very certain beliefs. Nevertheless, I think it is quite possible that some way of resolving the problem of the incommensurability between the evidential case and faith can be found. The key, I suggest, is to reject the implicit acceptance of a Lockean ethic of belief that regards belief as necessarily to be proportioned to internally accessible evidence. Certainly,

---

[44] Luke 14: 26.
[45] See Robert Adams, 'Kierkegaard's Arguments Against Objective Reasoning in Religion', and also 'The Leap of Faith', both in *The Virtue of Faith* (Oxford: Oxford University Press, 1987); and C. S. Lewis, 'On Obstinacy in Belief', in *The World's Last Night and Other Essays* (New York: Harcourt, Brace, & Co., 1960), 13–30.
[46] See Swinburne, *Faith and Reason*, 111, 115, 166–7.
[47] To be fair, Swinburne does say that *some* beliefs are necessary for faith and others are desirable; one cannot simply have 'acting-as-if' a proposition were true about everything.

from an externalist viewpoint, there is no reason to think that the degree of assurance for a belief must vary directly with the evidence. The problem of incommensurability does not therefore imply that the project of giving an evidentialist case is impossible, especially if the traditional epistemological assumptions that have burdened such cases are rethought.

10.4. CONCLUSIONS: VALUES AND LIMITS OF AN EVIDENTIALIST CASE

Richard Swinburne has shown, I think, that the traditional two-stage evidentialist argument for the historicity of the incarnational narrative can still be effectively mounted, even given the challenges of contemporary biblical scholarship. If one finds the existence of a God who loves his created humans plausible, and also finds it plausible to believe that there is something desperately wrong with the human race that requires divine action and communication, then it certainly seems that Christianity deserves serious consideration. Furthermore, Swinburne seems right that even given contemporary historical criticism of the Bible, there is enough historical evidence to take seriously the claims made there and by the Church about Jesus of Nazareth. To the degree that the historical documents can be shown to be basically reliable (more reliable than Swinburne himself thinks can be shown) and the more extreme sceptical claims challenged, the historical case will be strengthened even further, and I have suggested that prospects for this are good. Such an evidentialist case requires no claims that are not defended by reasonable scholars, and such cases continue to be convincing to many people, perhaps mostly to people who are already committed to Christian faith, but also to some who are converts. True, such cases are open to challenge at many points, as we have seen, but of what philosophical or historical arguments is this not true?

However, I think there are also reasons to explore the possibility of a different account of how incarnational knowledge is possible, one that makes more sense of what might be called the certainty of faith. Of all the difficulties that beset the evidentialist, the most serious in my own mind is the problem of incommensurability discussed in the last section, and it is with respect to this problem that the internal testimony of the Spirit is a particularly promising theme to explore.

Even aside from the difficulties evidentialism may face, it is a fact that a very different account of how knowledge of the incarnational narrative is gained already holds a prominent place in the Christian Church, particularly among Reformed thinkers. In the next chapter I shall examine this alternative theological tradition that places an emphasis on the internal testimony of the Holy Spirit in coming to knowledge of the incarnational narrative. I shall characterize this tradition as embodying a commitment to philosophical externalism, in contrast to the internalism which sometimes accompanies, though, as we have seen, is not essential to, the evidentialist approach. Externalist epistemologies, to recall the discussion in Chapter 9, claim that the conditions which make a belief warranted or justified, and which therefore are part of what converts a belief into knowledge, are not necessarily internal to the consciousness of the knower. If, as seems likely, a plausible version of an evidentialist account ultimately must appeal to externalism, than there is all the more reason to consider the theological tradition that emphasizes the role of the Holy Spirit.

Ultimately, I shall argue that we can indeed make good sense of this Reformed account, and that it basically gives us the outline of the correct story as to how Christians are able to gain the knowledge they claim. When we keep clearly in mind the subjective features of the evidentialist case we have bumped up against, then the apparent greater objectivity of evidentialism vanishes. However, my purpose is not to suggest that this other account should *replace* the story of evidentialist apologetics. Rather, I want to claim that the two stories are complementary. The evidentialist story can be considered as playing two different roles. It can be seen as providing one way in which the witness of the Holy Spirit operates. In this case the evidentialist story becomes a special case of the Reformed story.

The evidentialist story can also play the role of apologetic argument, an attempt to convince someone of the truth of the incarnational story. I shall suggest that this apologetic task is distinct from that of explaining how the believer knows the story to be true, a task which may best be fulfilled by an account that emphasizes the internal testimony of the Spirit (all the while remembering that an evidential case can be part of the work of the Spirit). When the evidential story is functioning apologetically, the two stories are answers to two different questions, attempts to carry out two distinct tasks, rather than rival answers to the same questions, or rival attempts to carry out the same task. I shall argue that each story can gain much-needed support from the other in carrying out these tasks, and thus that their complementary character is deep. The two stories are not only compatible but interdependent.

11

The Incarnational Narrative as Historical: Grounds for Belief

In the last chapter I looked in some detail at two-stage evidentialist apologetics, and examined some of the problems that face this approach. Four problems were found to be significant, though not unsolvable, especially if classical foundationalist epistemology is abandoned. (1) There are philosophical problems concerning the arguments for natural theology and miracles that are an essential ground of the strategy. (2) There are problems with sceptical biblical scholarship; since most of the evidence traditionally given for the resurrection is taken from the New Testament, we must have reason to think that there are good historical grounds for accepting some of the crucial claims in the Gospels. This may require some response to claims that these documents do not supply reliable historical testimony. (3) There are problems in determining the reasonableness of antecedent probabilities. The force of the argument depends heavily on estimates of the antecedent probability of such things as a revelation from God occurring in history, and the probability that such a revelation would have a particular character. (4) Finally, there is the problem of the incommensurability of living biblical faith and a tentative, probabilistic evidential case. Can passionate, whole-hearted biblical faith be rooted in such a complex argument, which at best results in a conclusion with some degree of probability?

11.1. THE REFORMED EMPHASIS ON THE TESTIMONY OF THE HOLY SPIRIT

Though I argued that these problems do not mean an evidentialist argument cannot be effective, they do give us good reason to examine an alternative theological account, one which lays stress on our knowledge of the historical Jesus as made possible through the internal testimony of the Holy Spirit, and makes evidence less central to the story, though it may play a role. I call this alternative to the standard apologetic approach to incarnational knowledge the Reformed account, since it is seen most clearly and prominently in the works of Protestant, especially Reformed, theologians. I do not of course mean to imply by this that such an account is the exclusive possession of Reformed theology. In fact, the themes sounded here are by no means lacking in Catholic theology. Thomas Aquinas, for example, besides giving the account I sketched in the last chapter, also emphasizes the internal testimony of the Spirit: 'One who believes does have a sufficient motive for believing, namely the authority of God's teaching, confirmed by miracles, and—what is greater—the inner inspiration of God inviting him to believe'.[1] I cite this in order to show that the two accounts may not be mutually exclusive, and I shall eventually try to show how to combine them.

Nevertheless, it is in Reformed thinkers that this theme figures most prominently. For Reformed thinkers the historical knowledge that can be part of saving faith is derived from the Bible. Thus, the question as to how we have such knowledge basically is the question of how we can know the Bible is the reliable revelation from God it is claimed to be by the Church. The Reformed creeds assert unanimously that this knowledge is due to the witness of the Holy Spirit in our hearts. The Belgic Confession, for example, says that '[w]e receive all these books ... believing, without any doubt, all things contained in them, not so much because the Church receives and approves them as such, but more especially because the Holy Ghost

---

[1] Thomas Aquinas, *Summa Theologiæ*, II-II q. 2 a. 9, trans. P. C. O'Brien (London: Blackfriars, 1964), xxxi. 99.

witnesseth in our heart that they are from God'.[2] Very similar statements can be found in the Westminster Confession, The French Confession of Faith, the Scots Confession, and the Helvetic Confession.[3]

The inspiration for all these creeds is to be found, of course, in the work of John Calvin. In his *Institutes of the Christian Religion*, Calvin claims both that the knowledge of God we need is to be found in the Bible,[4] and that we gain certain knowledge that the Bible is from God by the internal testimony of the Holy Spirit in our hearts.[5] Calvin does not deny that evidence could be adduced for these claims; on the contrary he says that 'so far as human reason goes, sufficiently firm proofs are at hand to establish the credibility of Scripture'.[6] He says that we could doubtless furnish many proofs of these things 'if we wished to proceed by arguments'.[7] He even proceeds to offer the arguments he says we do not need! Nevertheless, he says clearly that relying on such arguments is a mistake; those 'who strive to build up firm faith in Scripture through disputation are doing things backwards'.[8] The chief reason for this is that no human argument can produce the kind of certitude true faith demands; even the best arguments would be subject to doubts and possible objections. Here, I think it is clear that Calvin has in mind something closely related to the incommensurability problem that we saw as a difficulty for the evidentialist approach.

Furthermore, the witness of the Spirit produces not only intellectual certainty, but a distinctive quality of assent: through the work of the Spirit the conviction that God is the author of the Scriptures is 'sealed upon our hearts'.[9] Calvin

---

[2] The Belgic Confession, art. V in *The Creeds of Christendom*, iii. ed. Philip Schaff (New York: Harper & Bros., 1877), 386–7.

[3] See the following pages in *The Creeds of Christendom*, ed. Schaff, iii: The Westminster Confession (1647), 603; the French Confession of Faith (1559), 361–2; The Scotch Confession of Faith (1560), 450; Second Helvetic Confession (1566), 237.

[4] John Calvin, *Institutes of the Christian Religion*, ed. John T. McNeill, trans. Ford Lewis Battles (Philadelphia: Westminster Press, 1960) VI. 1 (pp. 69–71). All subsequent references to Calvin will be from this edition of the *Institutes*.

[5] Calvin, VII. 4–5 (pp. 78–81).

[6] Ibid. title of ch. VIII (p. 81).

[7] Ibid. VII. 4 (p. 78).

[8] Ibid. VII. 4 (p. 79).

[9] Ibid. VII. 5 (p. 80).

says that this means that our conviction is not rooted in human judgement or argument at all, but rather on the actual work of God.[10]

Lest we think that this account is exclusively found among Reformed theologians, it is worth noting that similar themes can be found in Lutheranism. Though the classical Lutheran creeds are not as explicit in addressing the issue, the general thrust is clearly to understand the knowledge of God in history that we need to be the result of the Holy Spirit, 'who worketh faith, where and when it pleaseth God, in those that hear the Gospel'.[11] The work of the Holy Spirit clearly involves the Bible, since the Scriptures constitute the authoritative 'judge, norm, and rule' and 'touchstone' for determining the truth of all doctrines.[12]

An interesting variation on this Lutheran theme is to be found in the writings of Kierkegaard. Kierkegaard gives an account of the formation of faith in which evidence appears to play no positive role at all. The individual comes to believe in the incarnation when there is a first-hand encounter with the incarnate God and the 'condition' of faith is created in the believer.[13] This account appears not only to regard evidence as unnecessary, but as positively harmful. I shall later argue that such a view is mistaken. Rather, evidentialist and Reformed accounts are best viewed as complementary.

---

[10] Calvin, VII. 4–5 (pp. 79–80).

[11] The Augsburg Confession, *Creeds of Christendom*, Art. V, ed. Schaff (p. 10).

[12] The Formula of Concord, ibid., 96.

[13] Strictly speaking the views attributed here to Kierkegaard are those of one of his pseudonyms, Johannes Climacus, the author of *Philosophical Fragments* (Princeton: Princeton University Press, 1985) and *Concluding Unscientific Postscript* (Princeton: Princeton University Press, 1992). However, much of the discussion of Kierkegaard's philosophical writings is grounded in discussions of these two pseudonymous works. For discussion of these two works that takes account of their pseudonymity and focuses particularly on the question of faith and how it arises in an individual, see my own *Kierkegaard's Fragments and Postscript: The Religious Philosophy of Johannes Climacus* (Atlantic Highlands, NJ: Humanities Press, 1983) and *Passionate Reason: Making Sense of Kierkegaard's Philosophical Fragments* (Bloomington, Ind.: Indiana University Press, 1992).

11.2. THE EPISTEMOLOGY OF THE REFORMED ACCOUNT

Now how we shall understand this Reformed account? Initially, it might appear to be a move toward fideism, an attempt to evade the hard intellectual work involved in justifying belief. Or if there is any appeal to evidence, the evidence in question looks like a private, unverifiable experience. Such an appeal looks too easy; perhaps, as Russell said on another occasion, it has all the advantages of theft over honest toil.

However, this quick dismissal of the Reformed account comes, I think, from trying to understand it in evidentialist terms, particularly an evidentialism that is rooted in internalism. To briefly review the discussion in Chapter 9, if we assume that knowledge is something like a true belief that is appropriately justified or warranted, and if we know what it is for a belief to be true, then the crucial question concerns what sort of justification or grounding must be added to a true belief I have in order for that belief to count as knowledge. The internalist says that what must be added is something internal to my consciousness. My belief must be based on good evidence, I must be aware of that evidence, aware that it is the basis of my belief, and I must be aware that the evidence is good evidence, and so on.

Now one might well try to understand the Reformed account as an attempt to measure up to these internalist demands. If we do so, I believe there are two possible interpretations. One is to claim that the Reformed view is maintaining that the truth of the biblical revelation is 'self-authenticating'. One way of taking this would be as a claim that the truth of the Scriptures is immediately obvious to someone who reads in the right way. For example, Calvin says that 'Scripture exhibits fully as clear evidence of its own truth as white and black things do of their colour, or sweet and bitter things do of their taste'.[14] Here the work of the Holy Spirit might be thought of as helping the individual to see what is immediately, experientially obvious.

---

[14] Calvin, *Institutes of the Christian Religion*, I. 7. 2.

The other option, if we wish to understand this Reformed view in evidentialist, internalist terms, is to try to characterize the internal testimony of the Holy Spirit as a kind of experience, and to view that experience as internally available evidence. The experience in question is one that might be described as a sense that one is being addressed by God, or perhaps as a feeling of certainty or assurance that one gains as one reads the Bible or hears the Gospel preached, a sense that the reader or hearer takes as coming from the work of God.

Neither of these options looks very promising, at least when measured by internalist standards, especially if we understand evidence as objective evidence in the classical foundationalist manner. The claim that the truth of the Scriptures is immediately obvious may be correct; however, it seems safe to say that the truth of the Bible does not seem immediately obvious to many, including many believers. The other option looks little better. Certainly, many people who read the Scriptures experience a feeling of certainty or assurance, or have a sense of being addressed by God, but how can we know that such a feeling or sense stems from the work of the Holy Spirit? As evidentialist apologetics, such claims seem weak.

Rather than dismiss the Reformed view as bad apologetics, I am inclined to think that we should reconsider the whole account. Rather than interpreting this doctrine as providing a weak form of internally available evidence, we ought to recognize it as providing a different type of story altogether.

I propose therefore to try to understand the Reformed account in the externalist terms defended in Chapter 9, where I argued that the factors that determine whether or not I am justified or warranted in holding my belief do not have to be internal to my consciousness. At bottom the externalist says that what properly 'grounds' a belief is the relationship of the believer to reality. There are many different kinds of externalism, of course. Some see a true belief as knowledge when it is caused in the right way, or produced by the right kind of process. William Alston speaks of a true belief as being justified 'in the evaluative sense' when it is held and maintained on the basis of a 'truth-conducive ground', which means roughly that most of the time someone who believes something on that kind of basis will have a true belief.[15]

Alvin Plantinga regards a belief as having what he calls warrant when it is the result of our God-given faculties operating properly in the kind of environment in which they were designed to function.[16] So on this view, if God has designed and created me with memory, for example, and I have a certain belief as a result of my memory functioning properly in the right kind of circumstances, that belief will have warrant for me. What all these externalist views have in common is that according to them what makes a true belief knowledge is a relation between the knower and the objective world; knowledge requires us to be so oriented to that world that our beliefs can be said to 'track' with that world, to use Robert Nozick's suggestive phrase.[17]

So on an externalist account, I now know that there is a computer in front of me, not because I have propositional evidence for its existence, even though I may have such evidence, but because I am so constituted that when I have experiences of a certain kind, namely those in which it appears there is a computer in front of me, then I find myself believing there is a computer in front of me, unless I have some special reason for doubting this to be the case. If this belief was formed in the right way and I am related properly to the reality of the computer, and if the belief in question is true, then I do indeed know the computer is present to me.

---

[15] Alston's own account is of course much more complex and nuanced than this. For example, he also holds that I must not have any strong reason to think the belief is false; where I do have such reason then the prima facie justification offered by the ground may be overridden. See his essay, 'Concepts of Epistemic Justification', in *Epistemic Justification* (Ithaca, NY: Cornell University Press, 1989). It should be noted that Alston's view is not purely externalist, in that he thinks that the justifying ground of the belief should be something to which the subject has access. However, despite this internalist component, Alston's view is externalist in that what turns out to be decisive for justification is the objective fact that the ground is truth-conducive. The subject must be aware of the ground, but does not have to know that the ground is truth-conducive, so long as it is in fact truth-conducive.

[16] Again, Plantinga's view is actually more complex than this. He also requires that the relevant portion of the design-plan that is operative be one that is directly aimed at truth. See Plantinga's *Warrant and Proper Function* (Oxford: Oxford University Press, 1993), esp. 31–47.

[17] Robert Nozick, *Philosophical Explanations* (Cambridge, Mass.: Harvard University Press, 1981), 172–288.

As we saw in Chapter 9, various externalists understand this relation differently, and also describe the outcome differently. Some might say, for example, that the belief-forming process is what justifies the belief; others might prefer to use the term 'justification' in the deontological sense, to describe the state of people who have 'done their best', to use Locke's phrase, to see whether a belief is supported by internally available evidence. In that case we might say that what the reliable process confers on the belief is warrant, to use Alvin Plantinga's term, or some other quality, such as 'putting us in a strong epistemic position', rather than justification.

Let us take Alston's position as a representative externalist view. On this view a belief is justified (in what Alston calls the evaluative sense) when it based on a truth-conducive ground (and when I have no good reason to think otherwise). Alston's view is not purely externalist since he thinks that at least in the normal case people have some awareness of the ground of their beliefs. However, it is externalism, since on Alston's view it is not necessary for them to know that the ground is truth-conducive; what is crucial is that the ground is in fact truth-conducive.

Now Alston clearly thinks the ground in some cases will consist of other beliefs; in that case my belief is derived from the ground by a process of inference. But the ground might also consist of an experience that is not itself a belief. In such a case the link between ground and belief may be more causal and constitutional than inferential in character. I do not infer there is a computer in front of me when I have computer experiences; rather the belief is formed immediately and naturally (given that I know what a computer is and how to recognize one). So Alston does not insist that the ground of a belief must consist of propositional evidence. I do not know whether Alston himself would wish to say this, but it seems to me that his view could be extended still further; the ground of a belief might consist not merely of other beliefs and experiences but the extended process that has given rise to the belief. In such a case the ground would be equivalent to the total situation that has given rise to the belief (taking 'situation' in a temporally extended sense). To the degree that we are aware of this situation, Alston's internalist constraint could still be

met; a person could still have *some* awareness of the ground of
a belief. If I have some awareness of a process that has produced
a belief in me, and if that process is one that reliably produces
true beliefs, then it would appear that I am aware of a truth-
conducive ground.[18] (It seems obvious that in most cases such
awareness would be only partial.)

It is possible to get bogged down at this point in semantic
questions. Is not this ground evidence, in that it is what makes
the truth of the proposition evident? In some sense of evidence,
the answer is probably yes. Still, it is clear, I think, that the
ground of a belief does not have to be viewed as evidence in
the sense in which evidence is what provides a premiss for an
argument or figures in a process of inference. Still less is it the
case that the knower must somehow know that the ground is
an adequate basis for an argument. A ground is not evidence
in the sense that it must be propositional and fully accessible
to consciousness, with its adequacy similarly accessible to consciousness. Hence a belief that is grounded may still be
regarded as a basic belief in one's epistemic structure.

Of course a ground may also be considered as propositional
evidence, or as providing one with such evidence. I have
already noted that one could try to construe the testimony of
the Holy Spirit as providing propositional evidence, and it
might be possible for me to take my visual experiences of my
computer as providing backing for some kind of inferential
argument that it exists. But the fact that it is possible for a
ground to be construed as evidence does not mean that it must
always be so construed. The fact that evidence can be given for
a belief does not mean that the belief is not in fact held as basic.

In the normal case I do not appeal to any experiences in
order to be justified in believing that my computer is in front
of me. The belief is not the conclusion of any process of
inference, conscious or unconscious. Rather, when I am in the
right circumstances, and my eyes and brain are functioning
properly, the belief that is formed within me is warranted by

[18] It is probably Alvin Plantinga who has done most to make sense of the idea that
a belief could be grounded though it is not based on propositional evidence. See his
discussion of belief in God in 'Reason and Belief in God', in Alvin Plantinga and
Nicholas Wolterstorff (eds.), *Faith and Rationality* (Notre Dame, Ind.: University of
Notre Dame Press, 1983).

the fact that beliefs formed in this manner are usually true. Though of course the warrant is defeasible, and will be defeated in the case where I have some special reason to doubt my senses, it is not the case that I must somehow understand and certify the reliability of the process before my belief is warranted.

In Chapter 9 I argued that externalism provides us with the best account we have of what knowledge is and how we get it. Many contemporary philosophers, religious and non-religious, agree with this assessment. If I am right in thinking that externalism provides us with our best account of knowledge for non-religious cases, then it makes sense to apply this theory to religious knowledge as well, and to view true religious beliefs that are formed in the right kind of ways, or that are rooted in truth-conducive grounds, as knowledge.

If we accept some form of externalism, then what will our religious historical knowledge look like? *If my belief that Jesus is the Son of God who atoned for sin by his death and resurrection, as taught in the biblical narrative, is the result of the work of the Holy Spirit, and if the work of the Holy Spirit is one that generally produces true beliefs, then my belief is justified in Alston's evaluative sense, or warranted if one prefers Plantinga's language.* Furthermore, if the belief is true, then it amounts to knowledge. An appeal to evidence is not necessary in every case, since the belief, though always grounded, may sometimes be basic in character.

What does this process by which the Holy Spirit produces a belief look like? It may look differently to different people; indeed, the process may *be* different for different people, since the Spirit 'bloweth where it listeth' and may work in many different ways. For example, in some cases the Spirit might testify by helping someone see the strength of evidence that points to the truth, while in other cases the belief may be formed in a more basic manner. In any case, the process whereby the Holy Spirit forms such a belief must not be identified with *how it appears to the believer.* The process must not be identified with an experience, particularly not with an experience that is being construed as evidence. Christians certainly believe it is possible to experience the work of the Holy Spirit, and they regard such an experience as a valuable and precious one. However, the work of the Holy Spirit cannot be regarded as identical with someone's experience of that work, and it is the work of the Spirit that counts.

In other words, the work of the Spirit can be described both objectively and phenomenologically. If one were committed to internalism, then the phenomenological account would be all-important. For an externalist, however, though the phenomenology may be valuable and important, especially in answering the question as to how one recognizes the work of the Holy Spirit, what is all-important is the objective reliability of the actual process whereby the Spirit produces belief.

Someone might object that in using the term 'testimony' for the total process whereby the Spirit of God produces faith, rather than simply an internal mystical experience, the term is being stretched beyond its proper sense. For surely there are many ways the Spirit could create such a belief in someone or guide a person in its formation that could not aptly be called 'testimony'. For example, in the case of belief based on historical evidence, even if the Spirit guides the individual's consideration of the evidence, this guiding does not itself look like a case of testimony.

My response to this is twofold. In part, I wish to concede that the terms 'testimony' or 'witness' may be used here in a somewhat extended sense. However, such an extended sense is by no means unprecedented. For example, the Scriptures themselves speak of the natural world 'witnessing' to the glory of God: 'The heavens are telling the glory of God; and the firmament proclaims his handiwork.'[19] But even if the term is being used in an extended sense, the appropriateness of it is grounded in the end product. The final result of the process is a conviction, an inner certainty that the story of Jesus is indeed the true account of the Son of God. That inner sense of conviction is not by itself the ground of the belief, especially not if it is construed simply as an experience that provides evidence. A subjective feeling of certainty is not necessarily powerful evidence. Nevertheless, that sense of certainty and conviction is regarded by the believer as the outcome of the Spirit's activity; it is properly said to be the Spirit's 'witness' because,

---

[19] Psalm 19: 1. (*NRSV*).

like a case of hearing a convincing witness, it leads to a conviction about the truth of the matter.

I still have not answered the question as to what the process by which the Holy Spirit is supposed to produce faith is like, except to say that the answer will be different for different people. However, this does not mean that nothing useful can be said about the process in general. One important point is that the work of the Holy Spirit should be conceived diachronically, not just synchronically, over time and not simply at a moment. To say that a belief is basic and not derived from other beliefs is not to say that the belief was acquired instantaneously, or that the ground must be a set of circumstances at some particular point in time. Rather, the ground of belief is the total process whereby God brings it into being and nourishes it.

When believers describe this process diachronically, our human response becomes a part of the story. God speaks to human persons through the story of Jesus Christ—speaks not only or even primarily in the sense that he reveals truths, but in many different speech acts: God commands, God promises, God questions. A belief that God has acted for us in Jesus is typically formed in those who hear and obey those commands, test those promises, answer those questions. When they respond to God's revelatory acts, then the authoritativeness of the commands, the reliability of the promises, the appropriateness of the questions posed by Jesus become evident to believers over the course of their lives. The work of the Spirit on this view is not necessarily a private experience accessible only to an individual, but manifests itself in a life in a public way that may become apparent to others.

In a typical case, an individual encounters the story, either by reading the Gospel, hearing it preached, or through the testimony of a friend. Imagine a concrete individual, Birgitta, is in such a situation. As Birgitta reflects on the story, it speaks directly to her; it insightfully describes her deepest needs and hopes and fears. Or, perhaps better, as she reads she learns what her deepest needs, hopes, and fears are for the first time. Birgitta sees in the story the solution to those needs, the fulfilment of those hopes, and the antidote to those fears. The story of Jesus becomes the story of one who offers to be her saviour, the story of one who has the authority to offer both new demands and the resources to meet those demands. The story takes on the ring of truth for Birgitta and she finds herself united with the crucified Lord who offers resurrection life, as she is baptized into the communion of those who are Christ's followers. Though there is certainly a ground to her belief, and Birgitta in the typical case will be aware of the ground, the belief still functions as basic in her epistemic structure. The ground is the total process which gives rise to the belief.

This fictional story, which has paid no particular attention to evidential arguments, has been repeated countless times over the centuries. Reformed theologians sometimes describe the biblical story as self-authenticating; I think this is best understood, not in the sense that the truth of the story is intuitively obvious or becomes so, but in the sense that through the work of the Spirit the story itself produces a conviction of its truth in persons, and it is in that sense epistemologically basic.[20]

An important question to consider here is whether the initial object of belief is the Bible itself as a reliable witness, or the narrative the Bible tells. Either is possible. If you tell me a story, it is possible for me to consider your reliability first, and come to believe your story as a result of believing you are a reliable witness. Alternatively, I might consider your story, and come to believe you are a reliable witness because I have come to believe in your story.

I am inclined to think that in the case of the incarnational narrative, it is normal for the second alternative to hold. Though belief in the reliability of the biblical narrative is logically connected to faith in Jesus, it is Jesus and not the Bible that is the primary object of faith. If I come to believe that the Jesus whom I meet in the biblical narrative rose from the dead, then I do implicitly accept the resurrection narratives as trustworthy and reliable. But I do not have first to consider the reliability of the Bible and then conclude that the story about Jesus is true, though this might be possible as well. Much less do I have to begin by considering whether the biblical narrative is inspired, infallible, or inerrant. Those who accept

---

[20] For an insightful discussion of what it might mean for a revelation to be self-authenticating in this sense, see Paul Helm, *The Varieties of Belief* (New York: Humanities Press, 1973).

such doctrines should see them as dependent on faith in Jesus and acceptance of his authority as Lord, and not the other way around. Certainly, one cannot have faith in the Jesus we meet in Scripture without accepting the scriptural account as basically reliable, but that belief in the general trustworthiness of the scriptural account is a belief that I can acquire in the course of coming to faith in Jesus; I do not have to possess it antecedently to such faith.

11.3. EPISTEMOLOGY SUPERNATURALIZED

Externalist epistemologies are different in several important respects from traditional epistemological theories. One of the most important differences is that externalism was developed as a form of 'naturalistic' epistemology; externalists try to understand the formation of beliefs as a natural process that relies on our normal belief-forming faculties. The work of the Spirit, however, clearly cannot be understood simply as another natural belief-forming process; by definition it must be understood as a supernatural work within the person.

This does not mean that the Spirit cannot employ natural belief-forming processes. One of our most important natural belief-forming processes is that whereby we come to believe something on the basis of someone's testimony, and it seems clear that this disposition to accept someone's testimony will be part of the process whereby the Holy Spirit works. Furthermore, one of the means the Spirit may employ is the consideration of evidence that supports the truth of the beliefs or the reliability of the testimony, and consideration of evidence is certainly a natural process. Hence, although a belief in the truth of the incarnational narrative can be basic, it can also be one that is grounded at least partly in inference from propositional evidence.

If such 'natural' processes are employed, what need is there for anything supernatural? The answer to this question requires some insight into the complicated way that beliefs about Jesus interconnect with beliefs about one's self, and with a person's deepest hopes, fears, and desires. Beliefs about Jesus are not 'mere' historical beliefs. Though the incarnational story certainly has historical content, it is a story with relevance and meaning for a person's life today. It is a story of how God himself entered human history to suffer with and for God's fallen humanity. The story implies that humans are fallen, that they are sinful, and that the cure for their condition lies in a relationship with Jesus, accepted as Lord and Saviour.

This is a story that sinful humans have ample reasons to reject, reasons that have nothing to do with evidence or the lack thereof. For it is painful for people who are sinful to recognize their sinfulness, and it is offensive to people who wish to be their own lords to recognize Jesus as Lord. However much evidence I have for the truth of the incarnational narrative, as long as the ground of the belief (evidence or belief-forming condition) is not absolutely coercive, it is possible that the story will be rejected. And as many theologians have noted, it is not surprising that a God who wishes a free response from his creatures as part of a mutual relationship should give grounds for belief that are less than coercive.

I think therefore that the work of the Spirit must be understood as having both epistemic and non-epistemic dimensions, as involving the will and the heart as well as the mind. The Spirit must be understood as producing an understanding of one's sinfulness and the horribleness of that condition, a desire for purity and wholeness, and a deep yearning for eternal life with God. It is not necessary to think of the Spirit simply as creating these conditions apart from the response of the individual; they too may be produced in a non-coercive manner, involving the consent of the individual. Without them, however, it will be impossible for an individual properly to grasp the grounds of the truth of the narrative. If the grounds consist of evidence, the evidence will not be appropriately interpreted and evaluated. Or if the individual does grasp the force of the grounds, it is an insight that can be and often is dismissed and explained away.

Such a process of belief-formation is indeed supernatural and not merely natural. However, I see no reason why the conclusions of externalist epistemology do not apply to this case. So long as the supernatural character of the process does not affect the ability of the individual who relies on it to reach the truth in most cases, and so long as the beliefs produced are true, why should the fact that such a belief is not possible for humans in their natural state imply that it is not knowledge? There are many beliefs, and many belief-forming processes, that require a transformation in the individual for their operation. People must be educated, must be trained and socialized into communities, in order to do science, history, and many other things. The fact that in this case God himself is involved in the education and transformation of the individual does not seem to me to imply that the result cannot be knowledge.[21]

11.4. HOW CAN ONE KNOW A BELIEF HAS A TRUTH-CONDUCIVE GROUND?

If a belief in the truth of the incarnational narrative is formed as a result of the Holy Spirit, and if beliefs formed in such a manner are usually true, then the testimony of the Holy Spirit produces knowledge. Or so I have argued. One may well think that these 'ifs' are very 'iffy' however. How can one know that such a process normally leads to true beliefs?

One could argue a priori here that God, being all-powerful, all-knowing, and all-good, can be counted on to produce beliefs in a reliable manner. For clearly it cannot be that God lacks the power to see that true beliefs are arrived at, unless this would require interfering with the freedom of the individual, and in the case of the believer we can imagine that God enjoys the believer's free co-operation. Nor can it be that God is ignorant of what truths must be believed. Nor will it do to imagine that God, if he undertakes to produce beliefs in a person, will exhibit a careless unconcern about the outcome. So an argument can be mounted that the work of the Holy Spirit must be reliable at least, even if we imagine that due to human finitude it is not infallible.

The critic is hardly likely to be content with this answer. Perhaps, the critic will say, it is true that the work of the Holy Spirit in producing beliefs is reliable. But how does one recognize the work of the Holy Spirit? How can one know

---

[21] See my article, 'The Epistemological Significance of Transformative Religious Experiences', *Faith and Philosophy*, 8/2 (1991).

for sure that it is the Holy Spirit, and not one's unconscious or one's desire to develop a relation with a Church-member of the opposite sex, that has produced the beliefs in question?

These are extremely important questions, and I shall presently sketch the type of answer I think they require. However, it is easy to see that it will not be easy to say how to recognize the work of the Spirit. The history of Christianity includes many people who believed they were being guided by the Spirit, even though they were manifestly mistaken or even deluded about many of their beliefs. Furthermore, even if the work of the Spirit can be recognized, because of human finitude and sinfulness it is impossible to stipulate some method whereby this recognition can be achieved with absolute certainty. Hence, before attempting an answer to the question as to how one can recognize the work of the Spirit, I want first to look at the situations in which a person is either unable to recognize the work of the Spirit, or else can do so but is unable to say how he or she does this.

Let us suppose, in a particular case, that an individual *cannot* answer the question as to how he recognizes the work of the Spirit? What follows from this?

First of all, it does not follow that the individual is not able to recognize the work of the Spirit. It is common for people to be able to make sensory discriminations without being able to say precisely how they were able to do so, and it seems quite possible that someone might be able to recognize the work of the Spirit without being able to say how he is able to do so.

Secondly, even if the person is not aware of the Spirit's work *as the work of the Spirit*, it is still possible that the individual is in fact aware of the work of the Spirit, and thus for the individual to be aware of a truth-conducive ground that makes possible knowledge. I have some inclination to agree with Alston, who requires that the individual have some awareness of the ground of a true belief in cases of knowledge.[22] My externalism is thus not complete; I am prepared to admit that some internal condition is necessary for knowledge, at least in the normal situation. Hence, to have knowledge in this case, I think it likely that the individual must have some awareness of

---

[22] See above, s. 9.5 and n. 27, and s. 9.6.

the work of the Holy Spirit. However, it does not follow that the individual must be aware of the work of the Spirit *as* the work of the Holy Spirit. What is important for knowledge is that the true belief be based on an adequate ground. Only if we were full-fledged internalists would it also be required that the individual know that the ground is adequate. So it does not follow in the case in which the individual cannot say how to distinguish the work of the Spirit from other factors that the individual cannot have knowledge of the story of Jesus as true.

The critic is likely to be unmollified by these claims. Surely, the critic worries, if I can't reliably tell whether it is the Spirit or my unconscious that is moving me, then I cannot really trust the mover. This critic is of course voicing the intuition that gives rise to internalism in epistemology, which insists that we must not only have good grounds for our beliefs, but must also know that those grounds are good ones. Suppose an individual cannot say for sure whether or not the prompter of a belief is a reliable ground or not? Does this undermine the possibility of knowledge? According to externalism, the answer should be 'not necessarily'. But let us test this externalist answer by looking at two kinds of case. In one case we shall consider an individual who is struggling to resolve doubts. The other case will be a situation in which the individual is a firm believer.

Let us take the case of the doubter first. If the individual is not aware of the Spirit as the Spirit, then that individual cannot appeal to the trustworthiness of the Spirit as a reason to trust the ground. However, such a case is *not* a case where the Holy Spirit has effectively brought about belief, since by hypothesis we are dealing with a case where there is significant doubt. Hence this case does not show that a person who has been guided by the Spirit still lacks knowledge because of an inability to recognize the Spirit's work; this is not a case where the Spirit has worked. This does imply that an appeal to the work of the Holy Spirit is unlikely to be helpful in a case where someone is struggling to resolve doubts through consideration of evidence. But we have already claimed that when considered as evidence, the appeal to the testimony of the Spirit may be weak. Some other evidence may be needed. In the next chapter

I shall try to show that this is precisely one of the places that the evidentialist story may be helpful to the Reformed account.

Let us then take the case of someone who has a firm belief in the truth of the incarnational narrative, and let us assume that this conviction has been in fact produced by the work of the Spirit, though in this particular case the person in question cannot reliably recognize the work of the Spirit. We must remember that in order to produce knowledge, the Spirit must produce true beliefs by providing a 'truth-conducive ground'. Awareness *that* the production of this ground is the work of the Spirit is *not* a necessary part of the picture. The ground is a situation in which the truth of the incarnational narrative becomes evident to a person. If the ground is trustworthy and functions adequately, then no evidential appeal to the authority of the Spirit on the part of the individual is necessary to shore it up. By hypothesis in this case the individual has firm beliefs and hence is not worried about the adequacy of the ground.

Of course we can easily imagine situations in which doubts about the adequacy of the ground arise, and in *that* situation it would be very desirable for the individual to be able reliably to recognize the work of the Spirit. And this also seems very desirable in the case where the individual would like to be able to show someone that a belief is justified in the evaluative sense. It is not necessary to be able to justify a belief to someone else, however, in order to be justified in holding it, and an ability to recognize the work of the Spirit as the work of the Spirit is not necessary for knowledge in all cases.

Alston frequently has recourse to a 'distinction of levels' in dealing with these kinds of issues. That is, it is important to distinguish the first-order knowledge that Jesus is the Son of God, who lived, died, and rose again to save the human race, from the second-order knowledge in which one knows that one knows these things about Jesus. Having the first-level knowledge does not always require the second-level knowledge, and certainly does not guarantee the possession of the second-level knowledge. In many cases at least, it may be necessary to be able to recognize the work of the Spirit reliably in order to have this second level knowledge, but it does not follow from this that the first-level knowledge will be lacking if this condition is not met.[23]

II.5. CRITERIA FOR RECOGNIZING THE WORK OF THE SPIRIT

We must recall that this whole discussion has been hypothetical. That is, given the difficulty of recognizing the work of the Spirit, and the likelihood of error about this, I have taken some pains to consider the situation in which a person either cannot say how he or she recognizes the work of the Spirit or is unaware of the Spirit as the Spirit. However, I am far from admitting that such recognition is impossible.

How then can a person recognize the work of the Spirit? It is important to recognize that the account of the work of the Spirit we have given is a theological account. It is an account of the work of the Spirit of God as the Spirit is understood in Christianity. The Spirit is not an unknown 'X' but the Spirit of God the Father and God the Son as made known in the Scripture. So one test will be coherence between the testimony of the Spirit in one's heart and what is taught about the Spirit by the Christian faith. The truth to which the Spirit attests must be consistent with the character of the Spirit that is doing the attesting.

Another test will be coherence between the work of the Spirit in one's own life and the outcome of the Spirit in other lives down through the centuries and today. Since this Spirit is the Spirit who is the centre of the Church, if the testimony of the Spirit in my life is disturbingly different from that of people recognized to be Spirit-filled in the Church, this will be grounds for suspicion.

Yet another test will of course be the practical fruits of the Spirit in one's life. Does the testimony of the Spirit lead to greater sanctity, increasing moral and spiritual maturity?

[23] See William Alston, 'On Knowing That We Know: The Application to Religious Knowledge', in C. Stephen Evans and Merold Westphal (eds.), *Christian Perspectives on Religious Knowledge* (Grand Rapids, Mich.: W. B. Eerdmans, 1993), 15–39. Also see the discussion of levels of knowledge later in this chapter and in the next chapter, where the role of evidence in dealing with this issue is discussed.

There are more distinctly phenomenological marks as well. One sign of the work of the Spirit may be a sense of confidence, even certainty, about Christian truth, as the Spirit works within a person. Of course a subjective feeling of certainty by itself carries little weight; many people who are insane or evil have been very sure that God was telling them to do things. Nevertheless, there may be more specific phenomenological indicators; the specific *kind* of confidence the Holy Spirit grants may be different, coupling that confidence with a quiet humility and sense of peace. Still, I myself think that such subjective indicators are probably not reliable unless used in conjunction with the more communal criteria.

11.6. PROBLEMS WITH THE REFORMED ACCOUNT

The Reformed account faces difficulties, just as was the case with the evidentialist account, though we shall see the difficulties are not the same ones. The first problem concerns whether on the Reformed account we can know that we know. What about the 'second-level knowledge' discussed above? The Reformed claim is that the average Christian has knowledge that Jesus is the Son of God, provided that this belief is true and that it has been produced with God's help in the right manner. But many will regard it as difficult to ascertain whether those conditions can be met. I have just argued that the work of the Spirit can provide a truth-conducive ground even if a person is unaware that it is the Spirit at work. If the Spirit is at work in my life and if the Spirit gives me access to an adequate ground, the result is knowledge. But here we have more 'ifs'. How can it be known that these conditions have been met? If externalism is true and these conditions are met, then *perhaps* average Christians have the knowledge they claim to have. But do they in fact have it?

Many philosophers would say that if I know *p* then I also must be able to know that I know *p*. It is sometimes alleged that internalist epistemologies make this possible, because I must be able to tell by reflection that the grounds for my knowledge are adequate. (I say only that it is alleged because it is not in fact possible to tell merely by reflection whether I know some *p*, since whether I know depends in part on the truth of *p* and that is something that cannot usually be determined simply by reflection.) Externalism must stoutly deny that to know I must be able to know that I know, for it claims it is possible that my reliable beliefs are produced by grounds that are adequate, but are not known by me on reflection to be adequate. There are various distinct levels of knowledge, and it may be possible to know some *p* even if we do not know that we know *p*. Average Christians may know what they know, even if they do not know that they know.

But might not the process that makes possible the first-level knowledge make second- level knowledge possible as well? It might be argued, for example, that the Holy Spirit not only reliably produces a belief in the Bible's teachings about Jesus, but also reliably produces a belief that beliefs produced in this way are reliably produced. I don't wish to deny this is possible; typically, in fact, the person who claims to know that Jesus is the Son of God makes just this sort of claim. However, that response simply pushes the worry that the doubter might be inclined to have about the first-level knowledge to the second level, for the same question can now be asked about this second-level knowledge. Of course such doubts do not necessarily affect the believer, for part of the work of the Spirit may simply be to produce a sense of conviction, a kind of certainty. But as we noted in the last section, such a subjective feeling of confidence does not appear to be a reliable ground for belief in itself. We seem to have a situation then in which a person might indeed know, but not know that she knows, and be unable to show others that she knows. Surely in this case those others may have justified doubts about the first-order knowledge claim.

If it is possible to know something without knowing that one knows, then even if someone does not know that she knows Jesus is the Son of God, she might still know that he is. However, there is a clear sense in which such a situation is less than optimal. All other things being equal, it seems better to know *and* know that I know than simply to know. This is especially true in a case where I am aware of possible 'defeaters' that might indicate to me that my belief that I have knowledge is mistaken, or where I have peers who tell me that my claim to knowledge is mistaken. Even a well-grounded belief may be undermined in a case where the individual comes to believe (mistakenly, perhaps) that the belief was not based on an adequate ground. It is possible in such cases that the original belief will become shaky or disappear. In such cases I naturally want to know that I know; the mere knowledge that I know *if* my beliefs are true and are well-grounded is less than satisfactory.

The second difficulty arises at just this point, for it looks very much as if any account of how I might obtain this second-level knowledge will be 'circular' in the broad sense that it will presuppose that I have some knowledge of the kind of which I am trying to give an account, and which a sceptic might see as doubtful. We might say, as mentioned above, that the Holy Spirit reliably authenticates his own work. However, it seems likely that anyone who has doubts about whether the Holy Spirit truly produces the first-level belief will not be reassured by the claim that the Holy Spirit also produces a belief that his testimony is reliable. Or, we might try to give criteria, as in the last section, for recognizing the work of the Holy Spirit, but those criteria clearly are in some sense 'internal' to the Christian life. They are theological criteria. They function only in the context of active, living faith.

William Alston, who defends an externalist account of knowledge in general and of historical Christian claims in particular, is inclined to think that any plausible account of how we have first-level religious knowledge is likely to be circular in just this way:

[I]t is a theological question whether the Bible or the Church is a trustworthy source of belief, and whether practices of forming beliefs on their basis are reliable. If we want to know whether, as the Christian tradition would have it, God guarantees the Bible and the Church as a source for fundamental religious beliefs, what recourse is there except to what we know about God, His nature, purposes, plans, and actions? And where do we go for this knowledge? In the absence of any promising suggestions to the contrary, we have to go to the very sources of belief credentials of which are under scrutiny.[24]

---

[24] William Alston, 'Knowledge of God', in Marcus Hester (ed.), *Faith, Reason, and Scepticism* (Philadelphia: Temple University Press), 42.

It is, I think, because of this circularity that Reformed accounts are often accused of being fideistic.

Alston has responded to this objection by pointing out that this circularity is a consequence of externalism in general, and does not stem from any peculiarity in religious knowledge. For externalism generally, we are 'much more dependent on other knowledge than is the case for internalism'.[25] This has the consequence that our knowledge that we have a certain kind of knowledge generally has just this circular character. For example, our knowledge that a perceptual belief-forming mechanism is reliable depends on knowledge that we have in such fields as psychology, physiology, and physics, knowledge that is gained in part by using our perceptual mechanisms.[26] Such knowledge presupposes that many of our ordinary perceptual judgements are reliable. We cannot know that our perceptual belief-forming mechanisms are reliable, and that therefore perceptual judgements are likely to be true, without presupposing that many of our perceptual judgements are correct. So, for externalism generally, 'there is no escape from epistemic circularity in the assessment of our fundamental sources of belief'.[27] So it is hardly surprising that the same thing holds for the case of religious knowledge.

In the final analysis, then, to show that such beliefs are justified or warranted there may be no escape from what we might call the circle of commitment. The difficulties caused by this circularity should not be overestimated. As we have seen, first-level knowledge may still be present even if second-level knowledge is lacking, and people may be justified in a belief even if they cannot show that they are justified. Nevertheless, doubts about second-level knowledge can affect first-level knowledge, and an inability to justify belief may create problems for the person who is indeed worried about whether a belief is justified. Hence it seems worthwhile to see if the evidentialist story can here offer any help to the Reformed account. In the following chapter, I shall examine a number of ways the two accounts might complement each other.

[25] Alston, 'Knowledge of God', 28.
[26] Ibid. 28–9.
[27] Ibid. 41.

12

Putting the Two Stories
Together

WE have examined two plausible accounts of how knowledge of the incarnational narrative might be gained. We have seen that both the evidentialist story and the Reformed story have difficulties, though in both cases the difficulties do not seem insurmountable. At certain points the evidentialist case seems less than compelling to many people, and there seems to be a gap between the kind of assent such arguments could produce and living Christian faith. The Reformed story, on the other hand, has difficulty in making clear how Christian claims to knowledge can be justified to others and in accounting for second-level knowledge, showing that Christians know what they claim to know. Its attempts to justify its knowledge claims and give accounts of how such knowledge is possible involve a kind of circularity. I am convinced that the fact that these two stories face different kinds of problems is a clue that they are not necessarily designed to do the same job. They offer complementary answers to different questions, not rival answers to the same question. (However, at the risk of sounding enigmatic, we shall later see that in some cases they may also be seen as offering alternative versions of the same answer to the same question.)

As a first and rough approximation, which will have to be substantially qualified, I propose understanding the two accounts as related in the following way: the Reformed story is the story that the Church tells when it is attempting to understand how Christians in fact gain the knowledge they claim to have. The evidentialist story is the story the Church tells when it is attempting to convince or persuade someone of what it takes to be the truth.

The primary purpose of telling the Reformed story is not to persuade or convince someone of the truth of Christian faith; it is not at bottom a piece of apologetics, though in some cases it could function in that way. Rather, it is a story Christians tell when they wish to understand how God has given them the knowledge they believe he has given them. This story has the theological merit that it helps to make clear that this knowledge is primarily due to the work of God rather than being something people achieve for themselves.

The evidentialist story, or rather evidentialist stories, for we shall see there is not one story but many, is primarily the story Christians tell when they want to defend the claim that Jesus is the Christ, the Son of God. The purpose of the evidentialist story is primarily apologetics, though the doubters to be convinced may be within as well as outside the Church. This task must not be understood as the task of providing a once-and-for-all justification of faith, one that would be convincing to any rational person in any time or place, but as the task of persuading or convincing particular groups of people by responding to particular objections and appealing to particular beliefs already held.

We can immediately see that there is promise here in dealing with the major difficulties of each approach. The fact that a story such as Swinburne's is not convincing to everyone is not really a difficulty if it is understood as one apologetic story. No such story can be expected to be universally convincing. The proper question to ask is not whether it ought to be accepted by everyone, but rather whether there are some people who find the argument persuasive. Nor is it a difficulty that there seems to be for most people a gap between the outcome of such arguments and the conviction and certitude that Christian faith demands, for Christian faith is not the result of human arguments taken by themselves, but the outcome of the work of the Holy Spirit, and it is the Spirit who produces certainty and conviction.

In a similar way, the circularity charge that is addressed against the Reformed story seems misplaced. As a piece of apologetics, an appeal to the witness of the Holy Spirit may appear circular and weak to some, but all that this entails is that such an account is not effective as an apologetic for such people. So I conclude there is much promise in seeing the two accounts as complementary. However, this initial suggestion is too simple, for it seems to presuppose that an evidential case is an *alternative* to the work of the Holy Spirit. It naturally seems to suggest that the real work is done by the Spirit of God, and raises the question: What use are human arguments? What room is left for apologetics?

12.1. CAN THE HOLY SPIRIT WORK THROUGH HUMAN ARGUMENTS?

It is not uncommon to hear Christians claim that if they appeal to evidence they are somehow relying on 'human reason' and *not* relying on God. Such a claim is sometimes found in Lutheran theology, with its strong commitment to salvation by faith alone, and is seen among other places in some of Kierkegaard's writings. Human reasoning to some looks dangerously like a human 'work', and thus something that has no part in coming to know God by faith.

Now it is possible to choose to rely on some human good or aptitude as a substitute for faith in God. Indeed, this is the essence of idolatry. However, reliance on human goods or skills as such is not necessarily a result or symptom of lack of faith in God. Think for example of human medicine. It is possible for someone to go to a human physician to be healed because the person lacks faith in God's healing powers; this amounts to trusting in human medicine *rather* than in God. However, it is surely possible for one to go to a human physician in faith that God will heal through the agency of the human physician, and to pray that God will give the physician skill and knowledge. Though it may be more difficult to ascertain the hand of God at work in a healing that is mediated through human agency, the eyes of faith may have no doubt that it is present, and it would be strange indeed to deny that an omnipotent being could choose to heal in this way.

In a similar manner, it seems to me to be a mistake to argue that the Holy Spirit could not operate by means of evidence. The Holy Spirit could be active in calling an individual's attention to evidence, and in helping an individual properly to understand and interpret evidence, as well as in producing the conviction of sin that motivates the individual to receive the forgiveness that God offers. It seems quite possible, in fact, that the Holy Spirit could operate in an individual in such a manner that the individual's consciousness might be so focused on the evidence that the person would be unaware that it was in fact the Holy Spirit at work. Nor would such an awareness be seen as necessary from the viewpoint of externalism, which requires that a belief be rooted in a 'truth-conducive' ground, but does not require someone to know a lot about this ground.

Though I see no reason to insist that the Holy Spirit must operate by way of evidence, I also see no reason to rule out such a case. It is plausible to claim, in fact, that the miracles recorded in the New Testament functioned in just this manner, though it is fashionable for theologians today to deny this. The writers of the Gospels, particularly the writer of the Fourth Gospel, seem to view faith in Jesus as the Messiah as something that was called for by the signs that Jesus did.[1] I therefore reject the assumption that one must choose between the Holy Spirit and rational evidence. The Christian who is convinced that faith is the result of the work of the Spirit in human hearts may none the less engage in apologetics, trusting that God may use human efforts in this area for his purposes, much as he may use the eloquence of a preacher, or the elegance of a Christian writer to draw people to himself. And, for some people, such apologetic arguments may be an essential part of the process whereby the Spirit of God produces faith. In those cases the evidentialist story becomes part of the Reformed story, part of the account of how faith comes into being.

Apologetics is a dangerous enterprise, in many ways. Not only may people be tempted to think that their own human abilities are the key to bringing someone to faith; they may

---

[1] See John 2: 23, 3: 2, 6: 2, 11: 47–8, and Acts 2: 22. The writer of this Gospel also clearly holds that despite the signs Jesus did, many refused to believe; see John 12: 37. Another subsidiary theme is that requiring signs as a condition of faith is not praiseworthy; see John 4: 48. Both of these subsidiary themes are quite consistent with the claim that the signs do in fact warrant a believing response.

also be tempted to subvert and distort the message for the sake of success. But these are temptations only, not necessities. There are no good theological reasons for viewing the two stories as mutually exclusive.

12.2. DETAILED COMPLEMENTARITIES

Nor are there any good philosophical reasons for doing so. If we opt for some form of externalism, there is no need to choose between the two accounts, at least if the evidentialist story is shorn of any imperialistic features. For of course good evidence would seem to be one kind of adequate ground for a belief. There is no reason why the practice of forming a belief on the basis of evidence should not be seen as a reliable source of beliefs. In fact, even an evidentialist who wishes to maintain that the evidentialist story is the only correct account of how knowledge of the incarnational narrative is gained, could interpret her account of historical religious knowledge in a Reformed manner, drawing on an externalist epistemology. In this case it is claimed that the Spirit works through the evidence and the inferences so as to lead people reliably to true beliefs.[2]

The evidentialist does not need to make an exclusivist claim for her story, as we noted in the case of Thomas Aquinas above.[3] Nor does the Reformed account need to deny there is evidence or deny the importance of such evidence. We can now qualify the initial characterization of the complementary character of the two stories. The basic account is that the knowledge of the career of Jesus as the Son of God in history is produced by the work of the Holy Spirit. If the beliefs in question are true, and if the process that creates the belief is objectively truth-conducive, then the beliefs in question amount to knowledge. However, there is no need to claim that

---

[2] See Stephen J. Wykstra, 'Is Theism a Theory? Externalism, Proper Inferentiality and Sensible Evidentialism', *Topoi*, 14 (1995) 107–21, for an interesting account of an evidentialist account of religious beliefs that is externalist. While Wykstra thinks that religious beliefs are based on evidence, he thinks that the evidence need not be available to every member of a community, and that neither the evidence nor the inferential paths must always be clearly present to the consciousness of the knower.

[3] See s. 11.1.

the beliefs are produced in only one manner. The Holy Spirit might produce the beliefs as basic ones, or they might be the outcome of a process that involves reflection on evidence.

I said initially that the evidentialist story was aimed at apologetics, while the Reformed story was aimed at understanding how the knowledge is gained. One might say that the evidentialist story is for outsiders, while the Reformed story is for insiders. However, even on the initial account things were not quite that simple. First of all, the story the Church tells itself may have real, if limited, value for outsiders, in helping them to see that the Church's message, including its account of how it gained knowledge of the message, is a coherent one, one that is internally consistent and powerful when taken as a whole. Secondly, the apologetic story has great value for the Church, and not just outsiders, for there is a bit of an outsider in almost all believers. The evidentialist story can have real value in strengthening and confirming faith.

It can also have intrinsic value for the life of faith itself as faith seeks understanding. However true it may be that faith may arise in a person without any special consideration of apologetic arguments, it is equally true that the person who has faith, and wishes a deeper understanding of that faith, is frequently driven to consider the evidential backing that can be provided for faith. And this is a good thing. It reflects one of the epistemological virtues, namely that a virtuous knower monitors and works on improving what might be called his epistemological equipment. Contrary to Kierkegaard, it does not appear that a concern for apologetics necessarily is a sign that faith is diminishing—though that could be the case—for it is a secure and confident faith that is more likely to embark on such an intellectual quest.

On the assumption that the process whereby the Spirit produces belief can include the evidential story, it is perhaps best not to speak of the Reformed and evidentialist stories as distinct, rival accounts, but as accounts that are given for different purposes or that perhaps reflect different emphases. However, speaking loosely, we can still treat them as two stories so long as we understand that one of the stories can function as part of the other. From this basis we can now see several possible ways the two accounts can complement each other:

1. First, and most obvious, one might simply see the two accounts as applying to different groups of people. Just as God may heal some people of physical illness directly, and others through the agency of a physician, so the Holy Spirit may produce a conviction of the truth of the Scriptures directly in some people as they read the Scriptures, and for others produce such a conviction by way of evidence.[4] It seems to me that this is not merely a possibility, but actually is the case. Some people seem to read the Scriptures or hear the Gospel preached, and form a belief as to the identity of Jesus without any conscious consideration of evidence, as they come to see the fit between the story and their own spiritual condition, and find the story 'grounded' over time by their own life experiences.

Others of a more reflective bent may view similar experiences evidentially, developing an argument along the following lines: 'A true religious story is likely to entail certain consequences for the life of the one who is committed to the story. The Christian story implies just such consequences, and as I have committed myself to it, I have experienced just what I should have expected. Hence the story is likely to be true.'

Still others might of course find apologetic arguments of a very different character convincing. Someone might find some version of the traditional two-stage argument convincing. One might, for example, find Swinburne's argument, or a variation on it, very plausible. One merit of the account I am developing is that it may allow for reinforcement of some of the possible weak points in Swinburne's argument. For example, Swinburne lays heavy weight on the authority of the Church, but yet it may be difficult to say which church is the true Church on his view.[5] If however, the evidential argument is viewed as a means whereby the Spirit of God induces faith, it is not clear that such a heavy weight needs to be placed on the Church.

---

[4] George Mavrodes makes this suggestion in his article, 'Revelation and the Bible', in *Faith and Philosophy*, 6/4 (1989), 409.

[5] Swinburne himself does not say that this cannot be determined, but he refrains from making any pronouncement about the identity of the true Church in his work so far. See Richard Swinburne, *Revelation: From Metaphor to Analogy* (Oxford: Oxford University Press, 1992), 119–45.

The Church may still be vital as the bearer and authorized interpreter of the story, but the witness of the Spirit can itself authenticate the story as the Church's story, bypassing a potentially long historical detour as one seeks to determine the historical credentials of various churches. For on an externalist framework, in order for a belief to be warranted it is sufficient that the ground in fact is adequate, not that it be evident on reflection that it is adequate. Thus if the Spirit produces in me a conviction that the story I encounter is the true Church's story, and that conviction is true, then I am warranted in the convictions I thus form, even if I have no strong evidence to decide the question of the true Church.

2. A second possibility is to see the two types of account as applying to different *levels* of knowledge. One might hold that the primary knowledge that Jesus is the Son of God who came to redeem us from sin is the result of the internal witness of the Holy Spirit, which in turn could be seen as mediated in some cases through historical evidence. Our second-level knowledge that we have this first-level knowledge could be seen, in some cases though not necessarily for all, as based on a more traditional evidential case. I say only some cases, because I do not wish to say that the simple believer whose faith has a more basic character and does not rely on evidence necessarily fails to know that she knows. The Holy Spirit may inspire not only knowledge but assurance that knowledge has been given.

However, there are cases where individuals are troubled by intellectual doubts that are grounded in the accusations of others. People in this condition may need to have some of those doubts resolved, and it is not clear that this can always be done without intellectual inquiry. We have seen that the Holy Spirit can operate by means of evidence, and that a need to look at the evidence honestly does not have to be seen as a lack of faith. So one option for the person who is troubled by the 'circularity' charge directed against the Reformed account is to seek to show that a belief is justified evidentially on premises that would be conceded by some opponent. This might remedy the problem, if it is a problem, of the circularity of this second-level knowledge that besets the externalist.[6] It should be clear that it is not inconsistent of the externalist to say that the second-level knowledge depends on evidence, since we have seen that holding a belief on the basis of evidence is one way a belief may be based on a truth-conducive ground.

Of course if we accept this suggestion, the second-level knowledge for those who thus depend on evidence will be vulnerable to the kinds of objections commonly made against evidentialist accounts such as Swinburne's. Their second-level knowledge may be subject to doubt because of the uncertainty surrounding the prior assumptions needed to generate the evidential case, for example, or the worries that stem from contemporary critical biblical scholarship. However, it is important to remember that on this suggestion it would only be the second-level knowledge of a particular group that would be threatened in this way; the people in question as well as ordinary believers may still know what they know, whatever problems may beset philosophical and theological arguments designed to show that they do know what they know. It is also important to remember that these difficulties are, for many people, resolvable. As we saw when we examined the evidentialist kind of case, the mere fact that objections are possible does not mean such arguments are not convincing to many people; no arguments of this type are absolutely convincing to everyone.

This level distinction may also help with the problem of incommensurability. Perhaps the certainty and quality that evidence is powerless to produce and that requires the direct witness of the Holy Spirit is present for our first-level knowledge. Doubts and uncertainty may be present for some when they reflectively try to see how they know what they know, but it is not obvious to me that this second-level uncertainty must necessarily seep down into the first-level knowledge. In any case, we must make some room for doubts and uncertainty within the life of faith, for even saints struggle at times with doubt. And once again we must remember that the problems

[6] I say 'only partially' because one of the problems that may beset the evidentialist account itself is apparent or at least partial circularity. It might be argued that the estimates of prior probability the evidentialist requires presuppose the truth of the first level beliefs.

that such an evidentialist account faces are by no means necessarily unsolvable; doubts and uncertainty are often resolved.

In fact, once we have banished the epistemological stance
of classical foundationalism, there are excellent prospects for
dealing with the objections raised against the evidentialist
story. We found that this account is convincing to some, but
not all. One factor that surely is part of the reason the account
is convincing to some and not others is the presence or absence
of faith. It is likely therefore that the person who looks on the
evidential account from the perspective of faith is a person
who will find the account convincing.

Take, for example, the issue of biblical criticism, which we
will examine in more detail in the concluding two chapters.
We have seen that scepticism about the incarnational narrative
on the part of biblical scholars may be linked to doubts about
the possibility of special acts of God in history. However,
believers who have experienced the power of God in their lives
have good reason to affirm that such special acts are possible
for God.

Nor is there any reason for the person of faith to attempt to
put aside her faith in examining the evidence, even if it were
possible to do so. Of course I may, in arguing with another
person lay aside my own convictions and attempt to use premisses the other will accept. It is then often advantageous for
apologists to use arguments which do not presuppose Christian faith, but this fact should not lead to a general policy of
thinking about such questions as if I knew nothing. In the case
where an individual is seeking the truth for herself, it is foolish
to set aside convictions about what seems true, even if it were
possible to do so. In any case, no one else has succeeded in
putting aside all convictions and assumptions in looking at the
historical records, least of all biblical scholars committed to
Troeltsch-like historical methods. So the believer should not
be intimidated into giving up faith's insights for the mirage of
an 'objective, impartial view'.

That is not to say that the believer should not try to look at
evidence fairly and impartially. There is such a thing as failing
to respect the evidence. But there is no looking at the evidence
that is not a looking from a particular point of view. Hence
evidence that is not appreciated by everyone can still be recog-

nized as good evidence, once the Enlightenment ideal of certainty has been set aside. Of course the believer may be wrong; others will claim this is the case. But that is a necessary feature of being epistemologically finite.

3. Suppose the two levels of knowledge are not so well insulated that doubts at the second level do not sometimes seep through so as to affect the first level. It follows that if these second level doubts can't be resolved, then faith is put into question. Doubtless there are cases where if I doubt whether I know what I know, my knowledge itself will be put in doubt. In such a case, the 'circular' kind of justification can still be offered. That is, one may give an account of the second-level knowledge that presupposes the truth of the theological perspective under consideration. Someone might say in the end, for example, that she can know that the story of Jesus is true because it is vouchsafed by the Church or taught in the Bible, and these are reliable sources. Nevertheless, even in this situation an evidential case may still have great value in rebutting or undercutting various alleged 'defeaters'. For example, one may need a response to objections that the Bible or the Church are not trustworthy authorities.

There are two different kinds of 'defeaters' to consider. In one sort of case a knower has good reason to think that a well-grounded belief is false; in the second kind of case a knower has good reason to think that the ground of the belief is not strong or truth-conducive. For example, someone who has formed a basic belief on the basis of a perception might have reason to believe that his perceptual apparatus is malfunctioning or is not operating in a reliable manner in the case in question. In a pluralistic religious society, it is not uncommon for religious believers to at least perceive themselves as being in an analogous situation. I may be a student who believes that Jesus is the Son of God on the basis of the witness of the Holy Spirit, but who also believes that my philosophy professor has given me a sound argument that God does not exist, and hence that there can be no Son of God. Or, I may be a student who believes, as a result of the internal testimony of the Holy Spirit, that the Bible is a reliable source of truth about Jesus as the Son of God, but who also believes that my religion professor has given me good reasons to believe that the Bible is full of contradictions in the fundamental claims it makes about Jesus.

In such cases it seems highly desirable to have rebuttals or undercutters.[7] A rebuttal, or 'defeater for the defeater', would show that the alleged defeater does not really undermine the belief or that the ground of the belief is not defective. An undercutter would be a way of casting doubt on the alleged defeater; even if we cannot show conclusively that the defeater fails, perhaps it can be shown that we have no very good reasons for accepting the defeater either.

One could of course simply maintain that whatever original story we tell about our knowledge will do the job; the internal testimony of the Holy Spirit will do the job of rebuttal or undercutting that is needed. Ultimately, I suspect that something like this is the case. It is more God holding on to people than people clinging to God. However, in the case where the individual is genuinely struggling with doubt, *advice* to this effect may possibly be unhelpful. It looks as if the individual is looking for an answer to a problem, and to be told that one knows because one has the testimony of the Spirit looks more like a denial of the problem than a possible answer. So it makes sense to turn to evidence in this situation. Moreover, if I am right in my contention that reliance on evidence is not necessarily supplanting the Holy Spirit, then offering evidence in such a case is not a denial of the adequacy or sufficiency of the work of the Holy Spirit.

It is my judgement that evidentialist accounts are well-suited to serve as rebuttals and undercutters. There are of course many evidentialist accounts, corresponding to the many different types of problems and the many different life-situations of the people who feel the weight of the problems, and the constraints on what is acceptable as evidence will depend in part on to whom the argument is directed. A person who does not see the relevance or importance of the incarnational narrative may need help in coming to see the significance of moral failings and the need for an atonement. A person who is

---

[7] My usage here is inspired by the distinction drawn by Alvin Plantinga between rebutters and undercutters in his article, 'The Foundations of Theism', *Faith and Philosophy*, 3 (1986), but my usage differs somewhat from his.

a convinced materialist but who accepts the reality of moral obligation may benefit from a moral argument for God's reality. A person who finds the exclusivist claims of Christianity intolerably arrogant may benefit from an argument that shows that so-called pluralistic views of religion may be even more arrogant and intolerant. A college student who is struggling with the reliability of the New Testament may benefit from philosophical criticism of the assumptions of sceptical biblical scholars, as well as the example of the work of scholars who take the biblical record more positively. And so on.

We should of course remember that apologetic arguments do not have to convince anyone, much less everyone, in order to be successful. There are many other goals for such arguments, that could be summarized under the rubric of 'softening up' the intended audience, such as lessening the grip of various objections, removing certain barriers that make it impossible fairly to consider faith, producing a disposition to hear with a more open mind or to seek to hear more about the faith, and many more.

Among this large group of apologetic arguments, the traditional two-stage comprehensive argument can continue to play a useful role, even though such arguments often have more value in strengthening faith that already is present than in convincing non- believers. Many of the problems that seem serious for such an evidential case if it is seen as the sole basis of our religious knowledge seem less serious or not to be present at all when such a case functions apologetically as a defence against 'defeaters' of various kinds. For example, when an evidentialist argument is functioning as a rebutter or undercutter, the 'incommensurability' problem does not arise, since the evidential case is not the source of faith and therefore cannot be expected to be the source of the quality and degree of certainty of faith.

Let us call the Swinburnian argument, in all its complexities and with all of its assumptions, 'Swinburne's story'. Rival accounts of equal complexity could be termed 'alternative stories'. Suppose that it is the case that Swinburne is unable to establish beyond reasonable doubt to an 'impartial observer', putting aside faith's perspective, the superiority of his story to the alternative stories. In order for Swinburne's story to function as an effective undercutter, however, it is not necessary for the story to accomplish this. If Swinburne's story could be established as being at least as plausible as its chief competitors, this might well be enough to create doubt that those alternative stories undermine the knowledge that one deems oneself to have. I think the prospects for this are bright indeed, especially if the case is revised to include a challenge to the Troeltschian assumptions of sceptical biblical scholarship. Comprehensive justifications of the Christian claims, viewed holistically, can then be seen as functioning as undercutters in the sense that they undermine the plausibility of rival stories.

Arguments such as Swinburne's constitute what Basil Mitchell has called cumulative case arguments.[8] In other words, the Christian view of things, including its crucial historical component, should be understood as a comprehensive world-view, and the arguments presented should be viewed as part of a comprehensive case for that world-view. The probability of such a world-view is estimated as a whole, and relative to rival world-views, as Swinburne himself has maintained,[9] not simply absolutely. Evidence for particular aspects of this world-view should be regarded as providing partial confirmation to a comprehensive theory. This makes rational evaluation more difficult in one sense, but as Cardinal Newman argued so forcefully, this procedure corresponds much more closely with the way we actually reason about ultimate religious commitments.[10]

When such a story is viewed as a rebuttal or undercutter, then its alleged weaknesses appear very differently. After all, the situation is not one where we are totally dependent on this kind of story to have any knowledge. The religious believer in question takes herself to have knowledge, true belief produced by a reliable process. The relative plausibility of the Swinburne story undercuts the claims of those who wish to show that this knowledge claim is spurious. In effect the individual may say

---

[8] Basil Mitchell, *The Justification of Religious Belief* (London: Macmillan, 1973).

[9] See Swinburne, *Faith and Reason* (Oxford: Oxford University Press, 1981), 173–97.

[10] Newman argues strongly that people may have good grounds for a belief but be unable to articulate those grounds. See *An Essay in Aid of a Grammar of Assent* (Notre Dame, Ind.: University of Notre Dame Press, 1979; first published in 1870), especially ch. 8.

to herself, 'Why should I not in this situation trust the work of the Holy Spirit, as I am inclined to do? After all, the reasons that have been offered me to doubt in this case are no stronger than the reasons I could give for my beliefs, even if I were to put aside my personal convictions and try to argue for my beliefs using premisses my critics would find acceptable'. And of course if the Swinburne story is more plausible than its competitors, even if the case is less than overwhelming, then its power as an undercutter is even stronger, and it may even function as a rebutter.

4. So far, we have mainly been thinking about how the Reformed account could be strengthened and supported in various ways by the evidentialist story, though we have briefly looked at the way the evidentialist story itself seems stronger when it is functioning apologetically and not as the basic account of how knowledge of the incarnational narrative story is gained. I now wish to discuss the situation from the point of view of what we might call a moderate evidentialism that takes account of the insights of the Reformed account. How is the evidentialist story strengthened when it tries to incorporate these Reformed insights?

In looking at evidentialist accounts, we noted four major problem areas, involving philosophical prologomena, estimates of antecedent probability, critical biblical scholarship, and the incommensurability between religious faith and the evidential case. It seems to me that the evidentialist might well draw on the Reformed account to help with all these problems.

Let us begin with the incommensurability problem. Even if one adopts an evidentialist view of historical knowledge such that one needs evidence to have such knowledge, it does not follow that *every* feature of the belief must stem from the evidence. This is particularly the case if we adopt an externalist account of knowledge, since such accounts were developed in part to emphasize the degree to which we lack voluntary control over our beliefs, in contrast with internalist 'ethics of belief' that claim we have an intellectual duty to proportion belief to evidence.[11]

---

[11] I don't mean to imply here that an internalist must be committed to such an ethic

In Chapter 9 we examined 'ethics of belief' that prescribe that the degree to which one believes something must always correspond directly to the evidence available, and found such views wanting. However, there is a bit more to be said on the issue. We might begin by noting that 'degree of belief' is not a clear notion. One might distinguish, for example, the *firmness* with which I hold a belief (perhaps understood in terms of degree of certainty) from the *tenacity* with which I hold a belief (perhaps understood as degree of reluctance to revise a belief). Neither of these qualities seems to be something we can always directly control, so any alleged ethical duty to govern them directly must immediately be seen as dubious. Nor does it seem plausible to claim that such a 'proportionality' between belief and evidence is always a good thing.

However we understand 'degree of belief' it seems to me it will not always correspond closely with degree of evidence, even if one claims that beliefs should be rooted in evidence. In other words, even if one is an evidentialist, the evidentialism could be construed as a 'threshold' requirement, not as a proportionality requirement.[12] Though one should not believe without evidence, the degree of belief does not have to correspond directly with the degree of evidence.

Let us consider first tenacity. Michael Banner, as well as others, has argued with great force that even in the natural sciences, investigators often justifiably hold on to beliefs with a tenacity that does not correspond to the available experimental evidence.[13] Often it appears that if a belief is not held with a certain determination, it is impossible properly to develop it and discover relevant evidence. Something of this sort seems clearly to be the case within the religious life as well, where theologians have long argued that a certain type of con-

---

of belief, but merely that many internalists have accepted such a view, and that it would seem to be one motivation for adopting internalism.

[12] In 'Intellectual Morality in Clifford and James', George Mavrodes discusses the idea of taking W. K. Clifford's evidentialism as such a 'threshold' account, arguing that if we do so, then Clifford's view turns out to be consistent with William James's defence of 'The Will to Believe'. Mavrodes's essay is found in Gerald McCarthy (ed.), *The Ethics of Belief Debate* (Atlanta: Scholar's Press, 1986), 205–19.

[13] See Michael Banner, *The Justification of Science and the Rationality of Religious Belief* (Oxford: Oxford University Press, 1990), 103–18.

firmation of truth claims is found through a commitment that allows those claims to be tested.

Nor does it seem plausible to claim that degree of psychological certitude or confidence must always correspond simply with evidence. There may be some beliefs that must be held with passion if they are held at all. For example, there are some beliefs that must be integrated into a complex emotional web because of the function the belief plays in the personality. Think of the belief that my wife loves me. Even if my evidence for this is less than perfect, if I continue to believe it, and continue to be committed to my marriage, I am best off believing this with all the gusto I can muster, in view of the role the belief plays in the relationship.[14] On any plausible account of belief there will be many 'pragmatic' aspects that have an impact on the manner in which beliefs are held.

The evidentialist who is willing to look at the value of the non-evidentialist story might well argue that though our faith rests on evidence, the certainty and conviction that accompany faith result from the internal testimony of the Holy Spirit, as the Spirit awakens us to our desperate need and the tremendous good offered to us by God's redemptive act. The belief may be based on evidence but the quality and intensity of the belief are not based solely on evidence.

Of the three remaining problems for the evidentialist, I am convinced that the difficulty of forming and justifying antecedent assumptions is by far the most significant. The other two may in fact collapse into this one, since it is plausible that arguments about miracles and disagreements about the reliability of Scripture usually boil down to differences in antecedent assumptions. It is a fact that it strikes some people as quite likely that God would offer some kind of revelation of himself, while this strikes others as quite unlikely. Those who think the latter is the case will naturally require more evidence to accept a particular alleged revelation as genuine. This situation in which arguments reach an impasse because of

---

[14] Of course this is not an argument that commitment justifies belief in the spouse in *any* circumstances. A spouse who is being abused does not have merely 'less than perfect evidence' of the other spouse's love, but instead has good evidence that he or she does not truly love or else that the love is pathological in character. Such evidence should not be ignored.

underlying intuitive disagreements is hardly an unusual one in philosophy.

The evidentialist who is also an externalist, and who accepts the story of the witness of the Holy Spirit as complementary to the evidentialist account, may take some comfort here, however. The evidentialist who is worried about the status of these antecedent estimates of probability is in the following situation. Some things strike him as probable that do not so strike others. The worry is that his acceptance of such an estimate of probability is therefore subjective and arbitrary. If, however, he believes in God's providential care and the internal testimony of the Holy Spirit, then he has a reason for not regarding his intuitive judgements as groundless and arbitrary. For he is likely to attribute the appeal these judgements have for him to the work of the Spirit.

That hardly constitutes impressive evidence to a sceptic. However, in the imagined case the person is not a sceptic, but someone who finds these judgements reasonable. The fact that he has available to him a coherent story about how he comes to make such judgements might stiffen his convictions if he is tempted to worry about the fact that his intuitive judgements are not universally shared. The evidential story that may fail as apologetical argument for some opponent who doubts some particular premiss may still be a correct account of how a person knows.

Here we must recall the distinction that William Alston insists upon: the distinction between being justified and showing that one is justified. If the believer's knowledge is rooted in a process (the work of the Holy Spirit) that is a truth-conducive ground, then whether the knowledge in question is basic or evidentially mediated, it can qualify as knowledge, *regardless of whether the believer can produce an argument that will satisfy some particular opponent*. Being justified or warranted in a belief is one thing; being able to justify a belief to someone else is another.

I conclude that if externalism provides a cogent account of knowledge, then the Christian community does not have to and should not make a choice between the evidentialist and non-evidentialist accounts of historical religious knowledge.

Whichever account one finds to be primary, one can still regard the other as a valuable complement. In the final two chapters I shall examine a case of an individual who claims to have such knowledge of the Christian story, sketching how the person himself understands the situation, and seeking to determine whether this person has violated any epistemological duties, and exhibits valuable epistemological virtues. I shall look particularly at the idea that claims to know about the historical components of the Christian story are undercut or even defeated by contemporary critical study of the New Testament.

13

Historical Scholarship and
the Layperson:
A Case Study

IT is time to survey the terrain covered. I began by a look at the problematic status of the incarnational narrative, and an argument that recent recognition of the limitations of Enlightenment metaphysics and epistemology opens the door to a reconsideration of the viability of the narrative as historical. I first tried to show that a great deal would be lost by giving up historicity. Readings of the story as non-historical myth or as illustrations of moral truth leave out some of the central dynamics of Christian faith: at the heart of Christianity is a conviction that in the life of Jesus of Nazareth, God acted so as to make possible human salvation and a new kind of relation between God and humans.

Nor can the significance of history be limited to the events. The relationship becomes actual for particular individuals through conscious faith in Jesus as God incarnate. Hence, though God is doubtless at work throughout human history, and though people who lack conscious faith in Jesus in this life will not necessarily be permanently excluded from God's fellowship, an understanding of what God has done in Jesus is none the less the path to eternal life for those who respond to the story in faith.

The story cannot of course be true if it is incoherent. Hence I next examined the central concept of the story, the concept of incarnation. Here I argued that though such an event is certainly surprising, even paradoxical, to human thought, we have no good reason to believe it is logically impossible. We have limited, reliable, a priori knowledge of God, and if there are no good arguments showing the concept is incoherent, we are reasonable to consider its possibility, and think through various plausible models, such as the kenotic and the two-minds accounts, for how such an incarnation could occur. A kenotic model offers particular promise in developing a reading of the story that has great religious power and does full justice to the humanness of the Jesus seen in the New Testament.

Another stumbling block to the viability of the incarnational narrative is its miraculous character. Here in particular the baneful effects of Enlightenment epistemology and misconceptions of science can be seen. Against such views I argued that we have no good reasons to rule out miracles as possible or knowable, nor any reason to believe that God cannot act in history. Such positive claims about miracles run strongly counter to what many theologians have claimed about the methods that must be followed in order to be 'critical historians', but a careful examination of those claims shows that the believer in the incarnation should not be intimidated by them. Claims about the impossibility of rooting religious truths in history often rest on unjustified a priori assumptions about the character of religious truth.

The principles that it is alleged must be followed by critical historians, dealing with such things as the uniformity of experience and the nature of historical causality, are systematically ambiguous. If interpreted platitudinously, they are acceptable to religious believers, but then do not rule out taking the incarnational narrative as historically true. When interpreted in ways that incorporate Enlightenment metaphysics, for example by ruling out miracles, they do undermine the narrative. However, when interpreted in this way such principles are not binding on religious believers who do not share the naturalistic world-view.

After a brief look at the contemporary epistemological scene, I then looked at two kinds of accounts of how knowledge of the narrative might be gained. The evidentialist story sees the knowledge as rooted in historical evidence, while the Reformed story sees the knowledge as grounded in the workings of the Holy Spirit in the life of the believer. The two stories turn out not to be rivals, but complementary in a number of ways.

If we assume the correctness of the Reformed account, the evidential story is valuable for multiple reasons. First, evidence can be one way the Holy Spirit operates so as to produce belief; hence the evidential account can be regarded as a special case of the Reformed story, though the Reformed account also allows for the knowledge of the Gospel to be epistemologically basic. The evidential story can also be the tale that is told when one is attempting to convince another of the truth of the narrative. The evidential story can be seen in some cases as providing a way of dealing with the question of how 'second-level knowledge' is possible by showing that the believer has the knowledge she has gained through the operation of the Spirit. Finally, and perhaps most significantly, the evidential case can be valuable in undercutting or rebutting alleged defeaters.

Someone who is committed to the evidentialist account as the primary one can also gain help from the Reformed account. The Reformed story which sees the crucial factor as the witness of the Holy Spirit can reasonably increase the confidence of the believer who relies on the evidentialist story but is worried about the fact that certain features of the evidential case are not convincing to everyone. The Reformed story may also account for certain aspects of faith, such as its tenacity and confidence, that do not seem to stem solely from evidence. And since all evidential arguments at certain points must appeal to premisses which appear doubtful to some, the Reformed account can help alleviate the worry that embracing these premisses is arbitrary by explaining the appeal of the premisses as due to the work of the Spirit.

From an externalist point of view, both these stories are viable accounts. If we assume William Alston's epistemological position, knowledge is seen as a true belief that is justified in the evaluative sense, or warranted (to use Plantinga's language, which I prefer), which simply means that the belief is based on a truth-conducive ground. From such a viewpoint, if the story of Jesus is true, and if it has been formed and continues to be held on the basis of an adequate ground, then the believer knows the story, whether the knowledge be basic or rooted in propositional evidence. To take the case where the knowledge is basic, if the Holy Spirit operates so as to produce belief by helping the individual come to understand her condition as one that needs precisely what the narrative seems to offer, and instils a confidence that the narrative is trustworthy because God speaks to her through it, then she really does know the story, if the story is true and if that Spirit-filled process puts her in a strong position to get at the truth. Or, to look at the evidential case, someone who has been guided by the Spirit to consider the signs and wonders done by Jesus and the trustworthiness of the historical testimony, and has thereby been led to faith, is similarly privileged, provided that the story is true and that the inferences in question are ones that reliably lead to true beliefs.

13.1. APOLOGETICS AND UNDERSTANDING HOW KNOWLEDGE IS GAINED

But is the story true? And is the process that leads to belief really a reliable one? We have already seen that it may not be possible to answer such questions in a non-circular manner, particularly if the knowledge is grounded in a fundamental belief-inducing process. This is because of the nature of human knowledge generally, and not because of any specific characteristics of religious knowledge. The circularity in question is not necessarily a vicious circularity, but simply shows that we cannot certify the basic processes that produce knowledge without assuming that we already have some knowledge of the type in question.

Nevertheless, the questions about the truth of the story are legitimate ones. One way of understanding them is to see them as challenges or perhaps as friendly enquiries from one who does not share the beliefs in question. Such a person may be taken as saying, 'How can *I* know the story is true? How can *I* know the process you speak of is a reliable one?' What must be seen is that an attempt to answer such questions is not identical with an account of how the knowledge is gained. What is called for by the questions is apologetics. Apologetics is a vital enterprise, but it is not identical with the task of gaining a reflective understanding of how the knowledge is gained. Once a person has come to know Jesus is the Son of God and has put her faith in Jesus, she may come to understand how the Spirit of God acted in her life to produce her beliefs. This understanding is valuable, but it is by no means the same thing as having an answer to a challenger or enquirer.

As I argued in Chapter 12, the task of the apologist must be understood to be specific and audience-relative. There is no once-and-for-all argument to demonstrate the truth of the incarnational narrative, but there are a variety of arguments and answers that can be given to objectors of various kinds.

What can link the task of apologetics and the task of understanding how one knows is the situation of the possible defeater. Obviously, if a belief is based on evidence, then it is vulnerable to counter-evidence, but even where a belief is basic, it is vulnerable in various ways. On the kind of moderate foundationalism I argued for in Chapter 9, basic propositions are not infallible or incorrigible, but are subject to being over-ridden or defeated. In a case where a belief conflicts with other beliefs, or is undermined by other evidence, then the same argument that might serve an apologetical function may become part of the story of how the individual has the knowledge in question.

For an educated person, the situation of encountering an alleged defeater in today's culture is by no means rare or unusual. I have in the course of this volume already responded to a number of such problems, such as the claim that the historicity of the narrative lacks religious significance, the claim that the concept of the incarnation is incoherent, and the claim that miracles are impossible or unknowable. There is, however, one problem area that I have not yet addressed in a systematic manner, and it is the crucial matter of contemporary historical New Testament scholarship.

It is easy to see that the New Testament plays a crucial role for the evidentialist story, whether this account be understood as a particular form of the Reformed account or as an alternative view. Though the philosophical first stage of the traditional 'two-stage' argument and the assumptions with which the New Testament are approached are also obviously crucial to this account, it remains true that the actual evidence that forms the heart of the case is centred on the New Testament. Hence the evidentialist cannot be indifferent to scholarly claims about what can be historically known on the basis of the New Testament. Even if the Holy Spirit is guiding the process by which the evidence is interpreted and assessed, one can imagine situations where the evidence accessible to an individual will either be insufficient for faith or positively count against faith.

It is less obvious, perhaps, but it is also vitally important for the version of the Reformed account that sees the knowledge of the incarnational narrative as basic to come to terms with New Testament scholarship, at least in the case of most educated believers. Beliefs cannot be insulated from other beliefs. Though I may have formed a basic belief that Jesus is the Son of God and that the New Testament is a reliable witness to his story through the witness of the Holy Spirit, and I may regard the witness of the Scriptures as 'self-authenticating' in the sense explained in Chapter 11, I am aware that people have made similar claims to know things on the basis of divine guidance that I would view as mistaken. I cannot regard myself or my own convictions, even—perhaps especially—my convictions about the workings of God in my life as infallible. Hence I may well be troubled by reasonable doubt of my convictions if respected authorities, New Testament scholars for instance, claim that my beliefs are false or at least historically dubious.

To some degree New Testament scholarship that takes a sceptical attitude towards the incarnational narrative is grounded in anti-supernaturalistic assumptions. To the degree that the sceptic is motivated by doubt about the possibility of miracles or even doubt about the possibility of divine action in history at all, these doubts may be alleviated by the kinds of considerations advanced in Chapters 7 and 8. However, it is by no means the case that all scholarly doubt about the historicity of the narrative rests on such philosophical assumptions. A good deal of scepticism is fuelled by such factors as discrepancies between the four Gospels, and features of the narrative that seem to reflect in a transparent way the needs of the Early Church rather than the historical situation in early-first-century Palestine.

I shall attempt to look at this difficulty in the remainder of this chapter and in the concluding chapter. In looking at the problem, I shall presuppose a case where the believer takes her faith to be directly grounded in the testimony of the Holy Spirit, in the manner described in Chapter 11. I choose this case, rather than the evidentialist case, for several reasons. First of all, it is more typical of Christian experience. Few people become Christians as a result of reading historical apologetics. Secondly, since the case of a person whose beliefs are based on evidence can be seen as a special case of the working of the Spirit, one way the Spirit works to produce faith, much of what can be correctly said about the case of basic knowledge will apply to mediated knowledge as well.

13.2. A CASE STUDY

Imagine a young man, call him James, raised in a non-Christian home, who begins to attend a Christian youth meeting. He hears the claims of the Gospel from the youth workers, such claims as the following: that he, along with other human beings, is sinful and in need of forgiveness and healing; that Jesus of Nazareth is the Son of God who came to be the Saviour of all humans, including James, through his life, death, and resurrection; that James can appropriate the gift of divine forgiveness and begin a new relationship with God if he becomes a part of the new community that Jesus established, by becoming a follower of Jesus in trusting faith.

As James reflects on these claims in the light of his experiences, he begins to read the New Testament, both the Gospel accounts of the life of Jesus and the understanding of the meaning of Jesus' life, death, and resurrection to be found in Acts and the Epistles. As he reads, he discovers that he is gripped by a conviction that the claims of the Gospel are true. As a result of his participation in the youth group, he publicly commits his life to Jesus, is baptized, and joins a local church.

As a high school student, James is aware in a vague way that many people do not believe the New Testament is entirely accurate, but he himself is content with a conviction that the entire Bible is 'the Word of God'. When he goes to the university, however, James encounters a crisis of faith when he takes an introductory religion class, and is exposed to sceptical claims about the New Testament.

He discovers, for example, that most New Testament scholars do not believe that the 'I am' sayings attributed to Jesus in the Gospel of John, in which Jesus says such things as 'I am the way, the truth, and the life', and 'I am the bread of life', are historically accurate. Much of the nativity story is widely regarded as non-historical legend. Many of the miracle stories are similarly regarded as legendary, with the possible exception of some healings and exorcisms, which in turn are often regarded as instances of psychosomatic healings which can be accepted as historically reliable without really admitting that miracles occur in a strong sense.

Even the resurrection of Jesus, while not usually denied outright, at least by Christian scholars, is often reinterpreted in a manner that significantly reduces or even eliminates its miraculous character. Instead of accepting the Gospel narratives that clearly imply that the tomb of Jesus was empty, and that Jesus' dead body had been miraculously transformed, the resurrection is often described simply as 'the Easter event', which is understood as a set of experiences enjoyed by the followers of Jesus. As James reads more of the scholarly literature about the New Testament, he discovers that some scholars doubt the authenticity of the visits to the empty tomb, regarding these narratives as stories invented much later. The descriptions of these resurrection experiences the scholars talk about seem somewhat vague to James, but he notices a definite tendency to interpret the experiences in ways that did not require anything miraculous.[1]

What should James do when he encounters such claims? In the remainder of this chapter, I will consider a number of possible responses, on the assumption that James lacks the ability to make an informed scholarly judgement himself. In the final chapter I shall push the question further, looking at the case in which James is able to do a deeper investigation of

[1] For an example, see John Hick's discussion of the resurrection in *The Metaphor of God Incarnate* (London: SCM Press, 1993) in which he speculates that the original experience of Peter and 'perhaps some others of the twelve' were experiences that are similar to the 'near-death experiences' which have been reported so abundantly in recent years' (p. 24).

the problems. In every case I shall try to look at them from the perspective of a responsible epistemic agent; that is, I shall ask whether if James holds on to his faith he would be violating some epistemic duty or failing to exhibit some important epistemic virtue.

13.3. DETERMINING WHAT IS ESSENTIAL TO THE STORY

Before looking at James's options with respect to the challenge posed by New Testament scholarship, there is one preliminary consideration that deserves attention, and that is to fix with more precision what the incarnational narrative he is committed to believing includes. What is essential to the narrative and what is inessential? What is important and what is unimportant? And what kind of accuracy is at stake? Just what must be the case for the narrative to be judged historically reliable?

Prior to his encounter at the university, James may have had a somewhat naïve view of what the story must include, and what it meant for it to be accurate. He might, for example, have vaguely pictured the Gospel accounts as providing word-for-word transcripts of the exact speeches of Jesus, and precise descriptions of the actions a video crew would have recorded had the crew followed Jesus continuously. Such beliefs about the accuracy of the story may have been linked to views James had been taught about the Bible when he became a Christian. Perhaps he had come to believe the Bible was inspired by God and that it was completely 'inerrant', and it was somewhat natural for James to understand such claims in terms of contemporary 'scientific' standards. (James was himself studying chemistry at the university.) If James did think something like this, it is likely that such a belief was held only vaguely and inarticulately, for it would not survive much careful scrutiny.

Even without the benefit of an encounter with critical biblical scholarship, a careful reader of the four Gospel accounts is struck by many differences between them. What appears to be the same incident is often described in significantly different ways, and as occurring at different times and in different orders. What appears to be the same speech differs from one account to the other. For example, James notices that in the account of the Sermon on the Mount given in Luke, Jesus says, 'Blessed are the poor', while in Matthew the blessed are described as 'poor in spirit'. Of course in some cases the narratives could be talking about two distinct though similar incidents, and it is very possible that Jesus as a teacher may have varied his teaching from occasion to occasion. However, attempts to 'harmonize' the differences in this way are not always plausible. For example, with respect to the story of the resurrection, there are differences in the number of people who are said to go to the tomb, the time of their going, and so forth.

As James thinks about the story in the light of these facts, he may reasonably conclude that his earlier understanding of the nature of the story and its truthfulness was somewhat naïve and anachronistic. Since the differences between the accounts are so obvious, if God did inspire these accounts, it cannot have been his intention to give a precisely accurate transcript of the life of Jesus. It occurs to James that the biblical accounts leave out entirely lots of information, including some information that James would very much like to know. There is, for example, no information about the physical appearance of Jesus or the character of his speaking voice. Almost no information is provided about the childhood and upbringing of Jesus. More surprisingly, there is precious little information about the psychological states of Jesus. Occasionally, the accounts describe Jesus as feeling compassion or anger, but by and large the narrative is terse and lean, with very little insight given into Jesus' own self-consciousness or thinking processes. (The latter omission is particularly surprising since James had noticed that many of the 'lives of Jesus' that have been written in the past by supposedly objective historical scholars had included a lot of information about the special character of Jesus' experience and 'God-consciousness'.) James begins to think about what aspects of the story are really important.

It seems reasonable for James to conclude that not every historical detail of the life of Jesus has significance. If the biblical narratives were inspired by God, and they are silent about so much, then clearly there is much that is of little or no importance. After all, God could have chosen to inspire a precise, complete record; the fact that God did not do so implies that the possession of such a record cannot be important. If this is so, then it occurs to James that some of the details that are included in the records may turn out to be unimportant as well, particularly if different accounts of those details are given in different Gospels. If the Gospels are inspired, and if the four Gospels show no particular concern for such details, then it seems reasonable to conclude that teaching about such things was not part of the divine purpose in inspiring the writings. It strikes James that what must really be important is the accuracy of the general picture given of the character, teachings, and actions of Jesus.

For example, did Jesus really teach the things attributed to him in the Gospels? Did he really proclaim that the kingdom of God was imminent and that his hearers should repent? Did he really consort freely with sinners and outcasts, and proclaim and offer forgiveness to all who truly repented of their ways? Did he really perform miraculous deeds and teach with an astonishing personal authority? Did he really select twelve disciples, and teach them to eat and drink bread and wine in a memorial meal, as the basis of a new community? Did he really foresee and predict his own death and see that death as a sacrifice for others? Did he really die on the cross, and was he really raised from the dead? James decides that the purpose of the biblical account was to answer such questions as these. Though theologians might give various technical accounts of what the 'inspiration' of the accounts might come to and what such inspiration would imply by way of accuracy, he decides that if someone who relies on these accounts arrived at true answers to such questions as these, then the accounts were indeed reliable. If they were inspired by God, the inspiration must have been directed at this kind of reliability and truthfulness.[2]

---

[2] For a careful attempt to spell out with some precision what it might mean to say the New Testament narratives are historically reliable, see Peter van Inwagen, 'Critical Studies of the New Testament and the User of the New Testament', in Eleonore Stump and Thomas P. Flint (eds.), *Hermes and Athena: Biblical Exegesis and Philosophical Theology* (Notre Dame, Ind.: University of Notre Dame Press, 1993). Van Inwagen characterizes historical reliability in three different ways, of which the first is most like my own view. This is the view that with respect to the acts and words of Jesus, the narratives recounting them are reliable provided two conditions are met: '(i) Jesus said and did at least most of the things ascribed to him in those narratives, and (ii) any false statements about what Jesus said and did that the narratives may contain will do no harm to those users of the New Testament who accept them as true because they

This focusing of the narrative by no means resolves all James's difficulties. At plenty of places, the answers given by the biblical narratives seem to him to be challenged by contemporary historical scholarship. There is still a degree of vagueness in his understanding of what is essential to the narrative; for example, in reading various orthodox theologians he notices some give much more importance to the details of the infancy narratives than others. To James the virgin birth seems important; after all, it had been included in the early creeds. It seems less crucial to him whether the story of the visit of the Magi is accurate, except in so far as doubt about such a detail might inspire doubt about the general credibility of the narrative. Nevertheless, he decides that he has a clear enough idea of what was important to think about the challenge that has been posed to his faith.

13.4. POSSIBLE RESPONSES TO SCEPTICAL HISTORICAL SCHOLARSHIP

What options are open to James at this point? I shall discuss several possibilities in a particular order, beginning in this chapter with responses that might be regarded as 'less critical' or reflective and moving towards increasingly reflective responses in the concluding chapter. However, these responses are by no means mutually exclusive. James might well find more than one of them attractive. In fact, I will discuss them

occur in the New Testament' (p. 169). The concept of 'doing no harm' is explained through an analogy with a military leader in Italy who relies on a map of Italy, one that is accurate enough in most respects, but that contains erroneous information about the founders and dates of founding of various Churches. If the general believes everything on the map, and thereby forms some erroneous beliefs about the dates certain Churches are founded, he has not been harmed as a military leader, so long as the map is accurate in other ways. Of course the relevant role and kind of harm in the case of the incarnational narrative would be spiritual and moral rather than military in character. The kind of historical truthfulness that I here attribute to my hypothetical James is intended to be a common-sense version of what van Inwagen spells out, the kind of view that an ordinary person such as James could reasonably be expected to have. An account by a New Testament scholar that resembles this view of van Inwagen's in certain ways can be found in Darrell Bock, 'The Words of Jesus in the Gospels: Live, Jive, or Memorex', in *Jesus Under Fire: Modern Scholarship Reinvents the Historical Jesus* (Grand Rapids, Mich.: Zondervan, 1995).

in an order such that later strategies can be seen as reinforcing or complementing earlier ones, though they may also be capable of independent use.

13.4.1. *Appeal to the Original Ground*

The hypothetical situation we have described is as follows. James has become convinced that the incarnational narrative is true; he believes that Jesus is the Son of God who became incarnate so as to die on behalf of humans and overcome sin and death through his resurrection, thereby establishing a new people of God. James's conviction that the story is true has developed as he has heard the story and reflected on its implications for his life. He believes that the Holy Spirit has developed this conviction as James has opened himself up to the story and begun to respond in faith to the person of Jesus. On an externalist account, if the story is true and the ground of James's belief—that is, the whole process and circumstances which have produced the belief—is a truth-conducive one, then James knows the narrative to be true.

The problem is that James has encountered an alleged defeater for his belief, a reason to think his beliefs, or at least some of them, are false.[3] The first possible response that James might take is simply to decide to ignore this defeater, because of his confidence in the original ground of his belief.

This may appear epistemically irresponsible, and in many cases such a response would be epistemically irresponsible. One of the epistemic virtues highlighted in Chapter 9 is a humility that takes seriously our human finitude and fallibility and therefore pays attention to others who wish to call our attention to what those others perceive as our mistakes.

However, I do not think a decision on James's part to discount the defeater is necessarily irresponsible on his part. It is true that a person who encounters such a defeater has some reason to doubt or reject what he believes on other grounds, and is therefore not in an ideal epistemic situation. If possible, it would seem good to try to resolve the problem by further enquiry or reflection. However, it is not always going to be the

---

[3] See pp. 293–4 for a brief account of overriders and defeaters.

case that further information will be available or that further reflection or enquiry will help. In that situation, what should a person do? The answer is not clear. Which response is more reasonable depends partly on the strength of the two competing beliefs. James now has grounds both for believing and for doubting the incarnational narrative. It would seem most reasonable for him to reflect on which grounds seem to him to be stronger. In some cases this doubtless means he will and should doubt his original belief. However, in other cases it would seem just as reasonable for James to doubt his doubts and hold fast to his convictions. If the conviction the Holy Spirit has produced in him is strong enough, he will probably simply decide that the defeater can be overcome in some way, even if he has no idea as to how it could be done.

It is important to point out here that a certain steadfastness or 'obstinacy' in non-religious beliefs is perfectly reasonable. Contrary to a popular view of science, expressed in 'falsificationist' theories for example, scientists do not necessarily abandon an accepted theory merely because they discover some data that appear to contradict the theory. Rather, they often regard such recalcitrant data as 'puzzles' to be solved, rather than as refutations of the theory.[4] In fact, it is clear that if theories were abandoned too quickly, they would never be adequately developed and we would lose the chance to see how certain problems can be solved.

Philosopher Basil Mitchell has considered a 'generic' version of James's problem in his essay 'The Layman's Predicament'.[5] James's problem is by no means unique: 'He (the layman) needs to make up his mind about innumerable issues, and yet he knows that he cannot conceivably muster the resources that are required to make a reasonable judgement.'[6] Think for example of the citizen who must decide whether scientific findings about damage to the ozone layer require new environmental laws. Mitchell says that one cannot always simply defer to experts in such cases.

---

[4] See Michael Banner, *The Justification of Science and the Rationality of Religious Belief* (Oxford: Oxford University Press, 1990), 177–82.
[5] Basil Mitchell, 'The Layman's Predicament', in *How to Play Theological Ping-Pong* (Grand Rapids, Mich.: Wm. B. Eerdmans, 1991).
[6] Ibid. 11.

First of all, what experts say sometimes is just nonsense. Secondly, the experts in a particular field often disagree. Thirdly, academic subjects seem to be subject to fads and other non-rational factors. Fourthly, knowledge is becoming so specialized that even 'experts' may not be expert with respect to many issues in their disciplines, and no one is really expert in the issues that people care most about. Finally, the experts from one discipline often contradict the experts from another.

In such a situation Mitchell argues the reasonableness of a moderate form of 'methodological conservatism'. In general methodological conservatism says that one should continue to believe what one already believes until there is clear evidence to the contrary. Mitchell points out, reasonably enough, that this cannot be the whole story. One must also be willing critically to evaluate established traditions. But in doing so one should continue to attach a significant weight to those traditions with their already established beliefs.

So I conclude that James may well be epistemically virtuous if, after encountering a challenge, he conservatively clings to his original beliefs, and decides his original ground is stronger than the reasons he has discovered to doubt the narrative. Of course it may be difficult for James to determine whether his ground is strong enough to bear this weight. He will realize, if he reflects on the matter, that his belief may be grounded in factors that are not truth-conducive, such as wish-fulfilment. However, he also sees that doubts may be similarly grounded in non-epistemic factors. His best option, if he cannot obtain further evidence, is simply to examine the situation as honestly as he can, and then hold to what appears true.

13.4.2. *Appeal to the Authority of the Church*

In some cases, exposure to claims that a belief one has is false may result in crippling doubts, and such doubts cannot always be resolved merely by appealing to the original ground of the belief. If James is in such a situation, then he may look around for some new evidence or ground to decide the question. Even if he is not crippled by doubts, he may well think his new situation calls for more reflection or consideration of new evidence if that is possible. Since he is a Christian and regards himself as a member of Christ's body, the Church, one thing James might do in this situation is consider the claims of the Church.

One might think that this kind of appeal to authority can have no legitimate bearing in such a situation, but this is a misunderstanding. Since we are assuming that James is not himself a historical scholar, his problem is generated precisely by what might be called an appeal to authority. Some people whom he has reason to consider competent authorities, such as his teachers and the biblical scholars whose books he has read, have made claims that some of his beliefs are false. Since the problem is generated by an appeal to authority, it is not unreasonable to respond by considering the testimony of an authority of a different kind.

Of course someone may challenge the competence of the Church to give testimony with regard to such matters, but such a challenge can in principle be raised with respect to any authority, including the guild of historical scholars.[7] Of course it may be desirable for James to examine the claims of the critics directly, and we will consider such responses presently. However, one should note that such a direct examination of the critical objections will not be a viable option for everyone. Not everyone will possess the educational prerequisites and time to undertake such study. Our hypothetical James is a university student, and thus might be thought to have the critical ability to pursue such study. However, if James is a student of science or engineering, as we have imagined, it is not clear that he will possess the necessary background for such study, even if he has the basic intelligence required, and of course it is very likely that he will not possess the time to acquire the necessary knowledge. In such a situation, the normal recourse is an appeal to competent authority, and James may well consider the Church to be such an authority.

For this kind of appeal to have weight, James must of course

---

[7] Jon Levenson, who is himself a first-rate historical scholar of the Hebrew Bible, in his book *The Hebrew Bible, the Old Testament, and Historical Criticism: Jews and Christians in Biblical Studies* (Louisville, Ky.: Westminster/John Knox Press, 1993), does an excellent job of arguing that the community of historical scholars, like various religious communities, is a 'tribe' with its own historical limitations and blind spots. Hence it is by no means the case that the insights of a religious community will always be inferior to the conclusions of scholars.

have some reason to think the teachings of the Church and its testimony to be true, but it is quite conceivable that this condition can be met. 'Church' here is ambiguous. It might mean primarily the teachings of James's present church, perhaps even his local church, which he of course sees as a particular segment of the universal Church, or the referent might be primarily to that historic, universal Church.

If James understands 'church' to refer primarily to his local church, he might for example be impressed by the lives of the people that he has encountered in the church, or by his own experiences with church life. Perhaps he has acquired a strong consciousness of meeting God in the communion services, or a strong sense of God's presence in times of prayer with others. Through these kinds of experiences James might well reasonably come to believe that the church is a visible instrument of the work of God and conclude that its teachings are likely to be reliable.

If the appeal is to the local church, this is probably best understood as a broadening of James's original conviction that his belief is based upon the work of the Holy Spirit, for James is in this case really assuming that his church provides a broader theatre for the work of the Spirit. Such a broadening is not necessarily valueless, even though the ultimate warrant is of the same kind as the original ground, since it provides some check on James's individual fallibility. If his church does teach that the New Testament narratives are truthful, and if James has reason to think that his church is a reliable authority about this, then James might well take that fact as settling the tension between the grounded belief he has and the alleged defeater.

If James takes the term 'Church' to refer primarily to the historic Church as it has existed down through the ages, then the appeal will be different, depending on how James understands the referent of 'Church'. In this case the appeal does not have to be simply to the immediate witness of the Holy Spirit, but can rest on the claim that the Church as an historical community has preserved a truth granted to its founding members. If James takes some particular church to be an authoritative embodiment of that historic, universal Church, then the appeal will be to the teaching of that church.

If James believes that no one church is the embodiment of

that universal Church, then the appeal is more complicated. He might in this case look for those teachings that are present universally or almost universally in all the branches of Christianity. Since in the contemporary situation some Christian theologians appear to deny many of the credal claims universally accepted in earlier times, there is a danger that almost nothing will pass this test. However, James might well decide that not every contemporary representation of Christian faith is part of the authentic Church, just as many versions of Christianity were judged heretical during the time of the Church Fathers. Contemporary theologians who deny elements of the creeds that seem both central to the faith and to have been universally accepted in earlier times may thereby exclude themselves from the relevant historical community, at least with respect to the question as to who is qualified to represent the Church's teachings.[8] If that community of faith is rooted in universal or near-universal Christian beliefs, then those who deny some of those beliefs cut themselves off from that tradition.

The Christian churches, at least until the advent of historical criticism, down through the ages do give virtually unanimous testimony that the Gospel narratives are historically reliable with respect to the central elements in the story of Jesus. Though many details in the biblical narratives were regarded as having allegorical interpretations, the possibility of such allegorical interpretations was never regarded as ruling out the historicity of Jesus' ministry, atoning death, and resurrection. The testimony of the Church to this is not only given in credal statements, but is present very powerfully in the preaching and liturgical practices of the Church. To the degree that James has reason to accept the testimony of the universal, historical Church, to that degree he has a reason to trust his original belief and discount any objections derived from New Testament scholarship. How strong these reasons are will depend on the

---

[8] I do not here wish to be seen as making any judgements as to who is 'in' the Church in the sense of being a member of the family of God. It is quite possible for a person to be accepted into God's family but fail to be a qualified teacher of the Church. On this point compare the argument in Ch. 5 that individuals who lack conscious faith in Jesus in this life, such as adherent of other faiths, may nevertheless be included in the kingdom of God.

strength of his reasons to accept the testimony of the Church, as compared with the strength of the objections from historical scholars.

This last comment concerning the relative strength of the objections from historical scholars suggests the desirability of James undertaking a critical examination of this scholarship, so as to determine for himself the strength of the objections. In the final chapter, I shall look at some possible outcomes of such an examination, along with some concluding thoughts on the defence of the incarnational narrative.

14

Conclusions: Deeper Encounters with Historical Scholarship and Prospects for Apologetics

I⊤ is now time to consider the outcome if James devotes some serious study to contemporary historical scholarship concerning the story of Jesus. Such an examination can be undertaken at many different levels, and at some levels, as we have noted, a great amount of preliminary knowledge is required in order to be competent to form critical judgements. I shall look at the situation by imagining various levels of study on the part of James.

14.1. REVIEW OF THE CONCLUSIONS OF IMPORTANT SCHOLARS

If James has the time, it certainly seems possible for him to do at least a study of the conclusions of historical New Testament critics. At a beginning level, even if he lacks the competence to follow the work of scholars in detail, much less evaluate their arguments, he might be able to examine the claims of recognized scholars and compare them. Such a comparative study would, I think, give James a possible way of undercutting the objections he has encountered. For one of the most striking facts that will be evident even on a superficial examination of such scholarship will be the fundamental and radical disagreements that permeate it.

Such disagreements are both synchronic and diachronic. At

any given time people who appear to be equally competent, well-trained, and respected scholars disagree fundamentally about many of the most crucial issues. Such disagreements can easily inspire and justify scepticism on the part of an outsider as to whether any of the parties to such disputes really have beliefs that are strongly grounded. Even where there is consensus at present among scholars, a degree of scepticism seems justified if one looks at the history of the discipline, for it seems clear that what was widely accepted by one generation of scholars is often doubted or rejected by the next.

A few examples of such disagreements will be helpful at this point. There is, for instance, a fundamental disagreement among scholars as to whether the teachings or the actions of Jesus are more likely to have been historically preserved. One scholarly group holds that the narratives about Jesus are highly coloured by mythology, but that at least some of the teachings of Jesus, perhaps those preserved in the hypothetical source Q, thought to have been a 'sayings gospel', are likely to have been preserved.[1] Other scholars are quite sceptical about this, doubting even the existence of Q.[2] Some argue that not only is it the case that we know little about what Jesus taught, but that there may have been little in the way of a 'teaching' that was important in the life of the Early Church.[3] Some of these scholars argue that actions are much more likely to have been remembered than words, and that these actions provide a context for reconstructing what Jesus must have taught, to the degree that this can be known.[4]

This disagreement is closely tied to another fundamental

[1] See B. H. Streeter, *The Four Gospels: A Study of Origins*, 2nd edn. (London: Macmillan, 1930), for a classic defence of the hypothetical source, Q. A recent defender of Q who regards it as an independent and to some degree reconstructible source is John Dominic Crossan. See his *The Historical Jesus* (San Francisco: HarperCollins, 1991). Burton Mack has published an attempted reconstruction of Q; see his *The Lost Gospel: The Book of Q and Christian Origins* (San Francisco: HarperCollins, 1993).

[2] William Farmer and his students are the most well-known critics of the Q hypothesis. See Farmer's *The Gospel of Jesus: The Pastoral Relevance of the Synoptic Problem* (Louisville, Ky.: Westminster/John Knox Press, 1994) for an overview of recent work that is critical of the Q hypothesis.

[3] John Muddiman argued very powerfully that despite the fact that Jesus was known as 'teacher' he may not really have presented anything that could be called a 'teaching', in a lecture at Oxford, Hilary term, 1994, in a course on 'The Historical Jesus'.

[4] See e.g. E. P. Sanders, *Jesus and Judaism* (London: SCM Press, 1985), 4–13.

disagreement, one that concerns sources. Most scholars regard the Synoptic Gospels as the most important sources for our knowledge of the historical Jesus. However, there is wide-spread disagreement about the character of the Synoptic Gospels and their relation to each other. The most widely accepted view is that Mark is the earliest of the three Synoptics, and that Matthew and Luke relied on Mark, as well as another common source, Q, besides their own individual sources. However, even though this 'two-source' hypothesis is widely accepted, there are excellent scholars who defend the priority of Matthew to Mark, or who argue that there is no literary dependence, at least between Mark and Matthew.[5] Such dis-agreements about the relations between the Synoptics have large implications for other issues, such as the dating of the Gospels and their independence as sources.

When one turns from the Synoptics to other sources, dis-agreements loom just as large. The historical worth of John's Gospel is, for example, much disputed, a noted defender of its value being John A. T. Robinson.[6] Similar disagreements exist about such sources as the Gospel of Thomas. Though many scholars would regard this non-canonical work as a second-century work that shows knowledge of the Synoptics, some scholars regard it as containing independent and very early

---

[5] William R. Farmer is well known for his attacks on the two-source hypothesis and championing of the so-called 'Griesbach theory'. See his *The Synoptic Problem: A Critical Analysis* (New York: Macmillan, 1964), and more recently, *Jesus and the Gospel: Tradition, Scripture, and Canon* (Philadelphia: Fortress Press, 1982); and *The Pastoral Relevance of the Synoptic Problem*, cited in n. 2. For others who doubt the two-source hypothesis see the work of classics scholar John M. Rist, *On the Independence of Matthew and Mark* (Cambridge: Cambridge University Press, 1978), who argues that though Luke probably knew the other Synoptics, there is no good evidence of a literary relationship between Matthew and Mark. Also see John Wenham, *Redating Matthew, Mark and Luke* (Downer's Grove, Ill.: InterVarsity Press, 1992). Works such as Rist's and Wenham's do not appear to be very well received among New Testament scholars. However, many of the arguments they mount with relevance to the logic behind the case for the two-source theory are quite understandable to a layperson and seem very powerful. Anyone who has been involved in an academic field has seen the ways in which what is currently accepted in a field may be due to accidental, non-rational factors and hence will not necessarily be intimidated by the dominant scholarly view, especially when the issues bear on logical and literary judgements which do not require expert historical knowledge.

[6] See John A. T. Robinson, *The Priority of John* (London: SCM Press, 1985). Also see his *Redating the New Testament* (Philadelphia: Westminster, 1976).

material, and even seem to prefer it in many cases to the Synoptics.[7]

As one might expect, in addition to these disagreements with respect to sources, there are also profound disagreements about what Jesus was actually like, disputes that are partly grounded in the disputes over sources. One currently fashionable view of Jesus sees him as a Hellenistic sage quite similar to a wandering Cynic philosopher.[8] Other scholars believe that Jesus is much better understood if his Jewish origins are made the major context for interpretation.[9]

There are many other basic disagreements. Jesus is seen as essentially apolitical; Jesus is seen as consciously challenging the oppression of the poor in the Roman empire.[10] Jesus was an apocalyptic preacher who thought the world would soon end; Jesus was a preacher of 'realized eschatology' who saw the kingdom of God as already present in embryonic form.[11] Jesus challenged the Mosaic law and thereby incurred sharp opposition; Jesus had no significant differences with the Mosaic law.[12] Jesus formed a community with the intention of

---

[7] Crossan's *The Historical Jesus* is again an excellent example, but much of the work of the so-called Jesus Seminar in the United States reflects this view of Thomas. The disagreement about *Thomas* often seems linked to disagreements about Q and its worth. Since *Thomas* is largely a collection of sayings, its discovery has provided ammunition for those who believe in the existence of Q as an early 'sayings gospel'. See James M. Robinson and Helmut Koester, *Trajectories Through Early Christianity* (Philadelphia: Fortress Press, 1971), for a strong defence of this view.

[8] See Burton Mack, *A Myth of Innocence: Mark and Christian Origins* (Philadelphia: Fortress Press, 1988), as well as *The Lost Gospel: The Book of Q and Christian Origins* (cited above). Also see John Dominic Crossan, *The Historical Jesus: The Life of a Mediterranean Jewish Peasant* (San Francisco: HarperCollins, 1991).

[9] E. P. Sanders, *Jesus and Judaism* (Philadelphia: Fortress Press, 1985), is a good example of a scholar who stresses the Jewishness of Jesus.

[10] Good discussions of Jesus in relation to politics can be found in Marcus Borg, *Conflict, Holiness, and Politics in the Teaching of Jesus* (New York: Edwin Mellen Press, 1984), and Richard A. Horsley, *Jesus and the Spiral of Violence* (San Francisco: Harper & Row, 1987). Sanders, on the other hand, tends to view Jesus as essentially apolitical in the sense of 'lacking a political strategy' in *Jesus and Judaism*.

[11] Albert Schweitzer, who followed J. Weiss, gave a famous interpretation of Jesus as an apocalyptic preacher who expected the end of the world very soon in his *The Quest of the Historical Jesus* (1910). See C. H. Dodd, *The Parables of the Kingdom* (1935), rev. edn. (New York: Scribners, 1978), for a defence of the idea of 'realized eschatology'. N. T. Wright subjects the view that Jesus expected the end of the world to devastating criticism in *The New Testament and the People of God* (Minneapolis: Fortress Press, 1992).

[12] See Sanders, *Jesus and Judaism*, for a spirited defence of the claim that Jesus had no significant differences with the laws of Judaism and for a polemic against the large

founding or re-establishing a 'new Israel'; Jesus had no such intention.[13] And so it goes on.

What do these disagreements imply? They do not imply that the scholars involved in the disputes are never justified in holding their views. Some of them may well have good reasons for their views, and indeed, if we reject classical foundationalist type epistemologies, some of the disputed views may even amount to knowledge. My own discipline of philosophy provides a close analogy. Disagreements in philosophy are pervasive, but I would not myself take this to imply that no philosopher has good grounds for philosophical beliefs or ever knows any philosophical claim to be true.

What is implied, I think, by the disagreements in both cases is that the views of scholars on such disputed questions cannot provide a strong basis for other people to form beliefs. Anyone acquainted with the history of philosophy would know that it carries little rational weight that a large number, even a majority of philosophers, at a particular time hold a certain view. In the 1950s, for example, the majority of philosophers in England and America probably thought some positivist form of the verifiability theory of meaning was correct, but today such a view is almost abandoned. Similarly, it seems to me that the views of a group of New Testament scholars, even if they constitute a majority, carry little authority for outsiders if respected scholars equally conversant with the facts continue to disagree with that majority.

Does the fact that the conclusions of New Testament scholarship with regard to such disputed questions have little authority for the layperson mean that the layperson should remain agnostic about the question of the historical Jesus? That would only follow if the conclusions of historical New Testament

body of literature that interprets Jesus through 'Protestant' eyes as someone who came into conflict with the 'legalism' of Judaism.

[13] Those who see Jesus as intending to found a community cite the calling of the twelve and the institution of the Eucharist as particularly significant, since the number twelve could only be understood as in some way a restoration or refounding of Israel, and a memorial meal presupposes a continuing society. Those who see Jesus with Schweitzer as apocalyptic preacher who expected the end of the world naturally interpret the data differently. See Stephen Neill and N. T. Wright, *The Interpretation of the New Testament*, 2nd edn. (Oxford: Oxford University Press, 1988), 205–15 for a critique of the Schweitzer view.

scholarship provided the only legitimate basis for having beliefs about these matters. Some would argue that this is so. Van Harvey, for example, has argued that the person who is not a historical scholar has no right to hold any views about the historical Jesus at all.[14] Such a claim presupposes that the methods of critical, historical scholarship are the only methods available for getting at the historical truths in question.

Whatever one might want to say about this claim, it is not itself a claim that can be warranted by historical, critical scholarship, for it is essentially a philosophical and theological claim. One can see this not only by unpacking the implicit epistemology and 'ethic of belief' it contains, but even more clearly by considering the position it is excluding. The denial of a philosophical or theological proposition must itself be a philosophical or theological proposition, and Harvey is clearly making such a denial.

Theologians such as Calvin wish to maintain that the Spirit of God is alive and at work within human life in such a way as to make it possible for ordinary people to understand and believe the truth about Jesus of Nazareth. Roman Catholics wish to maintain that the witness of the Church with respect to the life and teachings of Jesus is a trustworthy guide to the truth, and that ordinary people who rely on that authority are reasonable to do so. These claims of Reformed and Catholic theologians (which are not mutually exclusive) may well be false, but it is hard to see how their falsity could be established on the basis of historical scholarship. If it can be shown that there is no Holy Spirit, or that the Holy Spirit does not act reliably so as to produce true beliefs about Jesus, then the Reformed claim can be shown to be false. But what will be needed to do this is not historical scholarship, but theological and philosophical argument. Hence the claim that historical scholarship is the only means of arriving at true beliefs about

[14] See Van Harvey, 'New Testament Scholarship and Christian Belief', in *Jesus in History and Myth*, ed. Gerald A. Larue and R. Joseph Hoffmann (Buffalo: Prometheus Books, 1986). Harvey's view here has the curious implication that neither Harvey himself nor any other historical biblical scholar should address a lay audience with respect to the historical Jesus, since that audience has no right to believe the scholar's claims.

Jesus is not itself a claim that can be warranted by historical scholarship. The Christian believer who finds either the Reformed or Catholic claims, or both of them, plausible, will have good reason to reject such a dogmatic claim on the part of the historical scholar.

If the layperson had to rely solely on historical scholarship as the means of forming historical beliefs about Jesus, then agnosticism might be the most reasonable policy, at least with respect to some important issues, though I certainly do not want to say that it would be impossible to sort through the conflicts and arrive at reasonable convictions. However, in our hypothetical situation, James does not regard historical scholarship as the only source of knowledge. James takes himself to have a ground for his beliefs about Jesus, that ground being the total circumstances of his life in which the truth of the Gospel has become evident as he has responded in faith to the assertions, promises, and demands he perceives God to be making upon him in Jesus. The problem was whether or not these beliefs continue to be reasonable when challenged by critical historical scholarship. In this situation, the disagreements within critical historical scholarship undermine any pretension that historical criticism has some strong claim to be a sure authority for the layperson and leave the original ground for the belief undefeated.

One might wonder whether or not it is arrogant of James to rely on his own judgement when by hypothesis he knows much less than the scholars in the field. Should he not defer to the judgements of scholars? However, the illusory force of this rhetorical question dissipates as soon as one asks 'Which scholars should he trust?'

14.2. UNCERTAINTY AND CRITERIA OF AUTHENTICITY

The claim that the conclusions of historical scholarship about the life of Jesus are very uncertain is one that New Testament scholars themselves frequently assert. In fact, there seems to be more consensus about this uncertainty than about anything else. Hence, if James decides that the conclusions of New Testament scholarship have no strong authority for him, he is doing no more than echoing what many New Testament scholars themselves claim.

This uncertainty emerges clearly if James examines the 'criteria of authenticity' employed by many New Testament scholars. If one approaches the New Testament text with the assumption that it may contain some historically reliable information, but that much of it is unreliable, it is naturally helpful to have some criteria to help in sorting out the reliable information from the unreliable information. New Testament scholars have indeed employed a number of 'criteria of authenticity' in looking at the Gospels, but here both James's common sense as an educated layperson, and the scholars themselves, agree that these criteria can produce very uncertain results at best.

A good example of this uncertainty is provided by the criterion of 'dissimilarity' or 'discontinuity', a criterion much employed by form critics. Reginald Fuller explains this criterion as follows: 'As regards the sayings of Jesus, traditio-historical criticism eliminates from the authentic sayings of Jesus those which are paralleled in the Jewish tradition on the one hand (apocalyptic and Rabbinic) and those which reflect the faith, practice and situations of the post-Easter Church as we know them from outside the Gospels.'[15] The idea seems to be that teachings that are paralleled in first-century Judaism or in the Early Church may perhaps be attributed to those communities; one should only attribute to Jesus what cannot possibly be the work of either of those communities.

Many New Testament scholars have pointed out what common sense confirms, which is that such a criterion cannot safely be used to generate a reliable picture of Jesus. At best such a criterion would provide a picture of what was idiosyncratic about Jesus, rather than what was characteristic. One could only conclude that the picture of Jesus that emerged was accurate of him as a whole if one knew in advance that there was no continuity between Jesus and the Judaism that nourished him or between Jesus and the Church that grew up from

---

[15] R. H. Fuller, *The Foundations of New Testament Christology* (London: Lutterworth, 1965), 18.

his life and work. Far from being known to be true, both of these claims seem enormously implausible.

Besides these logical difficulties, New Testament scholar Morna Hooker points out the practical difficulties in applying this criterion. Use of the criterion seems to presuppose a great deal of reliable knowledge about first-century Judaism and about the Early Church. But in fact, as Hooker points out, knowledge of both those communities is quite scanty in many ways, so that a judgement that a particular saying of Jesus is 'discontinuous' with a community may simply reflect our ignorance of that community.[16]

As I have stressed, the difficulties with this criterion are frequently noted by New Testament scholars themselves.[17] However, despite the acknowledgement of uncertainty, this criterion, and others that are also subject to varying degrees of uncertainty, continue to be used, perhaps because, as Hooker asserts, they are the only tools available.[18] A clear example of this continuing use of uncertain criteria can be seen in the recent work of John P. Meier. Meier is a moderate, middle-of-the-road New Testament scholar, who is certainly aware of the difficulties besetting the criterion of dissimilarity. Nevertheless, in arguing that the story of Jesus' miraculous stilling of the storm is unhistorical, Meier appeals to the fact that the narrative is discontinuous with other Gospel miracles but continuous with the type of miracle alleged to have been done by the Early Church as part of his case.[19] This use of the criterion by Meier seems doubly dubious, for if the criterion has any valid realm of application, it would surely be to the teachings of Jesus. On what possible grounds could one argue

---

[16] Morna Hooker, 'On Using the Wrong Tool', *Theology*, 75 (1972), 575.

[17] For some examples of critical discussions of this criterion and others, in addition to the article by Hooker cited above, see Craig A. Evans, 'Authenticity Criteria in Life of Jesus Research', *Christian Scholars Review*, 19/1 (Sept. 1989), 6–31; ch. 1 of *Who Was Jesus*, by N. T. Wright (London: SPCK, 1992); Robert H. Stein, 'The "Criteria" for Authenticity', in R. T. France and David Wenham (eds.), *Gospel Perspectives: Studies of History and Tradition in the Four Gospels* (Sheffield: SOT, 1980), i. 225–63; and A. E. Harvey, *Jesus and the Constraints of History* (London: Duckworth, 1982), 1–10.

[18] Hooker, 'On Using the Wrong Tool', 580–1.

[19] John P. Meier, *A Marginal Jew: Rethinking the Historical Jesus*, ii (New York: Doubleday, 1994), 932–3.

that a miracle done by Jesus must be dissimilar to miracles performed by his followers?

The uncertainty attached to the criterion of dissimilarity seems to be the clearest case, but other criteria used by New Testament scholars are also uncertain in their results. Take, for example, the criterion of multiple attestation. This criterion rests on the common-sense principle that if more than one source testifies to a particular event, then it is more likely to be historical. In principle, this criterion, unlike the criterion of dissimilarity, appears objective and sensible. However, what is to count as a source? The fact that a particular story may be recounted in all three of the Synoptic Gospels often does not mean that scholars regard it as having multiple attestation, because of a belief that Matthew and Luke derived their versions from Mark. However, as I shall point out in the next section, this dependence on Mark is not an established fact but a theory that not all scholars accept. What is regarded as an independent source then depends in part on the theories of the scholars concerning the way that particular books were composed, and those judgements in turn often rest on other uncertain judgements about the purposes of particular authors, the situation of the Early Church, and many others. Thus, the probability of an event's historicity, as determined by the number of multiple attestations, is in turn affected by the probability of many other judgements.

Probability theory makes it evident how uncertain such conclusions can be. When an inference that has only a moderate degree of probability depends on a claim that in turn is merely probable, which depends in turn on the probability of others, the probability of the final conclusion must be determined by multiplying the probabilities of the various steps in the chain of inference. In such a case uncertainties quickly become enormous.[20] This point applies of course not merely to uncertainties about the independence of sources, but to many other claims made by historical biblical scholars.

Even if a particular narrative or saying in Matthew or Luke is dependent on Mark, it is not obvious that the passage lacks

[20] For a detailed critique of biblical criticism along these lines, see Humphrey Palmer, *The Logic of Gospel Criticism* (London: Macmillan, 1968).

multiple attestation. Many scholars in such a case are inclined
to say that the passage is only attested by one source, reasoning
that the other writers are dependent on Mark. The correctness
of this procedure seems open to question, however. Let us
assume we are considering parallel passages in Luke and Mark,
and that it looks as if in this case Luke is dependent on Mark.
It is true that if Mark is the only source Luke has, and if Luke
has no independent way of verifying Mark's information or
determining its reliability, then Luke's witness is not truly
independent of Mark's. However, how could a historical
scholar know that these things are the case?

Claims that Luke had no other source and no way of assessing Mark's information look quite speculative. In contrast we
know with a high degree of certainty that Luke and Mark are
distinct authors. Even if Luke has borrowed the literary form
of Mark, it does not follow that Luke had no access to information verifying the historical authenticity of the passage.
Luke may have copied this passage from Mark, if he did,
because he had independent grounds for accepting it as historical. The author of Luke's Gospel is almost certainly a
distinct writer from the author of Mark's Gospel, and in choosing to include a passage from Mark's Gospel, the author of
Luke is surely claiming, among other things, that the event
occurred. That we do indeed have two authors who both attest
to the events in question is a fact that is more certain than any
theory about the literary dependence between the two authors.
Furthermore, the fact that Mark and Luke are distinct authors
is logically consistent with and therefore not undermined by
any literary dependence, even if the dependence is genuine.

14.3. DEEPER REASONS FOR DOUBTS ABOUT HISTORICAL SCHOLARSHIP

If James has the time and ability to investigate critical historical
scholarship in a deeper manner, he will find confirmation of
the scepticism about such scholarship that emerged merely
from considering the disagreements of the scholars and their
own disclaimers about the criteria of authenticity often relied
upon. What he needs to do is investigate the grounds of the

disagreements. If he does so, James will discover that the parallel drawn between philosophy and historical critical scholarship earlier in this chapter is not accidental, because the disagreements between historical scholars often rest on philosophical, theological, and literary assumptions.

Now, on the assumption that James, like most ordinary people, lacks the scholarly tools possessed by the historical scholar, such as specialized knowledge of ancient languages, history, and texts, there will be sharp limits to his ability to evaluate a great deal of the biblical historian's work. However, in investigating disagreements on the part of scholars who do possess this knowledge, James may reasonably conclude that a good deal of this disagreement is rooted in factors where the scholars in question may not have any special expertise either. Philosophical, theological, and literary assumptions may appear as significant, and with respect to some of these matters James may be competent to evaluate the views of the scholars.

14.3.1. *The Role of Philosophical Assumptions*

For example, there seems little doubt that some of the judgements critical historical scholars have made about the reliability of the New Testament narratives rest partly on the assumptions about the miraculous that are embedded in the 'criteria for critical history', discussed in Chapters 7 and 8, championed by people such as Troeltsch and Harvey. Though James may not be a professional philosopher, he may well have good reason to doubt the philosophical assumptions about miracles that permeate this view of historical method.

A concrete example of what this might mean in practice would be helpful here. Some scholars have thought that Acts was probably written in the mid-60s AD on the grounds that the book concludes with the imprisonment of Paul, but does not mention his death, which probably occurred in the mid-60s. If this is correct, and if Luke was written earlier by the same author, then this seems to imply that Luke must be dated not much later than AD 64.[21] Since most scholars believe Mark

---

[21] See John M. Rist, *On the Independence of Matthew and Mark* (Cambridge: Cambridge University Press, 1978), 4–5.

and Matthew are earlier than Luke (though as noted before there is sharp disagreement about this) this would imply fairly early dates for all three of the Synoptics.

One of the reasons commonly given for doubting the above reasoning is that Luke gives internal evidence of having been written much later. Specifically, it is said that Luke's reference (21: 20) to Jerusalem being 'surrounded by armies', is a 'prophecy after the fact', and shows that Luke knew that such a thing had occurred when the Roman armies under Vespasian and Titus crushed the Jewish revolt between AD 66 and AD 70. It is also sometimes claimed that the language Luke uses in the beatitudes (6: 22), where it is said that 'they exclude you and revile you and cast out your name as evil', reveals a knowledge of a curse upon Christians that was instituted in the synagogues in the 80s.

Both these arguments actually can be criticized without even bringing up the issue of the possibility of miraculous prophecy. If Luke is writing in the early 60s, there is good reason to think that a modest amount of political insight could have anticipated the brewing trouble with the Romans and the likely outcome. For that matter, it is by no means incredible that Jesus himself could have possessed similar natural insight some years earlier. And the reference to persecution could just as easily reflect earlier episodes of tension between the early Christian movement and Judaism, episodes that are well reflected in Paul's Epistles, which undoubtedly are written at an earlier date.

However, putting aside these criticisms, it is important to challenge the implicit assumption that any accurate 'prophecy' must have been made after the events in question. Such an assumption makes it impossible to give the incarnational narrative, with its ineradicable miraculous elements, a fair historical test. One simply cannot begin by ruling out as impossible any supernatural knowledge or insight on the part of Jesus, if one wishes fairly to test the claim that God was at work in Jesus in a special way, or that Jesus was actually God incarnate. Even on a fully kenotic view of the incarnation, in terms of which Jesus as a human being had fully divested himself of his divine omniscience, it remains true that as God Jesus lived in an intimate relation with the Father and Spirit and it is thus quite coherent with the story to see Jesus as empowered with supernatural insight at times, just as he is empowered to perform miraculous healings. A refusal to take this possibility seriously is just as 'dogmatic' and 'uncritical' as is the view of the narrative taken by a theologian who refuses to consider the possibility that Luke invented the prophecy after the fact.

There are other philosophical assumptions frequently made by historical scholars in this area that are similarly open to doubt. One important assumption concerns the value of testimony. Some historical scholars argue quite explicitly that testimony is of little or no historical value. Thus, for them the fact that Luke or Matthew witness to some historical incident provides little or no evidential support for the historicity of the incident. On the contrary, the degree of suspicion and scepticism attached to ancient witnesses sometimes appears to be so great that testimony is weighted negatively, so that an assertion that an incident occurred is prima facie evidence that something else probably happened. The burden of proof is always on the Gospel accounts, and they are judged worthless or nearly so until we have independent confirmation or evidence of their veracity. This scepticism can be seen at two levels. First, there is a general scepticism about historical testimony, and secondly, a specific scepticism about the Gospel testimonies, since they come from Christian sources, and thus are biased in a number of ways. The New Testament records are regarded as reflecting the needs and situation of the Early Church, and as embodying little concern for historical accuracy.

This is not the place for a detailed critique of either the broader or the more specific assumption, but it is appropriate to point out that neither view is a historical claim supported by historical learning. The broader scepticism about testimony reflects a general philosophical view that testimonial evidence is subsidiary and requires foundational support, rather than regarding testimony as one of our basic sources of knowledge. This view has been discussed earlier, and it has been subjected to devastating criticisms by Coady.[22] It is certainly a mark of a reasonable person to recognize that testimony can be mistaken,

---

[22] See the discussion of testimony and of C. A. J. Coady in Ch. 8.

and people often have good grounds for being suspicious of the testimony of particular witnesses. However, that is quite consistent with accepting the general principle that testimony in favour of some proposition p tends to raise the plausibility of p. Many philosophers think that some form of what is called the 'principle of credulity' is a necessary feature of rational human life. This is the principle that, other things being equal, testimony in favour of some proposition at least makes belief in that proposition more reasonable. With respect to many points dealing with the life of Jesus, such a principle would seem to imply that the testimony of the Gospel narratives should be accepted unless we have good reasons to doubt it, and thus wholesale a priori scepticism is unjustified.

Of course some might think that the more specific scepticism that is rooted in recognition of the Christian character of the sources provides just such a reason for doubt. Here we encounter an assumption that is not exactly philosophical in nature; it seems closer to the kind of personal judgement that one makes that a particular person or group of persons is or is not trustworthy. But even if not strictly philosophical, this assumption surely resembles a philosophical claim in that it does not seem to be the kind of proposition that historical scholarship can support. Rather, as different individuals read the Gospel narratives, some gain a sense of the authors as trustworthy, believable individuals and others do not, just as jurors listening to a witness might form diverse judgements about the reliability of the witness.

One factor that may shape such judgements will be agreement or disagreement in basic moral and religious beliefs. Someone who shares the basic world-view and moral convictions of the Gospel writers will naturally be more disposed to trust them, or at least less disposed to be particularly suspicious of them, than someone who finds the authors alien. Our fictional character James, as a Christian, has just such an affinity with the Gospel writers. The fact that they are Christian writers does not give him any special reason to be suspicious of them. After all, he is himself a member of the same historical tradition, a later member of the same community.

One point James may have noticed in this connection is that the Gospel writers do include quite a lot of material that does not seem particularly helpful to the concerns and theological agendas of the Early Church. There is for instance a great deal of the Synoptic Gospels which, taken alone, seems to support a 'low' Christology. Some of it, such as the recording of the baptism of Jesus by John the Baptist, seems positively embarrassing to the Early Church, and yet it is included, though sometimes with what appears, at least to many scholars, to be a mitigating gloss.[23] Historical critics who are inclined towards a priori scepticism sometimes cite this kind of embarrassment as a criterion of historical authenticity. Material that lacks such character cannot be assumed to be authentic. This policy should strike James as curious and unreasonable.

If the Gospel authors include a fair amount of material that is embarrassing or not particularly helpful, why do they do so? Surely it is either because the authors themselves have a concern for historical truth, or else because the events in question are well known and the intended audience was assumed to care about historical reliability. If the facts were well known and if the audience did care about historical truth, then the authors' credibility as writers would have been undermined if they did not report the facts truthfully. If the embarrassing material is included because of the authors' own concern for accuracy, then the writers certainly do not warrant excessive scepticism, and if the material is included because of the writers' need to maintain credibility then this implies that enough was known about Jesus at the time of writing, and that there was enough concern for historical truth, that the authors were compelled to show some concern for the facts. Either way the assumption that there was little concern for historical truth on the part of the authors seems undermined.

It seems overwhelmingly likely that if authors preserve material that is embarrassing and unhelpful, then they are even more likely to preserve authentic material that is supportive of their agendas. Thus the fact that a particular passage from the Gospels seems to be helpful to the Church gives one no reason to doubt its authenticity, though many form critics seem to assume that it does. Of course it is possible such a passage was

---

[23] For a good example of the use of what is called the 'criterion of embarrassment' by a contemporary biblical scholar, see Meier, *A Marginal Jew*, ii. 19–233 provides a very extensive discussion of John the Baptist and his relation to Jesus.

fabricated, but its functional value gives one no particular reason to think that it was.

Recently, as I am writing this (1994) the Conservative party in England has announced a number of tax increases, after winning the last general election on the basis of a claim to be the party of low taxes. In the next election, it is highly likely that the Labour party will claim that the following historical facts are true: (1) The Conservatives promised to keep taxes low. (2) The Conservatives raised taxes. One can easily see the value of these historical claims to Labour in the next campaign, but the fact that the assertions so obviously serve the needs of Labour gives one no particular reason to doubt their truth.

The work of 'redaction critics', who assess a passage in the light of the theological intentions and other characteristics of the final author of a Gospel, also raises questions at times. Some critics are quick to assume that a passage that reflects the theological views or characteristic vocabulary of the final author are likely to be creations of that author. The work of John Meier, who is in many respects a model of moderation and good judgement among biblical scholars, on the miracle of the changing of water into wine at Cana, is a good example here.[24] Meier argues that there is strong evidence of the hand of the evangelist with regard to almost every element of this story; he then jumps to the conclusion that the passage as a whole is not likely to be historical: 'If we subtract from the eleven verses of the first Cana miracle every element that is likely to have come from the creative mind of John or his Johannine "school" and every element that raises historical problems, the entire pericope vanishes before our eyes verse by verse.'[25] Of course Meier may be completely correct in his claim about this particular passage, but it does not seem to me in general to be true that the fact that a passage reflects the characteristic 'voice' of the final author of the text, or that the incident recounted has symbolic meaning or serves the author's theological agenda, provides very strong evidence for that conclusion. A true story can well be told in a way that reflects a particular author's voice, and the way it is told, as well as the

---

[24] Ibid. 936–50.
[25] Ibid. 949.

reason the story was selected in the first place, may well be determined by an author's purposes.[26]

Much of the work of historical biblical scholars has been devoted to going 'behind' the text to discover earlier sources, either literary or oral, as well as to determine what parts of the text are due to the creativity of the community that passed on the traditions, and what parts are the result of the author's 'redactional' changes. Whatever be the outcome of such an endeavour, and though it certainly leads at times to interesting and helpful findings, it appears inevitably to be a speculative, uncertain enterprise in many cases. Such a quest for uncertain sources should not obscure facts such as these: The four Gospels exist as literary wholes, as contemporary 'canon critics' have emphasized.[27] *Someone* authored those Gospels, and in the case of the Synoptics at least, that someone wrote between twenty-five and fifty years after the events. It is therefore a certainty that positive historical testimony exists for the incarnational narrative. Since the factors that determine whether this testimony is regarded as reliable are by no means the sole province of scholars to assess, James is not necessarily irrational to believe that the authors are trustworthy, even if he does not have the support of the majority of scholars. It is true that James would be unreasonable to believe this if scholars had demonstrated that the narratives were unreliable, but we have seen that the conclusions of historical scholarship are very far from having achieved this.

It is vital to see that scepticism about accepting material in the Gospels as authentic cannot be justified on the grounds that it is a more 'cautious' policy that is less likely to lead to mistakes. From the point of view of a virtuous epistemic agent

---

[26] For a strong argument that theological symbolism is no reason to discount the historicity of a narrative, see Old Testament scholar Robert Alter's discussion of the Israelites' crossing of the river Jordan. Alter argues that the historicity of the crossing is quite consistent with the fact that the author has set it into a framework of symbolic meaning. See Robert Alter, *The World of Biblical Literature* (London: SPCK, 1992), 90.

[27] See Brevard S. Childs, *The New Testament as Canon: An Introduction* (Philadelphia: Fortress Press, 1984). Childs argues that regardless of how many historical strata there may be in the New Testament books, or what the purposes of the redactors may have been, we can look at these works as literary wholes, and not simply as patchworks of competing traditions, because that is how the Church which canonized the texts viewed them, and how the Church has continued to view them.

who is interested in finding truth and avoiding error, there is no more merit in making a mistake by failing to recognize a truth about the historical Jesus than in making a mistake by falsely believing something about Jesus. There is just as much risk in a sceptical policy as in a more trusting policy. This is particularly true if one avoids attributing something to Jesus by attributing it instead to the Early Church. New Testament scholar Morna Hooker makes this point very clearly: 'For we are being no more "cautious" or "safe" in our procedure if we discard doubtful material than if we retain it—and if we unknowingly attribute dominical sayings to the Church, our resulting pictures of Jesus and the developments of Christ-ology will be just as prone to error as if we wrongly attribute the Church's formulations of their belief to Jesus.'[28]

It is also worth noting that the recognition of the funda-mental importance of philosophical and theological pre-suppositions has been noted by many historical biblical scholars as well. Morna Hooker again provides a very clear example:

For in the end, the answers which the New Testament scholar gives are not the result of applying objective tests and using precision tools; they are very largely the result of his own presuppositions and prejudices. If he approaches the material with the belief that it is largely the creation of the early Christian communities, then he will interpret it in that way. If he assumes that the words of the Lord were faithfully remembered and passed on, then he will be able to find criteria which support him. Each claims to be using the proper critical method. Each produces a picture of Jesus—and of the early Church—in accordance with his presuppositions. And each claims to be right.[29]

14.3.2. *Questionable Literary Assumptions*

It is not merely philosophical assumptions in historical biblical scholarship that James might find objectionable. Historical critics often make literary assumptions that are not strictly warranted by their historical learning, but reflect judgements

---

[28] Morna Hooker, 'Christology and Methodology', *New Testament Studies*, 17 (1971), 485.

[29] Morna Hooker, 'On Using the Wrong Tool', *Theology*, 75 (1972), 581.

about the narratives as stories that have or lack unity. Recently, a new type of biblical scholarship, with its roots in literary criticism, has come to the fore.[30] This type of literary criticism of the Bible is very mixed in character; some of it simply displays a lack of interest in historicity. Nevertheless, some of the better literary-oriented critics have demonstrated how poorly historical critical scholarship has read many of the narratives it rejects as unhistorical.

A standard move in critical historical scholarship is to examine a particular unit, or pericope, with an eye towards seeing evidence of disunity in the text. Inconsistencies in the text may be a sign that the author is relying on diverse sources which he has been unable to make completely consistent. Or the fissures may not be outright inconsistencies, but simply elements that don't seem to fit together very well: pointless details, or mention of points that don't seem to connect with the major point. It is patently obvious, however, that this procedure rests not merely on historical learning, but also on a sense for how to read a story, an understanding of what is connected and what is not, what advances a story-line and what does not.

Eleonore Stump, for example, has recently shown how claims that a particular story is unhistorical may reflect poor reading.[31] One case study she examines is Raymond Brown's commentary on the Gospel of John's account of the raising of Lazarus.[32] Brown is a good example, partly because he is a well-respected scholar, and partly because his views would be considered moderate within the range of historical scholarship,

---

[30] See e.g. Robert Alter, *The World of Biblical Literature* (London: SPCK, 1992). Meir Sternberg's *The Poetics of Biblical Narrative* (Bloomington, Ind.: Indiana University Press, 1985) provides a powerful demonstration of the value of literary analysis, and what is more, Sternberg specifically argues against the idea that such analysis precludes historicity.

[31] The following material is taken from a seminar paper entitled 'Betrayal of Trust' that Stump delivered at St Olaf College in the summer of 1993. This material is to be included in Stump's forthcoming work on the philosophical and literary assumptions that permeate contemporary historical biblical criticism, tentatively entitled *The Knowledge of Suffering: Biblical Studies and the Problem of Evil*.

[32] The story of the raising of Lazarus is found in John 11: 1–44. Brown's discussion of this passage can be found in his work, *The Gospel According to John* (New York: Doubleday, 1966), which is no. 29 in the Anchor Bible Commentary series.

and thus Stump cannot be accused of having selected an extreme and unrepresentative scholar.

The story of the raising of Lazarus is a complex one. The main characters are Jesus, and three of his friends, Lazarus and Lazarus' two sisters, Mary and Martha. When Lazarus is taken ill, the sisters send Jesus a message, hoping he will come and help. Jesus delays, knowing that Lazarus will die but apparently planning to do a miracle. He eventually announces his intention to go to Bethany to help, even though such a journey risks death from the authorities in Jerusalem. Upon arriving, Jesus is met first by Martha, who reproaches him gently. He later has a similar conversation with Mary, who 'knelt at his feet' (John 11: 32). Finally, Jesus goes to the tomb and does indeed raise Lazarus from the dead. As John tells the story, this miracle directly precipitates the plot that will lead to the death of Jesus.

On Brown's reading of the Lazarus story, the major characters are Jesus and Lazarus. Though Brown does not pronounce dogmatically on the subject, he appears sympathetic to the claim of some scholars that the dialogues between Jesus and the two sisters, Martha and Mary, are later additions, and thus their historicity seems suspect. As Brown sees it, the dialogue with Martha does not seem to advance the story much, and the later dialogue with Mary seems repetitious and pointless.[33] However, as Stump shows clearly, a sensitive reading of the story sees it as concerned very centrally with the loving relation between Jesus and the two sisters, whose dialogues with Jesus reveal interestingly different personalities and a lot about Jesus as well. On Stump's reading Jesus may be seen as delaying his coming partly so as to reward the faith of the sisters with a glorious miracle. When he arrives, the distress of the sisters reveals his plans have not proceeded precisely as he wished and expected.

As an example of the power of Stump's reading, one could focus on the extreme frustration Jesus exhibits in John 11: 33, where the Greek literally implies that Jesus 'snorted within himself', like a horse. One of the merits of Stump's reading of the story is that it helps makes sense of this strong emotion of

---

[33] See *The Gospel According to John*, particularly 432–5.

frustration, an emotion that many commentators have found difficult to understand. On Stump's account, Jesus is here expressing extreme irritation and frustration because his wonderful plan to do a great miracle and reward the faith of his followers is just not working out. Instead he finds himself with a woman weeping at his feet, and he reacts as many men do who find themselves dealing with a woman they love who is overcome with tears. Here Stump obviously takes seriously the full humanity of Jesus.[34]

As Stump views the story, the conversations between Jesus and the two sisters, far from being 'interruptions', as many commentators have thought, are crucial in revealing the tensions in the relationships between Jesus and the two sisters, and the very interesting characteristics of those relationships that are tied to the differences in the personalities of the sisters. Martha, who is more practical and rational, is upset, but capable of discussing the matter. Mary, who seems more emotionally intense, cannot be dealt with in the same way. The story then is not just about Lazarus but about the intense relationship between Jesus and two women friends. It is a relationship that is put under severe strain, but one in which the mutual love and loyalty between Jesus, Mary, and Martha finally triumph, as seen in Jesus' miracle on the one hand, and the anointing of Jesus by Mary that follows in chapter 12 on the other.

Of course the fact that Stump is able to give the story a convincing reading as unified does not show it to be historical; the writer could have been a skilful composer of fiction. But it does reveal that one of the grounds for regarding the story as unhistorical is not itself historical in character. Rather, Brown's conclusion rests on a literary judgement about how the story should be read, and that literary judgement looks highly debatable, if not downright flimsy. The 'fissures' Brown sees in the narrative seem to be entirely his own creation.

Another example of what can only be regarded as wooden

---

[34] I should like to note that Stump's reading of this story by no means implies that there is any moral fault in Jesus' behaviour. Jesus acts with the best of intentions towards the sisters, and the frustrations that ensue presuppose only the finitude of Jesus' human understanding of the situation. The kind of kenotic understanding of the incarnation defended in Chapter 6 coheres well with this story.

reading is found in John Dominic Crossan's treatment of the parable of the Good Samaritan.[35] In the parable, of course, Jesus tells a story to a 'lawyer' who has asked Jesus the question 'Who is my neighbour?' By asking the question, perhaps the lawyer wanted to excuse himself from concern about some kinds of people. The story Jesus tells is that of a Samaritan who helped a robbed and injured Jewish man, who had been ignored by two of his fellow countrymen. The Samaritan's merciful action is noteworthy, especially given the fact that Samaritans were ostracized by Jews at the time. At the end of the parable, Jesus asks the lawyer a question in return: 'Which of these three, do you think, was a neighbour to the man who fell into the hands of the robbers?'[36]

In asking this question, Jesus transformed the category of 'neighbour'. Refusing to give the lawyer a boundary beyond which he need show no neighbourly concern, Jesus did not say who is and is not the neighbour who should be the object of concern. Instead, he forced the lawyer to think about other questions: What does it mean to be a neighbour? How can I be a neighbour? The twist in the ending, which is actually characteristic of many of Jesus' parables, is one of the factors that makes this story both memorable and profound.

At the hands of Crossan, however, the shift in meaning in the concept of neighbour is taken simply as 'logical inconsistency' on the part of the writer. He argues that Luke 10: 30–5 would fit well either with 10: 27–9, in which the neighbour is viewed as someone in need, or with 10: 36, in which the neighbour is viewed as someone who helps one in need, but cannot go with both passages. Thus, he claims the story is a composite of two distinct stories, only one of which probably goes back to the historical Jesus.

Of course Crossan's view is *possible*. Crossan may well be correct in thinking that this story is a composite. However, anyone who thinks the shift in meaning that 'neighbour' undergoes in this story provides *evidence* for Crossan's view exhibits a literary insensitivity that does not inspire confidence in his judgement. A reading of the Gospels that assumes that

[35] John Dominic Crossan, *In Parables* (New York: Harper & Row, 1973), 59, 60.
[36] Luke 10: 36.

paradox cannot be part of Jesus' teaching is as unhistorical as it is literarily flat, for nothing is more common in ordinary life than this kind of 'inconsistency', whether it be unintentional or intentional.

It seems then that the more James learns about the grounds of the disagreements among New Testament scholars, the more reason he has to question whether there are any assured conclusions of such scholars that could serve to undermine the convictions he has formed, and which he has taken to be reliable. This is not to say that there are no responsible scholars who regard the Gospels as historically reliable. As James explores those disagreements, he will be heartened to discover that there are outstanding scholars who take a high view of the historical reliability of the texts. He will encounter twentieth-century scholars such as James D. G. Dunn, N. T. Wright, Howard Marshall, and Robert Stein, who do possess an expert's view of the issues, and are persuaded that the historical reliability of the New Testament is well grounded.[37] The judgement of such respected scholars as A. E. Harvey may encourage his faith in the New Testament:

The Gospels must be compared, not with a hypothetical uncontaminated list of bare events (which would in any case be devoid of significance for religious purposes), but with other historical writings which come down to us from antiquity, and in which too we have to allow for the interpretative bias of their authors. On this test, we shall find that the information about Jesus which we can derive from the Gospels enjoys a high degree of historical reliability. The Gospels can be subjected to investigation with all the tools and methods of modern historical study, and come remarkably well out of the process. So far as their historical reporting is concerned, they bear

[37] See James D. G. Dunn, *The Evidence for Jesus* (London: SCM Press, 1985); Robert H. Stein, *The Synoptic Problem* (Grand Rapids, Mich.: Baker, 1987), 187–216; N. T. Wright, *The New Testament and the People of God* (Minneapolis: Fortress Press, 1992); I. Howard Marshall, *I Believe in the Historical Jesus* (Grand Rapids, Mich.: Wm. B. Eerdmans, 1977) and *Luke: Historian and Theologian* (Grand Rapids, Mich.: Zondervan, 1970); and F. F. Bruce, *New Testament History* (Garden City, NY: Doubleday, 1982). All the above authors are from the moderate to conservative wing of biblical scholarship, but it is of course noteworthy that scholars who are much less conservative in their theology often regard the basic historicity of the narrative as defensible. For a review of much literature that vindicates the historical reliability of the New Testament, see Craig Blomberg, *The Historical Reliability of the Gospels* (Downer's Grove, Ill.: InterVarsity Press, 1987).

comparison with the work of any ancient historian, and at many points the information they offer is not merely credible but impressive.[38]

If James is or becomes a New Testament scholar himself, the situation does not appreciably change. Of course in this case James will have an expert knowledge of the many points at which scholars will disagree with his convictions. However, he will have a correspondingly deeper knowledge of the grounds of his own convictions, and of the personal, philosophical, and literary presuppositions that underlie the disagreements. The fact that his convictions are not universally shared by other scholars and that he may be unable to convince some other scholars of his views may give James a reason to reconsider his beliefs; epistemological humility is indeed a virtue and James should recognize his fallibility. There is no reason, however, for James (or anyone else) to be seduced by the claims of classical foundationalist epistemology, and so, having considered the objections of peers, James may be quite justified in continuing to hold to his personal convictions as to the truth of the matter.

14.4. BIBLICAL HISTORICAL CRITICS AS AN INTERPRETATIVE COMMUNITY

Biblical historical critics have sometimes portrayed themselves as an objective community whose only concern is the truth, proceeding by induction from facts, 'evidence on which everyone can agree'.[39] This self-perception has often led to a superior attitude towards committed members of religious communities, whose readings of the evidence are regarded as constricted by 'dogma'. One of the insights that is regarded as defining the community of historical critics is an understanding of the relativity and pervasiveness of culture as a determinant of human thought and behaviour. Historical critics have rightly insisted that the first-century Mediterranean culture is in many

---

[38] A. E. Harvey, 'Christology and the Evidence of the New Testament', in *God Incarnate: Story and Belief* (London: SPCK, 1981), 46.
[39] Sanders, *Jesus and Judaism*, 5.

ways a different world from ours, one that requires special training and learning to understand.

Ironically, however, the community of historical critics has often failed to see the influence of their own cultural situation on their work. Jon Levenson, a scholar of the Hebrew Bible at Harvard, has recently levelled this charge in a powerful way at his own scholarly colleagues, and I believe Levenson is substantially right. His argument is that historical critics must come to see themselves as one more 'tribe', a community of interpretation that has a right and a duty to put forward its views into the conversation, but one which has no right to disparage and consider illegitimate other communities of interpretation, particularly religious ones.[40] As Levenson himself notes, at one level this charge is not completely fair. Historical critics have a keen grasp that what is called historical criticism has not always existed; it came into being at a particular time and place, and therefore presupposes a cultural framework. Even while recognizing this cultural setting, however, the members of this community, like every other, has tended to absolutize their own cultural assumptions. Thus, the epistemological and metaphysical assumptions of the Enlightenment were simply seen as the right way to look at the world. Members of this 'tribe' have tended to assume that only with the advent of the Enlightenment did human beings achieve the level of true, critical historical awareness; ancient peoples, with their cultural framework, are regarded disparagingly as utterly lacking in concern for objective truth.[41] In practice, then, the community of historical critics saw themselves as lifted above the relativities of history.

Levenson is himself a historical scholar and does not wish to question the idea that this particular community has a valuable contribution to make. He does wish to question whether the community of historical scholars is always in a better position than members of other communities to discern the truth, even

[40] See Jon D. Levenson, *The Hebrew Bible, the Old Testament, and Historical Criticism: Jews and Christians in Biblical Studies* (Louisville, Ky.: Westminster/John Knox Press, 1993).

[41] For a fine example of this kind of cultural condescension, see Ernst Troeltsch's essay, 'Historiography', in *Encyclopaedia of Religion and Ethics*, vi, ed. James Hastings (New York: Charles Scribner's Sons, 1922), 716–23.

though there is a strong tendency on the part of the community to see itself as the ones who get at the real meaning of documents. Such interpreters 'are claiming to have a definitive insight, not empirically derived into the meaning of things, even things that they have never directly experienced and that are interpreted very differently by those who have'.[42] Such a claim 'shifts the locus of truth from the practicing community to the nonpracticing and unaffiliated individual', without questioning whether such detachment might 'decrease one's insight and obscure one's vision'.[43]

Recently, William Farmer has given a provocative example of the relativity of scholarly criticism, focusing on the development in Germany of the idea that Matthew and Luke drew on Mark, regarded as the first of the canonical Gospels, as well as another 'sayings source', usually designated as Q.[44] Farmer argues that this view, which was only advanced as a tentative theory in the middle of the nineteenth century, acquired the status of a Protestant religious dogma in Germany because it served the needs of the Prussian state in its *Kulturkampf* with the Roman Catholic Church. If Matthew could be displaced as the earliest and most authoritative Gospel, then the claims to papal authority rooted in that Gospel's stories in which Jesus gives the keys of the Church to Peter and promises to build his Church on Peter could be minimized. Furthermore, the Prussian Chancellor Bismarck had the support of the German state universities in this culture war; there was no need for explicit pressure or direct censorship. In short, Farmer argues that a particular view became accepted as the 'assured result of German scholarship', for reasons that had little to do with the evidential support for the theory in question.

Farmer's argument here may or may not be right. Whether one agrees with his claim that non-rational factors led to this adoption of a particular source theory in Germany will depend in part on whether one agrees with Farmer's judgement that the actual evidence supporting the particular theory is insufficient,

---

[42] Jon D. Levenson, 'The Bible: Unexamined Commitments of Criticism', *First Things*, 30 (Feb. 1993), 28.
[43] Levenson, 'The Bible: Unexamined Commitments of Criticism', 29.
[44] See William Farmer, *The Gospel of Jesus: The Pastoral Relevance of the Synoptic Problem* (Louisville, Ky.: Westminster/John Knox Press, 1994), 146–60.

and that is a claim that many scholars will not grant. In particular, one might argue that the widespread adoption of the 'two-document' theory in England is due to the arguments of Streeter and other scholars, and cannot be explained simply as a carry-over from Germany.[45] But whether Farmer's view here is somewhat of an exaggeration or not, it seems right to look at the history of biblical scholarship as open in principle to this kind of 'relativizing' analysis. Interesting examples of the way cultural and political forces shaped the rather different world of American biblical scholarship can also be found in Mark Noll's *Between Faith and Criticism*.[46]

More recently, with the advent of 'post-modern' viewpoints, there is a tendency to give at least lip-service to this kind of self-critical view. It is easy enough to look back at nineteenth-century New Testament scholarship and see the pervasive way cultural assumptions shaped its conclusions. Whether Farmer's particular claim about the two-document source theory is right or not, it is true that Protestant German scholarship in the nineteenth and early twentieth centuries consistently showed a tendency to look for a 'Protestant' Jesus, who was seen as opposing both Judaism and Catholicism, which were given unsympathetic and inaccurate readings. Despite this recognition of their own cultural relativity, however, many New Testament scholars in practice still seem committed to Enlightenment ways of thought, and committed to seeing those ways of thought as *correct*.

There is, for example, little openness to miracles as a real possibility. Jesus is often viewed as a miracle-worker, but the miracles attributed to him are those, such as exorcisms, that can be explained by the modern mind as psychosomatic and that do not require any genuine supernatural power. Furthermore, there is still a widespread assumption that the community of historical scholars provides the best, or even the only route to gaining the truth about the issues in question.

---

[45] See B. H. Streeter, *The Four Gospels: A Study of Origins*, 2nd. edn. (London: Macmillan, 1930).

[46] Mark Noll, *Between Faith and Criticism* (San Francisco: Harper & Row, 1986). Though Noll's book deals chiefly with biblical scholarship among evangelicals, his narrative sheds a good deal of light on the history of the world of biblical scholarship generally in the United States.

Meier's 'unpapal conclave' and Sanders' appeal to 'evidence on which everyone can agree'[47] show that the Enlightenment assumption that beliefs must be constructed on objectively certain foundations has not really been rejected in practice, even if such a view is often recognized in theory to be naïve.

There is a curious feature of the community of critical, historical New Testament scholarship. In so far as this community aims at the 'historical Jesus' there is an incongruity between the aims of the quest and the assumptions that are regarded as essential to carry it on. A basic question one might ask is why there is such an intense concern for the historical Jesus. Granted, Jesus is an important historical figure, and so one can easily justify some historical attention, but none the less, when one looks at the tremendous amount of scholarly effort that has been devoted to determining just what are the 'authentic' words and deeds of Jesus, one can hardly avoid the conclusion that this quest is motivated partly by religious concerns. Many New Testament scholars want to know exactly what Jesus said and did, because they either believe that Jesus was God incarnate, or at least because they see him as a focal point of divine revelation and action in the world. One can't simply be content with the Jesus presented by the text; it is all-important to know just what the 'real' Jesus was like, and this seems to show an assumption that Jesus is somehow 'special', not an ordinary person.

Ironically, however, the historical assumptions governing this quest seem designed to make it difficult if not impossible to recognize anything really special about Jesus. If Jesus really performed miracles, or thought of himself as divine, the assumptions of historical criticism would make it nearly impossible to discern this. There is nothing illegitimate about such an historical quest, of course. Scholars are entitled to study the historical evidence in any way they think best, making whatever assumptions that seem right to them. However, it does seem illegitimate for scholars to require members of religious communities to divest themselves of their religious assumptions in order to be recognized as involved in a quest for historical truth. If the motivation for the quest is

---

[47] Sanders, *Jesus and Judaism*, 5.

religious in the first place, then it seems bizarre to say that the only interpretative assumptions that are legitimate are those which make it difficult, if not impossible, to recover the religious significance of the subject.

This is not to attack the value of historical critical scholarship. This scholarship has indeed discovered a tremendous amount about the ancient world and the New Testament that is of great value. Historical, linguistic, and textual scholarship deserve due credit for such discoveries, and laypeople, including religious people, owe such scholars a debt of gratitude. Nor is there anything wrong with *looking* for evidence upon which everyone will agree, so long as one does not insist that such evidence is the only basis upon which important conclusions can be achieved. When it comes to really important issues that have religious significance I doubt that very much of such evidence will actually be *found*. A more realistic policy is to look for evidence upon which one's conversation partners will agree. Such partners will always be particular people, not 'everyone', and the restriction may be limited to the purposes of the conversation.

Religiously committed individuals who are involved in such conversations will often find it useful to try to show that certain conclusions follow from premises that their opponents will recognize as true. Hence, it is often valuable, for apologetics, to make the kinds of assumptions about the New Testament that Swinburne makes in his argument, for example. A religious apologist might then adopt the following policy, at least while doing apologetics: begin with what one's critics are willing to admit about the New Testament and try to show that even on their views, the person of Jesus offers a challenge.

However, it is important to remember that the task of apologetics is not identical with the task of giving an account of how one knows. Apologetics is a matter of convincing an opponent; this remains true even if the opponent is one's alter ego. To do apologetics I need to be able to justify my beliefs, to show that I know what I know. However, if I fail in this task, this does not mean that I fail to know. To reiterate a conclusion of Chapter 9, justifying a belief is not the same as being justified in holding a belief.

There are of course circumstances in which the two become

intertwined. If my apologetic argument is directed against my own doubting self, then a failure to show that I am justified may cripple belief itself. However, the task of convincing myself is just as particular and concrete as any other apologetic task. The self I must convince is not 'everyone' but a particular human being with particular hopes and fears, convictions and doubts. There is no guarantee of success, no universal recipe for overcoming problems. Success is defined, however, as overcoming the particular difficulties I have, not as answering all the possible objections that could be mounted.

14.5. APOLOGETICS OLD AND NEW

When understood in this particularistic way, I believe the prospects for traditional apologetic arguments are good. Think for example of the 'trilemma' argument discussed briefly in Chapter 10. This tradition of argument, used very successfully by C. S. Lewis, for instance, centres on the claims to divinity that are implicit and explicit in the Gospel narratives. Jesus, for example, claimed the power to forgive sins, which is the prerogative of God alone. He taught with a unique authority, 'not as the scribes and pharisees'. Even in the Synoptics, he represents himself as having a particularly intimate relation with God. In his triumphal entry into Jerusalem, the cleansing of the Temple, and last meal with his disciples, he evidenced a clear view that his own person was closely connected to the coming kingdom of God. The argument is that such claims, if not true, can only be put forward by an evil person or a lunatic, and yet Jesus clearly was neither.[48]

Objections to this type of argument usually centre on the accuracy of the Gospel records. If we are right in maintaining that a person can reasonably take those records as at least generally reliable historical testimony, then there is no reason why such traditional arguments cannot be effective. In fact, in a recent spiritual autobiographical essay, philosopher and

---

[48] See C. S. Lewis, *Mere Christianity* (New York: Macmillan, 1952). For a more recent version of the argument, see Peter Kreeft, *Between Heaven and Hell* (Downer's Grove, Ill.: InterVarsity Press, 1982).

classics scholar John Rist explains how this argument was a key element in his own conversion.[49] Rist, as a classics scholar, examined the case for seeing the Gospels as early, reliable witnesses, and published his results in a monograph.[50] His scholarly work removed any objections he had to the classical argument:

Thus the full range of Christian claims must go back to the very earliest followers of Jesus, and in all probability to Jesus himself. The solution that either Jesus was a lunatic or his earliest followers were all blatant liars again seemed the only alternative possibility if their claims were false. I could no longer delude myself that 'real' scholarship told us that we have no evidence that Jesus himself, as well as the earliest generation of his followers, made claims for his divinity. The attempt of the Biblical critics to show that such claims grew up (or were fabricated) within the church seemed to be a tissue of bad argument, unhistorical treatment of the sources and wishful thinking.[51]

Another traditional form of apologetic argument centres on the resurrection of Jesus, perhaps the best-attested miracle in the story, and the one that seems singularly suited to attest that Jesus was indeed sent from God. Of course the resurrection alone cannot serve to establish the truth of the narrative as a whole. One cannot, for example, simply deduce from the claim that 'Jesus was raised from the dead' that 'Jesus was God incarnate'. However, the resurrection is a powerful witness that the claims Jesus made about himself, and the claims made about him by his earliest followers, are true. It seems a fitting sign that God was truly at work in Jesus, that both his message and his life, including his sacrificial death, were part of God's actions on behalf of a fallen humanity.

Recently, philosopher Stephen Davis has given a powerful defence of the Christian claim that Jesus was bodily raised from the dead.[52] Davis carefully sharpens the meaning of the

[49] John Rist, 'Where Else?' in Kelly James Clark (ed.), *Philosophers Who Believe* (Downer's Grove, Ill.: InterVarsity Press, 1993), 99–100.

[50] John Rist, *On the Independence of Matthew and Mark* (Cambridge: Cambridge University Press, 1978).

[51] John Rist, 'Where Else?', 100.

[52] Stephen Davis, *Risen Indeed: Making Sense of the Resurrection* (Grand Rapids, Mich.: Wm. B. Eerdmans, 1993).

claim and distinguishes the traditional Christian claim from others. He then, without any 'dogmatic' assumptions about the biblical testimony, looks at the evidence, which centres on the narratives describing the appearances of Jesus and the accounts of the discovery of the empty tomb. The empty tomb narratives are often attacked as late, legendary stories, full of contradictions, and probably created either for apologetic reasons, or to make the claim of resurrection intelligible to contemporaries.

Against such criticisms Davis responds powerfully: (1) The Gospel accounts 'agree to an amazing degree on what we might call the basic facts'.[53] Few of the discrepancies are serious, and in any case disagreement about details from independent sources does not affect the evidential force of testimony. (2) There is little evidence that the empty tomb stories are late; most of the arguments to this effect are circular. On the assumption that the empty tomb stories are late, narratives about the empty tomb are regarded as late. Contrary to critics, there are some reasons to think that Paul was aware of the empty tomb tradition.[54] (3) There is good reason to think that the empty tomb narratives were not created for apologetic purposes. They do not appear to have been used apologetically in the Early Church, and the event is presented in the New Testament more as an enigma than as powerful proof of the resurrection. Besides, if the Church were going to create an apologetic story, it surely could have done better than to create a story in which everything hinges on the testimony of women, who were not regarded as legally competent to testify in court at the time.[55]

The empty tomb tradition enjoys very broad support in the New Testament, notes Davis. Furthermore, he argues convincingly that in first-century Jerusalem, it would have been psychologically and apologetically difficult to proclaim the resurrection of Jesus without safe evidence of an empty tomb. As good Jews, the early disciples would most likely have conceived of the resurrection as a bodily event.[56] When we add the

[53] Ibid. 69.
[54] Ibid. 75–7.
[55] Ibid. 72–5.
[56] Ibid. 78–80.

testimony about the appearances of Jesus, and the willingness of the disciples of Jesus to die rather than to deny the truth of his resurrection, we see a strong historical case.

Does this evidence amount to a proof? Davis himself would be the first to deny this. In the nature of the case, he points out that the evidence will be seen as powerful only to those who approach it with the right philosophical assumptions.[57] To those who think miracles impossible, for example, the evidence will not be nearly enough. Of course those assumptions are not arbitrarily chosen; they can be philosophically defended as well, but once more, there is little prospect of arguments that will convince all 'sane, rational, people'. However, that is a feature that will be found in virtually all arguments dealing with historical, philosophical, literary, and moral judgements, and implies no adverse judgements about the ability of Davis's arguments to convince those who agree or can be brought to agree with the assumptions he brings to bear on the evidence.

So I conclude that traditional apologetical arguments, once the bogey of historical criticism has been whittled down to size, still have force. Of course there is no reason to think that only traditional arguments can and should be given. Since apologetics is a response to particular problems, new objections should give rise to new arguments. It is particularly important in today's world to respond to the 'scandal of particularity' and deal with the question of whether belief in the incarnational narrative of Jesus is intolerant or denigrative to other religious views, as I have briefly tried to do in Chapter 5.

In a culture in which religious faith is for many not a serious option, it is important to give arguments to show the relevance and power of the Christian story. The most effective apologetic arguments may be those that aim to show that the story of Jesus contains the solution to life's deepest problems, and to show that eternal life with the God Jesus reveals is what human beings at bottom really want.[58] In so far as humans are sinful, as Christianity claims, then it will also be true that the story contains what human do *not* want: the truth that they are not

[57] Davis, *Risen Indeed*, 168–90.
[58] For an example, see my own *The Quest for Faith* (Downer's Grove, Ill.: Inter-Varsity Press, 1986), 51–67.

their own gods, but are responsible to their Creator. In that case, the very offensiveness of Christianity may be seen as one indicator of its truth.[59]

I have argued that the Spirit of God can produce faith without such apologetic arguments, and that such faith can amount to knowledge. Nevertheless, the Spirit can also work through argument, and in those who have the advantages of learning, the faith that is formed will surely be a faith that seeks understanding, and thus will see such arguments as helpful. The faith the Spirit produces is a faith that is enriched by confirmation of its truth; the evidence that provides such confirmation is in turn illumined by faith.

---

[59] See Søren Kierkegaard, *Practice in Christianity* (Princeton: Princeton University Press, 1991). Also see David McCracken, *The Scandal of the Gospels: Jesus, Story, and Offence* (Oxford: Oxford University Press, 1994).

Works Cited

ADAMS, ROBERT, 'Kierkegaard's Arguments Against Objective Reasoning in Religion', in *The Virtue of Faith* (Oxford: Oxford University Press, 1987).
—— 'The Leap of Faith', in *The Virtue of Faith* (Oxford: Oxford University Press, 1987).
ALSTON, WILLIAM, in 'Knowledge of God', in Marcus Hester (ed.), *Faith, Reason, and Skepticism*, (Philadelphia: Temple University Press, 1992).
—— 'Yes Virginia, There is a Real World'. *Proceedings and Addresses of the American Philosophical Association*, 52/6 (1979), 779–808.
—— 'Concepts of Epistemic Justification', in *Epistemic Justification* (Ithaca, NY: Cornell University Press, 1989).
—— 'God's Action in the World', in *Divine Nature and Human Language* (Ithaca, NY: Cornell University Press, 1989).
—— *Perceiving God: The Epistemology of Religious Experience* (Ithaca, NY: Cornell University Press, 1991).
—— 'On Knowing that We Know: The Application to Religious Knowledge', in C. Stephen Evans and Merold Westphal, *Christian Perspectives On Religious Knowledge* (Grand Rapids, Mich.: Wm. B. Eerdmans, 1993).
ALTER, ROBERT, *The World of Biblical Literature* (London: SPCK, 1992).
ANDERSON, HUGH, *Jesus and Christian Origins* (New York: Oxford University Press, 1964).
AQUINAS, THOMAS, *Summa Theologiae*, i (Garden City, NY: Doubleday & Co., 1969); xxxi, trans. P. C. O'Brien (London: Blackfriars, 1964).
—— *Summa contra Gentiles*, trans. Anton C. Pegis (Garden City, NY: Doubleday & Co., 1955).
ARISTOTLE, *Categories. Complete Works of Aristotle*, i. ed. Jonathan Barnes (Princeton: Princeton University Press, 1984).
BAILLIE, D. M., *God Was In Christ* (London: Faber & Faber, 1948).
BANNER, MICHAEL C., *The Justification of Science and the Rationality*

of Religious Belief (Oxford: Oxford University Press, 1990).

BENNER, DAVID and EVANS, C. STEPHEN, 'Unity and Multiplicity Hypnosis, Commissurotomy, and Multiple Personality Disorder', *Journal of Mind and Behavior*, 5/4 (Autumn 1984), 423–31.

BLOMBERG, CRAIG, *The Historical Reliability of the Gospels* (Downer's Grove, Ill.: InterVarsity Press, 1987).

BOCK, DARRELL, 'The Words of Jesus in The Gospels: Live, Jive, or Memorex', in *Jesus Under Fire: Modern Scholarship Reinvents the Historical Jesus* (Grand Rapids, Mich.: Zondervan, 1995).

BONJOUR, LAURENCE, *The Structure of Empirical Knowledge* (Cambridge: Cambridge University Press, 1985).

BORG, MARCUS, *Conflict, Holiness, and Politics in the Teaching of Jesus* (New York: Edwin Mellen Press, 1984).

BRADLEY, F. H., *The Presuppositions of Critical History* (Oxford: J. Parker & Co., 1874); repr. in Lionel Rubinoff (ed.) (Chicago: Quadrangle Books, 1968).

BROWN, DAVID, *The Divine Trinity* (London: Duckworth, 1985).

BROWN, RAYMOND C., *The Gospel According to John*, Anchor Bible Commentary Series, 29 (New York: Doubleday, 1966).

BRUCE, F. F., *New Testament History* (Garden City, NY: Doubleday, 1982).

BULTMANN, RUDOLPH, *Kerygma and Myth* (New York: Harper & Row, 1961).

BURNS, R. M., *The Great Debate on Miracles: From Joseph Glanvill to David Hume* (Lewisburg, NJ: Bucknell University Press, 1981).

BUTLER, B. C., *The Originality of St Matthew* (Cambridge: Cambridge University Press, 1951).

BUTLER, JOSEPH, *Analogy of Religion* (Oxford: Clarendon Press, 1896; New York: E. P. Dutton, 1906).

CALVIN, JOHN, *Institutes of the Christian Religion*, ed. John T. McNeill, trans. Ford Lewis Battles (2 vols.; Philadelphia: Westminster Press, 1960).

CAMPBELL, JOSEPH, *The Hero with a Thousand Faces*, 2nd edn. (Princeton: Princeton University Press, 1968).

—— 'Mythological Themes in Creative Literature and Art', Joseph Campbell (ed.), *Myths, Dreams, and Religion* (New York: E. P. Dutton, 1970).

CAPON, ROBERT F., *Hunting the Divine Fox* (New York: Seabury Press, 1974).

CHILDS, BREVARD S., *The New Testament as Canon: An Introduction* (Philadelphia: Fortress Press, 1984).

CHISHOLM, RODERICK, *The Problem of the Criterion* (Milwaukee: Marquette University Press, 1973).

CHISHOLM, RODERICK, *Theory of Knowledge* (Englewood Cliffs, NJ: Prentice-Hall, 2nd edn. 1977; 3rd edn. 1989).

COADY, C. A. J., *Testimony* (Oxford: Oxford University Press, 1992).

CROSSAN, JOHN DOMINIC, *In Parables* (New York: Harper & Row, 1973).

——*The Historical Jesus: The Life of a Mediterranean Jewish Peasant* (San Francisco: HarperCollins, 1991).

CULPEPPER, R. A., *Anatomy of The Fourth Gospel* (Philadelphia: Fortress Press, 1983).

CUPITT, DON, 'A Final Comment', in John Hick (ed.), *The Myth of God Incarnate* (London: SCM Press, 1977).

DAVIS, STEPHEN, *Risen Indeed: Making Sense of The Resurrection* (Grand Rapids, Mich.: Wm. B. Eerdmans, 1993).

DEWEY, JOHN, *The Quest for Certainty* (New York: G. P. Putnam's Sons, 1929).

DILLEY, FRANK, 'Does the "God Who Acts" Really Act?', in Owen Thomas (ed.), *God's Activity in the World* (Chico, Calif.: Scholar's Press, 1983).

DODD, C. H., *The Parables of The Kingdom*, rev. edn. (New York: Scribner's, 1978).

DRETSKE, FRED I., *Knowledge and the Flow of Information* (Cambridge, Mass.: MIT Press, 1981).

DUNN, JAMES D. G., *The Evidence for Jesus* (London: SCM Press, 1985).

EVANS, CRAIG A., 'Authenticity Criteria in Life of Jesus Research', *Christian Scholar's Review*, 19/1 (Sept. 1989), 6–31.

EVANS, C. STEPHEN, *Kierkegaard's Fragments and Postscripts: The Religious Philosophy of Johannes Climacus* (Atlantic Highlands, NJ: Humanities Press, 1983).

——*Philosophy of Religion: Thinking about Faith* (Downer's Grove, Ill.: InterVarsity Press, 1985).

——*The Quest for Faith* (Downer's Grove, Ill.: InterVarsity Press, 1986).

——'The Epistemological Significance of Transformative Religious Experiences', *Faith and Philosophy*, 8/2 (1991).

——*Passionate Reason: Making Sense of Kierkegaard's Philosophical Fragments* (Bloomington, Ind.: Indiana University Press, 1992).

——'Empiricism, Rationalism, and the Possibility of Historical Religious Knowledge', in C. Stephen Evans and Merold Westphal (eds.), *Christian Perspectives on Religious Knowledge* (Grand Rapids, Mich.: Wm. B. Eerdmans, 1993).

FARMER, WILLIAM R., *The Synoptic Problem: A Critical Analysis* (New York: Macmillan, 1964).

——*Jesus and the Gospel: Tradition, Scripture, and Canon* (Philadelphia: Fortress Press, 1982).

——*The Gospel of Jesus: The Pastoral Relevance of the Synoptic Problem* (Louisville, Ky.: Westminster/John Knox Press, 1994).

FARRER, AUSTIN, *Saving Belief* (London: Hodder & Stoughton, 1964).

——*A Science of God?* (London: Geoffrey Bles, 1966).

FEENSTRA, RONALD J., 'Reconsidering Keontic Christology', Ronald J. Feenstra and Cornelius Plantinga (eds.), *Trinity, Incarnation, and Atonement* (Notre Dame, Ind.: University of Notre Dame Press, 1989).

FIDDES, PAUL, *Past Event and Present Salvation: A Study in The Christian Doctrine of The Atonement* (Louisville, Ky.: Westminster/John Knox Press, 1989).

FOSDICK, HARRY EMERSON, *The Man from Nazareth* (New York: Harper & Bros., 1949).

FREI, HANS, *The Eclipse of Biblical Narrative* (New Haven: Yale University Press, 1974).

FULLER, R. H., *The Foundations of New Testament Christology* (London: Lutterworth, 1965).

FUNK, ROBERT W., HOOVER, ROY W., and THE JESUS SEMINAR, *The Five Gospels* (New York: Macmillan, 1994).

GEACH, PETER, *God and the Soul* (London: Routledge & Kegan Paul, 1969).

GERHARDSSON, BIRGER, *Tradition and Transmission in Early Christianity* (Lund: C. W. K. Gleerup, 1964).

GOLDMAN, ALVIN, *Epistemology and Cognition* (Cambridge, Mass.: Harvard University Press, 1986).

GUNTON, COLIN, *The Actuality of Atonement: A Study of Metaphor, Rationality, and the Christian Tradition* (Grand Rapids, Mich.: Wm. B. Eerdmans, 1989).

HARVEY, A. E., 'Christology and the Evidence of The New Testament', in *God Incarnate: Story and Belief* (London: SPCK, 1981).

——*Jesus and the Constraints of History* (London: Duckworth, 1982).

HARVEY, VAN A., *The Historian and the Believer* (New York: Macmillan, 1966).

——'New Testament Scholarship and Christian Belief', in R. Joseph Hoffman and Gerald A. Larue (eds.), *Jesus in History and Myth* (New York: Prometheus Books, 1986).

HEBBLETHWAITE, BRIAN, *Evil, Suffering, and Religion* (London: Sheldon Press, 1976).

—— 'Providence and Divine Action', *Religious Studies*, 14 (June 1978).

—— *The Incarnation* (Cambridge: Cambridge University Press, 1987).

HEGEL, G. W. F., *Hegel on Art, Religion, and Philosophy* (New York: Harper & Row, 1970). Taken from a translation of *Lectures on the Philosophy of Religion* by E. B. Speirs and J. Burton Sanderson.

HELM, PAUL, *The Varieties of Belief* (New York: Humanities Press, 1973).

HICK, JOHN, *Theology*, 80 (May 1977), 205.

—— (ed.), *The Myth of God Incarnate* (London: SCM Press, 1977).

—— *The Metaphor of God Incarnate* (London: SCM Press, 1993).

HOOKER, MORNA, 'On Using The Wrong Tool', *Theology*, 75 (1972), 575.

—— 'Christology and Methodology', *New Testament Studies*, 17 (1971), 485.

HORSLEY, RICHARD A., *Jesus and the Spiral of Violence* (San Francisco: Harper & Row, 1987).

HUME, DAVID, 'Of Miracles', *An Enquiry Concerning Human Understanding* (Indianapolis: Hackett Publishing Co., 1977).

JAMES, WILLIAM, *Pragmatism* (Cambridge: Harvard University Press, 1975). Published with *The Meaning of Truth*.

KÄHLER, MARTIN, *The So-Called Historical Jesus and the Historic Biblical Christ*, ed. Ernst Wolf, trans. Carl Braaten (Philadelphia: Fortress Press, 1964).

KANT, IMMANUEL, *Religion Within the Limits of Reason Alone*, trans. Theodore M. Greene and Hoyt B. Hudson (New York: Harper & Row, 1960).

KAUFMAN, GORDON, *God The Problem* (Cambridge, Mass.: Harvard University Press, 1972).

—— 'On The Meaning of "Act of God"', in Owen C. Thomas (ed.), *God's Activity in the World* (Chico, Calif.: Scholar's Press, 1983). Originally published in *Harvard Theological Review*, 61.

KELLER, JAMES A., 'Contemporary Christian Doubts about the Resurrection'. *Faith and Philosophy*, 5/1 (1988), 57.

KELSEY, MORTON, *Myth, History, and Faith* (Rockport, Mass.: Element, 1991).

KIERKEGAARD, SØREN, *Samlede Værker*, 1st edn. (Copenhagen: Gyldendal, 1901–6).

——— *The Sickness Unto Death*, trans. Howard V. and Edna H. Hong (Princeton: Princeton University Press, 1980).

——— *Philosophical Fragments*, trans. Howard V. and Edna H. Hong (Princeton: Princeton University Press, 1985).

——— *The Concept of Irony*, trans. Howard V. and Edna H. Hong (Princeton: Princeton University Press, 1989).

——— *Practice in Christianity*, trans. Howard V. and Edna H. Hong (Princeton: Princeton University Press, 1991).

——— *Concluding Unscientific Postscript*, trans. Howard V. and Edna H. Hong. Princeton: Princeton University Press, 1992).

KIRKPATRICK, FRANK G., 'Understanding an Act of God', in Owen Thomas (ed.), *God's Activity in the World* (Chico, Calif.: Scholar's Press, 1983).

KREEFT, PETER, *Between Heaven and Hell* (Downer's Grove, Ill.: InterVarsity Press, 1982).

KÜMMEL, WERNER GEORG, *The Theology of The New Testament*, trans. John Steely (New York: Abingdon Press, 1973).

KURTZ, PAUL (ed.), *The Humanist Manifestos I and II* (Buffalo: Prometheus Books, 1973).

LEHRER, KEITH, *Theory of Knowledge* (London: Routledge, 1990).

LESSING, G., 'On the Proof of the Spirit and of Power', *Lessing's Theological Writings*, ed. and trans. Henry Chadwick (Stanford: Stanford University Press 1957).

LEVENSON, JON D., *The Hebrew Bible, the Old Testament, and Historical Criticism: Jews and Christians in Biblical Studies* (Louisville: Westminster/John Knox Press, 1993).

——— 'The Bible: Unexamined Commitments of Criticism', *First Things*, 30 (Feb. 1993), 28.

LEWES, G. H., *Comte's Philosophy of the Sciences* (London: G. Bell & Sons, 1904).

LEWIS, C. S., *Miracles* (London: G. Bles, 1947).

——— *Mere Christianity* (London: Collins, 1952).

——— 'On Obstinacy in Belief', in *The World's Last Night and Other Essays* (New York: Harcourt, Brace, & Co., 1960).

——— 'Modern Theology and Biblical Criticism', in *Christian Reflections* (London: Geoffrey Bles, 1967).

——— 'Myth Became Fact', in *God in the Dock* (Grand Rapids, Mich.: Wm. B. Eerdmans, 1970).

——— *They Stand Together: The Letters of C. S. Lewis to Arthur Greeves (1914–1963)*, ed. Walter Hooper (New York: Macmillan, 1979).

LINDBECK, GEORGE, *The Nature of Doctrine* (Philadelphia: Westminster, 1984).

LOCKE, JOHN, *An Essay Concerning Human Understanding*, ed. Peter H. Nidditch (Oxford: Oxford University Press, 1975).

LUEDEMANN, GERD, *The Resurrection of Jesus: History, Experience, Theology*, trans. John Bowden (Minneapolis: Augsburg Fortress Press, 1995).

Lumen Gentium (The Dogmatic Constitution of the Church), in *The Documents of Vatican II*, ed. Walter M. Abbott (New York: Herder & Herder, 1966).

MCCRACKEN, DAVID, *The Scandal of the Gospels: Jesus, Story, and Offence* (Oxford: Oxford University Press, 1994).

MACK, BURTON, *A Myth of Innocence: Mark and Christian Origins* (Philadelphia: Fortress Press, 1988).

—— *The Lost Gospel: The Book of Q and Christian Origins* (San Francisco: HarperCollins, 1993).

MCKINNON, ALASTAIR, ' "Miracle" and "Paradox" ', *American Philosophical Quarterly*, 4 (Oct. 1967), 308–14.

MACQUARRIE, JOHN, *Principles of Christian Theology*, 2nd edn. (New York: Charles Scribner's Sons, 1977).

MARSHALL, I. HOWARD, *Luke: Historian and Theologian* (Grand Rapids, Mich.: Zondervan Press, 1971).

—— *I Believe in the Historical Jesus* (Grand Rapids, Mich.: Wm. B. Eerdmans, 1977).

MARTIN, MICHAEL, *The Case against Christianity* (Philadelphia: Temple University Press, 1991).

MARTY, MARTIN, *History and Historical Understanding* (Grand Rapids, Mich.: Wm. B. Eerdmans, 1984).

MASCALL, E. L., *The Importance of Being Human* (New York: Columbia University Press, 1958).

MAVRODES, GEORGE, 'Intellectual Morality in Clifford and James', in Gerald McCarthy (ed.), *The Ethics of Belief Debate* (Atlanta: Scholar's Press, 1986).

—— 'Revelation and the Bible', *Faith and Philosophy*, 6/4 (1989), 409.

MEIER, JOHN P., *A Marginal Jew: Rethinking the Historical Jesus*, i and ii (New York: Doubleday, 1991 and 1994).

MEYER, BEN F., *The Aims of Jesus* (London: SCM Press, 1979).

MICHALSON JR., GORDON E., *Lessing's 'Ugly Ditch': A Study of Theology and History* (University Park, Penn.: Pennsylvania State University Press, 1985).

MITCHELL, BASIL, *The Justification of Religious Belief* (London: Macmillan, 1973).

—— *How to Play Theological Ping-Pong* (Grand Rapids, Mich.: Wm. B. Eerdmans, 1991).

MORGAN, ROBERT, and BARTON, JOHN, *Biblical Interpretation* (Oxford: Oxford University Press, 1988).

MORRIS, THOMAS V., *The Logic of God Incarnate* (Ithaca, NY: Cornell University Press, 1986).

MOULE, C. F. D., *The Birth of the New Testament* (London: A. & C. Black, 1962).

—— *The Origin of Christology* (Cambridge: Cambridge University Press, 1977).

MUDDIMAN, JOHN, 'The Historical Jesus'. Lecture at Oxford (Hilary Term, 1994).

NEILL, STEPHEN, and WRIGHT, TOM, *The Interpretation of the New Testament: 1861–1986*, 2nd edn. (Oxford: Oxford University Press, 1988).

NEWBIGIN, LESSLIE, *The Gospel in a Pluralist Society* (Grand Rapids, Mich.: Wm. B. Eerdmans, 1989).

NEWMAN, JOHN HENRY, *An Essay Aid of a Grammar of Assent* (1870; Notre Dame Ind.: University of Notre Dame Press, 1979).

NINEHAM, D. E., 'Schweitzer Revisited', *Explorations in Theology* (London: SCM Press, 1977).

NOLL, MARK (ed.), *The Princeton Theology: 1812–1921* (Phillipsburg, NJ: Presbyterian and Reformed Publishing Co., 1983).

—— *Between Faith and Criticism* (San Francisco: Harper & Row, 1986).

NOWELL-SMITH, PATRICK, 'Miracles', Anthony Flew and Alasdair MacIntyre (eds.), *New Essays in Philosophical Theology* (New York: Macmillan, 1955).

NOZICK, ROBERT, *Philosophical Explanations* (Cambridge, Mass: Harvard University Press, 1981).

PALEY, WILLIAM, *A View of the Evidences of Christianity* (New York: Robert Carter & Bros., 1854).

PALMER, HUMPHREY, *The Logic of Gospel Criticism* (London: Macmillan, 1968).

PARKER, P., *The Gospel before Mark* (Chicago: University of Chicago Press, 1953).

PENELHUM, TERENCE, *God and Skepticism* (Dordrecht: D. Reidel, 1983).

PHILLIPS, D. Z., *Faith and Philosophical Enquiry* (London: Routledge, 1970).

—— *Faith after Foundationalism* (London: Routledge, 1988).

PLANTINGA, ALVIN, 'How to be an Anti-Realist', *Proceedings and Addresses of American Philosophical Association*, 56 (1982), 47–70.

PLANTINGA, ALVIN, 'Reason and Belief in God', in Alvin Plantinga and Nicholas Wolterstorff (eds.), *Faith and Rationality* (Notre Dame, Ind.: University of Notre Dame Press, 1983).

—— 'Coherentism and the Evidentialist Objection to Belief in God', in Robert Audi and W. J. Wainwright (eds.), *Rationality, Religious Belief, and Moral Commitment* (Ithaca, NY: Cornell University Press, 1986).

—— 'The Foundations of Theism', *Faith and Philosophy*, 3 (1986).

—— *Warrant: The Current Debate* (Oxford: Oxford University Press, 1993).

—— *Warrant and Proper Function* (Oxford: Oxford University Press, 1993).

PLANTINGA, CORNELIUS, 'Social Trinity and Tritheism', in Ronald J. Feenstra and Cornelius Plantinga (eds.), *Trinity, Incarnation, and Atonement* (Notre Dame, Ind.: University of Notre Dame Press, 1989).

PRICE, ROBERT M., 'Is There a Place for Historical Criticism?', *Religious Studies*, 27/3 (1991), 371–88.

PURTILL, RICHARD, 'Justice, Mercy, Supererogation, and Atonement', in Thomas P. Flint (ed.), *Christian Philosophy* (Notre Dame: University of Notre Dame Press, 1990).

QUINN, PHILIP, 'Aquinas on Atonement', in Ronald J. Feenstra and Cornelius Plantinga (eds.), *Trinity, Incarnation, and Atonement* (Notre Dame, Ind.: University of Notre Dame Press, 1989).

RATZSCH, DEL, *Philosophy of Science* (Downer's Grove, Ill.: Inter-Varsity Press, 1986).

REID, THOMAS, *An Inquiry into the Human Mind* (Chicago: University of Chicago Press, 1970). Originally published (1764) as *An Inquiry into the Human Mind on the Principles of Common Sense*.

RENAN, ERNST, *The Life of Jesus* (1863; New York: Random House, 1972).

RIESENFELD, HARALD, *The Gospel Tradition and its Beginnings* (London: A. R. Mowbray, 1957).

RIST, M., *On the Independence of Matthew and Mark* (Cambridge: Cambridge University Press, 1978).

—— 'Where Else', in Kelly James Clark (ed.), *Philosophers Who Believe* (Downer's Grove, Ill.: InterVarsity Press, 1993).

ROBINSON, JAMES M., and KOESTER, HELMUT, *Trajectories through Early Christianity* (Philadelphia: Fortress Press, 1971).

ROBINSON, JOHN A. T., *Redating the New Testament* (London: SCM Press, 1976; Philadelphia: Westminster Press, 1976).

—— *The Priority of John* (London: SCM Press, 1985).

SANDERS, E. P., *The Tendencies of the Synoptic Tradition* (Cambridge: Cambridge University Press, 1969).

——*Jesus and Judaism* (London: SCM Press, 1985).

SANDERS, JOHN, *No Other Name* (Grand Rapids, Mich.: Wm. B. Eerdmans, 1992).

SCHAAF, PHILIP, *The Creeds of Christendom*, iii (New York: Harper, 1919).

SCHULZ, HANS-JOACHIM, *Die apostolische Herkunft der Evangelien* (Freiburg: Herder, 1993).

SCHWEITZER, ALBERT, *The Quest of the Historical Jesus* (New York: Macmillan, 1948).

SKINNER, B. F., *Beyond Freedom and Dignity* (New York: Bantam Books, 1972).

SMITH, A. D., 'God's Death', *Theology*, 80 (July 1977), 262–8.

STEIN, ROBERT H., 'The "Criteria" for Authenticity', in R. T. France and David Wenham (eds.), *Gospel Perspectives: Studies of History and Tradition in the Four Gospels*, i (Sheffield: SOT, 1980).

——*The Synoptic Problem* (Grand Rapids, Mich.: Baker, 1987).

STERNBERG, MEIR, *The Poetics of Biblical Narrative* (Bloomington, Ind.: Indiana University Press, 1985).

STRAUSS, D. F., *The Life of Jesus Critically Examined* (Philadelphia: Fortress Press, 1972). Originally published as *Das Leben Jesu*, 1835.

STREETER, B. H., *The Four Gospels: A Study of Origins*, 2nd edn. (London: Macmillan, 1930).

STUMP, ELEONORE, 'Atonement According to Aquinas', in Thomas Morris (ed.), *Philosophy and the Christian Faith* (Notre Dame, Ind.: University of Notre Dame Press, 1988).

——'Betrayal of Trust', Lecture at St Olaf College (Summer 1993).

——'The Knowledge of Suffering: Biblical Studies and the Problem of Evil', typescript.

SWINBURNE, RICHARD, *The Concept of Miracle* (London: Macmillan, 1970).

——*The Coherence of Theism* (Oxford: Oxford University Press, 1977).

——*Faith and Reason* (Oxford: Oxford University Press, 1981).

——*The Existence of God* (Oxford: Oxford University Press, 1979).

——*Responsibility and Atonement* (Oxford: Oxford University Press, 1989).

——*Revelation: From Metaphor to Analogy* (Oxford: Oxford University Press, 1992).

TALIAFERRO, CHARLES, 'The Intensity of Theism', *Sophia*, 31/3 (61–73).

TEMPLE, WILLIAM, *Christus Veritas* (London: Macmillan, 1924).

THIERING, BARBARA, *Jesus the Man: A New Interpretation from the Dead Sea Scrolls* (London: Doubleday, 1992).

THOMAS, OWEN (ed.), *God's Activity in the World* (Chico, Calif.: Scholar's Press, 1983).

TILLICH, PAUL, *The Courage to Be* (New Haven: Yale University Press, 1952).

——*Systematic Theology*, i (London: Nisbet, 1953).

Time Magazine, 'Jesus Christ, Pure and Simple', 10 Jan. 1994, 38–9.

TROELTSCH, ERNST, *Gesammelte Schriften*, ii (Tübingen: J. C. B. Mohr, 1913).

——'Historiography', *Encyclopedia of Religion and Ethics*, vi, ed. James Hastings (New York: Charles Scribner's Sons, 1922).

TYRRELL, G., *Christianity at the Cross-Roads* (London: Longmans, Green & Co., 1909).

VAN INWAGEN, PETER, 'Critical Studies of the New Testament and the User of the New Testament', in Eleonore Stump and Thomas P. Flint (eds.), *Hermes and Athena; Biblical Exegesis and Philosophical Theology* (Notre Dame, Ind.: University of Notre Dame Press, 1993).

VINCENT OF LERINS, *The Commonitories*, in *The Fathers of the Church*, vii (Washington: Catholic University of America Press, 1970).

WAINWRIGHT, ARTHUR, *Beyond Biblical Criticism: Encountering Jesus in Scripture* (London: SPCK, 1982).

WARFIELD, B. B., 'Inspiration', *International Bible Encyclopedia* (Chicago: Howard-Severance, 1915). Repr. in *The Inspiration and Authority of the Bible*.

——*The Inspiration and Authority of the Bible* (Philadelphia: Presbyterian and Reformed Publishing Co., 1948).

——and HODGE, A. A., 'Inspiration', in Mark Noll (ed.), *The Interpretation of the New Testament 1861–1986* (Grand Rapids, Mich.: Baker, 1983).

WELLS, G. A., 'The Historicity of Jesus', in R. Joseph Hoffman and Gerald A. Larue (eds.), *Jesus in History and Myth* (Buffalo: Prometheus Books, 1986).

WENHAM, JOHN, *Redating Matthew, Mark and Luke: A Fresh Assault on the Synoptic Problem* (Downer's Grove, Ill.: InterVarsity Press, 1992).

WHITE, VERNON, *The Fall of a Sparrow* (Exeter: Paternoster Press 1985).

—— *Atonement and Incarnation: An Essay in Universalism and Particularity* (Cambridge: Cambridge University Press, 1991).

WILES, MAURICE F., *The Making of Christian Doctrine* (Cambridge: Cambridge University Press, 1967).

—— *God's Action in the World* (London: SCM Press, 1986).

WILSON, A. N., *C. S. Lewis: A Biography* (New York: W. W. Norton & Co., 1990).

—— *Jesus* (London: Sinclair-Stevenson, 1992).

WITTGENSTEIN, LUDWIG, *Tractatus Logico-Philosophicus* (New York: Humanities Press, 1961).

WOLTER, ALLAN B., *The Philosophical Theology of John Duns Scotus* (Ithaca, NY: Cornell University Press, 1990).

WOLTERSTOFF, NICHOLAS, 'Tradition, Insight, and Constraint', *Proceedings and Addresses of the American Philosophical Association*, 66/3 (1992), 43–57.

—— *John Locke's Ethic of Belief: When Tradition Fractures* (Cambridge: Cambridge University Press, forthcoming).

WOOD, JAY, *Introduction to Epistemology: A Virtues Perspective* (Downer's Grove, Ill: InterVarsity Press, forthcoming).

WRIGHT, N. T., *The New Testament and the People of God* (Minneapolis: Fortress Press, 1992).

—— *Who Was Jesus?* (London: SPCK, 1992).

WYKSTRA, STEPHEN J., 'Toward A Sensible Evidentialism: On the Notion of "Needing Evidence"'. Repr. in William Rowe and William J. Wainwright (eds.), *Philosophy of Religion*, 2nd edn. (San Diego: Harcourt Brace Jovanovich, 1989).

—— 'Is Theism a Theory? Externalism, Proper Inferentiality and Sensible Evidentialism', *Topoi*, 14 (1995), 107–21.

ZAGZESBKI, LINDA, 'Religious Knowledge and the Virtues of the Mind', *Rational Faith: Catholic Responses to Reformed Epistemology* (Notre Dame, Ind.: University of Notre Dame Press, 1993).

Index